ANCESTRAL RECORDS
AND PORTRAITS

VOLUME II

MEMORIAL GATES AT JAMESTOWN, VA.
Erected by The Colonial Dames of America in commemoration of the settlement of Jamestown in 1607. They were dedicated May 9, 1907.

ANCESTRAL RECORDS
AND PORTRAITS

A COMPILATION FROM THE
ARCHIVES OF CHAPTER I.,
THE COLONIAL DAMES OF
AMERICA

PREPARED UNDER THE DIRECTION
OF THE PUBLICATION COMMITTEE
BY THE EDITORIAL DEPARTMENT
OF THE GRAFTON PRESS

VOLUME II

CLEARFIELD

Originally Published
New York, 1910

Reprinted
Genealogical Publishing Company
Baltimore, 1969

Reprinted for
Clearfield Company, Inc. by
Genealogical Publishing Co., Inc.
Baltimore, Maryland
1997

International Standard Book Number: 978-0-8063-1970-4

Library of Congress Catalog Card Number 68-57950

ILLUSTRATIONS

Illustrations

ILLUSTRATIONS

Facing page

ANCESTRAL RECORDS
AND PORTRAITS

XXV

WASHINGTON

ARMS: *Argent, two bars gules, in chief three mullets of the second.*
CREST: *A raven with wings indorsed proper, issuing out of a ducal coronet, or.*

Sulgrave, Northamptonshire, Eng., was the residence of the Washingtons from 1535 to 1606. That this branch of the family used the arms here given is assured by the escutcheon over the doorway of the Sulgrave Manor House; and is proven also by the stone inserted in the wall of the Brington home, when reverses compelled them to leave Sulgrave, and to occupy that dwelling (now standing), with this inscription over the entrance:

WASHINGTON

The church of St. Mary, the Virgin, at Great Brington, was the place of worship of the Earls Spencer, whose seat, Althorp Park, is near by, and of the Washingtons, as also the place of burial of both families, having intermarried.

THE LORD GEVETH
THE LORD TAKETH
AWAY BLESSED BE THE
NAME OF THE LORD
CONSTRVCTA
1 6 0 6.

The first grantee of Sulgrave Manor House, time of Henry VIII, Lawrence Washington, Gent., was the son of John Washington, Warton, Lancashire, and his

wife Margaret Kitson, the daughter of Robert, and
sister of Sir Thomas Kitson, Kt., whose daughter
Katharine, married Sir John Spencer. Lawrence
Washington died February 19, 1584 (26 Elizabeth),
and is buried in Sulgrave Church. He was a member
of Gray's Inn, and twice Mayor of Northampton from
1533 to 1546. He married Amée, the daughter of
Robert Pargiter, of Gretworth, Gent., who died October 6, 1564. Issue, four sons and seven daughters, of
whom there are effigies in the Sulgrave Church with
those of their father and mother. The brass on the
effigy of Amée Washington has been stolen, and the
enamel in color in the coat of arms has crumbled with
time. Two of their sons were Robert, of Sulgrave,
and Lawrence, of Gray's Inn, the father of Sir Lawrence, of Garsden, County Wilts. (See Collateral
line.)

The following is a facsimile of the inscription on
the tomb of Lawrence Washington and his wife, showing the places left for the date of the death of Lawrence, which places his executors neglected to have
filled in.

The elder son, Robert Washington, of "Souldgrave,
in the County of Northampton Esq.," was forty years
old in 26 Elizabeth, and his will was proved January 3,
1620. He married first, Elizabeth, the daughter of
Walter Light, of Radway, Warwickshire; second, Anne
Fisher, of Hanslop, County of Bucks. In his will (now
at Sulgrave), he provides for the burial of his body in

"the south isle of the church before my seat where I usually sit, under the same stone that my father lyeth buried under, and my funeral to be done in decente sort, and not with greate pompt according to the order of the world of these dayes"; and mentions the issue of two marriages, seven sons, four by the first and three by the second, as follows: "Christopher, William, Thomas and Lawrence deceased, Albane, Guy and Robert."

The youngest son of the first marriage, Lawrence Washington, of Sulgrave and Brington, married Margaret, the daughter of William Butler of Tees, Sussex. He died December 13, 1616, and is buried in Brington Church in the chancel. His grave is marked by a flat slab, deeply cut and originally filled with brass. It bears the impaled arms of the Washingtons and the Butlers—the three mullets and two bars, familiar to us to-day. The inscription reads as follows:

HERE . LIETH . THE . BODI . OF . LAVRENCE .
WASHINGTON . SONNE . & . HEIRE . OF .
ROBERT . WASHINGTON . OF . SOVLGRAVE ..
IN . THE . COVNTIE . OF . NORTHAMPTON .
ESQVIER . WHO . MARRIED . MARGARET .
THE . ELDEST . DAVGHTER . OF . WILLIAM .
BVTLER . OF . TEES . IN . THE . COVNTIE .
OF . SVSSEXE . ESQVIRE . WHO . HAD . ISSVE .
BY . HER . 8 . SONNS . & . 9 . DAVGHTERS .
WHICH . LAVRENCE . DECESSED . THE . 13 ..
OF . DECEMBER . A : DNI : 1616 .

THOV . THAT . BY . CHANCE . OR . CHOICE .
  OF . THIS . HAST . SIGHT .
KNOW . LIFE . TO . DEATH . RESIGNS .
  AS . DAY . TO . NIGHT .

BVT.AS.THE.SVNNS.RETORNE.
REVIVES.THE.DAY.
So.CHRIST.SHALL.VS.,
THOVGH.TVRNED.TO.DVST.&.CLAY.

Issue, Lawrence and others.

The son of Lawrence and Margaret (Butler) Washington, Rev. Lawrence Washington, was a brilliant Oxford University scholar, a Fellow, and Lector of Brasenose, Proctor at Oxford in 1631, and Rector of Purleigh, Essex, 1633 to 1643.[1] He married Amphillis Roades and died January 16, 1655.

An old charge that the Rector of Purleigh Church, Essex, Eng., was "deposed on the ground that he was a public tippler, and railed against Parliament," seems to have been refuted in these days of research, when proof is required, and President Woodrow Wilson, in his *Life of Washington,* states that the "Uncle of the gallant Colonel (Henry Washington) who was the King's Governor at Worcester has been cast out of his living at Purleigh in 1643 by order of Parliament upon the 'false charge' that he was a public tippler, oft drunk, and loved to rail against the Parliament and its armies, but really because, with all his race he was a loyalist, and his living one of the best in Essex." He was buried at Tring, Hertfordshire, Eng. Issue: JOHN; Lawrence, born 1635, one of the executors of John's will; Martha, whose will may be found in the *N. E. Hist. and Geneal. Reg.,* 1893; her brother John left her £1,000 for transporting herself to America, a

[1] "Brasenose College, Oxford, November 2, 1621, entered Lawrence Washington, Northampton, a gentleman's son, aged nineteen." (*Matriculation Register,* Oxford, Eng.)

"Lawrence Washington, Master of Arts, admitted Rector of Purleigh, March 14, 1633" (*Bishop's Certificate of the Diocese of London*); died before 1654-5.

year's accommodation after coming and four thousand pounds of tobacco and "caske."[3]

Another interesting inscription in Brington church, is on the tomb[2] of Robert Washington (a son of Robert, of "Souldgrave"), who married Elizabeth Chishull, of More Hall, Essex, who in her will makes the following bequest: "I doe give unto my Cosen Lawrence Washington who is nowe at Oxford my husband's seal ringe."

HERE LIES INTERRED ỹ BODIES OF Elizab: WASHINGTON WIDDOWE WHO CHANGED THIS LIFE FOR IM'ORTALITIE ỹ 19ᵗᴴ OF MARCH 1622. AS ALSO ỹ BODY OF ROBERT WASHINGTON GENT. HER LATE HVSBAND SECOND SONNE OF ROBERT WASHINGTON OF SOLGRAVE IN ỹ COVNTY OF NORTH. ESQ: WHO DEPTED THIS LIFE ỹ 10ᵗᴴ OF MARCH 1622. AFTER THEY LIVED LOVINGLY TOGETHER IN THIS PARISH

COLLATERAL ENGLISH WASHINGTONS

The second son of Lawrence Washington, Grantee of Sulgrave, Lawrence, of Gray's Inn, died January 17, 1661-62, and was the father of Sir Lawrence Washington, of Westbury, Bucks and Garsden, Wilts. His wife was Elienor, daughter of William Guise "of Elmore in ye County of Gloucester Esqr.," who died July 19, 1686. Elizabeth, their daughter, married Robert, first Earl Ferrars, who held Garsden Manor for many years.

The late Bishop Henry Codman Potter, of New

[2] H. F. Waters and others, 1889.

[3] One of the two "Memorial Stones" of which facsimiles are in the State House in Boston.

York, in a recent visit to Garsden, near Malmsbury, England, gives a list of the Washingtons buried there and the inscriptions on their monuments. Among them the name "Lawrence Washington Esq." is twice repeated, for father and son. It is a singular coincidence that Elienor Washington, wife of Lawrence, married second, Sir William Pargiter, of North Hampton, Kt., deceased July, 1685, a century after the death of Lawrence, Grantee of Sulgrave Manor, whose wife was Amée Pargiter. Elienor, wife of Lawrence Washington above, afterwards Lady Pargiter, in 1684 gave to that parish a magnificent set of communion plate in solid silver, weight ninety-two ounces. By request of Mrs. Potter, wife of the late Bishop of New York, a replica of this service was presented by her to the new Cathedral of St. John the Divine, in the city of New York.

Sir John Washington, son of Lawrence and Margaret (Butler) Washington, an uncle of the emigrants to Virginia, fought with the King against Cromwell at Edgehill.

His brother, Sir William Washington, married Anne, the daughter of Sir George Villiers (brother of the second Duke of Buckingham), and is buried in the old Church of St. Martins-in-the-Fields, on Trafalgar Square, once a fashionable place of worship in court circles. Sir William's tombstone gives the year of his death as 1643. His daughter Elizabeth (Lady Dartmouth), married the eldest son and heir of Colonel William Legge, a Royalist, who received license March 2, 1641-2, to marry "Elizabeth Washington of Kensington, Middlesex, Spinster, about twenty-two, daughter of Sir William Washington, Kt., of the same parish

CHURCH OF ST. MARY THE VIRGIN
Brington, where are buried ancestors
of George Washington

THE WASHINGTON HOUSE
Little Brington

TOMB OF SANDYS, AND OF PENELOPE WASHINGTON, AT WICKHAMFORD

St. Faiths." The other daughters of Sir William were Catherine, Penelope and Susanna.

Colonel Henry Washington, of the Royalist Army, and Lord Mayor of Worcester, son of Sir William, is buried at Richmond, Eng. He had been with Rupert when he stormed Bristol, and held Worcester even after he knew King Charles to be a prisoner in the hands of the Parliamentary forces. "Procure his Majesty's command for the disposal of the garrison," was Colonel Washington's answer to Fairfax, when asked to surrender; "till then I shall make good the trust imposed in me. The worst I know and fear not; if I had, the profession of a soldier had not been begun." Penelope, a daughter of Colonel Henry Washington, whose tomb is said to be one of the finest examples of marble in England, has the Washington arms on top—the five pointed stars and two bars—with the date February 27, An. Dom., 1697.

An aunt of the emigrants, Alice Washington, the daughter of Lawrence of Sulgrave, and Amée Pargiter, his wife, married Robert Sandys, a brother of the Treasurer of the Virginia Company, and son of Thomas Sandys. The latter, with his brothers Samuel and Sir Edwin (who was knighted by King James I.), were sons of the Archbishop of York. Samuel married the widow of Colonel Henry Washington. The stately Sandys monument is at Wickhamford, England.

In 1533, Lawrence Washington, Grantee of Sulgrave, an ancestor of General George Washington, was Mayor of Northampton, Eng.

In 1633, one hundred years later, at York, Va., Nicholas Martian, great-great-great-grandfather of George Washington, was living on the present site of Yorktown, a leader among the men of his time.

In 1782, ninety-nine years later, was born George Washington, Commander-in-chief of the American Army, and twice President of the United States, who received the articles of surrender of Lord Cornwallis on the ground owned by Nicholas Martian.

LIEUTENANT-COLONEL JOHN WASHINGTON, and Lawrence his brother, sons of the Rev. Lawrence and Amphillis (Roades) Washington, being of the Royalist party then out of power, came out of England, " across the Seas " to seek their fortunes in the Colony. JOHN, born prior to 1634, and died January, 1677, settled at Bridges Creek in the Northern Neck of Virginia, afterwards Westmoreland County, 1653.[4] Copies of the originals in the worn and moth eaten volume which contains the earliest records of Westmoreland County, Va., give information in regard to him. He came to America in a merchant ship belonging to Edward Prescott. In the *Archives* of Maryland, and recorded at Westmoreland Court House, are entries covering many pages of a law suit of " Mr. Washington ag⁺ Mr. Prescott." It is certain, however, that John Washington was established in the County prior to that time, for a commission to the military officers of Westmoreland, dated April 4, 1655, and recorded in the volume previously mentioned, includes Thomas Speke as Colonel, Nathaniel Pope, Lieutenant-Colonel, and John Washington, Major.[5] In a deposition, dated 1674 and recorded in Westmoreland, he stated that he was then forty-five years of age. September 30, 1659, John Washington wrote to Governor Fendall of Maryland,

[4] *N. E. Hist. and Geneal. Reg.*, 1893, p. 271, Woodrow Wilson.

G. W. Stanard, *Quar.*, 1893, p. 183.

Pedigree taken from Visitation of Oxfordshire Harl. Soc. Publications.

[5] *Col. Va. Reg.*, pp. 79 to 81, and *Quar.*, Vol. I.

SURVEY MADE IN 1674 FOR NICHOLAS SPENCER AND LIEUT. COL. JOHN
WASHINGTON. CERTIFIED BY THOMAS LEE

regretting his inability to attend Court on account of the arrangements to have his " Young Sonne baptised; all ye Company and ye gossips being already invited." The Westmoreland records state that he was made a Vestryman of Appomattox Parish, July 3, 1661, and at that period a Vestryman controlled both Church and State affairs. Commissioned a Justice of Westmoreland June 24, 1662, and a Burgess November, 1654, in the first session in which Burgesses sat for Westmoreland, he was also among the Burgesses of Virginia known as the "Long Parliament." There having been no elections since the restoration in 1660, the same Legislature continued to hold its session from that time by prorogation. In the session of October 23, 1666, Colonel Nicholas Spencer and Colonel John Washington were Representatives, and in 1673 John Washington was Commissioner to arrange boundary lines between Lancaster and Northumberland Counties. These two men were again associated with others to deal with the Indians in 1675, when Colonel Washington commanded the Virginia troops, and Major Thomas Truman the Marylanders, against the Susquehannocks. A grant[6] is recorded to Lieutenant-Colonel John Washington of five thousand acres in Stafford County, 1677. He had seven grants of land. Lord Culpeper's order to his agent in Virginia, dated March 1, 1674, conveys land to Nicholas Spencer and Lieutenant-Colonel John Washington, as shown in the illustration. The following are extracts from his will:

"In the name (of) God Amen, I John Washington of Washington parish in ye Countie of Westmoreland in Virginia gent. &c.

"My body to be buried in ye plantation wheire I

6 *Va. State Land Registry.*

now live, by the side of my wife y^t is already buried &
two children of mine.

A provision for his sons and daughter An. "Item
I give unto my sayd Daughter wch was her Mothers
desire & my promise ye cash in ye new parlour & the
Diamond ring & her Mother's rings & the white quilt
& the white curtains & Valliance." "In every case
reserving to my wife her thirds for Life."

"Item, my desire is y^t there be a funerall Sermon
preached at ye church & that be no other funeral kept
y^t will Exceed four thousand pounds of Tobacco."

"Item, I give unto the Lower Church of Washington parish ye ten commandments and the Kings arms
wch is my desire should be sent for out of w^t mony I
have in England."

"Unto my sister Marthaw Washington £1000
pounds money in England for transporting herself
into this Country, and a years accommodation after
the comeing in & four thousand pounds of tobb^{cc} &
Caske."

"I doe ordaine and appoint my bro Mr. Lawrence
Washington & my son Lawrence Washington & my
Loving wife Mrs. An Washington my whole soale
Executors of this my last will & testament as witness
my hand & seale this 21st of 7 ber, 1675.

JOHN WASHINGTON."

"Y^e 10th Jana: 1677 proved &c."
Buried in the Vault at Bridges Creek.

John Washington married second *Anne,* the daughter of Nathaniel and Luce Pope. Issue: three children, viz.: LAWRENCE, John, and Anne.

MAJOR LAWRENCE WASHINGTON, son of Colonel
John Washington of Bridges Creek, Va., and Anne

Pope, his wife, born in Virginia 1661, and died 1698, married 1690, *Mildred,* the daughter of Colonel Augustine Warner, of "Warner Hall," Gloucester County, Va., and Mildred Reade, his wife. He was educated at Appleby, North of England. Member of the House of Burgesses 1685. July 25, 1690, " Among those hereby empowered to procure subscriptions for the proposed college in Virginia, (to be called King William and Queen Mary), are the following: Capt. William Hardrick, Capt. Lawrence Washington and Capt. William Ball." [7]

By his father's will he inherited, as follows:

"Item, I give unto my son Lawrence Washington my halfe & share of five thousand acres of land in Stafford County, wch is betwixt Coll Nicholas Spencer & myself wch we engaged y^t there shall be no benefit by Service or ship, to him and his heirs forever."

His Will, beginning: "I Lawrence Washington, of Washington Parish, in the County of Westmoreland in Virginia Gentleman," after speaking of the uncertainty of life, etc., says in part:

"I Trust and believe assuredly to be saved and to have full remission & forgiveness of all my sins, through the Merits of Christ's Death and passion."

"My body to be buried if please God I depart in this County of Westmoreland, by the side of my Father and Mother & Neare my Brothers & Sisters & My Children."

After the settlement of his debts, there is a provision for some mourning rings, and to his Godson, Lawrence Butler, to his sister Anne Writts' children, and to his sister (in-law) Lewis, bequests, with many others.

"Item, I give to the Upper and Lower Churches of Washington Parish each of them a Pulpett Cloth & Cushion."

"Item, it is my will to have a Funeral sermon at the Church, and to have none other Funeral to exceed Three Thousand pounds of Tobacco."

His personal estate to be divided into four parts. "My loving Wife, Mildred Washington to have one part; my son John Washington to have another Part; my son Augustin Washington to have another Part and my daughter Mildred Washington to have the other part. To be delivered to them in Specie when they shall come to the age of twenty-one years old."

To his son Augustine, fell the "Wakefield" tract (with two others). To Mildred Washington Gregory, the only daughter, was given the present Mount Vernon tract, etc.

Will dated 11th day of March, Anno Dom. 1697-8. Proven at a Court held for this county (Westmoreland) 30th March, 1698.

Issue:

John, married Catharine Whiting, whose tomb at Highgate bears the Whiting Arms. The tomb of their daughter Elizabeth, has Washington Arms.

AUGUSTINE I.

Mildred, married Roger Gregory, and was the God Mother of her nephew, George Washington. She had three daughters, Frances, Mildred and Elizabeth, who married the three Thornton brothers. When widowed, Mildred Gregory married Colonel Henry Willis.[8]

CAPTAIN AUGUSTINE WASHINGTON I., the son of Major Lawrence and Mildred (Warner) Washington, was born in Virginia 1694, and died April 12, 1743.

[8] Spark's, Vol. I., p. 550.

Like his father he was educated at Appleby, Eng. The ancient Truro Parish vestry book shows that Augustine Washington was a Vestryman, August 19, 1736. He also recommended Mr. Charles Green to the vestrymen as a person qualified to officiate as minister in that parish. The Reverend Mr. Green served the Falls Church or as then called the "Upper" or "New" Church in Truro Parish as Rector for many years.

"Ordered that Geo. Washington, Esq., be chosen and appointed one of the Vestrymen of this parish in the room of Wm. Peake, gent., deceased."

Washington served the Falls Church as Vestryman in the Truro Parish and was also elected to its first Vestry when cut off from Truro and made part of Fairfax Parish.

"October 3, 1763. Ordered: That Geo. Wm. Fairfax, & Geo. Washington, Esqs., be appointed Church Wardens for the ensuing year."

It is here shown that both Augustine Washington and his son George, served as Vestrymen of Truro Parish; the former in 1736, and a memorandum in the *Diary* of George Washington of 1764, would prove him still in office in that year.

Augustine Washington was elected one of the Trustees of Fredericksburg, at a meeting held April 5, 1742, to fill a vacancy, as shown by an old record recently found among the papers of Judge Bushrod Washington, of the United States Supreme Court, by Mr. Bushrod C. Washington of "Claymont," Jefferson County, W. Va., who presented the paper to the city of Fredericksburg for its archives.

He was married twice; first, April 20, 1715, to Jane, the daughter of Caleb Butler, who was a Justice of

Westmoreland County, Va., in 1699, and of the
Quorum. In the family burial ground at "Wakefield,"
Westmoreland County, may be seen the monument to
Jane Butler Washington, with the following quaint
inscription:

> "Here Lyes ye body of Jane
> Wife of Augustine Washington
> Borne at Pope's Creek, Virginia
> Westmoreland ye 24" Xber
> 1699 and died ye 24" of 9 ber 1729
> She left behind her two sons
> And one daughter."

His second marriage March 6, 1730, was to *Mary,*
the daughter of Lieutenant-COLONEL JOSEPH BALL, of
Millenback, Lancaster County, Va., and his wife Mary
Johnson (widow). (See Ball line, pp. 134-137.)

Issue first wife, four children:

Butler, died young; Lawrence, born at Bridges
Creek in 1718; AUGUSTINE II.; Jane, born in 1722,
died January 17, 1735.

Children of Augustine and Mary (Ball) Washington:

George, General, and twice President of the United
States; Betty, Samuel, JOHN AUGUSTINE, Charles,
and Mildred (died young). Of these, Betty, who married Fielding Lewis, is given on pages 132 to 134.

Colonel Samuel Washington, the third child, born in
Stafford County, Va., November 16, 1734, was a Colonel in the army. He built Harewood, in Berkeley
County, in 1755, now standing and in the possession
of one of this family. He married respectively, Jane,
daughter of Colonel John Champe; Mildred, daughter
of Colonel John Thornton; Lucy, daughter of Nathaniel Chapman; and Anne, daughter of Colonel Wil-

liam Steptoe (widow of Willoughby Allerton), and
they had: Frederick, George Steptoe, Lawrence Augustine, and Harriet Parks.

After which, the dashing Colonel married the widow
Perrin, and died 1781. President Madison was married
at Harewood to Dolly Payne, the sister of Mrs. Anne
Steptoe, wife of Samuel Washington.

The fifth child of Augustine and Mary (Ball)
Washington, was Colonel Charles Washington, of the
American Army. He married Mildred, daughter of
Colonel Francis Thornton, Charles Town, in Jefferson
County (now), West Virginia, being named for him,
he having given much of the ground, and laid it out.
His old residence is in the confines of the town, in
good preservation. Issue: Frances, married Colonel
Burgess Ball; Mildred, married —— Hammond; his
sons being George Augustine and Samuel. His brother
George, in his will, bequeaths to him "the Gold-headed
cane left me by Dr. Franklin. I add nothing to it
because of the ample provision I have made for his
issue."

George Steptoe, son of Colonel Samuel and Anne
(Steptoe) Washington, was born at Harewood about
1773; married Lucy, daughter of Mr. Payne of Virginia and Philadelphia. Issue: Sons, George, Samuel
Walter, William Temple, and George Steptoe. His
widow married Hon. Thomas Todd, Associate Justice
of the Supreme Court of the United States.

Dr. Samuel Walter, son of George Steptoe and Lucy
(Payne) Washington, born at Harewood, and died
there, married, in Philadelphia, Louisa, a daughter of
Thomas G. Clemson. Issue: Lucy Elizabeth, George
La Fayette, Christine Maria, Annie Steptoe Clemson,
all born at Harewood.

Lucy Washington, married William Bainbridge
Packett; George, married Miss Clemson; Annie, married Thomas A. Brown, and Christine Maria, married
a cousin, Richard Blackburn, born at Blakeley, November, 1822, son of John Augustine and Jane Charlotte Washington. He lived at Mount Vernon, and
married at Harewood. Had issue:

Elizabeth Clemson, married George Flagg; John
Augustine, the present owner of Harewood, married a
daughter of the Rev. Charles Ambler; Anna M. F.
Blackburn, and Louisa, died young; Samuel Walter,
married Elizabeth Willis; Richard Blackburn, married
Nannie Scott; Christine Maria; George Steptoe, married in Philadelphia, May Alexander; and De Hertburn, all born at Harewood.

These collaterals are the descendants of JOHN AU-
GUSTINE, through his son Corbin, who married Hannah,
daughter of Richard Henry Lee, and also descendants
of Samuel Washington, who intermarried with the descendants of John Augustine.

The will of Augustine Washington I. is much too
long to give, and is complicated by the two sets of children, or to quote his own language:

"Item, Forasmuch as my children in this my will
mentioned being by several ventures cannot inherit
from one another, etc." The seven children had each
a good portion, that of Lawrence, the eldest was 2500
acres; Augustine II, had "Wakefield," and the five
children of Mary Ball had each a good estate. The
home of Betty, in Fredericksburg, built by Colonel
Fielding Lewis, her husband, is in good preservation.

AUGUSTINE WASHINGTON II., the youngest son of
Captain Augustine and his first wife Jane (Butler)

Washington, was born at "Wakefield," Va., 1720. He was educated at Appleby, Eng., and later his half-brother George, had the advantage of his tutor, spending considerable time with this brother. Augustine was a Member of the Virginia Assembly 1754, 1755, and 1756.[9] That he was on close and intimate terms with his brother George appears from their letters. He married, in 1743, *Anne,* the daughter and co-heir of CAPTAIN WILLIAM AYLETT, JR., and *Anne Ashton,* his wife. Issue:

Elizabeth, married General Alexander Spotswood of the Revolution, a grandson of the Governor and son of John Spotswood; Jane, married William Thornton; Anne, born 1755, married Burdett Ashton; WILLIAM AUGUSTINE.

COLONEL JOHN AUGUSTINE WASHINGTON, fourth child of Captain Augustine and Mary (Ball) Washington, born at "Wakefield," January 13, 1736, and died February 17, 1787, married *Hannah,* a daughter of COLONEL JOHN BUSHROD, of "Bushfield," Westmoreland County, Va., and his wife, *Jenny Corbin.*

In a letter from William Fairfax, Esq., to "George Washington, Wmburg," April 14, 1756, he says:

"Mr. Lewis told me it was expected yr Brother John would be married this Day. We wish He may soon carry his Bride to Mount Vernon to make ye neighborhood more agreeable to Belvoir and Beneficial to you." Again:

. . . "Your Brother John is espoused to the late Miss Bushrod. All your Friends Salute You in which Gratulations and cordial Wishes for every Fe-

Col. Va. Register, Vol. VI., July, 1907. *Quarterly,* Vol. VI., p. 174. Also Grigsby's *Convention,* 1775-6.

licity that can reward a soldier, None can succeed, Dear Sir

Yr Afft Friend etc.

W. FAIRFAX."

"Bushfield," the home of John Augustine Washington, is still standing, and the following description is given in the journal and letters of Philip V. Fithian, in 1774:

" .   .   . The most agreeable situation of any I have seen in Maryland or Virginia; the broad Potowmack, which they account between 7 and 8 miles over, washes his Garden on the North, the River Nomini is within a stone's throw on the West, a level open country on the East: A lane of a mile and three quarters accurately measured, lies from the house on the South East, it has from the house the whole distance a uniform Descent, and at the Gate, at the End of this Lane the Situation is just six feet lower than at the House—There are no Marshes near, which altogether makes the place exceeding Description," etc.

One of the Signers of the Stamp Act February 27, 1765, John Augustine Washington, was also a member of the Virginia Association of Westmoreland, Va., July 17, 1775, to May, 1776. On Tuesday, the 26th day of September, 1775, at a meeting of the committee of Westmoreland County at the Courthouse, at the nomination of the field officers of the militia, he was nominated Colonel, as follows:

"At a meeting of the Committee of Westmoreland County at the Courthouse on Tuesday the 26th day of Septr. 1775

The Committee proceeded to the nomination of the field Officers of the Militia of said County as followeth Richard Henry Lee Esquire County Lieutenant

WILLIAM AUGUSTINE WASHINGTON
From a portrait by St. Memin

HON. GEORGE CORBIN WASHINGTON
From the painting by Simpson

HANNAH BUSHROD
Wife of Col. John Augustine
Washington

COL. JOHN AUGUSTINE WASHINGTON

John Augustine Washington Esq Colonel ⎤
William Barnard Esquire—Lieut Col°.   ⎬ Nem. con.
Burdette Ashton Esq—Major   ⎦
      Copy
        Test
           James Davenport Clk of Com."

During the wars between Great Britain and France
and that of the Revolution, he had charge of his brother
George's estates as well as that of his mother. In his
will, George Washington thus refers to his brother,
John Augustine, and bequeaths Mount Vernon to his
son Bushrod:

". . . To my nephew Bushrod Washington and his
heirs, (partly in consideration of an intimation to his
deceased father while we were bachelors, and he had
kindly undertaken to superintend my estate during my
military services in the former war between Great
Britain and France, that if I should fall therein Mount
Vernon, then less extensive in domain than at present,
should become his property), I give and bequeath all
that part thereof which is comprehended in the following limits . . . containing four thousand acres, be
the same more or less, together with the Mansion
House and all other buildings and improvements
thereon. . . ."

In writing to Henry Knox, Washington refers to
him as " A brother who was the intimate companion of
my youth and the friend of my ripened age."[10] The
descendants of John Augustine Washington held
Mount Vernon from the time of the death of General
Washington until purchased by the Mount Vernon
Ladies' Association.

[10] Ford's *Letters*.

In 1785, Colonel Washington was chosen one of the Vestry of Cople Parish in Westmoreland. He died and was buried at his estate in Westmoreland. Issue:

Jane (or *Jenny*), married COLONEL WILLIAM AUGUSTINE, son of Augustine II. and Anne (Aylett) Washington.

Mildred C., born at "Bushfield" about 1760, married Thomas, eldest son of Richard Henry Lee, of "Chantilly," and Anne Aylett, his wife (there were altogether three Anne Ayletts). He was born October 20, 1758, went to school in England, and lived at "Park Gate," near Dumfries, Prince William County, and practiced law. He married second, Eliza Ashton Brent, and died between the last of July and the first of October, 1805.

Bushrod; Corbin, married Hannah, a daughter of Richard Henry Lee of "Chantilly"; William Augustine, Jr.

CAPTAIN WILLIAM AUGUSTINE WASHINGTON, son of Augustine II. and Anne (Aylett) Washington, born in "Wakefield," Westmoreland County, Va., November 25, 1757, died in Georgetown, D. C., October 2, 1810, was buried in the vault at Mount Vernon, October 4, 1810, and removed to the new vault in 1824. He married first, September 25, 1777, when but twenty years of age, his cousin *Jane* (or *Jenny*), eldest daughter of JOHN AUGUSTINE, of "Bushfield" (his father's half-brother), and his wife *Hannah Bushrod,* born 1757-8, and died in 1791. On October 18, 1777, George Washington wrote his brother John respecting this marriage:

"Tell the young couple after wishing them joy of their union, that it is my sincere hope that it will be as happy and lasting as their present joys are boundless."

No likeness existed of *Jenny Washington,* until the recent publication of the *Journal* of Philip Vickers Fithian (1774), at Princeton, where he was graduated in 1774, going to Westmoreland as tutor. Therefore, after a hundred and thirty years her descendants have a most graphic picture of her from his pen; it also shows the fashions and customs of that day.

"Friday June 24, 1774. Nomini Hall, Westmoreland, Seat of Col. Robert Carter.

"Came to breakfast Miss Jenny Washington . . . Miss Washington is about 17. She has not a handsome face, but is neat in her dress, of an agreeable size & well-proportioned, and has an easy winning behaviour. She is not forward to begin a conversation, yet when spoken to is extremely affable, without assuming any girlish affectation, or pretending to be overcharged with wit. She has but lately had opportunity of instruction in dancing, yet she moves with propriety when she dances a minuet, and without any flirts or vulgar capers when she dances a reel or country-dance. She plays well on the harpsichord and spinet; understands the principles of Music, and therefore performs her tunes in perfect time, a neglect of which always makes music intolerable; but it is a fault almost universal among young ladies in the practice. She sings likewise to her instrument, has a strong, full voice, and a well-judging ear; but most of the Virginia girls think it labour quite sufficient to thump the keys of a harpsichord into the air of a tune mechanically, and think it would be slavery to submit to the drudgery of acquiring vocal music. Her dress is rich and well-chosen, but not tawdrey nor yet too plain. She appears to-day in a chintz cotton gown, with an elegant blue stamp, a sky-blue silk quilt, spotted apron. Her hair is a light brown; it was craped up with two rolls at each side, and on the top a small cap of beautiful gauze and rich lace, with an artificial flower interwoven. Her person and carriage at a small distance resemble not a little my much respected Laura, but on close examination her features are something masculine, those of Laura are mild and delicate. The dancing master very politely requested me to open the dance by stepping a minuet with this amiable girl, but I excused myself by assuring him that I never was taught to dance."

WILLIAM AUGUSTINE WASHINGTON married second, July 10, 1792, Mary, the daughter of Richard Henry and Anne (Aylett) Lee of "Chantilly," born there July 28, 1764, christened by the Rev. Archibald Campbell, March 11, 1765. Seven intermarriages between the Lees and Washingtons have occurred, the ownership of Mount Vernon descending through some of them. He married third, May 11, 1799, Sarah (Sally), the daughter of Colonel John Tayloe, of Mount Airy, Richmond County, Va., who survived him.

"At a meeting of the Committee of Westmoreland Court, at the Court House on Tuesday 26th September, 1775, the Committee proceeded to divide the County into Districts and to nominate the officers as follows: . . . and William Augustine Washington are nominated as Captains in the Lower District."

His company formed a part of the third Virginia regiment.[11] In 1785, he was High Sheriff of Westmoreland County.[12]

He inherited "Wakefield" from his father,[13] and it

---

[11] From original manuscript owned by Mrs. H. W. Hunter, née Washington.

[12] *Calendar of Virginia State Papers*, Vol. IV., p. 509.

[13] *Family Bible* at "Wakefield," owned by Mrs. Wilson. Ford's *Letters*, Vol. VI., p. 125.

was during his occupancy that it was burned, while he was entertaining on Christmas day, 1780. He was guardian, with General Charles Lee, of the children of Richard Henry Lee.

That General Washington was not ignorant or uninterested concerning the genealogy of his family in this country and England, is proven by letters from him to William Augustine, his nephew, dated February 27, and October 3, 1798. Also, from General Washington's letters it is learned that he was instrumental in sending the sons of this nephew (Augustine and George C.) to Phillips Academy, Andover, Mass., and the entries for the same may be seen at Andover.[14] The will of General Washington contains the following provision:

". . . To each of my nephews, William Augustine Washington, George Lewis, George Steptoe Washington, Bushrod Washington and Samuel Washington, I give one of the swords or cutteaux of which I may die possessed, and they are to chuse in the order they are named. The swords are accompanied with an injunction not to unsheath them for the purpose of shedding blood, except it be for self-defence or in defence of their country and its rights and in the latter case to keep them unsheathed and prefer falling with them in their hands to the relinquishment thereof. . . ."

William Augustine Washington was one of the executors of the will of his uncle, General George Washington, in which he was also given bequests of land. As he was ill at the time the choice of swords was made, Judge Bushrod Washington chose for him.

Issue, first wife, four children, viz.:   Bushrod,

14 *Original Manuscript* owned by Mrs. H. W. Hunter, née Washington. Preserved in *Calendar of Virginia State Papers*, Vol. IV., p. 509.

George Corbin, William Augustine, Jr., and Jane. Issue, third wife, four children.

Issue of John Augustine and Hannah (Bushrod) Washington:

1st. *Jane,* married her cousin, WILLIAM AUGUSTINE WASHINGTON, and had: Bushrod, married Henrietta Spotswood; *George Corbin* (see p. 433); William Augustine, Jr., married Julia Bayard, of Princeton, N. J.; Jane.

2d. Mildred (see pp. 455-456), married Thomas Lee, son of Richard Henry Lee, of Chantilly. Their home was Park Gate. They had one daughter, who married General Alexander.

3d. Hon. Bushrod Washington was born June 5, 1762, in Westmoreland County, Va., and died November 26, 1829. He married at Ripon Lodge, Prince William County, Va., in 1785, Ann, the daughter of Colonel Thomas Blackburn. No issue.

In 1778, he was a student at William and Mary College, and soon after became a private soldier in the Revolution, under Mercer at Yorktown, and went to the assistance of General Lafayette in 1780, as appears from the following:

"With the assistance of Bushrod Washington, then a youth of twenty, and other young gentlemen, a corps was collected, armed and marched in less than a week. At first, it did not exceed thirty; it gradually, however, grew in numbers and reputation, but never exceeded fifty on duty at one time; they furnished their own horses and armed themselves, and paid their own expenses, until all their resources were exhausted. . . ."

This was in response to the appeal from the Marquis de Lafayette "stating his total want of, and great distress for cavalry."

At an early age Judge Washington was admitted to the bar of his native state, after studying law in Philadelphia with James Wilson. In 1787 he was a Member of the Virginia House of Delegates, and the next year, of the Convention to ratify the United States Constitution. He received the degree of LL.D. from the College of New Jersey, dated October, 1803.

In 1798, at the age of thirty-six, Bushrod Washington was appointed by President Adams an Associate Justice of the Supreme Court of the United States (an office that he filled until his death), during which time we find this letter to him from Brockholst Livingston in 1817:

"What is Congress going to do with the Judges? As it seems admitted that our Compensation is not worth more than half it was originally, our salaries of course will be doubled. And as the President has just discovered that some of us are too old for our itinerary labors, from these we shall no doubt be delivered, etc."

A note of invitation sent to Mr. Edmund Lee reads:

General Washington presents his compliments to Mr. Edmund Lee, and requests the pleasure of his company to dine today with Genl Marshall & Mr. B. Washington Monday Sept 3^d '98.[15]

Judge Washington was one of the executors of his uncle, General George Washington, from whom he inherited Mount Vernon, his father, to whom it would have gone, having died. He was left a fourth choice of the General's swords, received all the papers which related to General Washington's Civil and Military administration of affairs of the country, and his library of books and pamphlets. Judge Washington died in

15 Original in the possession of Mrs. M. W. Keyser, of Baltimore.

Philadelphia while attending Court, his wife surviving him only three days, and they are buried at Mount Vernon.

4th. Corbin Washington, fourth child of John Augustine and Hannah (Bushrod) Washington, born at Bushfield, Westmoreland County, Va., 1765. He resided at Walnut Farm. Died about 1800. His will dated October 19, 1799. Married at Chantilly to Hannah, daughter of Hon. Richard Henry Lee, Westmoreland County, Va. Children: Richard Henry Lee, Bushrod Corbin, John Augustine, Mary Lee, and Jane.

5th. William Augustine, born at Bushfield. He was killed while at school.

Bushrod Corbin, son of Corbin and Hannah (Lee) Washington, born at Walnut Farm 1790, and died at Claymont in 1851, married Anna Maria, daughter of Major Richard Scott Blackburn, U. S. Army, and had a daughter, Hannah Lee, who married William P. Alexander (issue: Jean Charlotte, Richard William, Thomas and Herbert), and Thomas Blackburn, born 1813, married Rebecca Cunningham (issue: George, born February 22, 1840, died; Bushrod Corbin, married first Katharine Blackburn; married second, Emma Willis; James, died; Thomas, died; Annie, married in England to Alfred Ewing, C. B.).

John Augustine, son of Corbin and Hannah (Lee) Washington, born 1792, at Walnut Farm; married Jane Charlotte, daughter of Major Richard Scott Blackburn, U. S. A., and inherited Mount Vernon from his uncle, Judge Bushrod Washington. Dying in June, 1832, he is buried at Mount Vernon, his monument being just in front of the Vault. Issue: George, died young; Anna Maria, born 1817, died 1850, married Dr. William Fontaine Alexander.

John Augustine, son of John Augustine and Jane Charlotte Washington, born at Blakeley, Virginia, May, 1821, married Eleanor Love, daughter of Wilson Cary Selden, of Exeter, Loudon County, Va., and they had: Louisa, married Colonel Roger Preston Chew; Jane Charlotte, married Nathaniel Willis; Eliza Selden, married Major R. M. T. Hunter; Anna Maria, married Beverly Dandridge Tucker, Bishop Coadjutor of Virginia; Lawrence, married Fanny Lackland; Eleanor Love, married Julian Howard, and George, married Rena Porterfield.

The son of William Augustine and Jane Washington, *Hon. George Corbin Washington,* born at Haywood, Westmoreland County, Va., August 20, 1789, and died in Georgetown, D. C., July 17, 1854, was buried in Oak Hill cemetery. This was formerly a part of his residence "Dumbarton," inherited by his wife from the Bealls. The cemetery was presented to the city of Washington by Mr. W. W. Corcoran. He married first, September 1, 1807, Eliza Ridgely Beall, born November 22, 1786, died July 1, 1820; the daughter of "Thomas Beall of Geo. Esq.," and his wife Nancy Orme; married second, Ann T. Peter, who died February 3, 1861. Issue, one daughter, Eleanor Ann.

He was a pupil of Phillips Academy at Andover, Mass., 1803 to 1805. He served several terms in the Maryland Legislature and represented Montgomery County in Congress from 1827 to 1833, and from 1835 to 1837. He was President of the Chesapeake and Ohio Canal Company and Commissioner for the settlement of Indian claims. He is number five in the pic-

ture (sixteen by thirty feet), which hangs in Faneuil
Hall in Boston, painted by George P. Healy, under
the following circumstances:

> "Washington, March 3d, 1848,
> "at Mrs. Whitewell's, 4½ Street.
>
> "Hon. George C. Washington,
>   "Sir:
>   "The Citizens of Boston, Mass., have commissioned
> me to paint a group of the U. S. Senate representing
> Mr. Webster replying to General Hayne in 1830. As
> you were in the Lower House at the time, I am de-
> sirous that you should be painted in my picture. You
> will do me a favor by sending me a line saying on
> what day and hour next week you will give me the
> first sitting in the Committee room of Private Land
> Claims to the Senate. I shall remain but a short time
> longer.
>   "I have the honor to remain Sir,
>   "Respectfully Yours,
>   "GEORGE P. HEALY.
>   "P. S. I make this request at the suggestion of Mr.
> Webster."

From his father, William Augustine, George C.
Washington received the sword left him by his uncle,
George Washington, also the Lafayette pistols, his
watch chain and seals, etc., etc., and "Wakefield," the
birthplace of George and others of this family, now
owned by Mr. and Mrs. J. E. Wilson, she being a
cousin, a descendant of William Augustine and Sally
(Tayloe) Washington. The birth spot and the graveyard were reservations left to Lewis William Washington by his father.

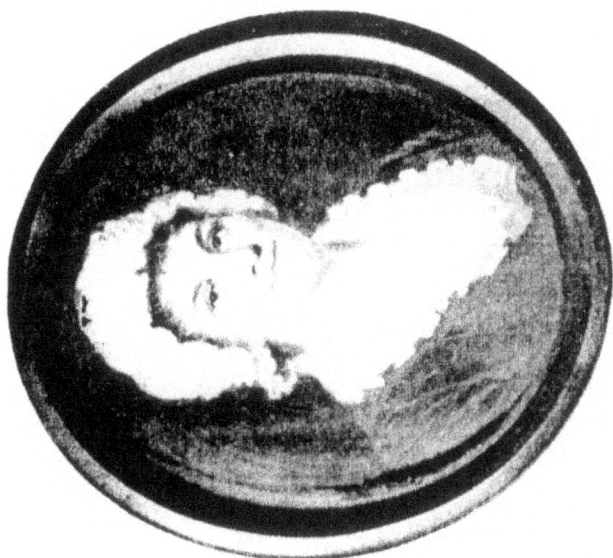

ANN ORME
Wife of Thomas Beall of Geo.
From a miniature taken in 1801

THOMAS BEALL OF GEO., ESQ.
From a miniature taken in 1801

From his uncle, Bushrod Washington of Mount
Vernon, George C. Washington inherited a fourth of
"All Liquors of every kind remaining in the house at
the death of my wife," etc. One-fourth went to his
brother Bushrod, and the remaining half to his two
first cousins, the grandsons of John Augustine, brother
of George Washington. He had one-fifth of lands,
and Judge Washington's will gave him "All the papers and letter-books devised to me by my uncle George
Washington, as well as the books in my study, other
than law books, I give to my nephew George C. Washington." Also, "The sword left me by Genl. Washington, I give to the aforesaid George C. Washington
under the same injunction that it was bestowed on me.
. . . The pistols which belonged to and were used by
Genl. Washington, to George C. Washington."

Issue, first wife, seven children, only one, *Lewis
William*, surviving to manhood; Eleanor Anne, born
October 30, 1822, and died April 13, 1849, was a
daughter of the second wife.

The only child of the Hon. George Corbin Washington and his first wife Eliza Ridgely Beall, who survived to manhood, *Lewis William Washington*, was
born November 30, 1812, and died at Beall-Air, October 1, 1871. He took his Bachelor's Degree at
Princeton 1833, and his Master's Degree in 1837.
Their home, inherited from his grandfather, "Thomas
Beall of Geo Esq.," lying in Jefferson County, Va.,
was an old stone house with walls literally three feet
thick, having for a background the Blue Ridge mountains, in the beautiful gap of which nestled Harper's
Ferry, later to play an important part in his experi-
ence. He married first, May 17, 1836, in Baltimore,

Md., by the Rev. William Edward Wyatt, D. D.,
S. T. D., Mary, the second daughter of James Barroll of Baltimore, and Mary Crockett, his wife. (He
was the son of the Rev. William Barroll, and Ann
Williamson, his wife, who was descended from the
Hynsons.) Mr. Washington's wife dying November 16, 1845, was survived by three of their four
children, who were taken by their Barroll grandparents in Baltimore; but they always visited their
father at his home "Beall-Air," in Virginia, in the
intervals of vacation.

During one of these visits to "Beall-Air," in the
fall of 1859, a man stopped at the house, claiming to
be a stranger travelling that way, representing himself
as a geologist, exhibiting specimens, and in turn asking
to see the relics of Washington that he had heard were
there. The cabinet in the first room to the left of the
portico where he was sitting, was opened and he was
shown a pair of pistols, the gift of Lafayette to Washington; also a sword allotted to Mr. Washington's
grandfather, said to have been presented by Frederick
the Great. The stranger expressed great interest in
these and other objects in the cabinet. Shortly afterward, a daughter, who was present at this interview,
left for Baltimore. After midnight of that day Mr.
Washington, who slept in the room just opposite in
the hall of the one containing the relics, was aroused
from sleep by a rap on the door. Opening it he saw
seven men, colored and white, with a lighted torch.
The spokesman, who was none other than the visitor
of the morning, informed Mr. Washington that he was
their prisoner, to be held as hostage by John Brown
at Harper's Ferry; that his carriage was being made

ready to convey him thence, while a large farm wagon was to transfer his servants. "Cook," the traveller, demanded the sword and pistols, taking them from the cabinet. This motley cavalcade arrived at Harper's Ferry about break of day and was met by Brown, who armed the servants with pikes (long poles with a spear on the end, a foot longer than a musket and bayonet) and told them they were free. The sword was taken by Brown, who issued all orders with it, and the pistols were appropriated by Cook. This was the morning of October 16, 1859, and on the 19th the prisoners in the engine house, who had been without food, were released by Colonel Robert E. Lee, commanding the United States marines. Brown was wounded in the storming of the engine house by the U. S. troops, but Cook escaped to the mountains in Maryland with the pistols, only one of which was recovered when Mr. Washington's servant led the scouting party that brought Cook back a prisoner. Mr. Washington, being a Colonel on the staff of Governor Wise of Virginia, was present at the execution of Brown, Cook, and their colleagues.

Mr. Washington married second, November 6, 1860, Ella More, daughter of G. W. and Betty Burnett (Lewis) Bassett. He died at "Beall-Air," and is buried in the churchyard of Zion Episcopal Church, in Charles Town, three miles distant. "Beall-Air" was confiscated during the Civil War, and restored later with here and there a valueless bit of furniture.

Issue, first wife, four children, viz.:

George Corbin, died young.

James Barroll, married Jane Bretney Lanier (widow Cabell).

MARY ANN, married H. Irvine Keyser. Issue: Henry Barroll, married CAROLINE FRANKLIN FISCHER; Lewis Washington, died young; Samuel Irvine, died young; W. Irvine, married Ethel Howard Whitridge; MARY WASHINGTON, married first, John Stewart, Jr., and second, De Courcy Wright Thom; William Williams, died young.

Eliza Ridgely Beall, married E. Glenn Perine, whose fourth daughter is ELIZA WASHINGTON.

Issue, second wife, two children, viz.:

A daughter, died an infant; William de Hertburn.

POPE

NATHANIEL POPE, in 1637 one of the twenty-four freemen of the "Grand Inquest" in Maryland, was exempted in 1643, with his nine menial servants, from all military service. Sent as agent to Kent Island 1647, in 1650 he removed to Virginia, on Pope's Creek. "On the 4th April, 1655, Commissioned for ye County of Westmoreland;" also, "Appointed by ye Governor & Council to be of ye Militia for ye said County Lieut Col. Nathaniel Pope." By Governor and Council made one[16] of the Quorum. The Will of "Coll. Nathaniel Pope of Appomattox, Westmoreland County, Gentleman, about to go to England," dated May 16, 1659, and proven April 20, 1660, contains bequests to son-in-law John Washington, and son-in-law William Hardidge.[17] His wife was Luce ——.

Issue of Nathaniel and Luce Pope: Thomas, Nathaniel, *Anne,* married Col. John Washington (issue, Lawrence, John and Anne), and Margaret, married William Hardidge.

[16] *Quarterly,* by W. G. Stanard, Vol. I., p. 188.
[17] *Quarterly,* Vol. I., p. 188; *Ibid,* Vol. II., p. 78.

WARNER

ARMS: *Vert, a cross engrailed, or.*
CREST: *A double plume of feathers.*

CAPTAIN AUGUSTINE WARNER, came to America about 1628. He was Justice of York County, and settled in Gloucester County at "Warner Hall." This estate retains the name, though the present house is not the original one, it having been destroyed by fire, 1845; the superb elms alone remain. Burgess for York 1652, and for Gloucester 1655, and "Satt as a Councellor" (to use a Colonial expression) 1659 to 1667.[18]

WARNER

In the graveyard at "Warner Hall" is the following:

"Mary Warner, ye wife of Augustine Warner, Esq., was Born the 13th day of May 1614 and dyed ye 11th day of August 1662." (Her surname unknown.)

His tombstone at Abingdon Parish, Gloucester County, reads as follows:

"Augustine Warner deceased ye 24th of December 1674 aged 63 years 2 Mth 26 D^s."

His name "Augustine" has been perpetuated to the present generation. Their daughter Sarah, married Lawrence Townley and was ancestress of General Robert E. Lee.

COLONEL AUGUSTINE WARNER of "Warner Hall," son of Augustine and Mary Warner, was born June 3,

18 *Wm. & Mary Quar.*, Vol. II., pp. 226-227, 1894.
Calendar of Md. State Papers, 1660-1661.

1642-3; and enrolled on the books of the Merchants
Tailor's School, London, in 1658, as the eldest son of
Augustine Warner, Gentleman, of Virginia, October
20, 1643; the former date is on his tomb-stone at
"Warner Hall," where his death is given June 18,
1681.

In 1676 he was made Speaker of the House of Burgesses & Councillor.[19]

The occupants of these old seats, "Warner Hall"
and the neighboring gentry, are characterized, says
a writer, as "families of first consequence in the
Colony, having good libraries, descended from English gentlemen, and all of them having Coats of Arms
of undoubted authority."

COLONEL AUGUSTINE WARNER married *Mildred,* the
daughter of Colonel George and Elizabeth (Martian)
Reade. Their daughter *Mildred,* married MAJOR
LAWRENCE WASHINGTON.

READE

COLONEL GEORGE READE, son of Robert Reade and
his wife, Mildred Windebank, has an interesting pedigree, as well as the record that he made in our American history. It may be remembered that his wife,
Mildred, was a daughter of Sir Francis Windebank
the obnoxious Secretary to Charles I., and also that
Robert (brother of Colonel George) was private Secretary to Sir Francis, his uncle.

In 1585 there was a conveyance of the Manor of
Linkenholt, County Southampton, England, to Andrew Reade. The Manor of Linkenholt at the time
of the Domesday survey, belonged to Ernalf de Hord-
ing, by whom it was given to the Abbey of St. Peter,
Gloucester County, coming into possession of Henry
VIII. by the dissolution of that house. The Manor

19 *Wm. & Mary Quar.,* April, 1901, p. 264.

was sold 1546 to Richard Reade, Esq., afterwards knighted. Andrew Reade in 1600, upon the marriage of his son Robert to Mildred Windebank, his last wife and mother of his children, conveyed the use of the Manor to Robert Reade, his wife Mildred and to Andrew Reade, son of Robert, in tail. Robert Reade and Andrew, his son, conveyed this Manor to Mr. Windebank, Mr. Henry Reade, Mr. Nicholas Blake and to said Robert Reade, who in 1627 by his deed appointed the Manor to be sold, etc. Shortly afterwards he died. This Manor was then, once possessed by a direct ancestor of George Washington's family. The name Mildred, traced through so many generations of the Warner, Lee and Washington families, has its origin as early as 1600, when Robert Reade married Mildred Windebank.

COLONEL GEORGE READE, the subject of this paper came to Virginia in 1637; died 1671; married Elizabeth, the daughter of CAPTAIN NICHOLAS MARTIAN of York County, Virginia. In 1640-1 he was made Secretary of State for the Colony; Burgess for James City County 1644-56, member of the Council from March 13, 1657-8 and April 3, 1659, holding this office until his death, with title and rank of Colonel.[20] Acting Governor and Acting Secretary of the Colony, during Kemp's absence. November 20, 1671, the will of George Reade was admitted to probate.

By the marriage of his daughter Margaret, and Thomas Nelson, George Reade was ancestor of Governor Thomas Nelson; and by the marriage of his daughter *Mildred* and Speaker Augustine Warner, was ancester of the *Washingtons*. He had at least a dozen children for whose record our space does not admit.

[20] York *Records*, March 27, 1660. *Quar.*, Vol. I., p. 194.

MARTIAN

CAPTAIN NICHOLAS MARTIAN, of York County in Virginia, was of French birth—born 1591—he was, however, a naturalized citizen of England, from whence he came to Virginia about 1620-1, with his wife and children. He was Justice of York 1630, and a Burgess of Kent Island and Kiskiach 1632. He patented land in York County March 14, 1639, which land was the present site of Yorktown, known then as Temple Farm.[21]

In the strife between Sir John Harvey, Governor, and William Claiborne, Secretary of State, such bitter feeling existed, that an indignation meeting was held on April 27, 1635, at the home of William Warren, in York, where the principal speaker was Nicholas Martian (formerly member of the House of Burgesses for Kent Island), Francie Pott, the Doctor's brother, and William English, Sheriff of York County; unfortunately space does not allow a repetition of this spirited interview, but it is regarded as an early protest against English tyranny. The house where this meeting was held 1635, was on, or near the site where, in 1781, the surrender of Cornwallis was arranged, and Nicholas Martian was direct ancestor of both Washington, who was commanding the Army, and of Thomas Nelson, who commanded the Virginia forces on that memorable occasion.

The will of Martian, dated March 1, 1656, recorded in York County, Va., proved 1657, divided his estate among his daughters: Elizabeth, wife of Colonel George Reade; Mary, wife of Lt. Col. John Scarbor-

21 Fiske, Vol. I., pp. 287, 296.
    Had land there Apr. 24, 1635. *Quar.*, Vol. II., pp. 3, 4.
    Neill's *Va. Carolorum.*
    Quar., July, 1893.

ough, and Sarah, wife of Capt. William Fuller, Governor of Maryland. William Fuller was one of the original appointees named by the Parliamentary Commissioners July 22, 1654, to fill vacancies made by the Provisional Court. In 1655 Fuller with one hundred and seventy-five men, had met Governor Stone and his force of a hundred and thirty men, and had come off victorious. Major John Scarborough, was a Justice of York; he married second, Jane, daughter of Thomas and Elizabeth Bushrod.[22]

Old York was a different place from Yorktown. Court was often held there during the early part of the 17th century. Kiskiach was the first settlement in York County 1630, York was next 1632, and Middle Plantation was the third.

DYMOKE

The Dymokes were hereditary champions of England. "There are Autograph letters Extant from Sovreigns, one from Henry VIII 1513, and also one from Queen Mary to the Knightly Dymokes—as Champions."

Frances, the daughter of Sir Edward Dymoke and Lady Anne Talbois his wife—concerns this narrative by marrying Sir Thomas Windebank August 20, 1566. Mildred Windebank, their daughter, married Robert Reade; these were the parents of the emigrant.

AYLETT

The family of Aylett, of King William County, Va., were of Saxon extraction, from County Essex, England, their ancient seat being Bocton Aloph, near Wye, in the County of Kent.[23]

22 *Sun Almanac*, p. 42 (1902).
    Quar., Vol. I., p. 82.
23 *Reign of Henry III.*
    Burke's *Extinct and Dormant Baronetcies.*

The name was originally Ayloffe of Braxted Magna, and variously spelled in the Journals of the House of Commons.

First, the eldest son of the third William Ayloff, was Sir William Ayloffe Knt., being knighted by King James I; later advanced by him to the degree of Baronet in 1612. Second, Sir Benjamin Ayloffe who for his fidelity to Charles I was made High Sheriff of Essex, at the beginning of the Civil War. After many vicissitudes, being a prisoner in the Tower until 1646, and surviving until after the Restoration, he served as Knight of the Shire of Essex in the Parliament succeeding that event. He was spoken of as a "deare olde friende" "of Colⁿ Richᵈ Lee," progenitor of the Lees of Virginia. Sir Benjamin married three times; Burke gives issue of the second marriage only. Margaret Fanshawe, his second wife, was the daughter of Thomas Fanshawe, Esq., (died 19 Feb., 1600), of Ware Neck, and Joan Smythe, his second wife, and sister of Sir Thomas Fanshawe, K.B., Supervisor General and Clerk of the Crown (died 1631). Sir Benjamin died 1662-63.[24]

The fourth son of Sir Benjamin Ayloffe, Captain John Aylett, was the Emigrant ancestor of the Ayletts in America, 1656, whence he came to escape "deathe or ye Tower," having raised and led as Captain, a troop of horse at the Battle of Worcester. Because of his extreme youth he was pardoned by Cromwell, but continuing active in plots against the Protector, in the Cavalier Rising of "55," he fled to Virginia in 1656, later taking up tracts of land in the present King William County. (Wilson M. Cary.) In the *Calendar of State Papers of Va.* we find him with others

[24] *Aylett Letters*, by Col. Wm. Winston Fontaine, written from Braxted Magna, 1658 to 1676, to Capt. John, in Va., by his elder brothers.

appointed to survey the County in 1660. His descendants intermarried with the Lees, Ashtons, Washingtons, and other families.

Letters from his family were, until 1662, in care of "Coll° Rich⁴ Lee," his father's "deare olde friende." His wife Anne was supposed to have been the daughter of "Coll° Rich⁴ Lee." Issue, three sons and two daughters: Philip, born 1658; Benjamin, born 1660, d. i.; William, born 1662; daughters' names not recorded.

The eldest son Philip, settled in King William County, Va., 1686, at "Fairfield," married and had issue among others:

CAPTAIN WILLIAM AYLETT, who bore the same arms as Aylett of Braxted Magna, England, from whom he descended, as shown by an old Book Plate in possession of the family. He was Clerk of King William County 1702 to 1714; member of House of Burgesses of Va. 1723 to 1726, and a Vestryman of St. John's Parish 1731. Had Patents of land in Essex 1704 and 1717. His wife was Sibylla, widow of Matt Hubard, living in 1749. Issue: Philip, married Martha Dandridge, whose son William, married Mary Macon, and their son Philip, married Elizabeth Henry, who built "Montville," WILLIAM II., John, Benjamin, and daughters who married eldest sons of the neighboring gentry.[25]

CAPTAIN WILLIAM AYLETT II., born 1700, of Westmoreland County, Va., son of William and Sibylla, died March 29, 1744; will proved August 28, mentions lands held as heir of his brother Benjamin. "Executors: Major Lawrence Washington, my Son-in-law Augustine Washington, My bro Philip Aylett, & Dan¹ McCarty, Gentlemen."

[25] *Genealog. Chart.* Francie J. A. Junkin.

He married, 1724, Anne (born 1706, died 1730), the daughter of Col. Henry Ashton and his wife Elizabeth Hardidge. Issue: Elizabeth, and *Anne,* who married in March, 1743, AUGUSTINE WASHINGTON II. Issue: WILLIAM AUGUSTINE, married Jane, the daughter of his half uncle, John Augustine Washington, and his wife Hannah Bushrod; Elizabeth, married General Alexander Spotswood, grandson of Governor Alexander Spotswood; Jane, married Colonel William Thornton, and Anne, married Burdett Ashton.

ASHTON

ARMS: *Argent, a mullet sable, on a fesse gules, a crescent for difference.*

CREST: *A boar's head argent couped sable.*

CHARLES ASHTON was in Virginia before 1650, being a Justice of Northumberland County in 1659, and of the Quorum, and Captain of Militia. He was born 1621-22, and died 1672.[26]

ASHTON

CAPTAIN JOHN ASHTON, an officer in King Charles' Army, and often mentioned in Virginia records, was a Justice of Westmoreland County and appointed by the Governor a Commissioner to treat with the Indians. He married, 1668, *G r a c e,* the daughter of COL. HENRY MEESE (of the Governor's Council); she died September 9, 1677. Issue: HENRY, Charles, Jr., John and Sarah.[27]

[26] *Wm. & Mary Quar.,* Vol. IV., p. 40.   *Col. Va. Reg.,* p. 56.

[27] *Quar.,* Vol. XV., p. 45.

WILLIAM AYLETT
From portrait by St. Memin

MEMORIAL TABLET
Dartmouth Arms, quartered with Washington at
the Minories, England

COLONEL HENRY ASHTON, their son, born July 30, 1671, died December 3, 1731, was High Sheriff of the County 1717 to 1718, Colonel, Justice, and Burgess 1702 to 1705. In 1696, he married first, *Elizabeth,* the daughter of COLONEL WILLIAM HARDIDGE, GENT., and Frances Gerard, his wife; she was born 1678, and died February 25, 1722; issue, four daughters: Frances, Elizabeth, *Ann* and Grace; the last only survived him; married second, Mary, the daughter of Richard Watts, Gentleman; issue, one daughter and two sons: Elizabeth, Henry and John.[28]

In an old graveyard upon Booth's plantation, in Westmoreland County, Va., is the monument with the Ashton Arms, to the memory of Col. Henry Ashton:

"Here lies ye body of Colonel Henry Ashton, Gentleman, Born in Westmoreland County, son of John Ashton Gentleman, by Grace his wife the 30th day of July Anno Domini 1670."

The will of Henry Ashton, recorded in Westmoreland County, Va., probated November 24, 1731, bequeaths to his daughter Grace one thousand acres of land inherited from Colonel William Hardidge. Grace married Philip Lee (son of Richard and grandson of Richard) of "Blenheim," High Sheriff of Charles County, Md.

Ann, daughter of Colonel Henry and Elizabeth (Hardidge) Ashton, married CAPTAIN WILLIAM AYLETT II., marriage contract in Essex County, Va., May 18, 1725. Their daughter *Anne,* married AUGUSTINE WASHINGTON II.

COLLATERAL ASHTON LINE

The second son of John Ashton, Charles Ashton II., (grandson of Charles), born May 3, 1712, and died

[28] Hayden; *Col. Reg. Quar.,* Vol. IV., p. 80.

April 2, 1781, married first Sarah Burdett, born July
9, 1715, and died October 28, 1772. His second marriage in 1706, was to Margaret Hart. Children of
first marriage, Burdett and Charles.[29]

The eldest son, Burdett Ashton, of Chestnut Hill,
King George's County, born November 21, 1747, married December 19, 1768, Anne, the daughter of AU-
GUSTINE WASHINGTON II.; she was born April 2, 1752.
He was member of State Convention 1788, Delegate
1799 to 1800, etc. Issue: Charles Augustine, died
1800; Burdett, Sarah and Ann.[30]

MEESE

"At a Committee of ye Association of Northumberland, Westmoreland, & Stafford Co's ye 1st of 9 [ber]
1667. Present Col Pett Ashton, Col Nich Spencer,
Lt Col Hen Meese &c."—(Abstract from the Records.)

"According to act of Assembly 25 Sep last a fort
was to be erected by the last of April next in Yeocomico
River, commissioners selected Levy Point, and Lt Col
Henry Meese was given charge of the money for dis-
bursement as ordered." [31]

COLONEL HENRY MEESE, first appearance in the
Colonial Council of Virginia, 1680, was Burgess from
Stafford County, in 1666. Date of his birth or marriage not forthcoming; that he left a daughter *Grace,*
who married CAPTAIN JOHN ASHTON, is well authenticated, as found on the tomb of their son, HENRY
ASHTON, who married *Elizabeth Hardidge,* whose
daughter *Ann,* married WILLIAM AYLETT II.; their
daughter *Anne,* married AUGUSTINE WASHINGTON II.

29 *Wm. & Mary Quar.,* Vol. VII., p. 174.
30 *Family Bible* of Burdett Ashton.
    Quar., Vol. VII., p. 115.
31 *Wm. & Mary Quarterly,* p. 227, April, 1901.

STURMAN-HARDIDGE

In 1645, Thomas Sturman, a Puritan, was prominent in the disturbances of Richard Ingle. He married Anne ——, whose will was proved in 1654. Issue: John, Richard, Anne, Elizabeth, and Rosanna.

Their daughter, Elizabeth Sturman, married William Hardwick, born 1618, deceased in Bristol, 1669.[32] Issue: Elizabeth and WILLIAM.

COLONEL WILLIAM HARDIDGE, their son, had a grant of a thousand acres of land in 1651. At a Committee, "By order of ye Grand Assembly for laying a Levy in the Northern Neck for suppressing ye late Rebellion," etc., August, 1677, were found acting together, " Coll. William Ball, Coll. John Washington and William Hardidge."[33] He was a Justice of Westmoreland County 1680 to 1692-93.[34]

He married first, Frances, the daughter of Colonel Thomas and Susanna (Snow) Gerard, and the widow of Colonel Thomas Speke (will dated 1659), and widow of her second husband, Colonel Valentine Peyton. She had one son Gerard, who willed his property to his half sister Elizabeth Hardidge.[35] (See pp. 547-548 for Gerard). Colonel William Hardidge married second, Margaret, the daughter of Nathaniel Pope, a sister of Mrs. John Washington.

His daughter Elizabeth (first wife), sole heiress, born July 20, 1671, and died December 3, 1731, married COLONEL HENRY ASHTON.

[32] *Quar.*, Vol. IV., pp. 40, 48.
　The name spelled at different times, Harditch, Hardwick, Hardidge.
[33] *Quar.*, Vol. II., pp. 48, 49.
　Wilson M. Cary.
[34] Hayden, p. 488, says Northumberland; *Quar.*, Vol. IV., p. 83, names Westmoreland.
[35] *Lee of Virginia*, p. 149.

BUSHROD

The colonist, Thomas Bushrod, first in Massachusetts, and afterwards in Virginia, married Mary Peircey, but left no issue. He was a Burgess 1659, and returned in 1660. There is among the Ludwell manuscripts a patent by Sir William Berkeley for three hundred and forty-five acres of land, to Thomas Bushrod in Westmoreland County, Virginia, dated July 2, 1669, framed and hanging in the State Library. His will, proved in York County in 1677, "Being a Quaker," enjoins that "'No Common prayers" be said at his burial.[36]

The brother of Thomas, Richard Bushrod, Gent., born 1626, in 1660 and 1665 patented large tracts of land in Westmoreland County, and was the progenitor of the family in America. He married Apphia, and had issue (named in will of Thomas Bushrod), Thomas, *John,* Apphia and Dorothy.

His widow Apphia afterwards married Dr. Whiting of Gloucester.

The tombstone of John Bushrod, son of Richard, at "Bushfield," reads as follows:

Here lies ye Body of
John Bushrod son of Richard Bushrod
Gent; by Apphia his wife
He was born in Gloucester County in Virginia
ye 30 January 1663.
He took to wife Hannah the daughter of
William Keene of Northumberland
County Gent, and Elizabeth his wife
and by her left two sons & four daughters
& died the 26th of February, 1719
in the 56th year of his age.[37]

[36] *Cradle of the Republic.*
  Wm. & Mary Quar., Vol. I., p. 195.
[37] *Quar.,* Vol. I., p. 9; *Lee of Virginia,* p. 550.

ANCESTRAL RECORDS AND PORTRAITS 451

The widow of John Bushrod of Nominy, Westmoreland County. Va., née Hannah Keene, married
Willoughby Allerton, Gent., Collector of Customs for
Potomac River, 1711 (grandson of Isaac Allerton, Pilgrim on the *Mayflower*).

COLONEL JOHN BUSHROD, son of John and Hannah
Bushrod, "of the Parish of Cople in the County of
Westmoreland Gent.," born 1718, married *Jenny,* the
daughter of COLONEL GAWIN CORBIN and *Hannah
Lee.*[38] He was Burgess for Westmoreland 1744 to
1755. His will, proved December 30, 1760, names
issue: *Hannah,* who married JOHN AUGUSTINE WASH-
INGTON, and Elizabeth.

KEENE

The will of Thomas Keene of Northumberland, was
dated November 22, 1652, and names wife Mary (will
1662), sons Thomas, William and Matthew, and
daughter Susanna.

His son, William Keene, born March 10, 1642, died
February 8, 1684, married *Elizabeth,* the daughter of
John Rogers, Gent. and Ellin his wife, of Northumberland County, in Virginia. On "Cypress Farm"
at the head of Garner's Creek, near the site of the
early Keene residence, two heavy slabs are to be seen.
On one is the following:

"Here lyeth the body of William Keene, the eldest
son of Thomas and Mary Keene Born in Kent in
Maryland the 10th day of March Anno Dom, 1642,
Who marryed Eliz[a], the Daughter of John Rogers
Gent, and Ellin his wife of Northumberland Co. in Virginia by Whome he had two Sons and four daughters
and dyed ye 8 day of Feb. 1684 in ye two and Fortieth
year of his age."

[38] Westmoreland County *Record.*

"On the death of William Keene, his widow Elizabeth, dau of John Rogers Gent, and Ellin his wife of Northumberland County in Virginia, was marryed the 8 day of december 1687 to Thomas Banks Gent, of Wiltshire, England."

On his tomb, after the above, we find:

"As I in Sorrow for thee have been distrest,
If God Permit Me Lye by thee to rest." [39]

In 1722, occurred the death of Elizabeth, widow of William Keene, and widow of Thomas Banks, her will being proved March 15, 1722. Issue, William, John, and a daughter, Hannah, who married John Bushrod of "Bushfield," in Westmoreland County.

ROGERS

JOHN ROGERS, will probated July 21, 1680; in Northumberland County, Va., this name first appears February, 1650, in connection with the Indians.[40]

"In the Indian War of 1676 is a Committee held for Northumberland County at ye Court Howse ye July 4, 1676, present Captain John Rogers, later known as Major."[41]

He was one of the early settlers of the County and long served as one of the early Justices, 1656. On a creek now known by his name, was the plantation and early home of the Justice. In 1676 he married Ellin, and had William (name often spelled Rodgers), who married Elizabeth, daughter of Edward and Diana Dale; and *Elizabeth,* who married first, William Keene, and second Thomas Banks.[42]

[39] *Quar.,* Vol. VIII., p. 45.
[40] *Records* of Northumberland Co., Va.
[41] *Wm. & Mary Quar.,* Vol. VIII., p. 25.
[42] *Va. Hist. Mag.,* Vol. I., p. 456.

CORBIN

ARMS: *Sable on a chief or, three ravens, ppr.*
MOTTO: *Provitas Verus, Honos.*[43]

As early as 1154 to 1161, one Robert Corbin gave lands to the Abbey of Ealesworth. From Robert are traced ten generations to Nicholas Corbin, seized of Hall End, and lands in the County of Warwick, etc.

Four generations after this is "Thomas Corbin of Hall End afors'd, born 24 May, 1594, died June, 1637; bur'd at Kingswinford." Thomas married 1620, Winifred, daughter of Gowen Grosvenor, of Sutton Colfield, County Warwick, England.

COLONEL HENRY CORBIN, third son of Thomas and Winifred Corbin, born 1629, died in Virginia January 8, 1675.[44] He was the progenitor of the Corbins in America, emigrating about 1654, and locating first in the parish of Stratton Major, in King and Queen County.[45]   Afterwards he had lands in Lancaster, Westmoreland, Middlesex, etc., as the ensuing will show. He was Burgess from Lancaster 1658, 1659, and 1660; one of the Council 1663, and Justice of Middlesex 1673, after which he was seated at "Pecatone" in Westmoreland County, patents for which were dated March 26, 1664. This estate was of such proportions that its gardens, with orange

CORBIN

---

[43] *Herald's College,* and Burke's *General Armory.*
[44] *Lee of Virginia,* p. 83.   [45] *Quar.,* Vol. III., p. 65.

trees, etc., were quoted in books of travel of that day.

He married, July 25, 1645, Alice, a daughter of Richard Eltonhead, of Eltonhead, County Lancaster, England, and the widow of Roland Burnham. After the death of Henry Corbin, she married third, Captain Henry Creek, who died at the home of Colonel Richard Lee, in August, 1684. Henry and Alice Corbin had issue:

Henry, died young; Thomas, lived in England unmarried, and his brother Gawin, in Virginia, inherited his lands; GAWIN; *Laetitia,* married RICHARD LEE, of Mount Pleasant, adjoining his father's estate; Alice, married Philip Lightfoot; Winifred, married Le Roy Griffin; Anne, married William Tayloe, and Frances married Governor Edmund Jennings of Virginia.

GAWIN CORBIN, married first Catherine Wormeley, but had no issue; married second, Jane (widow Wilson), and daughter of John Lane, of Laneville, Middlesex County, where in 1705 he was Naval Officer of the Rappahannock, afterwards Burgess, and later of the Council, and its President. Issue:

Richard, married Elizabeth Tayloe of Mount Airy; John, married Laetitia Lee (daughter of Richard); GAWIN II.; Joanna, married Major Robert Tucker; *Jenny,* married COLONEL JOHN BUSHROD of "Bushfield"; Alice, married Benjamin Needler; Ann, married Isaac Allerton, grandson of the *Mayflower* immigrant.

GAWIN CORBIN II., son of Gawin and Jane (Lane) Corbin, was Burgess 1720 to 1722, and Councillor 1740. He married *Hannah* (born 1701), the daughter of HON. THOMAS LEE, President of the Council, and his wife *Hannah Ludwell.* Their daughter, *Jenny,* married COLONEL JOHN BUSHROD; their daughter

Hannah Bushrod, married JOHN AUGUSTINE WASH-
INGTON, whose daughter *Jane* (or *Jenny,* named for
her Corbin grandmother), married her cousin, WIL-
LIAM AUGUSTINE WASHINGTON.

LEE

COLONEL RICHARD LEE, "Esqʳ.," was the first
Attorney-General of whom we have any notice. He
is referred to as such in the records of the General
Court in 1643, coming from Stratford, Langton, in
the County of Essex, England.[46] From the numerous
land grants we learn of his being in the Colony in 1642,
and also of the many offices that he held, Justice, Burgess, Councillor,[47] and that he succeeded Richard
Kempe as Secretary of State in 1649, and until April,
1652, when Claiborne was appointed. He served also
on many commissions. Living first in York, out of
which Gloucester County was afterward made, he was
later in Northumberland, 1651, at "Dividing Creeks."[48]
His will, proven in London, 1664-5, names his wife
Anna, and here are mentioned his sons, John, RICHARD,
Francis, William, Hancock; then Betsey, Anne and
Charles.

The application or order for head rights of his son
John, speaks of the transportation of ninety-four per-
sons into the Colony by "his ffather Collº. Richard
Lee, Esqʳ. whoe is now deceased."[49]

RICHARD LEE, son of "Collº. Richard Lee Esqʳ.,"
and Anna, his wife, was born 1647, died March 12,
1714, was educated at Oxford, and spent his life in
study, being a Greek, Hebrew and Latin scholar of

46 Only the members of this family are cited who are claimants of this
paper.
47 Neill's *Va. Carolorum.*   48 *Wm. & Mary Quar.,* Vol. X., p. 140.
49 *Lee of Va.,* p. 64.

note. He was one of the Council in 1675, 1680, 1683,
1688, 1692 to 1698; Burgess 1677. In a list of officers,
date 1699, "Rich⁴. Lee, Esqʳ. has been appointed
Naval Officer and Receiver of Virginia Duty's" on the
Potomac River, including three counties. Appointment made by Sir Edmund Andros, Governor. In
these Counties, Westmoreland, Northumberland and
Stafford, he is mentioned as "Coll. Rich⁴. Lee of the
Horse" in 1680. We learn through Governor Nicholson, in 1691, of his conscientious scruples in taking the
oath of allegiance to William and Mary, for which he
was dropped from the Council, but later reinstated.
Neill describes Nathaniel Bacon, Jr.,[50] as ordering
Richard Lee, among others, to surrender or be seized
as "Traytors to ye King and Country." He married
(it is said 1674), *Laetitia,* the eldest daughter of Henry
Corbin and his wife, Alice Eltonhead. Laetitia was
born 1657, and died before October 6, 1706. Their
tombstone is to be seen at "Mount Pleasant," the inscription almost effaced after one hundred and ninety-
five years' exposure. Translated, it reads:

"Here lieth the body of Richard Lee, Esq., born in
Virginia, the son of Richard Lee, Gentleman, descended of an ancient family of Merton Regis, in
Shopshire. While he exercised the office of Magistrate he was a zealous promotor of the public good.
He was very skillful in the Greek and Latin languages,
and other parts of polite learning. He quietly resigned his Soul to God, whom he always devoutly worshipped, on the 12th day of March, in the year 1714, in
the 68th year of his age."

"Near by is interred the body of Laetitia, his faithful wife, daughter of Henry Corbyn, Gentleman. . . .

50 *Va. Carolorum.*

COL. RICHARD LEE

MRS. RICHARD LEE

RICHARD LEE

LAETITIA CORBIN
Wife of Richard Lee

She died on the 6th day of October 1706 in the 49th year of her age."

Richard Lee's will was dated March 8, 1714. Issue: John, Richard, Philip, Francis, THOMAS, Henry and Ann.

HON. COLONEL THOMAS LEE, " Commander-in-Chief and President of His Majesties Council for this Colony," was the fifth son of Richard Lee and Laetitia Corbin, his wife, born at Mt. Pleasant in Westmoreland County 1690; died at " Stratford," [51] as his tomb there will show. He was a Burgess, and one of the Judges of the Supreme Court of Judicature in his Majesty's Colony of Va. One of the incorporators of the Ohio Company February 9, 1748, he took the lead at the outset, and by many has been considered its founder.[52] Associated with him among others, were Lawrence and Augustine Washington. He became Acting Governor of the Colony in 1749, by the death of John Robinson, appointed Governor, but died before his commission reached him. Lawrence Washington succeeded him as President of the Ohio Company, Thomas Lee married, in May, 1722, *Hannah,* the second daughter of Colonel Philip Ludwell II., of " Greenspring," James City County. She was born at " Rich Neck," in Bruton Parish, James City County, December 5, 1701, and died at " Stratford," Virginia, January 25, 1749; buried in the family burying-ground called the " Burnt House Fields," at Mount Pleasant. Her tombstone is now at " Stratford," whither it was removed probably by General Henry Lee, who built the new vault.

At Stratford, that landmark of American history,

[51] *Lee of Va.,* p. 108.
[52] Irving's *Life of Washington,* Vol. I., p. 46.

were born men who were to make their mark in after life: Richard, Philip Ludwell, Hannah, John, Lucy, Thomas Ludwell, Richard Henry, Francis Lightfoot, Alice, William and Arthur. The slab now at "Stratford" reads:

"Here lies Buried the Honble Col. Thomas Lee, who dyed 14 November, 1750, Aged 60 years; and his beloved wife Mrs. Hannah Lee. She departed this life 25 January, 1749-50. Their monument is erected in the lower Church of Washington Parish, in this County, five miles above their Country seat Stratford Hall."

Their daughter, *Hannah Lee,* married GAWIN CORBIN II. (nephew of *Laetitia Corbin* who married RICHARD LEE of Mount Pleasant, who were the grandparents of Hannah).

Their daughter, *Jenny Corbin,* married COLONEL JOHN BUSHROD, whose daughter *Hannah,* married JOHN AUGUSTINE WASHINGTON, and their daughter *Jenny,* married her cousin WILLIAM AUGUSTINE WASHINGTON. (See Washington line.)[53]

LUDWELL

PHILIP LUDWELL, and Thomas his brother, were sons of Thomas and Jane (Cottington) Ludwell. Jane was a daughter of James Cottington, of Discoe, in Bruton Parish, England; in America about 1660.[54] James was the son of Philip Cottington, Gent., of Godminster, whose brother was Lord Cottington, time of Charles II. Bruton was also the birthplace of Sir William Berkeley, between whom and the Ludwells there were long and intimate relations.

[53] The genealogical data here given shows that this Member has lines of descent from the Lees through the Ludwells and through the Corbins.
[54] *Quar.,* Vol. I., p. 110. English extract of Chancery Proceedings verify this genealogy.

In 1678, Thomas Ludwell, Philip's brother, died, and his tombstone, at the door of Bruton Church, Williamsburg, Va. (one of the oldest there), bears the Ludwell arms. He was Secretary of the Colony, and the name of Bruton Parish is thought to be in his honor.

PHILIP, was Deputy Secretary under his brother, and succeeding to that office, retained it for life. His first appearance in the records as Councillor is in 1670, rendering efficient service to Governor Berkeley. When attacked by Bland (with Bacon's adherents), Ludwell boarded the vessel, capturing Bland, and later the vessels of his squadron.[55] He was of the Civil and Martial Courts which tried Bacon's supporters. His fiery temper kept him in constant feuds, resulting in the Lords of Trade and Plantations, February 10, 1678-9, ordering his exclusion from the Council. While in England 1681, December 12th, Lord Culpeper writes from Virginia that at the request of the whole Council, he has appointed Colonel Ludwell to the Council in the room of Colonel Parke, deceased.

June 9, 1682, "thought fit and likewise ordered, that Coll. John Page may have the privilege to sett a pew for himself and his ffamily in the Chancell of the New Church at Middle Plantation," "Although the church was yet built." The privilege of setting up a pew in the Chancel was subsequently accorded to the HON. PHILIP LUDWELL. He was in the Vestry of Bruton Parish, 1684.[56]

In 1686, when Governor Effingham urged the House of Burgesses for the laying of levies by the Governor and Council, Ludwell and others utterly refused, and

55 Campbell's *History of Virginia*, p. 306.
56 Goodwin's *Bruton Church*.

disputed the King's authority. On June 12, 1687, the King confirmed the Governor's action, and Ludwell had his dismissal, which only added to his popularity, as he was requested in 1688, October 12th, to petition the King for a relief that they sought.[57] On March 28, 1689, he delivered a petition to the Privy Council in England, from the House of Burgesses, and on May 7, 1691, the House of Burgesses passed a vote of thanks to him, with £250 sterling, in acknowledgement thereof. December 5, 1689, he was appointed Governor of Northern Carolina, in Albemarle, and in 1691 at Charleston. In 1693 he was Governor of both the Carolinas, but their quarrels caused him to retire to Virginia in 1694.

He was twice married, first to *Lucy*, the daughter of Captain Robert and Joanna (Tokesey) Higginson, born between 1643 and 1649, and died November 6, 1675. (She married first, Major Lewis Burwell; second, Colonel William Bernard.) Of this union there was a son PHILIP II., and a daughter Jane.

He married second, Lady Frances Berkeley (née Culpeper), widow of Governor Sir William Berkeley. Lord Culpeper, writing Ryland in October, 1680, says: "My Lady Berkeley is married to Mr. Ludwell, and thinks no more of our world." Sir Maurice Berkeley (father of the Governor), and Sir Edwin Sandys, son of the Archbishop of York, were among those interested in the colonization of Virginia. George, a brother of Sir Edwin, came to the colony in 1621 as Treasurer.

There were two marriages in England between the Sandys' and the Washingtons, and here we find history repeating itself, for among those active in the first colony (afterwards known as the London Company),

57 *Col. Va. State Papers.*

LUCY HIGGINSON
Wife of Hon. Philip Ludwell

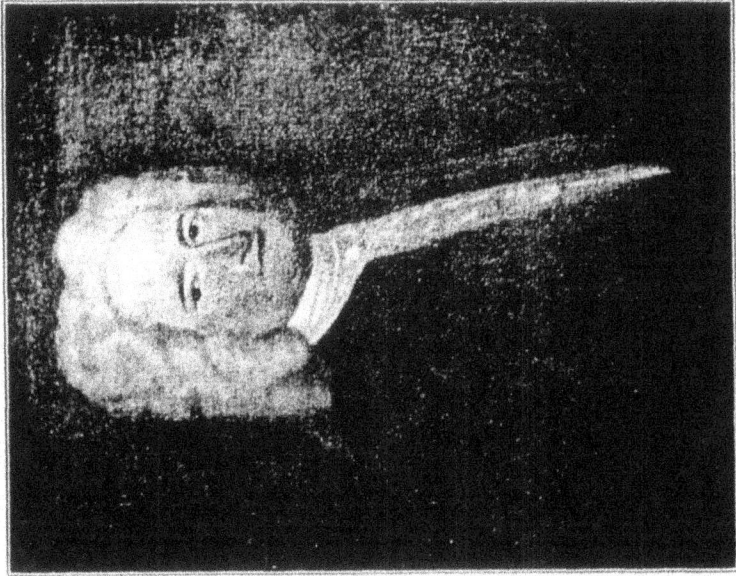

HON. PHILIP LUDWELL

were the Sandys', and of those interested and active in the Ohio Company, its survivor, were the two elder brothers of Washington, Lawrence and Augustine.

Lady Frances, always called "Lady Berkeley," had no issue, but Sir William Berkeley's tribute to her in his will was unusually handsome.

"First, I make my deare and most virtuous wife, Lady Ffrances Berkeley, my full and whole Executrix of the goods God has blessed me with in this world. Next, with my goods, I give her all my lands, houses and tenements, whatsoever, and not only to her but to avoid all cavil, to her and her heirs for ever."

At her death this property passed to the possession of the Ludwells, and was occupied by them for three generations, known as "Greenspring." By the will of his brother "Thomas Ludwell, of Bruton, in Somerset, Gent., Jan' 1676," Philip Ludwell inherited all of his land and other estates in Virginia.[58]

"Colonel Ludwell is, I think, in a declining way; he is at present in London."[59] He died in London, and was buried in the Ludwell Vault, in Bow Church, near Stratford (Middlesex).

There are two interesting links, one showing that Jane, a daughter of Governor Philip Ludwell, was ancestress of Martha Washington, by marrying Daniel Parke, Aide on the staff of Marlborough, who, carrying the news of the victory of Blenheim to London, was rewarded by Queen Anne with her miniature set in diamonds. They had two daughters, Frances, married John Custis, and were the parents of Martha Washington; Lucy was mistress of "Westover," marrying Colonel William Byrd.

58 II. Hening, p. 559; *N. E. Hist. Reg.*, April, 1893.
59 *Letters to Washington*, Vol. III., p. 214.

In Boswell's *Life of Johnson,* John Paradise is mentioned as one of the Literary Club, at the Essex Head, in Essex Street, London, December 4, 1783. He married Lucy, granddaughter of Hon. Philip Ludwell II., on May 14th, 1769, in London, England. The Rev. Hugh Jones, in his *Present State of Virginia,* 1724, speaks of this Literary Club, while the Quarterly gives a letter from Jefferson when Minister to France, introducing Lucy Ludwell Paradise, in which he gives her pedigree for three generations.

THE BOOKPLATE OF PHILIP LUDWELL II.

ARMS: *Gules between two towers on a bend argent three eagles displayed sable.*

MOTTO: *I pensieri stretti edil viso sciotto.*

The Ludwell papers in the Virginia Historical Society show that the second Philip Ludwell habitually used, on his seal to deeds, the arms described in the bookplate.[60]

60 *Quar.,* Vol. II., pp. 79, 159.

PHILIP LUDWELL II., the son of Philip and Lucy
(Higginson) Ludwell, "was born at Carter's Creek,
Abingdon Parish, Gloucester County, in Virginia,
Feby, 1672, died 11 Jany 1726-7 in the 54th year of his
age. Married 11 November, Thursday, 1697, to Han-
nah, daughter of Benjamin Harrison of Southarke
Parish, Surry County in Virginia Esquire. Born at
Indian Fields in the said Parish 15 December 1678.
Died 4 April 1731."[61] He was a member of the Vir-
ginia Assembly 1688 to 1697, and one of the Council
1702. The same year he is recorded as Vestryman of
Bruton Parish. "Some time Auditor of His Majesty's
revenue and twenty-five years Member of the Council."
Issue:

Philip Ludwell, Esq., III., only son and heir, mar-
ried, July 29, 1737, Fanny Grymes, daughter of
Charles Grymes; *Hannah,* married HON. THOMAS
LEE.

MEMORIAL GATES

On May 9, 1907, at Jamestown, Va., these Memorial
Gates were dedicated. They were erected by "The
Colonial Dames of America," in commemoration of the
"Birth of the Nation" in 1607, and are shown as the
frontispiece of this volume.

They mark the entrance to an old Church Yard, surrounding what was the oldest American Church. For
centuries, nothing remained but the ruins of a stone
tower, recently converted into a beautiful Chapel, by a
kindred society.

Lying in the shadow of this ivy-covered ruin, may be
seen to-day a monument with this inscription:

61 *Cradle of the Republic,* p. 127.

Under this stone lies interred
The Body of
Mrs. Hannah Ludwell
Relict of
The Hon[ble] Philip Ludwell Esq[r].
By whom she has left
One Son and Two Daughters
After a Most Exemplary Life
Spent in Chearful Innocence
And The Continual Exercise of
Piety, Charity and Hospitality
She Patiently Submitted to
Death on the 4th Day of April 1731 in the 52nd
Year of Her age.[62]

HIGGINSON

From John of Wem in the County of Salop, England, whose Will was dated 1640, descended the family known as the Barkeswell Higginsons in Warwick.[63]

CAPTAIN ROBERT HIGGINSON, son of Thomas and Ann Higginson of Barkeswell in Warwick, married Joanna Tokesey and about 1643 they came to America, in Virginia, where he died, August, 1649, leaving a widow, and an only daughter and heiress *Lucy*. In 1650 his widow returned to England. In 1644 he was commander at Middle Plantation, a pallisadoed Settlement (now Williamsburg) and was spoken of as "One of the first Commanders to subdue the Country of Virginia from the power of the heathen." In 1646 as a reward of Valiant service, he received from the Colony one hundred acres of land. He lies buried at Carter's Creek, Virginia.[64]

[62] *Cradle of the Republic.*
[63] *Quar.,* Vol. V., p. 186.
[64] York Co. *Records;* Neill's *Va. Carolorum,* p. 142.

Mrs. Thomas Lee

Thomas Lee

His only daughter, *Lucy,* born between 1643 and 1649, died November 6, 1675. She married first, Major Lewis Burwell; second, Colonel William Bernard; third, COLONEL PHILIP LUDWELL.[65]

On the tomb at Abingdon Parish, erected by her grandchildren, are the Arms and the following·inscription:

[In per]petual Memory of yᵉ virtuous
[Lucy B]urwell the Loveing and Beloved
[Wife of] Major Lewis Burwell of yᵉ County
[of Glos]ter in Virginia (long since deceased)
[She was de]cended from the Ancient family
[of the H]igginsons. She was yᵉ only Daughter
[of the V]alliant Capt Robert Higginson
[One of th]e first Commandʳˢ that subdued
[the Cou]ntry of Virginia from the power of
[the heat]hen who not being more worthy in her
[birth th]an Vertuous in her life Exchanged this
[World for] a Better one on the 6th November, in
[the —] yeare of her Age, Anno Domini 1675.
. . . buried on the . . ght hand of her
. . . d . . her M . . . . . . ll of her owne
Grand Children [66]

BEALL

COLONEL NINIAN BEALL, born in Dumbartonshire, Scotland, in 1625, was in the battle of Dunbar against

⁶⁵ *Quar.,* Vol. II., p. 231.

⁶⁶ This tombstone is much injured and the portion of the inscription in brackets is supplied from Campbell (Southern Literary Miss. xiii, p. 464). The last lines (Campbell does not give them), were doubtless: "She is buried on the right hand of her husband. Erected to her memory by several of her own grandchildren." (*Wm. & Mary Coll. Quar.* Vol .II., No. 1, July, 1893).

Cromwell 1650, where he was made a prisoner and soon transported to Maryland. His will at Annapolis bears date of January 15, 1717. He had married Ruth, the daughter of Robert Moore, as James Moore, in a deposition of August 15, 1708, speaks of Colonel Ninian Beall as his brother.[67]

He was Captain of Militia of Calvert County, Md., 1678; Major before 1688; in 1689 the Assembly had re-appointed Ninian Beall as Major; 1690, one of the twenty-five Commissioners for regulating affairs in Maryland, until the next Assembly; High Sheriff of Calvert County 1692; designated Colonel 1693, and Commander in Chief of Maryland forces; frequently engaged against the Indians; represented Prince George's County in the House of Burgesses 1696 to 1699. In this last year an Act was passed by the Assembly which reads: "An Act of gratitude to Colonel Ninian Beall."[68] As a member of the Assembly in 1699, he signed the petition to King William III., for the establishment of the Church of England in Maryland, although he was a Presbyterian Elder, he gave the land on Patuxent for "Ye erecting and building of a house for ye Service of Almighty God."

In 1703, Ninian Beall received a grant of seven hundred and ninety-five acres from Lord Baltimore, called the "Rock of Dumbarton," which includes much of the ground on which Georgetown now stands. He was a very large land holder. January 18, 1720, his son received a grant of thirteen hundred and eighty acres, known as the "Addition to the Rock of Dumbarton."[69]

[67] *Liber* P. C. 2 *Chancery Recs.*, 1671-1712, p. 626.
[68] *Colonial Wars Pedigrees; Liber* LL., No. 2, p. 228, P. R.
[69] *Liber* C. D., fol. 121, M'd. Land Office, Annapolis.

His deeds mention sons, Charles, Ninian, Jr., Thomas, John and GEORGE, and daughters, Hester, Mary, Rachell and *Jane.*

COLONEL GEORGE BEALL, youngest child of Ninian and Ruth (Moore) Beall, born at Upper Marlboro, in Prince George's County, Md., 1695, and died in Georgetown, D. C., March 15, 1780, aged 85. His tomb is at Georgetown. He was appointed a Major, September 21, 1776.[70] By an Act of May 15, 1751, the Legislature of Maryland provided for laying out a town on the Potomac River above Rock Creek, and a part of George Beall's land was taken, and divided into lots, he being allowed the privilege of first selecting two lots; he sent the following answer:

"If I must part with my property by force, I had better have a little than be totally demolished. Rather than have none, I accept these lots ' 72 ' ' 79.' I do hereby protest and declare that my acceptance of said lots, which is by force, shall not debar me from future redress from the Commissioners and others, if I can have the rights of a British subject. God save King George! George Beall."

He married *Elizabeth,* the daughter of Thomas and Barbara (Dent) Brooke. Among his many children there were three named "Thomas," two of whom died young.

The last and youngest child, *"Thomas Beall of Geo Esq.,"* was born September 27, 1748, and died October 5, 1819. He married, September 26, 1773, *Ann* (or *Nancy*), the daughter of John and Elizabeth Collett

---

[70] *Jour. of Correspondence* of the Md. Council of Safety. July 7th to Dec. 31, 1776, p. 293. (Baltimore, 1893.) *Arch.* of Md. (Baltimore, 1897), pp. 296, 373.

Orme. She was born July 29, 1752, and died April 9,
1827. He built the house known as "Dumbarton," on
the heights of Georgetown, that was occupied by his
son-in-law until his death in 1854.

His daughter, *Eliza Ridgely Beall,* married *George Corbin Washington.*[71]

ORME—EDMONSTON

The credentials of the Rev. John Orme were received
by the Synod in Philadelphia 1720. He was born in
Wiltshire, England, 1691-92; married March 14, 1720,
by Rev. Hugh Conn, to *Ruth* (born 1705), the daughter of Colonel Archibald Edmonston and *Jane Beall,*
his wife, daughter of NINIAN BEALL.

Their son, *John Orme,* born 1722, married first, Elizabeth Collett, a widow, and second, Lucy Beall, a
widow. His daughter *Ann* or *Nancy* (first wife),
married *Thomas Beall of Geo Esq.*

A settler in Talbot County, Md., 1685, Archibald
Edmonston (son of Thomas, son of John), is first
mentioned in the land records at Annapolis in a transfer of an assignment of one thousand acres, called
"Beall's Camp," by Colonel Ninian Beall's patent,
dated 1689. He was known after 1700, as "Colonel,"
and patented extensive tracts of land in Prince
George's County, later divided into Frederick, Montgomery and Washington Counties. He married *Jane,*
the youngest daughter of NINIAN BEALL, and is said
to have succeeded his father-in-law as Commander

71 *Family Bibles.*

of Prince George's County Militia.   He died 1733.
Issue:

James, married his cousin Mary Beall; he was Justice of Montgomery County, and Captain of Colonial Militia; Archibald, married Dorothy Brooke; *Ruth*, married the Rev. John Orme.[72]

BROOKE

Pedigree of Brooke is as follows:
Richard Brooke (1552), married Elizabeth Twyne.
Thomas Brooke, married Susan Forster.
GOVERNOR ROBERT BROOKE, married Mary Baker.
MAJOR THOMAS BROOKE, married Eleanor Hatton.
COLONEL THOMAS BROOKE, married *Barbara Dent.*
Elizabeth Brooke married COLONEL GEORGE BEALL.
(See pp. 553-558 for Brooke.)

DENT

HON. THOMAS DENT, was County Commissioner 1661 to 1669; High Sheriff, 1664 for Anne Arundel County; September 5, 1664, he was of the Quorum, St. Mary's County, Md.; July 27, 1666, appointed Justice; Burgess for St. Mary's, 1669, 1674, 1676.

He married Rebecca Wilkinson and their daughter *Barbara* (1676-1754), married as his second wife, THOMAS BROOKE, whose daughter *Elizabeth,* married COLONEL GEORGE BEALL of Prince George's County, Md.

---

72 *Chart* of Dr. Francis Orme.

HINSON

ARMS: *Azure, a chevron between three suns or, and a brodure ermine.* [73]
CREST: *A fleur de lis, per pale azure.*

These arms are otherwise described: The sun in full splendor face surrounded by rays, being the cognizance of the Duke of York to which Shakespeare's famous lines apply:

> "Now is the winter of our discontent,
> Made glorious by this Sun of York."

In 1651, "Lieutenant Thomas Hinson, High Sheriff for ye Countie of Kent," arrived in the Province of Maryland, accompanied by his wife Grace, his children, John, Grace and Anne Hinson, and three servants. He settled in Kent County, and in the year 1652 was filling the important office of Clerk of the County. On July 31st, 1652, the Parliamentary Commissioners, Richard Bennett, Edward Lloyd, Thomas March and Leo. Strong issued a commission to Thomas Hynson and others to be Commissioners of the Island of Kent, in which very great power and authority was given them. On March 1st, 1654, William Fuller and Wm. Durand issued a new commission to Thomas Hynson and others for the same important post. As High Sheriff of Kent, Lieutenant Hinson was the leading gentleman of Kent, and his

HINSON

[73] In ordinary parlance we would say, three suns look up.

mansion was the meeting place of the Court—as the old records of the County amply testify. In addition to the above offices, Thomas Hinson, who changed his name to Hynson in 1652, was Justice of the County Court in 1654—member of the House of Burgesses 1659—after which he was debarred from office by Lord Baltimore for serving under the Commonwealth—particularly as a member of the Assembly of 1659. Thomas Hinson, who was thirty years old upon his arrival in Maryland, according to a deposition regarding his age made March 29, 1655, was a man of means and high social position. He died in the year 1668, intestate, leaving a large family.

His son, Colonel John Hynson, was born in England. As a young man he is on record as High Sheriff of Kent, in which office of dignity and power his father had rendered years of service and in which Colonel Thomas Hynson, brother of Colonel John Hynson, also distinguished himself in Talbot County. He was a Member of the House of Burgesses from Kent County from 1681-1688. Although he included in his dignities the offices of Justice of the Peace, and Military Commander of the County of Kent, he served Church as well as State, as a Vestryman of St. Paul's Parish.[74] It was probably his close association with the affairs of the Church that brought both Rectors of Old St. Paul's a wooing at the Hynson Mansion. The Rev. Stephen Bordley on October 14th, 1702, claimed Anne Hynson for his bride, and two years after his

---

[74] *Original Settler's List*, Annapolis, Md.; Land Warrants, Annapolis. Old *Liber* A, Clerk's Office, Chestertown, Kent Co., Md., fols. 45-49-57, and *Liber* A. C. P., fols. 100, 102. *Arch.* of Md., including Provincial Court Assembly *Proceedings*, Vols. 1-10.

death when Rev.[75] Alexander Williamson responded
to the call from the Colonial Church, he promptly succeeded not only to the Living, but also won the widow
of his predecessor, as is shown in the settlement of the
estate of Stephen Bordley.[76] Nathaniel Hynson, son
of Col. John Hynson, in his will proved January 26,
1721 (Liber E. C. No. 1, Fol. 213, Register of Wills
Office, Kent County, Md.), mentions his nephew
"Thomas Bordley," to whom he leaves a legacy. This
proves that the Ann Hynson who married Stephen
Bordley was the daughter of Col. John Hynson,
which is further proved by a deed of gift from him to
his daughter Ann, wife of Stephen Bordley, of a piece
of land called "Bounty." (Kent County *Deed,* Clerk's
Office.) October 6th, 1709, "Ann Bordley Admx of
Stephen Bordley clerk, her adm'on bound in common
form, with Nathaniel Hynson and Thomas Bordley,
her sureties in 300 lbs. sterling."[77]

February 27, 1711, "Mr. Alex". Williamson and
Ux". Adrx (his wife administratrix) of the goods and
chattels wc" were of the Reverend Mr. Stephen Bordley late of Kent County, dead, charge themselves w"
all and singular the goods, chattles and credits of the
said deceased as per Invty of sum of £309:2:5, &c."
"The above Rev. and Mrs. Ann Williamson make oath
yet ye above is a just and true acct of her adm. in common before me by virtue of a spial Com" to me for
that end directed. Thos. Smyth. D. Com'y—Conet.
Kent."

[75] St. Paul's *Parish Register*, Kent County, Md., page 240: "Stephen
Bordley and Ann Hynson were married October 14th, 1702."
[76] *Ibid.*, p. 242: "Stephen Bordley buried August 23, 1709."
[77] Test. Proceed., Book No. 21, fol. 197, Land Office, Annapolis, Md.

August 25, 1713, "Additional account of Mr. Alexander Williamson and ann his wife, administratrix of Mr. Stephen Bordley, late of Kent County deceased."[78]

John Hynson, Testator   *Test:*
Will dated Dec. 29, 1704   Gorades Wessells
Proved June 5, 1705   Henry Phillips
                             Henry March

"To son, John Hynson, for his natural life, the plantation where I now dwell and all the land I have in the Eastern Neck, with reversion to my grandson, John Hynson, and failing his heirs the reversion to pass to all the heirs in the male line of testator's son, John Hynson."

Testator directs his debts to be paid out of the crop of corn, and what remains of the said crop after debts are paid "to be equally divided between my wife and daughter, Sarah Hynson.

"To my wife, Ann Hynson, all the estate that was hers when I married her that shall be in being when I die, and my horse called 'Phenix' and certain household goods.

"I appoint the Rev. Alexander Williamson and Mr. James Smith, or either of them, to make over to William Graves, 100 acres of land, being part of 'Buck Neck'—as also I leave Mr. Alexander Williamson and Mr. James Smith the care of my children, whom I appoint executors of this my last will and testament, and my daughter, Hannah Hynson, executrix, but she

[78] Inventories and Accounts, *Liber* 34, fol. 72, Land Commissioner's Office, Annapolis.

is not to act until she arrives at the age of seventeen
years or the day of her marriage."

Signed—NATHANIEL HYNSON.[79]

The daughter of Colonel John Hynson, *Ann Hynson,* married Rev. Alexander Williamson, whose son,
ALEXANDER, married *Sarah,* the daughter of Thomas
and Rebecca (Wilmer) Ringgold.

WILLIAMSON

ALEXANDER WILLIAMSON, son of the Rev. Alexander and Ann (Hynson) Williamson (she being the
widow of Rev. Stephen Bordley), was Speaker of the
Lower House Legislature, 1752, 1753, 1754, 1757, and
1758. His will was dated 1760. He married Sarah,
the daughter of Thomas and Rebecca (Wilmer) Ringgold. Issue: Alexander, James, Henrietta, and *Anne.*
The youngest child, *Anne Williamson,* married the
Rev. William Barroll, born at Hereford, England. He
was a son of William and Abigail (Jones) Barroll.
Abigail Jones was the sister of the Rev. Hugh Jones,
Chaplain at Jamestown, and later Professor of Mathe-
matics at William and Mary College.

RINGGOLD—WILMER

THOMAS RINGGOLD, came to Kent County, Md.,
when he was forty years old, in 1650, with his two sons,
JAMES and John. In 1661 he deeded to them one-half
of his lands, east side of Chesapeake Bay.

MAJOR JAMES RINGGOLD, son of Thomas, married
first, —— ——, and had one son; married second,

[79] *Register of Wills Office,* Kent Co., Md., *Lib.* E. C., No. 1, fol. 213.

JAMES BARROLL.

MARY A. CROCKETT
Wife of James Barroll

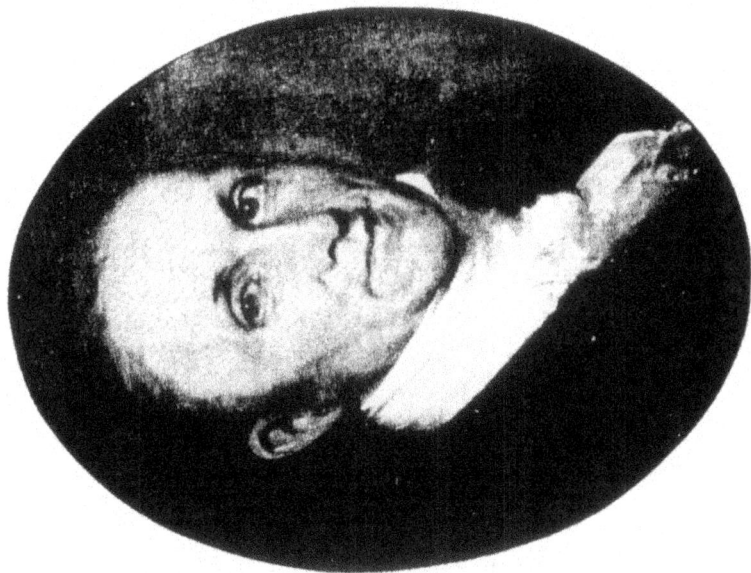

Mary, the daughter of Captain Robert Vaughan, of Kent County. He was Commissioner from 1647 to 1652, and died 1686. Issue, four sons: THOMAS, John, James, and Charles.

THOMAS RINGGOLD II., eldest son of James, died October 10, 1711; married, first, Sarah Ringgold, who died April 20, 1699, and they had one son:

THOMAS RINGGOLD III., who married, May 1, 1712, *Rebecca,* the daughter of Simon and Rebecca Wilmer. Issue: Thomas, Rebecca, William, and *Sarah,* who married ALEXANDER WILLIAMSON.

SIMON WILMER, of Kent County, Md., was one of the first Vestrymen for St. Paul's Parish, January 24, 1693. "On the 27th of November, 1694, he took the oath of allegiance and abhorency and qualified as Clerk of the County." He was a Member of the Legislature 1698.[80] He married Rebecca ——, and their daughter *Rebecca,* married THOMAS RINGGOLD III.

Their daughter, *Sarah Ringgold,* married ALEXANDER WILLIAMSON, whose daughter *Anne,* married Rev. William Barroll.

BARROLL

The Barroll pedigree is as follows:

Robert Barroll (will 1554), married Alys ——.

Robert Barroll (will Apr. 3d, 1580), married Maulde ——.

John Barroll, married Bridget Phillips.

Colonel James Barroll (1639, Mayor of Hereford), married Susan Denys.

Major James Barroll (see Visitation 1634), married Susan ——.

---

[80] *Old Kent,* pp. 325, 385.

William Barroll (will May 31, 1698; died June 3, 1698), married Mary —— (died June 11, 1698).

William Barroll (will Nov. 13, 1729), married Anne ——.

William Barroll (will May 2, 1754), married Abigail Jones (sister of Rev. Hugh Jones; will Nov. 28, 1761).

Rev. William Barroll, married *Ann Williamson.*

James Barroll, married Mary Ann Crockett.

Mary Ann Barroll,[81] married *Lewis William Washington.*

MARY ANN WASHINGTON, married Henry Irvine Keyser. (See Washington line.)

MARY WASHINGTON KEYSER,

MARY WASHINGTON THOM,

CAROLINE FISCHER KEYSER (Paper not inserted),

ELIZA WASHINGTON PERINE, JR.,

Members of Chapter I., The Colonial Dames of America.

---

[81] *Barroll In Great Britain and America,* 1554-1910. By Hope H. Barroll.

XXVI

BOWDOIN

" In the ancient records of La Rochelle, the name of Bowdoin was variously spelt Bauldouyn, Baudouyn, Baudouin, and finally, in Massachusetts, it became Bowdoin.

" The Boudouin family, of La Rochelle, was one of the most ancient and important of that city, and was among the first disciples of the Reformed faith. Several of the family distinguished themselves by their services to the Protestant cause during the ' Civil Wars.' Its different branches were known by designations taken from the numerous Seigneuries which they possessed. One of the family, Peirre Baudouin Ecuyer, Sieur de la Laigne, de la Fonte, Lousillon, Le Pere, Le Puy-sur-la-Creuse, in 1502, married Demoiselle Phillippe, daughter of Jean Bureau, Mayor of La Rochelle in 1448, Treasurer of France, and Master of Artillery of France. At the period of the ' Revocation of the Edict of Nantes,' one of its branches took refuge in Prussia, another in the Netherlands, and a third in Great Britian."

The ships that sailed nearly every month from London to Boston, were bringing over families whose names have become historical, and not a few of them had inherited wealth and ancestral rank. Such were the Bernons, Baudouins, Casineaus, Sigourneys, Faneuils and Allaires, who were here by the autumn of 1668.[1]

THE MASSACHUSETTS FAMILY

The colonist, Pierre Baudouin, was a native of La

[1] *History of the Huguenot Emigration to America,* by Rev. C. W. Baird.

Rochelle, and lived on a handsome estate in the neighborhood of that city, which he forfeited by his flight, when the severities practiced in France towards the Protestants, compelled him to depart from his native land. He took refuge in the city of Dublin, Ireland., with his wife and four children.[2]   There he obtained a position in the Royal Customs, but a change of officers left him without employment, and he was induced to come to America in 1687, where he settled in Casco, now Portland, Me.

In the summer of the same year, he petitioned Governor Andros for one hundred acres of land, and his prayer was granted, but the patent for the land was temporarily withheld by the surveyor, and in the autumn of the next year, 1688, he was compelled to seek redress. His letter to the Governor is on record in the Archives of Massachusetts, and like the writings of other refugees that have come down to us, almost uniformly show that the petitioner was a man of intelligence and cultivation. He obtained the grant, but only remained two years and a half in Casco, owing to hostile attacks of the French and Indians. Hearing of the establishment of a church in Boston by his fellow refugees from France, he removed to that city, and twenty- four hours after his departure, the fort at Casco was attacked and destroyed, followed by a general massacre. A race which had survived the massacre of Saint Bartholomew and the siege of La Rochelle, was not destined to perish ignobly in the wilderness. Pierre Baudouin's death occurred in Boston, 1706.

His youngest son, James Baudouin, remained in Bos-

---

[2] In the records of the French church in Dublin is the following: memorandum: 'Pierre Beaudouin parain for Marie Tourneux 25th March, 1682-83.

THE BOWDOIN ARMS
Drawn from the tombstone of James Bowdoin in the Granary Burying
Ground, Boston

ton and by his energy and perseverance rose to the very
first rank among the merchants of that place. He was
chosen a member of the Colonial Council before his
death, and left to his children, as the fruit of a long
life of industry and integrity, the greatest estate possessed at that day by any one person in Massachusetts.
He died September 8, 1747.

His son, James, succeeded John Hancock, as Governor of Massachusetts in 1785, and died 1790, leaving
a daughter, Elizabeth, who married Sir John Temple,
eighth baronet of Stowe, and a son, James III., who
was a gentleman of liberal education and large fortune,
and held several diplomatic positions. He, was a generous benefactor of Bowdoin College, Maine, named for
his father. He died childless, and with him, the name
of Bowdoin by direct descent passed from the annals
of New England.

THE VIRGINIA FAMILY

The progenitor of this line, " Pierre Baudouin, was
one of the same noble stock which gave three Presidents
out of nine to the old Congress of the Confederation,
which gave her Laurences, and Marions, her Hugers
and Manigaults, her Prileaus and Gaillards, and
Legares to South Carolina, her Jays to New York, her
Baudinots to New Jersey, her Brimmers, Dexters and
her Peter Faneuil, and the Cradle of Liberty to Massachusetts." [3] His wife's name was Elizabeth, and they
had two sons and a daughter.

The eldest son, (John) Jean Bowdoin I., died 1717.
He settled in Virginia, and his name occurs in the

[3] *History of the Huguenot Emigration to America,* By Rev. Charles
Baird.

records [4] of Northampton County, October 28, 1698. He seems to have had the energy and ability which characterized his father, brother, and the Huguenots generally, for at his death, he had acquired, if not wealth, that which was its equivalent in Colonial times, servants and lands. His wife was Susannah ——.

PETER BOWDOIN II., son of Jean, died in 1745. He was a member of the House of Burgesses in Virginia 1736.[5] He married Grace Harmonson. Their son:

JOHN BOWDOIN II. (1731-1775), was also a member of the Virginia House of Burgesses, 1774. He purchased the beautiful estate of "Hungars," built in 1743 of brick, with carving of leaves and grapes above the windows. It stood on a slight elevation and commanded a magnificent view of the Chesapeake. Broad steps led up to a portico tiled with black and white marble, the roof being supported by pillars. The Court, in front, was surrounded by brick walls fourteen feet high, overgrown with multiflora, roses, and planted with large box trees. A brick walk led to the entrance gate, and on each side were offices, used respectively as the house-kitchen, quarter-kitchen, school-room, laundry, flax room, and infirmary for sick servants. During the Civil War, some of the sheets and towels made at "Hungars" were sent to the hospitals. During the War of 1812, a British cannon ball struck the wall, injuring two crayon portraits of the owners of the house. Officers afterwards came ashore, were hospitably received, and in excuse for the shot said that they had no idea such extensive buildings could be a private residence. He married, January 10, 1754, Grace Stringer, and they left five daughters and two sons, John III. and *Peter III.*, a son, James,

[4] *Records of Northampton County*, Book XII.
[5] *Palmus State Papers*.

MARY TEMPLE
Wife of Robert Nelson

ROBERT NELSON

JAMES BOWDOIN AND HIS SISTER
Who afterward married Sir John Temple

Robert Nelson

Gary Cooper
Wife of Robert Nelson

having died before his father. As the name of James
was transmitted from father to son in the Boston branch
of the family, so the names John and Peter were alter-
nately borne through four generations in Virginia. John
Bowdoin left "Hungars" to JOHN III., his eldest
son, and was very explicit that in case his widow should
remarry, she must leave "Hungars" and renounce the
guardianship of her children. She remained a widow.

Their son, *Peter Bowdoin III.*, (1761-1825), married
first, Margaret Smith; second, August 4, 1801, *Leah,*
the daughter of Thomas and Elizabeth (Upshur)
Teackle. They had two daughters and three sons, one
of whom was *George Edward Bowdoin.*[6]

The Bowdoin family have been in each generation,
staunch Episcopalians. Three generations have served
as vestrymen in " Old Hungars Church," and the families with whom they have intermarried have belonged to
that communion. The name is now extinct in Northampton County.

TEACKLE

REV. THOMAS TEACKLE (1624-1695), the first rector
of Hungars Parish, lived and died on his estate called
"Craddock." He married second, Margaret, the daughter of Robert Nelson, of Gray's Inn, London, and his
wife, Mary Temple. (See pp. 343-344.)

JOHN TEACKLE I. (1693-1721), their son, married
1710, *Susannah,* the daughter of Arthur and Sarah
(Brown) Upshur.

Their son, *Thomas Teackle* II. (1711-1769), married *Elizabeth,* (Betty), the daughter of John Custis
and his wife Anne Upshur. Their son:

THOMAS TEACKLE III., died 1784. He was a member

[6] *Family Records.*

of Accomac County Committee of Safety, December
23, 1774. During the Revolution, he returned from an
absence spent with the troops, to visit his wife and child,
just as a British man-of-war landed at the foot of the
garden. He secreted himself and escaped, but the soldiers, acting under orders to burn the houses of rebels,
proceeded to destroy the Teackle house, after apologiz-
ing for their brutality, and removing the mother and
infant to the barn. After the war, Thomas Teackle
III., built the house which is now standing.[7] His wife
was *Elizabeth,* the daughter of Abel and Rachel (Revell) Upshur.

Their daughter, *Leah,* married Peter Bowdoin III.

The eldest son of Thomas III., *John Teackle II.*
(1762-1811), married, 1783, *Anne Stockley,* the daughter of Thomas and Anne (Stockley) Upshur, whose
eldest son, Thomas, sold Craddock, and removed to
Baltimore. Their daughter, *Lavinia,* married Captain
William Graham.

UPSHUR

Some of the descendants of Arthur Upshur (1624-
1709), who married, first, Mary Clark, are as follows:

ARTHUR UPSHUR II., who died 1738, married *Sarah,*
daughter of *Thomas Brown,* and his wife *Susannah,*
the daughter of LEVIN DENWOOD. Thomas Brown was
the son of JOHN BROWN, whose wife was Ursula ——.
(See pp. 344-345).

Thomas Upshur I., who died 1751, married Sarah
——.

Thomas Upshur II. (1739-1792), married, 1761,
Anne, the daughter of Eyre and Mary (Bell) Stockley.

[7] American Archives. Series IV, Vol. I.
Upshur Papers. Thomas Teackle Upshur, Genealogist.

PIERRE BOWDOIN

ELIZABETH UPSHUR
Wife of Thomas Teackle III

PETER BOWDOIN III
Reproduced from a miniature

DAVID GRAHAM
Reproduced from a miniature

Anne Stockley Upshur, married *John Teackle II.*[8]

CUSTIS

The following are descendants of John Custis, of Rotterdam:

MAJOR-GENERAL JOHN CUSTIS (1630-1696), of Arlington, married second, *Tabitha,* the daughter of Colonel Edmund and Mary (Charlton) Scarborough (Scarburg.)

COLONEL JOHN CUSTIS (1653-1713), married first, *Margaret,* the daughter of Captain John and Elizabeth (Thoroughgood) Michael.

Elizabeth Custis, married her cousin, *Thomas,* the eldest son of EDMUND CUSTIS and his wife, *Tabitha,* the daughter of COLONEL WILLIAM WHITTINGTON and his wife Tabitha, the daughter of William and Tabitha Smart. Colonel William was the son of CAPTAIN WILLIAM WHITTINGTON, and his wife, Elizabeth Western.

JUDGE JOHN CUSTIS IV., who died 1732, married second, Anne Upshur.

Elizabeth (Betty) Custis, married *Thomas Teackle II.*[9] (See pp. 345-350).

SCARBOROUGH-WEST

CAPTAIN EDMUND SCARBOROUGH, died 1634 or 1635; his wife was Hannah Butler.

COLONEL EDMUND SCARBOROUGH, died 1671; he married *Mary,* the daughter of STEPHEN CHARLTON. Their daughter, *Tabitha,* married MAJOR-GENERAL JOHH CUSTIS.

Another daughter, *Matilda Scarborough,* married,

8 *Ibid.*   9 *Ibid.*

1679, LIEUTENANT-COLONEL JOHN WEST, Gent.,
(1638-1703), the son of Anthony West, who died about
1652. *Anthony West II.*, the son of John, died about
1716, and his daughter, *Mary Scarburg,* married Nathaniel, the son of Robert Bell, of Accomac County, Va.
Their daughter, *Mary,* married Eyre, the son of Francis
and Elizabeth (Eyre) Stockley, whose daughter, *Ann
Teackle,* married *Thomas Upshur II.*[10]   (See pp. 337-
341, 345-347.)

THOROUGHGOOD-MICHAEL.

CAPTAIN ADAM THOROUGHGOOD married Sarah Off-
ley.   She was the daughter of Robert and Anne
(Osborn) Offley, and the granddaughter of Sir
Edward Osborn, Lord Mayor of London, 1583, and his
wife, Anne Hewitt, the daughter of Sir William
Hewitt, Lord Mayor of London, 1559.

Their daughter, *Elizabeth Thoroughgood,* married
CAPTAIN JOHN MICHAEL, and their daughter, *Margaret* married COLONEL JOHN CUSTIS III., whose
daughter, *Elizabeth,* married her cousin, *Thomas,* the
son of Edmund and Tabitha (Whittington) Custis.[11]
(See pp. 347-350).

REVELL

RANDALL REVELL, was a member of the House of
Burgesses in 1660. He married Katharine Scarburg.

EDWARD REVELL, their only son, who died 1687, was
commissioner of Accomac County, Va., 1666 to 1670.
He was twice married, first to Frances ——, and second
to Rachel ——, whose son, *John* died in 1727, leaving a
daughter, *Rachel,* (1702-1749), who married Abel Up-

[10] *Ibid.*   [11] *Ibid.*

shur (1702-1753). Their daughter, *Elizabeth Upshur,* married THOMAS TEACKLE III.[12]

EYRE-STOCKLEY

The Quaker, Thomas Eyre (will dated 1657), married *Susannah,* the daughter of John and Ann (Elkington) Savage. His sons and most of his grandsons were Quakers.

CAPTAIN JOHN EYRE, (son of Thomas), who died 1719, was justice of Northampton County, March 28, 1687.[13] His daughter, *Elizabeth,* married Francis, the son of Francis and Sarah Stockley.

The name of Francis Stockley, who died 1655, appears first in the records of Northampton County, Va., in 1634. He seems to have been a valuable addition to the colony.[14] He married Joane, whose surname is supposed to have been Hall. Their son, John, who died before 1690, was the father of Francis, who died 1698, whose son, Francis, married *Elizabeth Eyre,* and died 1744.

Their son, *Eyre Stockley,* married *Mary,* the daughter of Nathaniel and Mary Scarburg (West) Bell, and their daughter, *Anne Teackle,* married *Thomas Upshur II.*

SAVAGE

The colonist, Ensign Thomas Savage, died before 1627. He arrived in Virginia 1607 or 1608, then a boy, and was given to Powhatan, as a hostage for Namontack, a young Indian, whom Captain Newport took to England. Savage settled eventually on the Eastern

12 Hening's State Papers.
  Northampton Co. *Records,* Vol. I, p. 10.
13 *Ibid.*
  Northampton Co. *Records.* Vol. XII, p. 276.
14 Upshur *Papers.*

Shore of the Chesapeake Bay, at a point still known as
" Savage's Neck " and was an invaluable interpreter.[15]
John Perry mentions that he served the public without
recompense, and in the discharge of his duty, an Indian
arrow was shot through his body. He married Hannah,
the daughter of Edward Tyng, of Massachusetts.

CAPTAIN JOHN SAVAGE, their son, born 1624, in
1665 was Lieutenant.[16] He married first, Ann Elkington, and their daughter, *Susannah,* married three
times, her first husband being Thomas Eyre.

BOWDOIN (*Continued*)

The youngest son of Peter and Leah (Teackle) Bowdoin, *George Edward Bowdoin* (1816-1892), married
November 2, 1841, *Mary Anne,* the daughter of Captain William and Lavinia (Teackle) Graham. Issue,
two sons and three daughters. One son, Henry J.,
married JULIA MORRIS MURRAY. The elder son, *William Graham,* married KATHARINE GORDON, the daughter of James Edward and Catharine (Gordon) Price.
Their two daughters are: MARION GORDON, who married Dr. J. H. Mason Knox, Jr., and KATHLEEN GOR-
DON, who married Dr. John Staige Davis.

GRAHAM

The Graham family, of Scotch descent, took refuge
in Ireland, it is said, to escape religious persecution,
when James Graham, Earl of Montrose, and his kinsman the Duke of Hamilton, headed rival factions. Philip
Graham married Jane Hamilton.

Their son, David Graham, came to America, and
settled in Philadelphia, with his wife, who was Mary

---

[15] Smith's *History of Virginia*, Book IV, p. 18, etc. Upshur *Papers.*
[16] Northampton County *Recs.*, Vol. VII, p. 12.

Mollen, and four children. Removing to Alexandria, Va., he and his wife died there of cholera. The children were claimed and tenderly cared for, by their uncle, Mr. Hamilton Graham, living in Baltimore.

GRAHAM

One of the sons, Captain W i l l i a m G r a h a m (1 7 8 8 - 1864), having loved the sea from his boyhood, determined to make that his profession in which he continued until 1831. Subsequently, he was President of the Marine Insurance Company, until a short time before his death.

He married *Lavinia,* the daughter of John and Anne Stockley (Upshur) Teackle, and their daughter, *Mary Anne,* married *George Edward Bowdoin,* whose son *William Graham Bowdoin,* married KATHARINE GORDON PRICE.[17] (See pp. 167, 168, 186, for Price lines.)

PRICE

In the sixth generation of this family in America, James Price, the son of John and Rachel (Benson) Price, was born in Kent County, Md. He married *Margaret,* the daughter of Joseph and Elizabeth (Lea) Tatnall.

Their youngest son, *James Edward Price* (1809-1898), married *Catharine,* the daughter of John and Anne Catharine (Sharpe) Gordon, and their daughter was KATHARINE GORDON PRICE, who married *William Graham Bowdoin.*

17 *Family Records.*

TATNALL.

EDWARD TATNALL (1704-1790), married *Elizabeth,* the daughter of Joseph and Mary (Levis) Pennock.

Their son, *Joseph Tatnall,* (1740-1813), married *Elizabeth,* the daughter of James and Margaret (Marshall) Lea.

Their daughter, *Margaret,* married second, James Price.

PENNOCK-LEVIS

JOSEPH PENNOCK, the son of Christopher and Mary (Collett) Pennock, married *Mary,* the daughter of Samuel and Elizabeth (Clator) Levis. *Mary Collett* was the daughter of GEORGE COLLET.

Their daughter, *Elizabeth,* married EDWARD TATNALL.

SAMUEL LEVIS, the son of Christopher and Mary (Nede) Levis, married Elizabeth Clator. Their daughter, *Mary,* married JOSEPH PENNOCK.

LEA-FAWCETT-PASCALL (PASCHALL)

JAMES LEA (1723-1798), was the son of Isaac and Sarah (Fawcett) Lea. He married *Margaret,* the daughter of John and Joanna (Pascall) Marshall, and their daughter, *Elizabeth,* married *Joseph Tatnall.*

WALTER FAWCETT died January 29, 1704-05. He married second, Rebecca, the daughter of Robert and Elizabeth (Egginton) Fearne. Their daughter, *Sarah,* married Isaac Lea.

THOMAS PASCALL (1634-1718), was the son of William and Johanna (Collins) Pascall. He married Joanna Sloper.

Their second son, *Thomas Pascall* married *Margaret,* the daughter of William and Elizabeth (Griffith) Jenkins.

WILLIAM JENKINS, the colonist, a large land owner in Delaware County, Penn., married Elizabeth, the daughter of Lewis Griffith, and their daughter, *Margaret,* married *Thomas Pascall II.,* whose second child, *Joanna,* married John Marshall IV.

Their daughter, *Margaret Marshall,* married JAMES LEA, whose daughter, *Elizabeth,* married Joseph Tatnall.

Their daughter, *Margaret Tatnall,* married James Price. Their son, *James Edward Price,* married *Catharine Gordon.* (See pp. 167-186 for details of Price, Tatnall, Pennock, Levis, Lea, Marshall, Fawcett, Jenkins and Pascall).

GORDON

COE GORDON, who died 1787, was commissioned Second Lieutenant of the Flying Camp, at Perth Amboy, N. J., November 14, 1776. He married, 1777, Sarah, the daughter of Nimrod and Elizabeth (Taylor) Maxwell.

Their son, *John Gordon,* married Anne Catharine, the daughter of William and Anne Catharine (Parlin) Sharpe.

Their daughter, *Catharine Gordon,* married *James Edward,* the son of James and Margaret (Tatnall) Price, whose daughter, KATHARINE GORDON, married *William Graham Bowdoin.* Their daughters are:

MARION GORDON BOWDOIN KNOX.

KATHLEEN GORDON BOWDOIN DAVIS.

Members of Chapter I., The Colonial Dames of America.

XXVII
READ

ARMS: *Gules on a bend argent wavy, three shovelers sable.*
MOTTO: *Indefessus vigilando.*

The first of this family who came to America was Sir William Read, a Baronet. He lost his fortune because he married Jane Spalding of a London family, which displeased one from whom he had expectations. He emigrated to Delaware where he was appointed Sheriff by the King, but dropped his title. He was several times Warden of Emanuel Church of New Castle, Del., from 1720. On his death 1736, the rector of that church, Mr. Ross, wrote to the home secretary: " Sir, The Church in this place has lately lost two of its chief supporters, particularly one William Read, a person of singular piety and the greatest benefactor I had in all my parish." [1] He is buried in a vault in the churchyard of Emanuel Church, under an altar tomb carved with the Read arms, and another coat of arms, and a long and quaint inscription in memory of his wife Jane.

"Here lyes the Body of Jane, wife of William Read late sheriff of this county, with the remains of three of their children who died in their Infancy. She was born in London of the ancient creditable family of Spalding. Many were her exemplary virtues. Her temper meek and carriage obliging—strict Chastity—Prudent Economy, Piety without ostentation and Hospitality without grudging. Her grateful loving Husband caused to hew and here to place this lasting monument of real conjugal affection—Obit 5 Julii M. D. C. C. XXXII Anno, Aetatis XXXVI."

[1] *Hist. of Emanuel Church,* New Castle, Del., by Thomas Holcombe.

There was also a marble slab erected in his honor by the people of New Castle that stood a long time against the wall of the church, but being removed, for repairs to the church, it was broken in two parts which were leaned against the wall and subsequently lost.

HON. JAMES READ, their son, was a Lieutenant of the Royal Navy.[2] After his marriage with *Ellen,* the daughter and heiress of JAMES BOND, a man of wealth in Georgia, and of the King's Council, he resigned from the navy. Having distinguished himself he was urged

READ-BOND ARMS

to remain but declined. He always bore the title of Captain thereafter, though he resigned as a Lieutenant. He was later engaged in a gallant exploit, capturing a French Privateer that had beaten off a King's ship, boarding her in the night with boats and himself shooting the captain. He afterwards entertained the captain in his own house in Savannah, who was exceedingly grateful to James Read for his generous conduct, and

[2] *Hist. of S. C.,* Appendix.

presented him with a handsome sword which is still in the family. Issue: JACOB, George Padden, died s. p., Dr. William, James, died s. p., Susan.

SENATOR JACOB READ,[3] the eldest son, was born in South Carolina 1752, and died in Charleston, July 17, 1816. He was educated at Princeton and studied law in England from 1773 to 1776. During the Revolution he served as Major of the South Carolina Volunteers, was taken prisoner and confined for four years at St. Augustine, Fla. He was a member of the Legislature, and 1783 was a delegate from South Carolina to the Continental Congress, remaining a member of that body until 1786. He was elected as a Federalist to the United States Senate, taking his seat on December 7, 1795. At the end of his term, March 3, 1801, President John Adams appointed him Judge of the United States Court for the district of South Carolina which office he held till his death.[4] He married, September 13, 1785, *Catharine,* the daughter of David and Anna (French) van Horn. They had four children:

Jacob, married Nancy Williamson, and had three sons.

Catharine, married Commodore Morgan, and had a daughter Virginia, who died s. p.

Cornelia, married *John Eager,* the son of JOHN EAGER HOWARD, of Belvidere, Baltimore; had a son, *John Eager,* who died s. p.

William George.

[3] *Book* of Baltimore.

General Read was burned in effigy for voting in favor of Jay's treaty. His brother Dr. William Read married Miss Harleston, and left a number of children who have many descendants in South Carolina.

[4] Appleton's *Cycl. of Am. Biog.*

VAN HORN

As early as 1647 Cornelis van Hoorn was in this country. His name is among the signers of the petition 1664 to Governor Stuyvesant for the surrender of New Netherlands to the English. He married, October 4, 1659, Anna Maria Jansz von Jamerica. His son:

ABRAHAM VAN HORN was one of the leading wealthy men of New York and lived on Wall Street. June, 1722, Governor Burnet recommended him to the Lords of Trade as one of the Councillors of New York,[5] and July, 1723, he was appointed to that office, holding it until his death, January 14, 1741. He married, September 16, 1700, *Maria,* the eighth daughter of David and Zyntje (or Tryntri) (Laurens) Provoost of Amsterdam. Issue: Anna Maria, Catharine, *David,* Margaret, Samuel, Anna.

Their eldest son and third child, *David van Hurn,* was baptized July 20, 1715. He was said to be descended from a collateral branch of the family of Philip de Montmorency, Count van Horn, who was beheaded with Count Egmont in the Netherlands. Forty-two portraits of the van Horn family and many records were destroyed with the van Horn residence in the great New York fire of 1836. He married, September 25, 1744, Anna, the daughter of Philip and Anetjie (Philipse) French, baptized April 8, 1722. Issue:

Mary, married Levinus Clarkson.

Cornelia, married Philip Livingston.

Catherine, married GENERAL JACOB READ, of South Carolina.

Elizabeth, married Charles Ludlow.

Susan, married George Trumbull.

[5] *Recs.* of N. Y. Gen. Soc.

Anna, married William Edgar.

David, later Captain, seems to have died without issue, as the records of the New York Genealogical Society do not contain the names of any of his children.

FRENCH

ARMS: *Argent, a chevron between three boars' heads erased azure.*
CREST: *Fleur-de-lis.*
MOTTO: *Nec timeo, nec sperno.*

Printed and oral statements as well as armorial bearings confirm the Scotch descent of this family and the coat of arms in their possession from the time of the immigration is that given here with a change in the tinctures. These are the arms of the Frenches of Thorndike and Frenchland, County Berwick.[6]

JOHN FRENCH died at Braintree Manor, N. Y., August 6, 1692. According to early records, he arrived in New England previous to 1640.

PHILIP FRENCH, his son married Anetjie, the daughter of FREDERICK PHILIPSE, and his first wife, Margaret

6 Mrs. Lamb's *Hist. of N. Y.*

(Hardenbroek) de Vries. (His second wife was Catherine van Cortlandt.)

The Philipse family owned large estates around Tarrytown and were buried in the church there, the family on one side and their slaves on the other. Being Tories, at the time of the Revolution they disposed of all their property, and returned to England.

The daughter of Philip and Anetjie French, *Anna French,* married *David van Horn,* whose daughter, *Catherine,* married JACOB READ, of South Carolina.

PROVOOST

DAVID PROVOOST I., was born in Holland, and died January 16, 1656. He was Commander at the Fort Good Hope 1642 to 1647; first of the nine men, 1652; and Sergeant of the Blue Flag Company, Burgher Corps, New Amsterdam 1653, first separate Schont at Bencoolen (Benkulen) 1655, Secretary of Bencoolen, Amersfort (Amersfoort), and midwont until his death.

DAVID PROVOOST II., his son (died 1724), was Captain in Colonel Abraham de Peyster's regiment, New York City, 1700; Major 1710; Lieutenant-Colonel 1716; member of the General Assembly 1702 to 1711, and member of the Council 1708 to 1710. He married Zyntje (or Tryntri) Laurens from Amsterdam. Their eighth daughter, *Maria,* married ABRAHAM VAN HORN, whose daughter, *Catherine,* married JACOB READ.

HOWARD

In the year 1686, Joshua Howard, a young Englishman of the House of Howard, near Manchester, Eng., came to Maryland. He obtained several grants of land and married Johanna O'Carroll, a lady of Irish descent.

One of his sons, Cornelius Howard, married Ruth

(1723-1798), the daughter of John and Jemima (Murray) Eager, a family which had been long settled in Maryland.

COLONEL JOHN EAGER HOWARD, their son, was born June 11, 1752, and died October 12, 1827. He was buried in Old St. Paul's Church Yard, Baltimore. His funeral was attended by President Adams and the military and civil authorities. At the time of the Revolution he was appointed one of the Committee of Observation for Baltimore County and later to be Colonel in the Militia, but declined because of inexperience; he accepted after a time the commission of Captain, which was dated January 25, 1776, and signed by Mathew Tilghman who was President of the Convention. Captain Howard had then completed his twenty-fourth year, and within two weeks had raised a company which was incorporated with Colonel Beall's Brigade of the Maryland Flying Camp, then in active service at the front. At the battle of White Plains, October 28, 1776, this force with Howard in command of his company co-operated with Smallwood's First Maryland and covered the retreat. In December of the same year the Flying Camp was dismissed, and on the organization of the seven regiments furnished by Maryland, Captain Howard became Major in the Fourth, under his former commander, Colonel Hall, his commission dated April 10, 1777. He was appointed June 1, 1799, Lieutenant-

ARMS OF
JOHN EAGER HOWARD

DESIR N'A REPOS

Colonel of the Fifth and the following spring was transferred to the Sixth.   Finally, after the battle of Hol-
brook's Hill, he succeeded to the command of the Second
after the death of Lieutenant-Colonel Ford.   He was
with General Greene in the South, who gave him the
highest praise, pronouncing him " as good an officer as
the world afforded," and to have deserved "a statue of
gold, no less than Roman and Grecian heroes."   At the
battle of Cowpens, he seized the critical moment, and
turned apparent defeat into victory by his coolness and
courage.   At one time he had in his hands seven swords
of the officers of the 71st Grenadiers who surrendered to
him.   November, 1788, Colonel Howard was chosen
Governor of Maryland and in 1796 he was elected to the
Senate of the United States to fill a vacancy, and was
subsequently elected for the full term which expired
March 4, 1803.   He was chosen a member of the Baltimore Committee of Defence in 1813.   To the over timid
at this time he replied scathingly that he had as much
property as any at stake, and four sons in the field, but
that he would give up all rather than capitulate.   He
made the address of welcome to General Lafayette on
his landing at Fort McHenry, and with other members
of the committee entered Baltimore with the Marquis,
in whose honor he gave a public reception at Belvidere.
Congress voted Colonel Howard a medal at the close of
the Revolution, for his valor at the battle of Cowpens.
The inscription is as follows:
" Quod in mutantem hostium aciem subito virmens
praeclarum bellicae virtutis specimen in pugna ad Cowpens XVII Jan. M. D. CCLXXXI."
He made liberal public and private gifts without regard to denomination.   His gifts to the city of Baltimore included the ground for the first monument erected

to Washington, and the beautiful squares surrounding
it, which are known as Mount Vernon and Washington
Place; also the ground for the Methodist-Episcopal
Church on Eutaw Street, and the lot on which the
Cathedral is built deeded to the Roman Catholic Church;
to the Presbyterian Church, the ground on Fayette
Street between Green and Paca Streets, known as
Westminster Church; in the corner of this burying-
ground lie the remains of Edgar Allan Poe; to
Old Saint Paul's Church he gave the ground for its
beautiful Rectory on Saratoga Street, built in 1792,
which reverts to the family if otherwise used. Beside these
are his gifts of the ground for the Liberty and Howard
engine houses, and the markets, known as Lexington
and Richmond, and a lot for the interment of strangers.[7]

He married, May 18, 1787, " at Cliveden," *Margaretta,* the daughter of BENJAMIN CHEW, of Philadelphia, and Elizabeth Benson his wife. Margaretta
Chew has historic notoriety as having won the heart of
Major André, who, on the eve of the famous Mischianza
1781, indited these lines to her:

> " If at the close of War and strife
>   My destiny once more
> Should in the various paths of life
>   Conduct me to this shore—
>
> Should British banners guard the land
>   And faction be restrained,
> And Cliveden's mansion peaceful stand
>   No more with blood be stained,
>
> Say wilt thou then receive again
>   And welcome to thy sight,
> The youth who bids with stifled pain
>   This sad farewell to-night? "

[7] These are all worthy of record, making a part of the history of the
City of Baltimore, which is in Saint Paul's Parish, as is an old Church
twelve miles from the city.

John Eager and Margaretta (Chew) Howard had eight children as follows:

John Eager, married Cornelia, the daughter of JACOB READ, of South Carolina.

George, married Prudence Ridgeley, of Hampton.

James, married first, Sophia Ridgeley, of Hampton; second, Catherine Ross, of Frederick.

Benjamin, married Jane Gilmor.

Juliana, married John McHenry.

William, married Rebecca Key, of Cedar Point.

Charles, married Elizabeth Key, the daughter of Francis Scott Key, author of the " Star Spangled Banner."

Sophia C., married *William George Read,* of South Carolina.

EAGER

Prior to 1668, George Eager came to Maryland, as in that year the estate near Baltimore was purchased. The records give little information before this time.

His son, John Eager, was born 1723, and died November 17, 1798. He married Jemima Murray, and their daughter, Ruth, married Cornelius Howard. Their son, JOHN EAGER HOWARD, inherited large estates from his mother. He married *Margaretta,* the daughter of BENJAMIN CHEW, and their daughter, *Sophia C.,* married *William George Read.*

CHEW

ARMS:[8] *Gules, in chief or three leopards' faces proper, a chevron of the second or.*

The Chews have been settled in America longer than

[8] These are the arms of the Chews of Somersetshire, England, Maryland, Maidstone and Cliveden.

any other family represented in the Provincial Councils of Pennsylvania.[9]

JOHN CHEW came to Virginia 1622 in the vessel *Charitie,* with three servants, followed by his wife Sarah 1623, in the "*Seafloure.*"[10]

He settled at James City and a deed of 1624, granted him "for the better convenience and commoditie of his new house by him, now over see, and builded, one rood & 9 perches of land lying and being about the same house." He was a member of the Assembly from Hogg's Island until 1623 and from Jamestown 1623.

COLONEL SAMUEL CHEW, of Maryland, his fifth son, married Anne, the daughter of William Ayres, of "Ayres Addition," Baltimore County, surveyed for Edward Ayres on the west side of the Bush River.[11] She died April 13, 1695. Samuel Chew was great-grandfather of the Councillor, residing in Maryland as early as 1648. (See pp. 219, 248-249.) He had seven sons and two daughters.

The fifth son, *Benjamin Chew,* was born the "13th day of ye 2 mo 1671," and died in Maryland, March 3, 1699-1700. He married "8th day of ye 10th mo 1692," Elizabeth Benson. They had three daughters and one son:

SAMUEL CHEW II., their son, was born August 30, 1693, and died June 16, 1743. He was known as "Samuel Chew of Maidstone," an estate near Annapolis. He practiced medicine, became a Quaker and removed to Kent County on the Delaware. He had a residence in the town of Dover which is still standing, and was also the owner of a plantation about three miles from there.

9 *Provincial Councillors of Penn.*
10 Hotten's *List of Emigrants, Lieut. Berkeley's Muster.*
11 *Baltimore County Rent Roll.*

Rear view   Front view

"BELVIDERE," THE HOME OF COL. JOHN EAGER HOWARD

COL. JOHN EAGER HOWARD

"CLIVEDEN," THE HOME OF THE CHEW FAMILY
Germantown, Pa.

His influence was strong in the neighborhood and his abilities were recognized by the government. He was Chief Justice of the lower counties from 1741 until his death. Though a Quaker he was not opposed to lawful war, and was therefore very valuable to a Governor, ordered by the Crown to fit out troops, yet who met with constant opposition from the Quakers. He married first, October 22, 1715, Mary, the daughter of Samuel and Anne Galloway: second, September 28, 1736, Mary Galloway, the widow of his brother-in-law, Samuel Galloway. By his first wife he was the father of the Councillor and eight other children, of whom six died young.

CHIEF JUSTICE BENJAMIN CHEW, of Cliveden, their son, was born at his father's seat on West River, Md., November 29, 1722, and died January 20, 1810. He was appointed Judge and President of the High Court of Errors and Appeals of Pennsylvania, his commission being dated respectively the third and fourth day of October, 1791.[12] He married first, Mary, the daughter of John and Mary (Thomas) Galloway; and second, Elizabeth, who died in May, 1819, the daughter of James and Mary (Turner) Oswald. His daughter, *Margaretta,* married JOHN EAGER HOWARD.

The parents of Mary Turner, who was a sister of Joseph Turner, the Councillor, are not known to have been in this country. Joseph was born at Andover, Hampshire, Eng., May 2, 1701, and came to America January 13, 1713-14. One of their sisters married James Simmes, a merchant in Jamaica.

READ (*Continued*)

The son of Jacob and Catharine (van Horn) Read,

12 *Provincial Councillors* of Penn.

William George Read, married, May 15, 1825, *Sophia
C.,* daughter of John Eager and Margaretta (Chew)
Howard of Belvidere, Baltimore. She was born March
6, 1800, and died November 1880. Issue:

William George II., married Elizabeth Waters Howard.

Mary Sophia, married Arthur Thomas Weld, of
England.

MARY CORNELIA, married first, Albert H. Carroll,
and second, James Fenner Lee.

MARY CORNELIA READ LEE,

Member of Chapter I., The Colonial Dames of
America.

XXVIII

DE VEAUX

At the time of the revocation of the Edict of Nantes, Colonel Andrea de Veaux, of a Huguenot family of Brittany, left that country, and settled in South Carolina, where he married, March 24, 1757, *Catherine Barnwell*, who was descended as follows:

COLONEL JOHN BARNWELL, married Anne Berners.

John Barnwell, married Martha Chaplin, and their daughter, *Catherine*, married Andrea de Veaux. (See pp. 378-381 for Barnwell line.)

When the British, under Major-General Prevost advanced to Charleston in 1779, Andrea de Veaux and his son *Andrea II.*, then about eighteen years old, joined it, and both father and son were distinguished officers in that army. The latter recaptured the Island of New Providence, April, 1783.[1] In a letter to Sir Guy Carleton, dated New Providence, June 6, 1783, Colonel de Veaux says:

" I have the pleasure to inform your excellency that on the first of April last, not having heard that peace was concluded, I formed from St. Augustine an expedition against New Providence to restore its inhabitants, with those of adjacent islands, to the blessings of a free government. I undertook this expedition at my own expense and embarked my men, which did not exceed sixty-five, recruited at Harbor Island for four or

---

[1] *Recapture of the Island of New Providence*, by R. MacKenzie.

five days, & sailed for Providence which I carried about
daylight with three of their formidable galleys on the
14th. . . . My force never at any time consisted of
more than 220 men and not above 150 of them has mus-
quets, not having it within my power to procure them
at St. Augustine. . . ."

Leaving the English army at the time of his marriage
to *Anna Maria,* the daughter of Philip and Effie (Beekman) Verplanck, Colonel de Veaux settled in "Red
Hook," Dutchess County, N. Y., where he built a large
house surrounded by a park of two hundred and ninety-
eight acres, called "Almont." This estate was sold to
the Livingston family in the latter part of the eighteenth century by Andrea de Veaux II.

" It was the career of this man of mystery which made
the estate famous throughout the country in his day.
Favored of the nobility and a protégé of the Crown, he
was given considerable grants of land in South Carolina, but soon, for reasons best known to himself, he
purchased from General John Armstrong, of Revolutionary fame, his country seat in Dutchess County
known as 'Almont.' Apparently possessed of limitless
wealth, none of his neighbors cared to inquire its source,
for de Veaux brought with him into the heart of this
centre of the old aristocracy a reputation as a duellist
and fire-eater, which discouraged undue curiosity about
his affairs. He had been commissioned by the Crown
to suppress some of the rebellions in the Bermudas and
other English dependencies in the West Indies, and
captured a number of the forts which were in rebellion.
Reproductions of the forts so captured were afterwards cut in stone and adorned the mantels in the old

COL. ANDREA DE VEAUX II

ANNA MARIA VERPLANCK
Wife of Col. Andrea de Veaux II

mansion. . . . De Veaux chose 'Almont' as his per-
manent home more on account of the good anchorage
and the shelter for his ships provided by the deep cove
in front of the property.; and back of the island now
known as 'Cruger's,' de Veaux's sloops always came
under cover of darkness, and the unloading was surrounded with the deepest mystery. He brought from
the West Indies a corps of natives as slaves or servants,
whose chief duty it was to keep the inquisitive off his
possessions. When he came into possession of the Hudson River property, about one hundred and fifty of the
four hundred acres surrounding the mansion had been
cleared. The rest was a dense forest of huge oak and
hickory, which was carefully preserved by the Living-
stone family, and there remains to-day some two hundred acres of virgin forest on the property. . . . The
site of the mansion commands a magnificent view for
miles up and down the Hudson River. The Catskill
Mountains lie directly across the river, the Overlook
Hotel being in plain view. . . . The famous old mansion was burned in 1878, leaving only the old farm-
house and barns. . . . The walls of the ruins are still
standing. It was in the deep bay adjoining 'Almont'
that Robert Fulton, who married a member of the Livingston family, conducted the experiments with his
steamboats. . . . He lived in a house on the adjoining estate, which still remains."

Their daughter, *Julia,* married John Hare Powel.

VERPLANCK

ARMS: *Ermine on a chief engrailed sable, three mullets argent.*
CREST: *A demi wolf proper.*
MOTT: *Ut vita sic mors.*[2]

An ancestor of this family was Isaacsen Verplanck, of Holland.

ABRAHAM ISAACSEN VERPLANCK[3] married Maria Roos (née Vigue). He was born in Holland 1616, and came to New York 1635; died 1690. He was a member of the first representative Assembly of the Dutch in New Netherlands, one of twelve. His son:

ENSIGN GELYN VERPLANCK was born 1637, and died 1684. He was Ensign 1673; Schepen of New Amsterdam and Alderman of New York 1679. He married, June 25, 1668, Hendrika Wessels.

Their son, *Jacobus Verplanck,* was born 1671, and married, 1691, *Margaret,* the daughter of CAPTAIN PHILIP PIETERSE SCHUYLER, and his wife, *Margaritta*

---

[2] The arms used by the branch of the family descended from "Gulian" son of Abraham.

[3] Verplanck *Family Record* and *Md. State Colonial Dames,* p. 156.

van Slichtenhorst, who was the daughter of BRANT ARENTSE VAN SLICHTENHORST. (See pp. 232-234 for Schuyler and van Slichtenhorst lines.)

PHILIP VERPLANCK I., their son, was born June 28, 1695, and died October 13, 1771. He was Ensign 1711, in the Colonial Forces; Commissioner to the Six Nations 1746; in the New York Provincial Assembly 1734 to 1768. He married, April 10, 1718, *Gertrude,* the daughter of Johannes and Anna Maria (van Schaick) van Cortlandt.

Their son, *Philip Verplanck II.,* married *Effie,* the daughter of Gerardus II. and Catherine (Provost) Beekman.

Their daughter, *Anna Maria,* married Colonel *Andrea de Veaux II.*

VAN CORTLANDT

An ancestor of this family was Stephanus van Cortlandt, of Holland, who married Catrina ———.

HON. OLOFF STEVENSE VAN CORTLANDT (1600-1684) married Annatje Loockermans.

HON. STEPHANUS VAN CORTLANDT (1643-1700), their son, married *Gertrude Schuyler.*

Their son, *Johannes van Cortlandt,* married *Anna Maria,* the daughter of CAPTAIN GOOSEN GERRETSE VAN SCHAICK, the first settler of Bederwyck (Albany), 1663.

Their daughter, *Gertrude,* married *Philip Verplanck I.,*[4] whose son, *Philip II.,* married *Effie Beekman.* (See pp. 230-232 for van Cortlandt line.)

BEEKMAN

The marriage of Cornelius Beekman and Christiana

[4] *N. Y. City and State Records.*

Huygens, occurred at Cologne, Germany, and their son, Gerardus, was born 1568, and died 1625; he married Agnes Steening. Their son, Hendrick, married Mary Bandartins. Their son:

GOVERNOR WILLIAM BEEKMAN, was born in Holland 1623, and came to New York, 1647. He was Lieutenant of the Burgher Corps of New Amsterdam, 1652-1658; Vice-Governor on the Delaware, 1658 to 1664, Lieutenant of Militia under the Dutch 1673, and Deputy Mayor of New York, 1681 to 1683. He married Catherine Van Borg. Their son:

COLONEL GERARDUS BEEKMAN I., was born 1653, and died 1728. He was Captain 1681, Major 1689, Lieutenant-Colonel 1698, and Colonel, 1700 to 1703. He was a member of the Council 1705 to 1723, and Deputy Governor 1709 to 1710. He married *Magdalena,* the daughter of STEOFFLE JANSE ABEEL, and his wife, Neetie Janse Croon, whom he married in 1660. He was Komneissario at Renssaelaerwyck, from 1664 to 1667, and died in 1681. Their son:

GERARDUS BEEKMAN II., born in 1693, and died in 1742, was Lieutenant-Captain, 1738. His wife was *Catherine,* the daughter of William and Aiffe (Van Exveen) Provoost.

Their daughter *Effie* married *Philip Verplanck II.*[5]

PROVOOST

DAVID PROVOOST I. was born in Holland, and came to New York before 1639, where he died 1656. He married Grittse Gillis.

DAVID PROVOST II., their son (died 1724), married Tryntri Laurens.

Their son, *William Provoost,* married Aiffe Van Ex-

[5] Beekman *Papers.*

JOHN HARE POWEL
Reproduced from a painting by Sir Thomas
Lawrence

DE VEAUX POWEL
Reproduced from a painting by Jane Stuart
daughter of Gilbert Stuart

veen, whose daughter, *Catharine,* married GERARDUS
BEEKMAN II. Their daughter, *Effie,* married *Philip
Verplanck II.,* and their daughter, *Anna Maria Ver-
planck,* married *Andrea de Veaux II.*

HARE-POWEL

The colonist, Robert Hare, a son of Richard and

Martha Hare, was born in England, 1752, and died
March 8, 1811. He came to Pennsylvania in 1773, and
was a member of the Assembly 1791, and Lieutenant-
Governor of Pennsylvania 1795. He married *Mar-
garet,* the daughter of Charles and Anne (Shippen)
Willing.

Their son, *John,* changed his name by act of Assembly from Hare to Powel, and married, October 20,
1817, *Julia,* the daughter of *Andrea de Veaux II.,* and
his wife *Anna Maria Verplanck.*

Their son, *De Veaux Powel,* married *Elizabeth,* the daughter of George and Eleanor Addison (Dall) Cooke.

Their daughter, *Elizabeth Cooke Powel,* married Gustav W., the son of Gustav W. and Frances (Donnell) Lürman.

WILLING-SHIPPEN

In Gloucestershire, England, resided Joseph Willing II., who had married for his second wife, Anne Lowle.

Their son, Thomas, married Anne, the daughter of General Harrison (the regicide), and his wife, Dorothy Mayne, who was a daughter of Simon Mayne, also a regicide.

CHARLES WILLING, a son of Thomas, was born in Bristol, England, 1710, and came to Philadelphia, where he died November 30, 1754. He married, January 21, 1730-31, *Anne,* the daughter of Joseph and Abigail (Grosse) Shippen, and their daughter, *Margaret,* married Robert Hare.

EDWARD SHIPPEN, the colonist, was a son of William Shippen, of Yorkshire, England. He came to Boston, Mass., 1668, and died in Philadelphia, October 2, 1712. He married Elizabeth Lybrand. Their son, *Joseph,* married Abigail Grosse, whose daughter, *Anne,* married CHARLES WILLING. (See pp. 155-158, for details of Willing and Shippen.)

COOKE

A representative of this family, John Cooke, married *Sophia,* the daughter of Nicholas and Susanna (Burgess) Sewall.

Their son, *William Cooke,* married *Elizabeth,* the daughter of Richard and Susanna (Frisby) Tilghman.

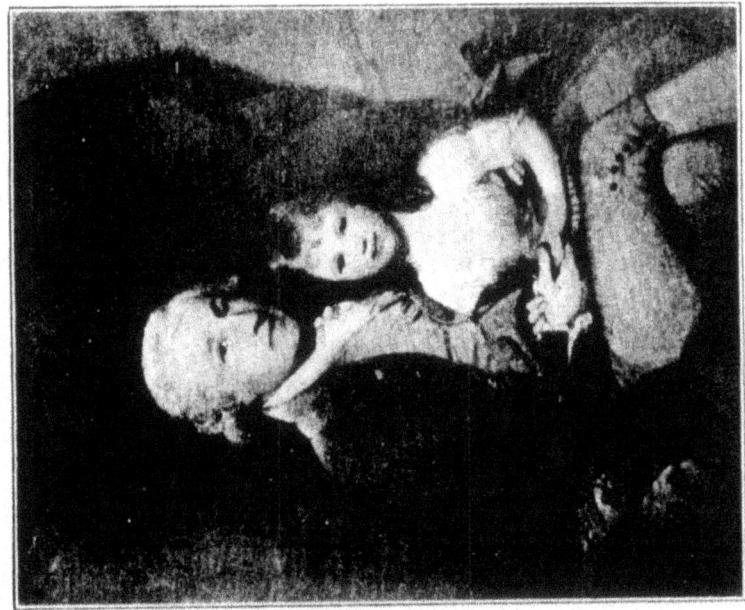

ROBERT HARE AND HIS DAUGHTER
Reproduced from a painting by Gilbert Stuart

Their son, *George Cooke,* married Eleanor Addison Dall.

Their daughter, *Elizabeth S. Cooke,* married *De Veaux Powel,* whose daughter, *Elizabeth Cooke Powel,* married Gustav W., the son of Gustav W. and Frances (Donnell) Lürman. Their daughters are FRANCES DONNELL and KATHARINE LURMAN.

The parents of Frances (Donnell) Lürman were John and Ann Teackle (Smith) Donnell, and through her mother she was descended from a number of colonial families, as follows:

SHEPPARD-SMITH

THOMAS SHEPPARD was the first of this line in America.

LIEUTENANT-COLONEL JOHN SHEPPARD, his son, married Jean ——, and their daughter, Ioane, married John Smith, whose son, *Isaac,* married *Sarah West.*

ISAAC SMITH II., their son (1734-1813), married *Elizabeth Custis Teackle.*

Their daughter, *Ann Teackle Smith,* married John Donnell. One of their daughters, *Elizabeth,* married *James Swan,* and another, *Frances,* married Gustav W. Lürman.

WEST-SCARBOROUGH-YEARDLEY

LIEUTENANT-COLONEL JOHN WEST, the son of Anthony, the emigrant, married Matilda Scarborough, the daughter of COLONEL EDMUND SCARBOROUGH and his wife *Mary,* the daughter of STEPHEN CHARLTON, and the granddaughter of CAPTAIN EDMUND SCARBOROUGH.

MAJOR JOHN WEST, their son, married *Frances Yeardley,* and their daughter, *Sarah,* married *Isaac Smith I.*

SIR GEORGE YEARDLEY, married Temperance West.

COLONEL ARGALL YEARDLEY, married Anne Custis.

CAPTAIN ARGALL YEARDLEY, married *Sarah Michael,* the daughter of CAPTAIN JOHN MICHAEL, and his wife, *Elizabeth Thoroughgood,* who was the daughter of CAPTAIN ADAM THOROUGHGOOD. Their daughter, *Frances Yeardley,* married JOHN WEST II., whose daughter, *Sarah,* married *Isaac Smith I.* (See pp. 335-342, 347, for Sheppard, Smith, West, Yeardley, Michael, and Thoroughgood lines.)

TEACKLE-CUSTIS

REV. THOMAS TEACKLE, the colonist, married, second, Margaret Nelson.

JOHN TEACKLE, their son (1693-1721), married *Susannah Upshur.* She was the daughter of ARTHUR UPSHUR II., and the great-granddaughter of JOHN BROWN.

Their son, *Thomas Teackle II.* (1711-1769), married *Elizabeth Custis.*

Their daughter, *Elizabeth Custis Teackle,* married ISAAC SMITH II., and their daughter, *Ann Teackle,* married John Donnell, whose daughter, *Frances,* married Gustav W. Lürman.

EDMUND CUSTIS, son of Thomas, of Baltimore, Ireland, married *Tabitha,* the daughter of COLONEL WILLIAM and the granddaughter of CAPTAIN WILLIAM WHITTINGTON.

Their son, *Thomas Custis,* married *Elizabeth,* the daughter of COLONEL JOHN CUSTIS III., and his wife *Margaret Michael,* the daughter of CAPTAIN JOHN MICHAEL.

JUDGE JOHN CUSTIS IV., their son, married Ann Upshur, whose daughter, *Elizabeth,* married *Thomas Teackle II.*

Their daughter *Elizabeth Custis Teackle,* married ISAAC SMITH II.

MAJOR-GENERAL JOHN CUSTIS II. married, second, Tabitha (Scarborough) Smart, the widow of William Smart, and they were the parents of COLONEL JOHN CUSTIS III. (See pp. 343-350 for Teackle, Custis, Whittington, and other connecting lines.)

SEWALL

ARMS: *Sable, a chevron between three bees argent.*
CREST: *A bee or.*

During the early part of the reign of King Richard II. (1381), one John Sewall was Sheriff of Essex and Hertfordshire, England, whose coat-of-arms was the same as that shown to-day.

In Coventry, Warwickshire, Henry Sewall was born 1544, and was alderman and mayor of Coventry 1589 and 1606. He married Margaret Gazebrook, of Middleton, and died 1629. Two of their sons were Henry and Richard.

The first named, Henry Sewall II., married Anne Hunt, emigrated to New England, and died, leaving an only son, from whom the New England family are descended. The other son, Richard, married Mary, the sister of William Dugdale (Garter King at Arms), and had issue nine children. The third son:

HON. HENRY SEWALL, died 1665. He was termed, in the notice of his emigration, as " of London." He was Secretary of Maryland 1661 to 1665. He married Jane Lowe, who afterwards married the third Lord Baltimore.[6] Their son:

6 *Arch.* of Md.

MAJOR NICHOLAS SEWALL (1640 or 1655-1737), was a member of the Council 1683 to 1689; Secretary of State and Deputy Governor 1689. He married *Susanna,* the daughter of COLONEL WILLIAM BURGESS. (See pp. 248, 533.) A daughter of this marriage, *Sophia Sewall,* married John Cooke, whose son, *William,* married *Elizabeth Tilghman.*

TILGHMAN

ARMS: *Per fesse sable and argent, a lion rampant regardant double-queued, crowned or counter charged.*

CREST: *A demi lion issuant and statant sable, crowned or.*

The Tilghman family of Holloway Court, Kent County, England, who were living there early in the fifteenth century, trace their descent twelve generations back to John Tilghman, contemporary with William the Conqueror.

Richard Tilghman of Holloway Court lived in 1400.

Thomas Tilghman.

William Tilghman, died 1541.

Richard Tilghman, died 1518.

William Tilghman II., died 1594.

Oswald Tilghman, of London, born 1579 and died 1628.[7]

DOCTOR RICHARD TILGHMAN, born September 3, 1626, was a colonist to America in 1660, and died at " The Hermitage," Maryland, January 7, 1675. He was a surgeon in the British navy, and one of the parliamentarians who signed the petition to have justice done King Charles I. He first settled upon " Canterbury Manor," a tract of a thousand acres, granted him by Lord Baltimore, July 17, 1659. The fact that the patent was issued before his arrival, indicates that Doc-

[7] *Old Kent.*

tor Tilghman was offered a special inducement to come
to the province. Being a man of family, he brought
with him a heritage still treasured by his descendants of
to-day, in the form of a "record book," begun in the
year 1540, during the life of his great-great-grandfather, William Tilghman I.[8] In this book he gives an
account of his voyage to Maryland. Each generation
has added its entries, and it is one of the most complete
family records in the State of Maryland. Prior to his
death, Doctor Tilghman received numerous patents for
land, which aggregated, in Talbot County alone, over
eight thousand, two hundred acres. One of these patents was for " The Hermitage," in the year 1666. To
this estate he removed, and it has ever since been the
family seat. He was High Sheriff for Talbott County,
1670 to 1671. He married Maria Foxley. Their son:

HON. RICHARD TILGHMAN II., born in 1672, and
died in 1738, was Burgess for Talbot County, 1698 to
1702; a member of the Council from 1711; Chancellor
1725. He married *Anna Maria,* the daughter of PHI-
LEMON LLOYD, and his wife Henrietta Maria (Neale)
Bennett (the daughter of JAMES NEALE). Anna Maria
was also the granddaughter of EDWARD LLOYD, of Wye
House. (See pp. 548-551, for Neale, and pp. 354-356
for Lloyd lines.)

RICHARD TILGHMAN III., their son, born in 1705,
and died in 1768, was Justice of the Provincial Court
1746 to 1754. He married *Susanna,* the daughter of
COLONEL PEREGRINE FRISBY, a member of the House
of Burgesses, Cecil County, Md., 1713.[9] Their daughter, *Elizabeth,* married *William Cooke.*

[8] *Old Kent,* p. 230.
  Md. Heraldry, Baltimore Sun.
[9] *Arch.* of Md.
  Old Kent.

Their son, *George Cooke,* married Eleanor Addison Dall, whose daughter, *Elizabeth S.,* married *De Veaux Powel.*

Their daughter, *Elizabeth Cooke Powel,* married Gustav W. Lürman, whose daughters are:

FRANCES DONNELL LÜRMAN,

KATHARINE LÜRMAN,

Members of Chapter I., The Colonial Dames of America.

XXIX
KILTY

CAPTAIN JOHN KILTY, was born 1756, and died May 27, 1811. He was Captain of the first regiment of Light Dragoons, 1783, with a record of six years and eight months' active service, in the war of the Revolution. He was a brother of Chancellor William Kilty, of Maryland, who was first Chief Justice of the District of Columbia. He married Miss Middleton, but had no issue. Both John and William Kilty were taken prisoners, and confined in separate prisons until the close of the war[1]. John Kilty was made Brigadier-General and Adjutant-General of Maryland, and was one of the original members of the Society of the Cincinnati, whose certificate, with the signature of Washington, is in the possession of Allan MacSherry, of Baltimore. He was well educated, with a musical talent, which has been inherited by most of his children. He held the civil office of Supervisor of the Revenue of the General Government, within the State of Maryland, appointed by President Washington. After the war, General Kilty settled in Annapolis. In 1808, he published *The Landholders' Assistant* and *Landholders' Guide.* He had issue, nine children, five sons and two daughters of whom died unmarried. A younger daughter, Ellen Ahearn, married Major Smack of the United States Army.

The elder daughter, *Elizabeth,* married Robert Wilson, a member of the Maryland bar, whose daughter *Catherine Somerville,* married Richard MacSherry.

[1] It is said the first intimation they had of the close of the war was brought to John Kilty by a mouse on a scrap of newspaper.

MAC SHERRY

A physician of Baltimore, Dr. Richard MacSherry was commissioned assistant surgeon in the United States Navy, and detailed surgeon to the marines at the breaking out of the Mexican War, serving under General Winfield Scott. He was present at the capture of Chapultepec and the City of Mexico. Dr. MacSherry was a Spanish scholar and a writer of note. He made a trip around the world in the frigate *Constitution* (*Old Ironsides*), under Captain Jack Percival. April 17, 1851, he resigned from the navy, being stationed at the Naval Hospital, Norfolk, and removed his family to Baltimore, where he resided the remainder of his life, dying October 9, 1885. He was president of the Medical and Chirurgical faculty of Maryland, 1883, and was one of the founders of the Baltimore Academy of Medicine, and its first president.

He married *Catherine Somerville,* the daughter of Robert and Elizabeth (Kilty) Wilson. Issue, eight children (four of whom died young):

William Kilty, married Charlotte Combs, and died without issue.

Richard Meredith, died 1898; married *Emily Hillen.* Issue, now living: Emily, Richard, KATHARINE, Soloman Hillen, and Clinton Kilty.

Henry Clinton, married Anna Wiester.

Allan, married his sister-in-law, *Emily* (*Hillen*) *MacSherry.*

WYNNE

DOCTOR THOMAS WYNNE, was born in northern Wales. The seal attached to his will, probated February 20, 1692, bears the design of a triple towered castle.[2]

2 Phila. *Book* A, p. 200.

ELEANOR PASCAULT
Wife of Columbus O'Donnell

GEN. JOHN KILTY
From a painting by Sharpless

LEWIS PASCAULT

SARAH BOND
Wife of Benjamin Chew

He came to this country with William Penn, in the ship *Welcome*, landing at New Castle, October 24, 1682, and in December, at Chester. At the preliminary Assembly, held at Chester, December 4, 1682, Thomas Wynne was appointed one of a committee of three, to request the Governor to form a constitution. Dr. Wynne and his wife became Quakers. He was present at the first meeting of the religious Society of Friends, held in Philadelphia, November 9, 1683, and was appointed one of a committee to build a meeting-house. He was a Member of the Pennsylvania Assembly, 1683. According to one account of Philadelphia, his house was among the first built in that city on Front Street, west side above Chestnut Street, which was once called Wynne Street. He married, 1665, Martha Buttall, whose family was identified with the town of Wreyham, Eng.

Their daughter *Sidney* married, December 20, 1690, William Chew. Issue: BENJAMIN.

CHEW-O'DONNELL

BENJAMIN CHEW, the son of William and Sidney (Wynne) Chew, was born in Anne Arundel County, 1700, and died in 1763. He removed to Cecil County, prior to 1744, where he was Justice of the Peace, 1743 to 1762.[3] He married, in January, 1726, Sarah Bond.

Their daughter *Mary* was born 1748, in Cecil County, Md.; married Thomas Elliott.

Their daughter, *Sarah Chew Elliott,* was born 1766, in Cecil County; died in Baltimore, 1857; married Colonel John O'Donnell, born in Limerick, Ire., 1743, and died in Baltimore, 1805.

---

[3] *Com. Recs.*, 1743–1762, pp. 60–148.

Their son, *Columbus O'Donnell,* married Eleanor, the daughter of Lewis Pascault. Issue:

Josephine, married Thomas S. Lee, of Needwood Forest, Md.

Eleanora, married Adrian Iselin, of New York.

Columbus, married Caroline Jenkins.

Oliver, married, first, Lucinda de Sodrie, a Portuguese, and second, Helen Carroll, a sister of Governor John Lee Carroll, of Maryland.

Emily, married Soloman Hillen, Mayor of Baltimore, 1842. Issue, eight children, of whom all but two died young. Their son, Thomas Hillen, married Sophia Frick, and had one child, Thomas O'Donnell Hillen. The daughter, *Emily Hillen,* married, first, Richard Meredith MacSherry, and second, Allan Mac-Sherry. Her daughter by first husband is:

KATHARINE MACSHERRY,

Member of Chapter I., The Colonial Dames of America.

COL. JOHN O'DONNELL

SARAH CHEW ELLIOTT
Wife of Col. John O'Donnell

XXX
BRENT

ARMS: *Gules, a wivern passant argent.*
CREST: *A wivern's head and wings couped.*

It is said that their ancestors in their arms recommended to their posterity—by the serpent, prudence; by his color, innocence; in a red field, a bloody and troublous world; with this motto or inscription, " Silentio et Diligentia." [1]

According to Collison, the name Brent (from an Anglo-Saxon word, meaning to burn), as applied to certain portions of the coast, occurs in the annals of Glastonbury before the time of the Danish invasions. It was, he says, to the devastations caused by the Danes that some had traced a fancied origin of the name. But

[1] *Va. Hist. Mag.* Vol. XII, No. 4, pp. 443 and 489. (For this passage and others that follow).

the Duchess of Cleveland in her book[2] says the name of "Brent is from Breaunt, Breant or Brente, near Havre." The family remained in Normandy in the sixteenth century as Viscounts of Holot. This would appear to be the more probable origin of the name, as the earlier de Brents were clearly Norman, as indicated by their name, by its being on the Roll of Battel Abbey,[3] and also from the Norman names of their wives, viz.: Malet, de Montecute, de la Ford, Deneband, le Eyre, Beauchamp, Latimer. "It is recorded in the 'Red Book of Knights fees, in the Exchecquer,'[4] that Odo de Brent, at the time of the Conquest, was Lord of Cossington, now in the County of Somerset, England."

The name of Odo de Brent's son is not known, but that of his grandson was Jeffry, whose son, Nicholas, was the father of Sir Robert, who died in 1262 (46 Henry III.), having married Millicent ———. (She married, second, Raymond Malet.[5]) Their son, Sir Robert, married Isabella, the daughter of Simon de Montecute; she survived him, his death occurring in the second year of Edward II. When Edward I. went into Gascony, 1277, Sir Robert attended him, as he did in most of his expeditions into Scotland, being then a Knight. In 1297 he was a Knight of the Shire of Som-

[2] *The Roll of the Battle Abbey*, by the Duchess of Cleveland, pp. xx. & 188-9.

[3] Battel Abbey was erected by William the Conqueror, to commemorate his victory over the Saxons in the battle of Hastings. In it he hung a roll containing the surnames of those of his Norman Knights who took part in that battle. Among the names is that of "Brent."

[4] *The Red Book of the Exchecquer* was compiled in the reign of Henry III, A. D. 1264, and contains the returns of the tenants in capite, in 1166, who certified how many knights' fees they held; also much matteer from Pipe Roll of Henry II and copies of inquisitions returned into the Exchecquer in 13 John. *Brewer's Dictionary*, &c.

[5] Collinson's *History of Somerset*, quoted in *Va. Hist. Mag.*, vol. xii, No. 4. p. 445.

BATTLE ABBEY, HASTINGS

MARIA FENWICK
Wife of William Leigh Brent

WILLIAM LEIGH BRENT

ROBERT JAMES BRENT

erset, at the Parliament then held at Westminster. He is said to have been the first to use a seal of his arms, viz., a Wiven, as it is now borne and has generally been used by his descendants.[6]

His son, also Sir Robert de Brent, married Claricia, the daughter and heir of Sir Adam de la Ford, of Ford, in the Parish of Bawdrip, by whom he had the Manor of Ford, and other lands, in this County, Wilts, Hants and Essex. Sir Robert is buried on the north side of the choir of the Abbey Church of Glastonbury. This Robert was also a knight and a great benefactor to the Abbey of Glastonbury.

DE MONTECUTE

His son, Sir Robert de Brent, married Elizabeth Deneband, and died 1357 (25 Edw. III.). One of their sons, also Sir Robert, succeeded his father at Cossington. Another son, John, settled himself at Charing, in Kent, on some lands which were Sir Adam de la Ford's, and became the progenitor of a family which continued there with great dignity for many generations.[8]

DE LA FORD [7]

Their son, Sir John Brent, married Joan, the daughter and heir of John le Eyre, of Midlezoy, by whom he

[6] Collinson, in *Va. Hist. Mag.*, Vol. II, p. 105.

[7] Borne by Sir Adam at the siege of Caerlaverock, 1300. *Foster's Feudal Coats of Arms.*

[8] Collinson's *Somerset*, in *Va. Mag. of Hist.* Vol. XIII, No. I, p. 105.

had a manor in that parish. The arms of Le Eyre
were: Ar, on a chevron, sable, three quatre foyles or.[9]

Their son, Sir John Brent of Cossington, married,
first, Ida, the daughter of Sir John Beauchamp, of Lil-
lisdon, Knt., by whom he had Sir
Robert, who succeeded him in the
estates of Cossington; and, second,
Joan, the daughter of Sir Robert
Latimer, Knt.

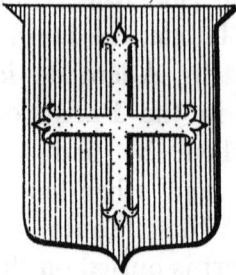

A son of the second marriage,
Sir John, succeeded to the estate
of Cossington (upon the death and
extinction of the line of his half-
brother, Sir Robert Brent).[10]

LATIMER

His son, Sir Robert, married Margaret, the daughter
of Hugh Malet, of Currypool.

Their younger son, Robert, married Margery, the
daughter of George Colchester, Lord of Stoke and
Admington, and died 1531. This Robert Brent
founded the Brent family of Stoke and Admington,
whose place of burial was in the church at Ilmington,
in Warwickshire, where a memorial tablet in brass
gives an account of their marriages and deaths.

A son, Sir William Brent, Lord of Stoke and Admington, married Elizabeth ———, and died 1595.
Their son, Sir Robert, married, 1572, Mary, the daughter of John and Katharine (Hennage) Huggeford, and
died 1587. The will of Mary Brent, widow,[11] bequeathed silver to her grandchildren, Elizabeth, Elinor, Anne, Jane, Richard, Gyles, William, Edward,
and George Brent.

9 Foster's *Feudal Coats of Arms.*
10 Collinson's Somerset, Va. Mag. of Hist. Vol. XIII, No. 1, p. 106.
13 *Va. Mag. of Hist.*, vol. xiv, No. 2, p. 213.

The elder son, Sir Richard, married, 1594, Elizabeth, the daughter of Giles Reed, Esq., Lord of Tus-

COLCHESTER [12]

burie and Witten, and Katherine Greville, his wife.
Sir Richard died 1652, and was buried at Ilmington.
He had thirteen children, a number of whom were con-
spicuously connected with the early history of Mary-
land and Virginia, viz.: Foulke, Giles, Mary, and
Margaret.

Their sixth child, George, was granted administration on his father's estate, May 21, 1652. He is mentioned in his grandmother's will and in a conveyance of
1663, as of "Defford." He married Marianna, the
daughter of Sir John Peyton, of Doddington; she was
twice married after George Brent's death, and died
after 1663. Their son, GEORGE, was the colonist, who
went to Virginia.

DENEBAND

The Denebands were an old English family descended from Sir John Deneband, Lord of Porscenet, in Wales, who married Alice, the daughter and heir of Thomas Gifford of Hinton. Philip Deneband, their son, married Cicely, the daughter of Simon Grandham al's Grandynham, and William, their son, married Agnes ———, and was the father of Elizabeth,[13] the wife of Sir Robert de Brent.

PEYTON

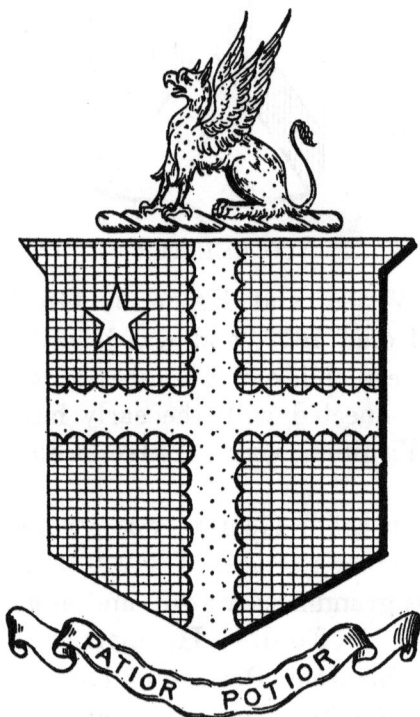

ARMS: *Sable, a cross engrailed or in the first quarter a mullet argent.*
CREST: *A Griffin sejant or.*
MOTTO: *Patior Potior.*

The Peytons were descended from Sir Robert Peyton of Isleham, one of whose sons, Sir Robert, was the

---

[13] From *Visitation of the County of Somerset*, by F. W. Weaver, Exeter 1885, p. 20.

ancestor of the baronets of Isleham and all the Virginia
families of the name. The other, Sir John, of Knowl-
ton, Kent, who married Dorothy, the daughter of Sir
John Tindall, K. B., was the father of two sons, Sir
Thomas, and Sir John, the younger, who was of Doddington, Cambridgeshire, and Governor of the Tower
in the reign of Elizabeth; member of the Privy Council,
and Governor of Guernsey and Jersey in the time of
James I. He married Dorothy, the widow of Sir Robert Bell, and the daughter and heir of Edward Beau-
pre, of Outwell, Norfold. He was the father of Sir
John Peyton of Doddington, in the Isle of Ely, whose
wife was Alice, the daughter of Sir John Peyton of
Isleham.[14] Issue, among others, Marianna, who married George Brent.

BRENT (*Continued*)

CAPTAIN GEORGE BRENT, Gent., of "Woodstock,"
Stafford County, Va., who came to Virginia before
1671, was the son of George Brent of England and his
wife, Marianna (Peyton) Brent, and grandson of Sir
Richard Brent, Lord of Stoke and Admington. He
was Captain of a Troop of Horse 1667; appointed May
2, 1683, by the Governor and Council, Receiver-General
north of the Rappahannock, and appointed July 10,
1690, Ranger-General of the Northern Neck. He died
either in 1699 or 1700.

Among other large estates, George Brent acquired
"Woodstock," now "Acquia," and "Brenton," Staf-
ford County, Va. He was land agent for Thomas,
Lord Culpeper,[15] and associate land agent with Colonel
William Fitzhugh, of Virginia, for Lady Culpeper and

14 *Va. Hist. Mag.*, vol. xii, No. 4, p. 441.
15 *Va. Hist. Mag.*

Lord Fairfax. In *Virginia Historical Magazine,* vol. I., No. 3, January, 1894, is a list of attorneys,—among them, thirty-three in all, are the names of George Brent and William Fitzhugh. "George Brent (and others) purchased from Thomas, Lord Culpeper, thirty thousand acres of land between the Potomac and Rappahannock, and applied to King James II. for freedom of religion, and by patent dated February 10th, 1687, the King granted to the petitioners and to all who should settle in said town and tract of land &c. the free exercise of their religion," [16] etc. He married, first, Elizabeth, the daughter of Captain William Green, and niece of Sir William Layton of England; she died March 26, 1686; second, March 27, 1687, Mary Chandler, the widow of Colonel William Chandler.

Issue, first wife: George, Nicholas, *Robert* of "Woodstock," Marianne, and Elizabeth.[17] Issue, second wife: A number of children, of whom only three survived, viz.: Henry, Mary and Martha.

OTHER CONSPICUOUS BRENTS

Four of the children of Sir Richard Brent and his wife, Elizabeth Reed (grandparents of GEORGE BRENT, the colonist), came to America, viz.: Foulke, Giles, Margaret and Mary.

The elder, Foulke Brent, emigrated to Maryland 1638, married Cecelia ——, and died without issue 1650. He was a member of the Fourth General As-

[16] Shea's Catholic Church in the Colonies, p. 96-7.

[17] "William Green of Bermuda, half brother of Elizabeth Green, first wife of Captain George Brent, of 'Woodstock,' by his will proved October 27th, 1692, devised his estate to the children of said George and Elizabeth, viz: George, Nicholas, Robert and Elizabeth. Personalty inventoried at £1285. He also devised his law books to Captain George Brent."

sembly of Maryland, October 12 to 24, 1640, and also that of 1641.

His brother, Giles Brent, emigrated to Maryland 1638, married Mary ——, and died in Virginia 1676. He was sworn in as one of the three Privy Councillors to Leonard Calvert, March 20, 1638-39. He was appointed Treasurer, the same day, May 29, 1639-40, was Captain of the Military band of St. Mary's, "to lead and command them and exercise them in discipline and military," training all the inhabitants but the Councillors on "Holy days and at other needful times." February 3, 1639-40, he was Commander of Kent, and granted the Manor of Kent Fort, on Kent Island, with right to hold a baronial court. Governor of the province, during the absence of Leonard Calvert in England, April 15, 1643, to September 10, 1644. In 1665-66 commanded in Virginia, a military force against Bacon.

An unmarried sister of these two men Margaret Brent, was left by Leonard Calvert his sole executrix, and she and (her sister) Mary Brent, who were present at his death,

"Having sworn that Leonard Calvert, by word of mouth on his death-bed did appoint Thomas Green, one of the Council, to be his successor. Green assumed the reigns of Government; and on November 16, 1647, This day the question was moved in Court whether or no Mr. Leonard Calvert, remaining his Lordship's sole attorney within the province, and then dying, the said Mr. Calvert's administrator was to be received for his Lordship's attorney within this province, until such time as his Lordship had made a new substitution, or that some other remaining upon the present commission was arrived in the province."

The Governor demanded Mr. Giles Brent's opinion
upon the said query, and in accordance with his reply,
"The Governor conceived, and it was ordered that the
administrator of Mr. Leonard Calvert aforesaid, should
be received as his Lordship's attorney to the intents
above stated." [18]   At the session of 1648, Mistress
Brent, relying upon this order, made an application to
the Assembly "to have a vote for herself and *another*
as his Lordship's attorney."   This was refused per-
emptorily by Governor Green, and the lady protested
in form against all the proceedings of that Assembly,
unless she might be present and vote as aforesaid.

"Lord Calvert being much displeased with Mistress
Margaret Brent's conduct (distributing cattle among
the soldiers) expressed bitter invectives against her.
The Assembly, however, in their spirited address and
letter, generously defended her.[19] . . ."

Of Mary Brent, another sister, there is a record of
a court-baron held at St. Gabriel's Manor, 1659, by her
steward. A tenant appeared, did fealty to the lady,
and took seisin of a messauge of thirty-seven acres by
delivery of a rod, "according to the custom of the
manor," engaging to pay yearly "fifteen pecks of good
Indian corn and one fat capon or a hen and a half;
and for a heriot half a barrel of like corn or the value
thereof." [20]

BRENT (*Continued*)

The youngest son of George and Elizabeth (Green)
Brent, *Robert Brent,* of "Woodstock," Stafford
County, Va., who was living in 1715, married, July 8,

[18] *Council Proceedings* 1636, et seq.

[19] *Terra Mariae* by Neill.

[20] *Maryland, The History of a Palatinate,* by William Hand Browne,
p. 177.

GEORGE CALVERT
First Lord Baltimore

THE LANDING OF LEONARD CALVERT AT ST. MARY'S

1702, *Susannah,* the daughter of Captain Daniel Seymour, of Bermuda. " It was in regard to the interest devised to himself, brothers and sisters by his mother's half-brother, William Green, of Bermuda (which has been previously mentioned), that Robert Brent, of ' Woodstock,' receiving a power of attorney from Nicholas, his brother, dated October 22, 1701, visited Bermuda, and while there married *Susannah Seymour.* February 28, 1688, this Robert Brent received from King James II., the grant of ' all wrecks in and upon any of the rocks, shelves, seas or banks, near the coast of America, between Bermuda, Porto Rico or between Cartagena and the Havana.' " [21]   Their son was *Robert Brent,* of Virginia.

SEYMOUR

In 1617 William Seymour was foreman of the Grand Jury of Assize Court.   In 1619 he was Sergeant Major under Governor Nat. Butler, and in 1623, he was Councillor for Sandys Tribe.   The last official mention of him is August, 1628.

In 1638, Captain William Seymour, Jr., was Councillor of State and Commander of Paget Fort, 1653. The last reference to him is May 3 and 4, 1653, as Councillor and Commander of Southampton Fort.

HON. FLORENTIUS SEYMOUR, was Governor-General of Bermuda, 1663 to 1668, and 1681, in which year he died, on November 3.   Bermuda was at that time part of the Virginia Colony.   He was Councillor of State and Captain of Southampton Fort, 1661.

CAPTAIN DANIEL SEYMOUR, his son, was Com-

[21] Indices of Patent Rolls, beginning 1606 and ending 1702. In *Md. Hist. Lib.*

mander of Paget Fort under Royal government, 1686, and in 1702, he was again Commander of Paget Fort, St. George's, Bermuda. His daughter, *Susannah,* married *Robert Brent,* of "Woodstock."

BRENT (*Continued*)

A son of Robert and Susannah (Seymour) Brent, *Robert Brent,* "of Virginia," was born 1704, and died in Maryland, February 4, 1750. He married in Maryland, May 6, 1729, *Mary,* the daughter of Henry and Jane (Doyne) Wharton, who died in Maryland, January 15, 1773. By this marriage he became brother-in-law to Joseph Pile II. who died previous to July, 1748, as appears by renunciation of administration by his widow Jane, in favor of his brother, Dr. Francis Parnham. This marriage is recorded in Durham church, Charles County, Md., Trinity Parish, an Episcopal church, where the children were baptized. Their eldest daughter, May, however, was a Carmelite nun, and her brother bequeathed money to the nunnery in case of her death. Their son was *Robert,* of Charles County, Md.

WHARTON

ARMS: *Sable, a maunch argent.*
CREST: *A bull's head erased sable armed or.*

COLONEL JESSE WHARTON, who came from the Barbadoes and died in 1676, was President of the Council of Maryland, 1672 to 1676. He was appointed by Charles, third Lord Baltimore, to be Deputy-Governor of Maryland 1676, and guardian of his eldest son

Cecil.[22] He married *Elizabeth,* the daughter of Hon.
Henry Sewall. After Colonel Wharton's death, she
married, second, —— Digges. Her sister, Mary Sew-
all, was the second wife of George
Brent, of "Woodstock," but the
Brents descend from his first wife.
The will of Mrs. Digges was dated
September 20, 1700, proved July,
1710,[23] mentions her son, Henry
Wharton, who was granted "Not-
ley Hall," July 1, 1708, will proved
February 4, 1745. He married
Jane, the daughter of JOSHUA
DOYNE and his wife Jane, of the
Barbadoes, he being High Sheriff
of St. Mary's County, Md., 1683.
He died 1693, and his wife 1739.

WHARTON

A daughter, *Mary Wharton,* married *Robert Brent,*
" of Virginia."

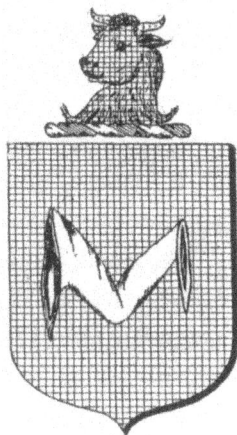

SEWALL

The Sewalls of Maryland have the following pedigree:

William Sewall, of Coventry, married Matilda
Horne.

Henry Sewall, married Margaret Gazebrook.

Richard Sewall, married Mary Dugdale, the daughter of John, and the sister of William Dugdale, Garter
King of Arms, and Historian of Warwickshire. Their
son:

HON. HENRY SEWALL, of Mattapany-Sewall, Md.,
was born in Nuneaton, Warwickshire, Eng., and died
in England 1665. "Near the mouth of the Patuxent,

[22] *Arch. of Md.,* 1676-77.
[23] *Lib. W. B. 5,* p. 96.

originally the dwelling place of the Matapanients, was 'Matapany-Sewall' given by the Proprietary to Hon. Henry Sewall, the Privy Councillor, and afterwards occupied by Lord Charles Baltimore, upon his marriage with Sewall's widow, as his residence, and as the Government House of the Province. There also once stood a fort and magazine." [24]

August 27, 1661, Cecil, Lord Baltimore, appointed Hon. Henry Sewall, a member of the Council, Chief Justice of the Province, Principal Officer and Secretary of the State and Keeper of the "Acts, Recorded of Grants and Wills and Chancellor." He was Commissioner to sign Treaty between Province and Delaware Bay Indians, and Commissioner to confer with Virginia about tobacco legislation.[25] He married Jane, the daughter of Vincent Lowe, Esq., of Denby, County Derby, Eng. (born 1593, died after 1634, in the eighth generation from Thomas Lowe, who died January 10, 1415), and his wife Ann, the daughter of William Cavendish, whom he married 1614-15. After the death of Henry Sewall, his widow married the third Lord Baltimore, and she is buried at St. Giles. *Elizabeth Sewall*, their daughter, married JESSE WHARTON.

BRENT (*Continued*)

A son of Robert and Mary (Wharton) Brent, *Robert Brent,* "of Charles County, Md.," was born May 6, 1734, and died January 6, 1790. These dates were recorded by him in the Bible now in possession of the family of the late Judge George Brent, of Charles

[24] Davis' *Day Star*, p. 169.
[25] Hening, Vol. II, 200-12.
    Arch. of Maryland. Proc. 1637-1667, pp. 441, 486, 492.

County, Md.; also in records of Durham Church, Trinity Parish, Charles County, Md., also in Hanson's *Old Kent.* He married October 5, 1750, *Anna Maria,* the daughter of Dr. Francis Parnham, of Charles County, Md., and the granddaughter of John and Elizabeth (Pile) Parnham, of " Parnham Hall," Charles County; she was born 1739, and died December 10, 1776. Their son was *Robert,* "of Brentfield," Charles County, Md.

PARNHAM

The marriage of John Parnham, of "Parnham Hall," Charles County, Md., to *Elizabeth Pile,* is proved by deed of Joseph Pile and Luke Gardner to John Parnham and Elizabeth, his wife, March 9, 1713.[26] Mary Parnham, the wife of Philip Briscoe, was administratrix of Dr. Francis Parnham's estate. Dr. Parnham, of Charles County, was living in 1748.[27] His daughter, *Anna Maria,* married *Robert Brent,* of Charles County, Md.

PILE

HON. JOHN PILE, Gent., of " Salisbury," on the Wicomico River, Md., arrived in Maryland before 1648 with his wife, Sarah. He was living 1665. His grant " Salisbury " was originally for four hundred acres, but was afterwards increased to a thousand acres. It was the home of his posterity for generations. He was a Catholic, as were his relations, the Tettershalls, who came during the year 1648, apparently from the

26 *Charles Co. Recs.,* 1714-19, *Lib.* F. 2, now in Annapolis *Land Recs.*
27 *Charles County Recs. Lib.* 8, of *Inventories,* p. 527.

sàme English county, Wilts, and under his immediate care. John Pile was Privy Councillor of Maryland 1649 to 1650. His commission [28] is dated 1648. During the ascendency of the Puritans, at the period of a bitter persecution, he came forward and "Confesseth himself in Court to be a Roman Catholic, and hath acknowledged the Pope's Supremacy."[29] By 1660 he had issue: JOSEPH, Ann and Mary.

CAPTAIN JOSEPH PILE, Gent., of "Salisbury," was Commissioner for trial of Causes and Justice of the Peace 1676, and was reappointed each year from 1677 to 1680.[30] He was a member of the Assembly from St. Mary's November, 1688. Was a Committee with Mr. John Stone from the Lower House to consult with the Upper House in relation to oath of allegiance.[31] Joseph Pile died 1692 and his will is in Annapolis.[32] His only son, Joseph, inherited Salisbury. His daughter, *Elizabeth,* married John Parnham; through her, the descendants of *Robert Brent,* of Charles County, are of the blood of the Privy Councillor.

BRENT *(Continued)*

A son of Robert and Anna Maria (Parnham) Brent, *Robert Brent,* "of Brentfield," Charles County, Md., was born June 17, 1759, and died 1810. He married, February 26, 1783, Dorothy, the daughter of William Leigh, of Charles County (living May 11, 1789), and his wife née Doyne. The fact that Dorothy (Leigh) Brent was the daughter of William Leigh, appears by

---

[28] *Proceedings of the Council,* 1631-1667, p. 41, *Md. Arch.* No. 3.
   Bozman, vol. 2. p. 650.
[29] *Land Office Rec. of the Prov. Court,* Lib. No. 3. p. 161.
[30] *Proceedings of the Council,* 1671-81, pp. 85, 86, 223, 224, 255, 326.
[31] *Proceedings of the Assembly,* 1659-92, pp. 158, 161, 183, 209.
[32] *Lib.* H. 6-64.

a deed of a tract of land, called St. Bernard's (Brentfield) by William Leigh[33] to Robert Brent; the will
of said Robert Brent, of Brentfield, whereby he re-

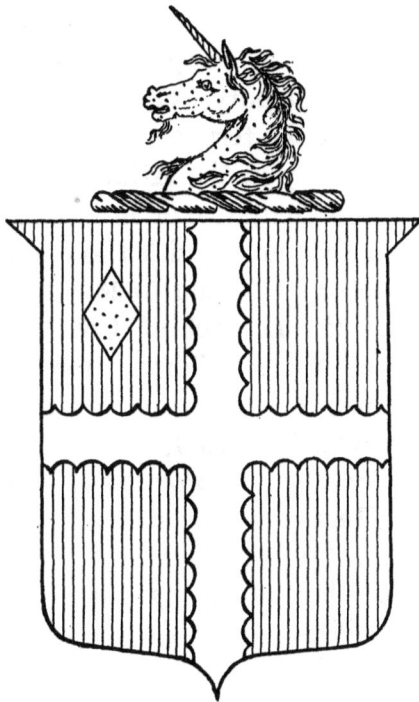

LEIGH

ARMS: *Gules, a cross engrailed argent in first quarter a lozenge or.*
CREST: *An unicorn's head couped or.*

quires Anna Maria, his daughter, to release her rights
to said tract derived from her mother, and by the further fact that in 1805-6, the said Robert purchased from
William Leigh Brent, his son, all his right in said

33 William Leigh was tax collector in St. Mary's Co. in 1780, as appears
by his bond, for 12,000 pounds current money, found at p. 602, *Liber*
D.D., No. 6. in *Land Records, Annapolis.*

land.[34] and thus the said Robert was able to devise St. Bernard's (Brentfield) to his son, George Brent."

Their son, *William Leigh Brent,* was born February 20, 1784, in Maryland, and died in Martinsville, La., July 3, 1848. He was a lawyer and went to Louisiana just after his marriage, being commissioned by President Madison as Deputy Attorney-General for the western District of the territory of Orleans. He practised law successfully in the Attakapas, and 1822 was elected as the Representative of Louisiana, in Congress, that state being then only entitled to one Congressman. He was re-elected 1824 and 1826. He remained in Maryland, and the District of Columbia, practising law, and educating his children, from 1826 to 1844, when he returned to Louisiana and died there. He married in Maryland, April 4, 1809, *Maria,* the daughter of James Fenwick, of "Pomonky," Charles County, and his wife, Henrietta Maria Lancaster. Maria was born February, 1791-92, and died January 1, 1836. "Pomonky" on the Potomac, just above Indian Head, the country residence of William Leigh Brent, was devised by will (dated January, and proved April 1, 1771), of James Cole, son of Edward Cole III., and half-brother to Sarah Taney, who married Ignatius Fenwick, Jr., to his nephew, James Fenwick, after his mother Sarah's death. James Fenwick, by will proved October 14, 1823, devised "Pomonky" to William Leigh Brent and his wife, née Maria Fenwick, for life, then to their son, *Robert James Brent.*

[34] *Charles County Records.*

FENWICK

ARMS: *Per fess gules and argent six Martlets counter changed.*
CREST: *A phoenix with the wings expanded and a coronet about the neck or.*

CUTHBERT FENWICK,[35] Gent. (1614-1655), an early Virginia colonist, became one of the original band of Pilgrims of 1634, in Maryland. All the known facts of his career prove him to have been a sincere believer in the faith of the ancient Roman Catholic Church, and one of the most loyal of her children. He was the special protegé of one of the noblest spirits in the band of

[35] Compiled from the *Day Star*, by George Lachlan Davis.

Pilgrims, Captain Cornwallis, the Chief Councillor of the Governor, in 1634. During Captain Cornwallis' frequent voyages to England, Cuthbert Fenwick lived at " The Cross," which was the name of Captain Cornwallis' manor-house (the Manor itself was called " Cornwallis' Cross " [36]), where he transacted faithfully all business relating to the manor.

"So intimate was the relationship that he was summoned on one occasion (the only case of so peculiar a kind of representation . . . upon the records) by a special writ, to sit as the ' Attorney' of the Councillor, at a meeting of the General Assembly . . . in 1640." [37]

Largely because of enmity toward Cornwallis, rather than any personal reason, Cuthbert Fenwick was surprised by the pirate, Captain Ingle, and his party, and confined as a prisoner on the pirate's ship; the manor-house was much injured, and servants, furniture and other property stolen. When traveling to Accomac, Va., on one occasion, Fenwick was robbed.[38] He was intimate with the Rev. Thomas Copley, and often in contact with Governor Leonard Calvert; took part in the little engagement of 1635 upon a tributary of the Chesapeake, between the pinnace commanded by Warren (the lieutenant of Clayborne), and the two armed boats, under the command of Cornwallis;[39] and sat in the Assembly of 1638,[40] the earliest of which we have a satisfactory account. As an individual freeman, he had a seat also in the Legislature of the subsequent

---

[36] *Rent Roll for St. Mary's County;* also Lib. No. 1, pp. 115-117.

[37] *Bozman,* vol. ii, p. 171.

[38] *Lib.* No. 1, pp. 432, 433, 572, 573, 582, 583, and 584.
   Lib. No. 2, pp. 354, 616, and 617.

[39] *Bozman,* vol. ii, p. 35 and 65.

[40] *Ibid.,* vol. ii, p. 65.

year.[41] Few, if any, of the original colonists were members more frequently of the legislative body than he. Again, he aided the government in the regulation of the Indian trade with the colonists;[42] and about the same time, reported the information he had obtained respecting the murder of Rowland Williams of Accomac,[43] a case which engaged the prompt attention of the Governor, and resulted in the union of Maryland with her sister colony[44] in the punishment of the Nanticokes.

In 1644,[45] he held a commissionership at St. Mary's—an office out of which grew that of the early County Court Judge. He was the foreman of many of the most important trial juries, at the provincial court (in the case, for instance, of the Piscataway Indians already quoted); the first member of the Financial Committee,[46] and probably the Speaker[47] in the Lower House of the Roman Catholic Assembly, of 1649; and in the Protestant one of 1650, he was Chairman of a joint Committee upon the "Laws," including Governor Green and Colonel Price from the Upper House. Although present at the time, he did not sign the Protestant Declaration; upon the questions arising between the two religious parties, in the Protestant Assembly of 1650, he voted with the Roman Catholic members; gave a legacy to each of the Roman Catholic priests, in testimony of his faith in the Church of Rome,[48] to

[41] *Ibid*, p. 103.

[42] *Ibid*, p. 115.

[43] The report is dated May 8, 1638. See *Lib. No. 2*, pp. 83-84.

[44] *Lib. No. 1*, p. 159.

[45] *Bozman*, vol. ii, p. 280.

[46] *Lib. No. 2*, p. 489.

[47] From the report of the financial committee, the only remaining fragment of the Journal, it is evident that he performed some special honorable service, besides that of an ordinary member.

[48] See Mr. Fenwick's *Will*, *Lib.* S. 1658-1662, *Judgments*, p. 219.

say nothing of the further evidence derived from the fact that so many of his descendants are still members of the same communion. The latter part of his life, he resided upon " Fenwick Manor," and died about the year 1655;[49] will dated March 6, 1654. He held a tract bounded by St. Cuthbert's Creek.[50] 'Fenwick' was the seat of a distinguished family of the same name in the County of Northumberland, Eng.,[51] and 'Fenwick' was the manor erected for the early colonist in what was subsequently Resurrection Hundred, St. Mary's County." "Fenwick Manor," upon the Patuxent, was surveyed for Cuthbert Fenwick, in 1651.[52]

In 1649, Cuthbert Fenwick was a widower, and the father of several children (Thomas, who probably died young, Cuthbert, Ignatius, and "Teresa"[53]). That year he married Jane (Eltonhead) Moryson,[54] the widow of Robert Moryson, of "Kecoughtan" County, Va., and the daughter of Richard Eltonhead of Eltonhead.

Under the will of Cuthbert Fenwick, the lordship of Fenwick Manor was held by Cuthbert, Jr., the eldest son of his first wife. The children of his second wife were Robert, *Richard* and John. The descendants of the original Lord of the Manor are many in the United States, and are to be found in civil[55] and military serv-

[49] *Lib. S.,* 1658-1662, *Judgments,* Court of Appeals (in the armory) p. 219.

[50] *Rent Roll* for St. Mary's and Charles, vol. i, fol. 55.

[51] Burke's *Gen. Arm.;* Art. Fenwick, at Fenwick, in Northumberland.

[52] *Rent Roll* for St. Mary's and Charles, vol. i, fol. 55.

[53] *Land Office Records, Lib.* No. 2, p. 515.

[54] *Lib. S.* 1658-1662, *Judgments,* p. 218.

[55] Ignatius, of St. Mary's County, was a Member of the Convention which framed the Constitution of the United States; Athanasius, closely connected with the "Cherryfield" branch, and James, the brother of the Bishop of Cincinnati, and the ancestor of the Fenwicks, of "Pomonky," were in the Senate of Maryland.

ice, in the priesthood[56] and in the hierarchy[57] of the American Catholic Church.

A son of Cuthbert Fenwick, by his second marriage, *Richard Fenwick,* Gent., of St. Mary's County, died in April, 1714. He married twice, but his wives' names are unknown.

His son, *Ignatius* (second wife), was also of St. Mary's County, and died 1732. His wife was Elinor ———, who died 1737.

Their son, *Ignatius,* of "Cherryfields," St. Mary's, who died 1776, married *Mary,* the daughter of Edward and Anne (Neale) Cole. Their son:

COLONEL IGNATIUS FENWICK, Jr., of "Wallington," St. Mary's County, great-great-grandson of Cuthbert Fenwick, was commissioned a Major of the Lower Battalion of St. Mary's Militia, Colonel Barnes commanding. The Battalion was called into service to repel the attack of Lord Dunmore's fleet in July, 1776, who sought to occupy St. George's Island and the territory adjacent.[58] As Major Fenwick, he was a member of the Committee of Observation of St. Mary's County. He was commissioned Colonel of the Battalion, August 26, 1776.[59] As Colonel Fenwick, he was a member of the Convention which framed the Constitution of the State of Maryland, 1774 to 1776. In 1761-62, he married *Sarah,* the daughter of Michael and Sarah

[56] John, the uncle of the Bishop of Cincinnati; Enoch the President of Georgetown College; George late professor of Rhetoric in the Novitiate of the Society of Jesus at Frederick.

[57] Edward, the first Bishop of Cincinnati, and a near relation of the Fenwicks of "Pomonky," and Benedict, the second Bishop of Boston, the brother of President Fenwick, and Professor Fenwick.

[58] *Md. Arch., Council of Safety,* July 7 to December 31, 1776, pp. 41, 43, 65, 97, 119, 122-3, 223, 232.

[59] *Journal of Correspondence of Council of Safety.* March 20, 1777, to March 28, 1778, pp. 345-6.

(Brooke) Taney, of Calvert County, Md., who was born in 1743-44.

Their eldest son, *Colonel James Fenwick,* of "Pomonky," Charles County, Md., was born in January, 1764, and died September 3, 1823; will proved October 14, 1823. His tombstone is in the graveyard at "Pomonky." His brother, Edward, was the first Bishop of Cincinnati. James was in the Senate of Maryland. He married *Henrietta Maria,* the daughter of John Lancaster, Jr., of Cob Neck, Charles County, whose mother was *Elizabeth,* the daughter of Raphael Neale. Their daughter, *Maria Fenwick,* married *William Leigh Brent.*

ELTONHEAD

ARMS: *Quarterly, per fesse indented, sable and argent, on first quarter three pallets.*

The Eltonhead (or Eltonhed) family were of Lancashire County, England,[60] and descended from Henry of Eltonhed through Thomas, Henry, Nicholas, John, Richard, William, to Richard of Eltonhed, Gent., in the eighth generation from Henry. Richard was aged eighty-two, September 23, 1664. He married Ann, the daughter of Edward Sutton, of Rushton Spencer, County of Stafford. He was the father of Jane, who married Cuthbert Fenwick. She was the sister of Richard of "Eltonhead" and William Eltonhead. The latter was Privy Councillor of Maryland and was shot in cold blood after the battle of Severn, "for treason," by the Puritans. His uncle, Edward Eltonhead, was one of the "Masters" of the English "High Court of Chancery."

[60] Hayden's *Va. Geneal.,* p. 227.

The first marriage of Jane Eltonhead was to Robert Moryson of " Kecoughtan " County, Va.,[61] and her second, 1649, to Cuthbert Fenwick. She died in 1660, and her will sheds much light on the social and domestic life of that day, and "enables us to form some idea of the degree of comfort in the family of this early colonial legislator, Cuthbert Fenwick, and gives a very good key to a bedchamber, a lady's wardrobe, headdress, and other articles, in 1660. She bequeaths to her step-daughter, ' Teresa,' a little bed, a mohair rug, a blanket, a pair of sheets, and 'the yellow curtains '; her taffeta suit and serge coat; all her ' fine linen,' consisting of aprons, handkerchiefs, head-clothes, &c.; her ' wedding-ring '; her hoods, scarfs (except her ' great ' one), and gloves (except three pair of cotton) ; and her three petticoats, one of which is a ' tufted-holland,' and another a ' new serge,' and the third a ' spangled one.' She gives to her own three children, Robert, Richard and John, her ' great scarf,' all her jewels, ' plate,' and rings (except the ' wedding' one) ; and to each of them a bed and pair of cotton gloves. To her stepsons, Cuthbert and Ignatius, she wills an ' ell of taffeta '; to the Rev. Francis Fitzherbert, a hogshead of tobacco, for five years. To her negro-servant, Dorothy, her ' red cotton coat' and some ' old linen '; to Esther, her ' new maid-servant,' all the linen of ' the coarser sort '; to Thomas, the Indian, two pairs of shoes, a matchcoat, and some other things; to Anthumpt, another Indian, several articles of clothing; to Thomas's mother (the ' old Indian woman') three yards of cotton. To William (a negro), the right to his freedom, provided he pay a hogshead every year to the church, and continue

a member, and to the church the same negro as a slave
' for ever,' if he leave her communion." [62]

COLE

The Cole family were first represented in St. Mary's
County, Md., by Robert Cole who died in 1663. He
married the widow of —— Knott.

His son, Edward Cole, a merchant, of St. Mary's
(1657-1717), will proved December 20, 1717, married
Elizabeth, the daughter of Robert and Susannah (Gerard) Slye, born 1669, living in 1722.

Their son, *Edward Cole II.,* Gent., of " De la Brooke
Manor," will proved May (?) 26, 1761, married, 1715,
Anne, the daughter of James Neale and his second wife,
Elizabeth Lord.[63] Edward devised to wife Anne, all
his lands and a part of De la Brooke Manor during her
life, and after her death to "my grandson, Ignatius
Fenwick." The marriage of Anne Neale and Edward
Cole is shown by wills; in 1727, that of James Neale,[64]
and in 1784, that of his wife, Elizabeth.[65] Also, January
10, 1715, two negroes are given "in consideration of
marriage lately had between Edward. Cole, of St.
Mary's, and my beloved daughter, Anne." [66] Their
daughter *Mary* married *Ignatius Fenwick,* of " Cherryfields."

Their son, *Edward III.,* married *Sarah (Brooke)
Taney,* widow of *Michael Taney III.,* (and the daughter of John Brooke.)

[62] Excusable, by the fact that some of her dearest friends had fallen
by the hands of the Puritans, including her own brother, the Hon. William Eltonhead.

[63] *D. D.* No. 1, p. 977.

[64] *Liber C. C.* No. II, p. 246.

[65] *Liber T & D.* p. 54.

[66] *Charles County Records,* XXVIII, p. 85 (95?).

SLYE

CAPTAIN ROBERT SLYE of "Bushwood," St. Mary's, Md. (1615-1670), was a Member of the Council of State in Maryland 1655, and a Burgess from St. Mary's County, 1658. He was also Captain of Militia. His wife was *Susanna,* the daughter of Doctor Thomas and Susanna (Snow) Gerard, of "St. Clement's Manor," St. Mary's. Their daughter, *Elizabeth,* married Edward Cole, Sr., whose granddaughter, *Mary Cole,* married *Ignatius Fenwick,* of "Cherryfields." Their descendant, *Maria Fenwick,* by her marriage with *William Leigh Brent,* connected that family with the Cole and Slye families.

GERARD

ARMS: *Azure a lion rampant ermine crowned or.*
CREST: *A lion's gamb erect, and erased ermine holding a lure gules garnished and lined or, tasselled argent.*

DOCTOR THOMAS GERARD, "ESQ.," Lord of "St. Clement's Manor," St. Mary's County, Md. (1600-1673), was a Member of the Assembly of Maryland from St. Mary's Hundred, and also in 1641, of the Council. He seems to have been a fearless and determined man, and to have acted on his conviction irrespective of all parties.[67] "With the grant of a manor, there was frequently granted a right for the Lord of the Manor to hold a ' Court Leet and Court Baron.' There is a record of the holding of several of such Courts at ' St. Clement's Manor,' from 1659-72,[68] which gives an interesting insight into the life and customs of that time. It was in the session of Assembly that met on February

[67] *Liber S,* 1658-1662, p. 1082; Davis' Daystar, p. 55.
[68] *Ground Rents in Md.* by Lewis Meyer, p. 151 et seq.

28th, 1659-60, (which convened at Thomas Gerard's) [69] that Governor Fendall, Thomas Gerard and Nathaniel Utie (Utye), the latter two were of the Council, and the majority of the house of Delegates, struck their blow for the overthrow of the Lord Proprietor's power and attempted to make the house of Delegates supreme. By this means a Commonwealth, similar to that which had existed in the Mother country, was to be established." [70]

He married Susanna, the sister of Justinian and Abell Snow, Gents., Abell being grantee of " Snow Hill Manor," Md. Their daughter, *Susanna Gerard,* married CAPTAIN ROBERT SLYE, whose daughter, *Elizabeth,* married Edward Cole, Sr.

NEALE

ARMS: *Argent a fesse gules in chief two crescents of the second, in base a bugle horn of the last, stringed vert.*
CREST: *Out of a ducal coronet or a chaplet of laurel vert.*

NEALE

CAPTAIN JAMES NEALE, Gent., of " Wollaston Manor," Charles County, Md., came to Maryland 1638 to 1645, and died 1684. He was a member of the Provincial Council of Maryland 1643 to 1644, 1660 to 1661; Burgess 1666; Commissioner of Treasury 1643. Attorney of Lord Baltimore at Amsterdam; was commissioned Captain by Lord Baltimore to raise troops against the Dutch on Delaware Bay. " On the first of September, in this year

[69] The lower house on March the first adjourned to Robert Slye's. *Terra Mariae,* by Edward D. Neill.
[70] *Maryland as a Proprietary Province,* by Mereness, p. 26.

(1642), Captain James Neale, an experienced mariner, who had lived in Spain, now settled on a large estate near the mouth of the Wicomico River, not far from St. Mary's, and a prominent citizen, arrived at Boston with two pinnaces, commissioned by Governor Calvert to buy mares and sheep."[71] "The visit of the Commissioners (1659, Virginia boundary dispute) did not tend to the solution of the question in dispute, and the next year Captain James Neale, of Maryland, as the attorney of Lord Baltimore, appeared before the directors of the West India Company, in Amsterdam, to urge the claims of the proprietor."[72] He married Ann Gill, the daughter and heiress of Benjamin Gill of Charles County.[73] She died in 1698. In 1666, James Neale petitioned the Assembly for the naturalization of his four children, "Henrietta Maria, *James, Dorothy,* and ANTHONY NEALE, born in Spain, of Ann his wife, during his residence there as a merchant, and when employed there by the King and Duke of York in several emergent affairs."[74] One of James Neale's descendants was Archbishop Neale, the successor of Archbishop Carroll.

His son, *James Neale II.,*[75] Gent., of "Wollaston Manor," Md., died 1768. He married twice, first Elizabeth, the daughter of William Calvert; second, Elizabeth, the daughter of Captain John Lord, of Westmoreland, Va.[76] His daughter, *Anne,* married *Edward Cole II.,* and their daughter, *Mary,* married *Ignatius Fen-*

71 Bacon's *Laws of Maryland*, p. 73.
72 *Terra Mariae* by Edward D. Neill, p. 160.
73 *Harleian Soc. Pub.*
74 Bacon's *Laws of Maryland.*
75 For this line of Neale, see *Md. Hist. Mag.*, March, 1906.
76 *Westmoreland County Records*, II, 48.

wick, Sr., whose great-granddaughter, *Maria Fenwick,* married *William Leigh Brent.*

It was supposed for some time, that Anne Neale was the daughter of James Neale's first wife, Elizabeth Calvert, the original marriage contract having been found among the papers of Robert James Brent. The dates, however, indicate that she was a daughter of the second wife, Elizabeth Lord.

ANTHONY NEALE, Gent., son of Captain James and Ann (Gill) Neale, died 1723. He was Lieutenant of His Lordship's Troops of Charles County, Md., January, 1686. He married Elizabeth,[77] the daughter of William Roswell, whose wife was Emma Turner, the widow of Thomas Turner.

Their son, *Raphael Neale* (1683-1743), married *Mary,* the daughter of Baker and Ann (Calvert) Brooke. The will of Raphael Neale was proved July 20, 1743. His wife's will was proved in May, 1763.

Their daughter, *Elizabeth,* married John Lancaster, Sr., who was appointed Justice of the Peace in Charles County, November 21, 1778, and reappointed July 24, 1779. Their son, *John Lancaster, Jr.,* of Cob Neck, Charles County, was appointed first Lieutenant of Captain Yeakes' Company, May 28, 1779. He married Mary ——, who died in December, 1803, and his daughter, *Henrietta Maria Lancaster,* married *James Fenwick* of "Pomonky," whose daughter, *Maria Fenwick,* married *William Leigh Brent.*

A daughter of James and Ann (Gill) Neale, *Dorothy Neale,* (a sister of James and Anthony), married (first wife), *Roger Brooke,* of Calvert County, (a half-brother of Baker Brooke.) A daughter, *Dorothy*

---

[77] Shorter *vs.* Boswell; Harris & Johnson, *Md. Reports,* pp. 359-361.

Brooke (1676-1730), married *Michael Taney II.*, whose granddaughter, *Sarah Taney*, married COLONEL IGNATIUS FENWICK; their granddaughter, *Maria Fenwick*, married *William Leigh Brent.*

ROSWELL, OR ROSEWELL

A patent was issued September 8, 1666, to William Roswell, of two hundred acres of land five miles from Chaptico,[78] for transporting four persons into the Colony; also, on the same date, a patent for three hundred acres, adjoining land of Emma Turner, called "St. Barbara's," for transporting William Johnson and three others. "St. Barbara's Addition," one hundred and twenty acres was surveyed for him December 28, 1680 (?).[79]

He was Commissioner for St. Mary's County, March 22, 1663, and August 29, 1668. Commissioned Justice of the Peace for St. Mary's County, September 5, 1664. March 2, 1675, he was appointed of St. Mary's Commission with Joseph Pile; reappointed and of the Quorum, March 4, 1678.[80]

He married Emma Turner, the widow of Thomas Turner, as recited in patent to her for St. Barbara's, dated July 26, 1664. Mrs. Turner was also the widow of William Johnson, planter.

Their daughter, Elizabeth Roswell, married ANTHONY NEALE, as set out in an affidavit of her mother, in the case of Shorter vs. Boswell.[81]

78 *Liber* 10, p. 70.
79 *Rent Roll*, Charles County, No. —— p. 16.
80 *Proceedings of Council* No. III, pp. 490-503; *Liber* V, L. 33; 1671-81, pp. 66, 153.
81 2d Harris & Johnson, Md. *Reports*, pp. 359-361.

TANEY

ARMS: *Azure three bars argent.*

CREST: *A hind's head erased, gules, a coronet about the neck or.*[82]

MICHAEL TANEY came to Maryland about 1660. His will was dated May 18, and proved June 21, 1692.[83]   He

was High Sheriff of Calvert County, Md., 1685-89. "On the third of August the Assembly met at the house of Philip Lynes, at the head of Britton Bay, and Michael Taney, the Sheriff of Talbot County, was brought before them on the third of September, and imprisoned at Charleston because he would not acknowledge their authority."[84]   Michael Taney, although a Protestant, refused to prostitute his office of High Sheriff and do the behest of Cood and Jowels in furtherance of their insurrectionary schemes, for which he was arrested, but defended himself with courage and spirit before the Protestant Assembly 1689."[85]   His first wife was named Mary, and was living in 1685.

TANEY

His son, *Michael Taney II.,* of Calvert County, Md., who died 1702, married *Dorothy,* the daughter of Roger and Dorothy (Neale) Brooke. She was the granddaughter of Captain James Neale and Ann Gill, his wife. Her will (being then Mrs. Dorothy Smith, having married second, Mr. Blundell, and third, Colonel John

[82] A copy of the arms of Taney; original written in 1769 by Colonel Ignatius Fenwick, Jr., who married Sarah Taney. Original in possession of family of the late Robert J. Brent.

[83] *Annapolis Wills, Lib.* 6, f. 1, back.

[84] *Terra Mariae* by Edward D. Neill. (Account of Coode's Rebellion.)

[85] Davis' *Day Star,* p. 96.

Smith), was dated August 18, 1730, and proved February, 1730-1."[86] "Dorothy, widow of Michael Taney, 2d., gave bond January 9, 1702-3, for administration of his estate, her sureties being Roger Brooke and Thomas Taney."[87]

Their son, *Michael Taney III.*, of Calvert County, Md., died in 1743. In his will dated June 2, 1743, and proved March 24, 1743,[88] he mentions his wife Sarah, his son, Michael, and daughter, Dorothy Brooke, and his son-in-law, Basil Brooke. He also makes provision for his unborn daughter, *Sarah.* He married, as his second wife, *Sarah,* the daughter of John, and the granddaughter of Roger Brooke. (She afterward married Edward Cole III.) Their daughter, Sarah, married COLONEL IGNATIUS FENWICK, whose granddaughter, *Maria Fenwick,* married *William Leigh Brent.*

BROOKE

ARMS: *Checky or. and azure on a bend gules a lion passant or.*
CREST: *On a wreath azure and or, a demi-lion erased or.*

The Herald's Visitation in the year 1634, shows that

86 *Annapolis Wills, Lib.* C. C. No. 3.   87 *Test. Proc. Liber,* 19, f. 131.
88 *Ibid, Liber 23,* fol. 465.

Richard Brooke, of Whitchurch, County Hampshire, Eng., was born 1530, and died 1593. His will was proved May 6, 1594. The old house in which the Brookes lived at Whitchurch, is still standing. Symonds, in his diary mentions that during the civil wars, King Charles I. passed two days and nights as the guest of Sir Thomas Brooke. He married Elizabeth Twyne, sister and heiress of Sir John Twyne, of Whitchurch, Hants. Her will, dated May 16, was proved June 2, 1599. Both wills are recorded at Somerset House, London. In the church at Whitchurch, there is Memorial Brass for this family.

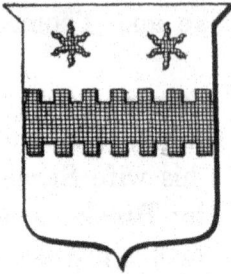

TWYNE [89]

A son of Richard, Thomas Brooke (1561-1612), received the degree of B. A., May 4, 1584, at New College, Oxford. As a member from Whitchurch he sat in Parliament from 1604 to 1611. His will was proved November 30, 1612. He married Susan, the daughter of Sir Thomas Forster of Etherstone, County Durham. Their third son:

ROBERT BROOKE, ESQ., of "De la Brooke Manor" (1602-1655), received at Wadham College, Oxford, the degree of B. A., July 6, 1620, and that of M. A., four years later. He emigrated to America in 1650.

" So impressed was Cecilius Calvert by the coming of Robert Brooke (to Maryland) that he made it the subject of a special message to Governor Stone and to the Privy Council, with instructions to them to enroll and register his grant to Robert Brooke in the common

[89] Wm. Berry's *Co. Gen. Hants*, pp. 222, 223, 339.

registry of the said province for the better confirmation and manifestation thereof." The grant consisted of a whole county and Mr. Brooke was endowed with " such honors, dignities, privileges, fees, perquisites, profits and immunities as are belonging to the said place and office of commander of the said county, etc." He was further given the power to call Courts for the purpose of hearing civil causes, etc. Lord Baltimore also appointed Robert Brooke commander-in-chief under him, " of all the forces which shall be armed, levied or raised in the said county and to lead and conduct them against the Indians and other foreign enemies." The Proprietary also forwarded to Maryland a commission naming Robert Brooke as a " Member from Privy Council to meet and assemble himself in Council upon all occasions."

"Therefore, when on the last day of June, 1650, Robert Brooke, lineal descendant of King Fergus II. (A. D. 404), sailed into the Patuxent River in his own ship, with a retinue of 28 servants, he was accorded, no doubt, the welcome which the heralding of Lord Baltimore naturally insured to him. Charmed by the picturesque shores of the Patuxent, he sailed many miles farther up than any adventurer had sailed, and chose for his abiding place the two thousand acres known as the Manor of De la Brooke, of which his eldest son, BAKER, was created lord, while his father became commander of the new county named Charles, in honor of the King."

"The fact that he came to Maryland as a friend of King Charles and was an adherent and Privy Councillor of the Lord Baltimore and changed his allegiance to the Cromwellian party when they deposed Governor Stone, in 1652, has caused much surmise among his descend-

556 ANCESTRAL RECORDS AND PORTRAITS

ants. Robert Brooke was, however, not the only man who changed his politics at this time, and it is quite impossible to judge at this distance whether he thought he could best serve Lord Baltimore's interests as acting-Governor under Parliament, or whether he really was diplomatic and accepted the goods the gods provided. Certain it is, however, that Lord Baltimore resented the change of front by annulling his commission as commander of Charles County in 1654, at which time Calvert County was erected in its place."

"Ten of his children came to Maryland from England with Robert Brooke and Mary, his wife. It is, therefore, not surprising that it took a ship of his own to bring his family across the ocean. . . . Although Robert Brooke lived only five years after coming to Maryland, he left a lasting impression upon the history of his day."[90]

The settlement founded by Robert Brooke, in 1650, (who was a Protestant), twenty miles from the mouth of the Patuxent, was probably Anglo-Catholic. There were originally forty persons in the company, including Brooke's own very large family, now represented by the Brookes of Brooke-Grove, in Montgomery, and by a vast number of descendants in Prince George's, and in other counties of the western shore.[91] The settlement was erected into a county, under the name of Charles; and one of Mr. Brooke's sons created lord of the manor, called "De la Brooke," which formed the chief seat of the little colony. Under a commission from the proprietary, Mr. Brooke was the first commander of the County, he also held a seat in the Privy Council, and at

[90] Compiled from the Publications of Hester Dorsey Richardson.

[91] Roger Brooke Taney, Chief-Justice of the United States, is a descendant in the female line.

a later period, but during the ascendancy of the Puritans, was elevated to the post of President, which was a position analogous to that of lieutenant-general or Governor.[92]

The first wife of Robert Brooke, whom he married February 25, 1627, was Mary, the daughter of Thomas Baker "of Battle, Esq.," in Sussex County; he married second, May 16, 1635, Mary, the daughter of Roger and Cecilia (Proper) Mainwaring, who died November 29, 1663. Issue, first wife, two sons, and two daughters, the elder son being BAKER BROOKE; issue second wife, eleven children, seven of whom were sons, one being *Roger Brooke.*

COLONEL BAKER BROOKE (1628-1679), of "De la Brooke Manor," Calvert County, was born in Sussex, Eng., and arrived in Maryland 1650. He was a member of the Council of Maryland from 1658 until his death, and Surveyor-General 1671 to 1679. Also Colonel of the Calvert County Militia. He married *Ann,* the daughter of Governor Leonard Calvert and the granddaughter of the first Lord Baltimore. Their daughter, *Mary,* married *Raphael Neale,* and through her descendants, the Brooke and Calvert families are connected with the Brents. (See Calvert, Neale, Lancaster and Fenwick.)

One of the sons of Robert Brooke, by his second marriage, *Roger Brooke,* Gent., of Battle Creek, Calvert County, Md., a half brother of COLONEL BAKER BROOKE, was born September 20, 1637, and died April 8, 1700. He was Justice 1674 to 1684; High Sheriff, April 18, 1684,[93] to May 30, 1685, and of the Quorum

[92] Compiled from *The Day Star* by G. L. Davis, Chap. viii, pp. 74, 76.
[93] *Lib. C. D.* fol. 396.

1679-1684.[94] His will[95] was proved May 3, 1700. He married, first, *Dorothy,* the daughter of Captain James Neale, Gent., of "Wollaston Manor," and his wife Ann Gill; second, Mary, the daughter of Walter, and the granddaughter of Sir Thomas Wolesley, of Staffordshire, Eng., niece of Anne Wolesley, the first wife of Philip Calvert.

One of the sons of Roger Brooke's first marriage was *John,* and one of the daughters was *Dorothy.*

The son, *John Brooke* (1687-1735), will proved March 21, 1735, married Sarah ——, born 1691.

Their daughter, *Sarah,* was twice married, first to *Michael Taney III.,* the son of Michael and Dorothy (Brooke) Taney, and second to *Edward Cole III.,* the son of Edward and Ann (Neale) Cole.

The daughter of Roger and Dorothy (Neale) Brooke *Dorothy Brooke,* was born 1676, and died 1730. She married *Michael Taney II.,* and their grandaughter, *Sarah Taney,* married COLONEL IGNATIUS FENWICK, JR., of "Wallington."

[94] *Md. Arch.* xv. 37, 68, 71, 268, 327, 395.
[95] *Annapolis Liber H.* fol. 384, *Md. Hist. Mag.* March, 1906.

FORSTER

FORSTER OF IDEN

ARMS: *Argent on a bend engrailed sable, three stags' heads caboshed or.*

FORSTER OF EGAN

ARMS: *Argent a chevron vert between three bugle horns stringed sable.*

CREST: *A stag, statant sable horned or.*

As early as 1587 Sir Thomas Forster, of Etherstone, County Durham, Eng., descended from the Forsters of Northumberland is spoken of as a barrister in both Coke's and Croke's Reports. He became a reader of the Society of the Inner Temple 1596; called November 24, 1607, to the Bench as a Judge of the Common Pleas, and sat in Court four years and a half; was named one of the first governors of Charter House Hospital.[96] He was knighted by King James I. Sir Thomas died May 18, 1612, aged about forty-three. He married Susan, the daughter of Thomas Forster, of Iden.

Their daughter, Susan, married Thomas Brooke

96 From Brooke Family by T. W. Balch.

(1561-1612), the son of Richard Brooke, of Whitchurch, Eng.

BAKER

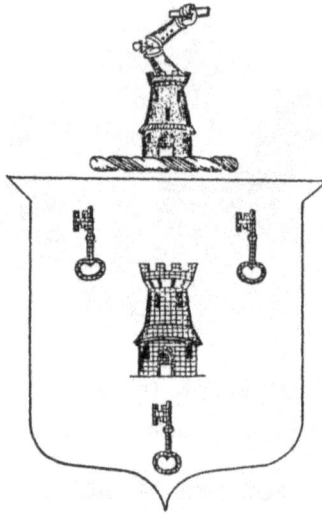

ARMS: *Argent a tower, between three keys, erect sable.*

CREST: *On a tower sable an arm embowed, in mail, holding in hand a flintstone, proper.*[97]

Pedigree of the Bakers of "Battel," Sussex County, Eng.

John, living there 1375, (49 Edward III.)

Simon, 1377-1399, (Richard II.)

John, 1399-1413, (Henry IV.)

John, 1422-1461, (Henry VI.)

Thomas, 1461-1483, (Edward IV.)

Henry, 1485-1509, (Henry VII.)

John, 1509-1547, (Henry VIII), was of Duckings, or Duckinghouse, in Wittyham.

John.

[97] Berry's *Co. Gen. Sussex*, pp. 225-26.

Thomas, whose daughter Mary, married, as his first wife, ROBERT BROOKE, of "De la Brooke Manor." [98]

MAINWARING

The Bishop of St. David's, England, Roger Mainwaring, was born at Stretton in Shropshire (though of a Cheshire family, which Lloyd says was a noble one). He received the degree of B. A. at All Souls College, Oxford, February, 1607-8; M. A. July 5, 1611; B. D. and D. D. July 2, 1625. He was Vicar of St. Giles in the Fields, and Chaplain to King Charles I. . . . "Before whom preaching (July 27), those sermons which he afterwards published and entitled, *Religion and Allegiance,* he was called in question for it by the Parliament charged with endeavoring to destroy the King and Kingdom, by his Divinity and censured to be Imprisoned; was fined £1000, and ordered to make his submission, and was Disabled to have or enjoy any Preferment or office. However, the King soon after Pardoned him, and gave him the rich living of Stamford-Rivers in Essex, 1633. Made him dean of Worcester, and two years after nominated him to this Bishoprick." [99]

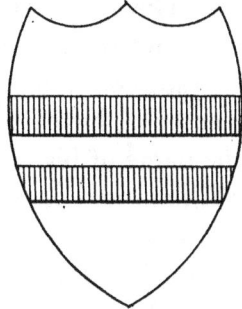

MAINWARING

He died at Caermarthen, July 1, 1625.[100] Bishop Mainwaring was the father of Mary, the second wife of ROBERT BROOKE, of "De la Brooke Manor."

[98] *Brooke Family* by T. W. Balch.
[99] *Sufferings of the Clergy of the Church of England,* by John Walker, M.A., p. 76.
[100] *Brooke Family,* by T. W. Balch in *Md. Hist. Soc.*

CALVERT

One of this family, Leonard Calvert, married Alicia, the daughter and heiress of John Crosland, of Crosland, whose son, Sir George Calvert, Knight, first Lord Baltimore, married first, Ann, the daughter of John Mynne, of Hartingfordbury.[101] Their second son:

GOVERNOR LEONARD CALVERT, was born 1606. He was Governor of Maryland from its first settlement 1634, until his death, June 9, 1647. Governor Calvert was supposed, until recently, not to have married. Late researches have disclosed the fact of his marriage, though the name of his wife is unknown. He left two children, William and *Ann*.

" 1647 June 19th.   Then came Margaret Brent Gent.[102] & desyred the testimony of the pr'nt Governor Mr. Tho. Green concerning the last will & Testam't of the late Governor Leonard Calvert Esq'r. And the s'd Governor did authorize Giles Brent Esq'r. one of his Lo'ps Councell to administer an oath unto him the s'd Governor concerning the fores'd business.

" The s'd Governor Thos. Green Esq'r. answered upon oath concerning the last will & Testam't of Leo Calvert Esq'r. afores'd. That he the said Leo. Calvert lying uppon his death bed, some 6 hours before his death, being in p'rfect memory directing his speech to Mrs. Margaret Brent sayd in pr'nce of him the s'd Mr. Green & some others. I made you my sole Exequutrix, Take all and pay all. After w'ch words hee the s'd Leon. Calvert desyred every one to depart the room & was for some space in private conference with Mrs. Marg. Brent, afores'd. Afterwards the s'd Mr. Green come-

101 *Md. Hist. Mag.*, vol. iv, 1907.
102 *Va. Mag. of His.* vol. xv. No. 3, p. 326.

ing into the room againe, he heard the said M. L. Calvert appoint certain Legacies in manner following viz. I doe give my wareing clothes to James Linsay & Richard Willam my servants, specifying his cloath suit to Rich. Willam & his black suit to James Linsey, and his waring Linnen to be divided between them allso I give a mare colt to my God-sonne Leon. Greene allso he did desyre th't his Exequutrix should give the first mare colt th't should fall this yeare (& if none fall in this yeare, then the first th't shall hereafter fall) unto Mrs. Temperance Pippet of Virginia and further he deposeth not. Recognit teste me Will'm Bretton Clk."

"Father Andrew White in his narrative speaks of Governor Calvert who died at St. Mary's City 9th June, 1647, as being most tenderly ministered to in his last moments by his kinswomen Margaret & Mary Brent." [103]

"The first mention of William Calvert, is contained in the record of a suit, begun at an uncertain date, but which was in progress in April, 1661.[104]   The case was one of William Calvert, an infant suing by Cecilius Lord Baltimore, his guardian, the heirs of Wm. Stone for the recovery of certain lands. . . . The Petition alleges, that Leonard Calvert, the late Governor, died seized of a tract of land &c.; that William Calvert was his son and heir, and that the Defendants entered in his absence, and prays recovery. The Defendants asked a Jury trial; the title of Leonard Calvert was not denied; but the Plaintiff could only recover by proving the marriage of Leonard and his own heirship, which he

[103] *Va. Mag. of Hist.*, vol. xv, No. 3, pp. 326, 329.
[104] *Original Manuscript record of Prov. Court*, 1658-1662, p. 459, now in the custody of the *Md. Hist. Soc.*

must have succeeded in doing as the Plaintiff had judgment. This record therefore establishes the marriage
of Leonard and the legitimacy of his son. But the
records of the Province are full of confirmation of these
facts. Leonard Calvert must have married shortly after
his arrival in England, perhaps June, 1643, so that
William, born 1644, would have been still an infant, age
about 17, 1661. As alleged in this suit, Leonard Calvert
returned to Maryland without his wife in November or
later in 1644, and she must have given birth to *Ann
Calvert* 1645. . . .   In addition to these record proofs,
Lord Baltimore, Cecilius Calvert, his son Charles Calvert and his brother Philip, constantly recognize the relationship, especially as set forth in Proceedings of the
Council, 28th July, 1669, where a commission of Lord
Baltimore to him as Councillor, was issued as follows:
" His Lordship's dear nephew to be of the Council and
to take rank directly after the Chancellor." (Philip Cal-
vert, who had been Governor.)

A member of House of Burgesses, and of the Council,
William Calvert was also Judge of Testamentary Court
and one of the Deputy-Governors and principal Secretary of Province, from October 20th, 1669, until May,
1682, when he was drowned in the Wicomico.

GOVERNOR CALVERT's daughter, *Ann Calvert,* received
the same recognition as her brother (See Calvert papers,
244 et se.)   She married BAKER BROOKE who thereafter
was always recognized as a nephew of Lord Baltimore.
Ann, after the death of Baker Brooke, married Henry
Brent, brother of CAPTAIN GEORGE BRENT, a nephew
of Giles.[105] Her daughter, *Mary Brooke* married
Raphael Neale.

[105] Compiled from a sketch prepared from notes left by Gen. Joseph
Lancaster Brent.

The wife of William Calvert, was Elizabeth, the daughter of Governor William Stone, and the proof of this marriage is found in the land records.[106] Their daughter, Elizabeth, married (first wife), *James Neale II.*

BRENT (*Continued*)

An eminent lawyer, the *Hon. Robert James Brent,* of "Pomonky," Charles County, Md., the son of William Leigh and Maria (Fenwick) Brent, was born in Louisiana, May 12, 1811, and died in Baltimore, Md., February 4, 1872.

". . . The reports of the Supreme Court of the United States and of the Court of Appeals of Maryland show the large number of cases he argued before those tribunals. He was the last of the Attorney-Generals of Maryland under the old constitution, when the appointment was for life, and when the office carried large powers of appointment of deputies in the several counties and also large emoluments by way of fees. He was appointed Attorney-General of Maryland February 12, 1851, and was a member of the Constitutional Convention of that year, and being opposed to the large power reposed in the hands of one man, in the person of the Attorney-General, under the then law, and also to the system of fees by which the Attorney-General was paid, he voted to abolish the office, and thus with great civic virtue legislated himself out of office."[107]

He married, 1835, *Matilda,* the daughter of Upton and Elizabeth (Hager) Lawrence, of Hagerstown, Md., who was born in August, 1815, and died October

---

[106] *Lib. W. R. C.* No. 1. p. 300.
[107] *Debates of the Reform Convention,* vol. 1, p. 532.

4, 1894. Their daughter, *Mary Hoke Brent,* married *William,* the son of Samuel S. and Elizabeth (Wyman) Keyser.

LAWRENCE

ARMS: *Argent, a cross raguly gules.*
CREST: *Two laurel branches vert, forming a chaplet.*

The first of the line in this country, Benjamin Lawrence, Gent., of "Desart," Calvert County, went from Virginia to Maryland 1668, where he died 1685. In 1676 he married *Elizabeth,* the daughter of Richard and Elizabeth (Ewen) Talbot. Her father, Richard Talbot, of Anne Arundel County, Md., died 1663.

Their son, *Benjamin Lawrence, Jr.,* of Anne Arundel County, Md., died 1719. He married Rachel, the daughter of Edward and Honor Mariartee of the same county.

Their son, *Leven* (or *Leaven*)

LAWRENCE   *Lawrence* (1711-1756), who lived at Elk Ridge, Md., married *Susannah,* the daughter of John and Honor (Elder) Dorsey, the son of Edward and Sarah (Wyatt) Dorsey, of Anne Arundel County, Gent. Their son:

JOHN LAWRENCE, of "Linganore Hills," Frederick County, Md., was born October 26, 1743, in Anne Arundel County, and died 1782. On April 20, 1766, he married Martha, the daughter of Stephen West, Gent., born in Prince George's County, Md., (who came to Maryland 1711), and his wife Martha (Hall) West, of

Prince George's County. Sir John West, Stephen's father, was of Horton, Buckinghamshire, Eng. John Lawrence was a member of the Committee of Observation, Frederick County, 1775, and a Justice 1777.

Their son, *Upton Lawrence,* a lawyer of Hagerstown, was born in Frederick County, July 21, 1779, and died March 31, 1824. He married, January 31, 1803, *Elizabeth Hager,* "Proprietress" of Hagerstown, and the daughter of Jonathan, Jr., and Mary Magdalena (Ohrendorf) Hager, born August 1, 1785, and died August 5, 1867. Issue, nine children, one of whom, *Matilda* married *Robert James Brent.*

EWEN

MAJOR RICHARD EWEN,[108] one of the eight who first took up lands on the Patapsco River, on the south side a little above its mouth, was of Anne Arundel County, Md. Three hundred and fifty acres were taken up November 19, 1652, and again six hundred acres on November 26, 1652, which was called "Scotland," on the Bay Shore, a little above the Severn River. Subsequently, six hundred and forty acres were taken up in three tracts on the West River. He was a member of the Council of Maryland; Speaker of the Assembly of 1657, which was called by the Puritans at Patuxent, and one of the High Commissioners to govern Maryland under Lord Protector Cromwell, also Major in the forces of the Colony. In 1657, Richard Ewen was Judge of the Provincial Court; 1658, was named as a member of the first board of Commissioners of Anne Arundel County, but declined the honor. In 1659 he became a member of the General Assembly (which was

108 *Md. Hist. Mag.* vol. III, No. 1, p. 56.

called by Lord Baltimore's direction) and was elected
Speaker. Was Commissioner of Anne Arundel County
1664, and on April 13, 1664-5, he was appointed by
Governor Calvert, High Sheriff. In November following, he again became one of the Commission, and afterwards a County Justice. He married Sophia ——.

Their daughter, *Elizabeth,* became the wife of Richard Talbot of Anne Arundel County, who died 1663,
after which she married, second, William Richardson.
Her daughter, *Elizabeth Talbot,* married Benjamin
Lawrence, Sr.

DORSEY

COLONEL EDWARD DORSEY, of Anne Arundel County,
Md., died in 1705. He married Sarah, the daughter of
Nicholas Wyatt, of Virginia, and Anne Arundel
County, Md. Edward Dorsey was Justice of his county,
1686 to 1689; Associate Judge of High Court of Chan-
cery, 1694 to 1696; commissioned Major 1694, and a
Burgess 1692 to 1697, and 1700-1705.

JOHN DORSEY, their son, died 1764. He married
Honor, the daughter of John Elder, of Maryland, and
their daughter, *Susannah,* married *Leaven Lawrence.*

HAGER

" The Hager family is of old Saxon origin; the very
name denotes its source and its antiquity. The ' Heger '
was one of the ' sworn and knowing freemen,' called
' Vierherren,' holding the Folkmoete or Thing, which
was legislature, divine-service and court of justice com-
bined. The mystic-square of the Thing, on which sat
or stood the officers, was called ' Die Hegung,' and one
of the Vierherren, who had to look to it that no un-

initiated person overstepped the boundaries of the square, was the Heger; afterwards, the representative of the Count or Graf, when holding court, was called Heger. Such offices in very early times became hereditary . . . and it is obvious that the office of Heger very early furnished the name for a family connected with the same for several generations."

CAPTAIN JONATHAN HAGER (HEGER) was born in Germany 1719, and came to America 1730. He died November 6, 1775. He was wounded as Captain of Volunteers in Braddock's Defeat, near Fort Duquesne, July 9, 1755. He was founder of Hagerstown, Md., 1750 and a member of the Assembly 1771-73. Also a Member of the Committee for raising money for the Revolution and of the Committee of Correspondence and Observation.[109]

He was married in 1740, to Fraulein Elizabet Kirshner, who died in April, 1765. The town now known as Hagerstown was named by its founder "Elizabethtown," for his wife, and it was so incorporated and known for a long time. Custom brought about a change, and in 1813 the present name was made legal.

The cause of Captain Hager's death was an accident at his saw mill on the Antietam Creek near the town. He had given a lot of land on which to build a German Reformed Church and he was superintending the preparation of timber for the same, when a log slipped, knocked him down and crushed him. As soon as he could be rescued, he was carried into a house near by and laid upon the floor. His great-grandaughter, Miss Martha Lawrence, had in her possession the silver watch he wore at the time and which had the dent made by the log in passing over it.

[109] *Gentlemen's Mag.* Aug., 1755.

Contributing more than any other citizen to develop the country in which he had settled, he died in the midst of his usefulness. Had he lived a year longer, he would have seen the town he founded the county seat of a new county named in honor of General Washington. His son:

CAPTAIN JONATHAN HAGER, JR., "Proprietor" of Hagerstown, born December 13, 1755, and died from disease contracted in the dungeon of a prison in Nova Scotia, December 18, 1798. He went into the revolutionary army at the age of about twenty having raised and equipped a company of soldiers at his own expense, and was captured by the enemy at the battle of Long Island and carried to Annapolis Royal, Nova Scotia. His brother-in-law, General Daniel Heister, visited him in prison, and prevailed upon his captors, owing to his extreme youth, to allow him employ instructors to complete his education. His brother-in-law also carried away with him a writing, conveying to Jonathan's sister, General Heister's wife, the portion of his father's estate, which the young prisoner thought should be rightfully hers, although, according to the law then in force, he, as the eldest son, received the whole estate. But at this time, he had not attained his majority, and the deed of agreement had no binding force. After he had passed his twenty-first birthday, while still in prison, General Heister got leave of the Board of War to go to Halifax and get his brother-in-law to make a good deed. This was done. It was impossible, however, to have deeds drawn up and executed in Halifax, with proper formality, and on his return, General Heister took the matter to the Legislature, which passed an act to cure the defects in the said deed. On five hundred of the fourteen hundred acres thus conveyed to Mrs. Heister, her

husband laid out the addition to Hagerstown, known as
Heisterboro.

His marriage to *Magdalena,* the daughter of Major
Christian and Elizabeth Ann (Hoffman) Ohrendorf,
of "Pleasant Valley," Md., occurred November 17,
1783.   She was born October 20, 1767, and died June
8, 1845, and was very beautiful.   (She married, second,
Captain Henry Lewis.)

Their daughter, *Elizabeth,* "Proprietress" of Hagerstown, married *Upton Lawrence,* whose daughter,
Matilda, married *Robert James Brent.*

OHRENDORF

Major Christian Ohrendorf, of "Pleasant Valley," Md., was born in Prussia, November 23, 1726,
and died December 10, 1796.   He came to America in
1741, and November, 1774, was appointed representative of Frederick County, in regard to the new expor-
tation policy agreed upon by the Continental Congress.
He was commissioned Major of the 36th Battalion of
Frederick County, April 20, 1776.   "He was First
Lieutenant 2nd Maryland Battalion Flying Camp,
June to December 1776; Captain April 1st, 1778;
transferred to 1st Maryland (Line) January 1st, 1781,
and served to close of war."   Major Ohrendorf was one
of the Committee of Safety, and in June, 1794, was appointed a Major in an expedition fitted out against the
Indians on the Western Frontier.   He married, April
2, 1749, Elizabeth Ann Hoffman, who died July, 1829.

Their daughter, *Mary Magdalena,* married Jonathan Hager, Jr., "Proprietor" of Hagerstown, and
their daughter, *Elizabeth,* married *Upton Lawrence,*

whose daughter, *Matilda Lawrence,* married *Robert James Brent.*

KEYSER

The first one of the male line, of whom there is certain knowledge, is Leonhard Keyser, of Scharding, in Bavaria. In the early part of the sixteenth century he separated from the Catholic Church. He was a Mass priest in Bavaria, a man of learning, or what passed for such, in the monasteries. He accepted the writings of Zwingly and Luther and went to Wittenberg, and there held converse with the doctors, partook with them of the Lord's Supper, and joined himself to the Separated Cross-bearing Church of the Anabaptists in 1525. He returned to Bavaria, spreading the work of the Gospel with great zeal and power. He was taken at Scharding in Bavaria, by the Bishop of Passau, and by the other priests and capitulates of the Church, and condemned to be burned alive. On his trial he repeatedly refused to speak in the Romish language. He would answer them only in the German language—the people's tongue. Three days before Laurentis, in August, 1527, he was taken to his execution.[110]

The colonist, Dirck Keyser, was born in Holland, 1635, and died in Pennsylvania, November 30, 1714. He married Elizabet ter Himpel. Their descendants are as follows:

Peter Dirck, was born November 26, 1676, and died September 12, 1724; married Margaret Souplis, born 1682, died 1700.

Dirck II. (1701-1757), married Alitze De Neuss (1702-1756).

Michael, was born August 30, 1745, and died October

110 Compiled from the *Keyser Book.*

5, 1825; married, November 25, 1767, Catherine, the daughter of John George Knorr; she was born July 28, 1728.

Samuel, of Baltimore, was born March 12, 1778, and died July 11, 1839; married, 1804, Mary, the daughter of Henry and Barbara (Close) Stouffer; she died 1805.

Samuel S., of Baltimore, was born February 18, 1805, and died February 20, 1871. His wife, *Elizabeth,* the daughter of William and Ruth (Davis) Wyman, whom he married in 1834, was born September 17, 1812, and died February 29, 1886.

William, also of Baltimore, was born November 23, 1835; married in Baltimore, November 10, 1858, *Mary Hoke,* the daughter of Robert James and Matilda (Lawrence) Brent.

MATHILDE LAWRENCE KEYSER, was born February 26, 1870, and married, April 23, 1902, William Maurice Manly.

WYMAN

The colonist, Francis Wyman of Woburn, born 1618, and died November 28, 1699, was one of the thirty-two inhabitants of Charlestown who established the town of Woburn, December 18, 1640. He was an early proprietor of Billerica. He married, second, October 22, 1650, Abigail, the daughter of William Read of Woburn.

Their son, William Wyman (1656-1705), married Prudence, the daughter of Thomas Putnam of Lynn and his wife Ann, the daughter of Edward Holyoke. Their son was Joshua (1692-1770), who married Mary Pollard.

The colonist, John Putnam, was of Salem, 1640, and

married Priscilla ———. Their eldest son, Thomas, of Lynn, was born in England, and early removed to Salem. His wife, Ann Holyoke, died September 1, 1665. He was a lieutenant and deacon, 1681, and died May 5, 1686. Thirteen of the family had, in 1832, been deacons of the First Church of Danvers, and of the name (sometimes perverted to Putmun), in 1828, there had been twenty-five graduates of Harvard, two of Yale, and seven of other New England colleges.[111]

WILLIAM WYMAN, the son of Joshua and Mary (Pollard) Wyman, was born January 2, 1739, and died March 3, 1820. He was "in Patterson Regiment at the Battle of Bunker Hill, June 17, 1775." He married, in 1765, Mary, the daughter of Doctor George Griggs and Alice, his wife.

Their son, *William Wyman III.,* of Lowell, Mass., was born February 10, 1782, and died August 15, 1864. He married, September 11, 1806, Ruth, the daughter of Colonel Adam Davis, of Roxbury, Mass. She was born in 1786, and died September 6, 1864.

Their daughter, *Elizabeth,* married *Samuel S. Keyser,* of Baltimore, whose son, *William Keyser,* married *Mary Hoke Brent,* and their daughter is:

MATHILDE LAWRENCE KEYSER MANLY,

Member of Chapter I., The Colonial Dames of America.

[111] For Wyman and Putnam, see Savage's *Gen. Dict. of N. E.* Vol. III., 496; IV, p. 664.

XXXI
GOUGH

The first record of this family is in 1707, when Peter Colleton, Landgrave, disposed of all his property in South Carolina to John Gough, Dominick Arthur and Michael Mahon, all of Barbadoes. October 12, 1709, " John Gough sen. of the Island of Barbadoes " received a grant of land, proving that he was in South Carolina by this time; will dated November 29, 1738, and proved February 7, 1739. In this he mentions his sons John, Richard, Edward, O'Neal and Francis, and his daughters, Ann and Mary. (He leaves bequests also to Ann Lejau, daughter of Francis Lejau, and her sister Mary.)

The will of O'Neal Gough, dated March 11, 1750, was proved August 30, 1751. In it he names his wife Mary, a daughter Mary, and a son JOHN. He married Mary, the daughter of John Parker II., and widow of William Clifford (died 1744). After O'Neal Gough's death, she married, third, September 12, 1754, Thomas Jones.

JOHN GOUGH, born about 1748, died at his plantation, Cane Acre, St. Paul's Parish, S. C., 1786. His name appears as Ensign in William Clay Snipe's company, in the Colleton Regiment of Foot, August 5, 1775, and was Lieutenant in Captain James Skirving's company of the Berkeley Militia, 1776. His will, dated April 11, was proved June 22, 1786; his wife was probably dead. Two of his children were: John Parker, who married Emma Lightwood, and *Jane Caroline,* who married, first, Ferguson Parker; second, Dr. Edward Washington North. Their son, *John Gough North,* married Jane Gibert Petigru, whose daughter, *Jane Caroline,* married Charles Lockhart Pettigrew.

PARKER

The earliest known member of this South Carolina family, is "John Parker, late of the Island of Jamaica, mariner," whose estate was administered in Charleston, February 20, 1694-95, by Thomas Barker and his wife Sarah, widow of John Parker. (Thomas Barker was a Captain of militia and was killed in the Yemassee War. His children were Charles, Mary and Anne.) It appears from the will of Mrs. Sarah Barker, dated March 30, 1728, and proved October 23, 1729, that John Parker had a son John, to whom she leaves a silver tankard.

This son, John Parker II., died 1737 or before, as in that year the inventory of his estate was filed. His wife Jane, who died 1755, married, second, Hugh Grange, her will being written July 15, 1754, and proved November 1, 1755. From the wills of his mother and his wife, it appears that he had the following children: Susannah, Dorothy, Mary, married first, William Clifford, second, O'Neal Gough, third, Thomas Jones; Anne; Jane, married ——— Saunders; Dorcas; Rebecca; John III., and Sarah, who married Charles Lowndes.

NORTH

EDWARD NORTH, the founder of this South Carolina family, was born in England, March 20, 1747, and died in America after 1794. He was captain of a fine merchantman, but settled in Bermuda. Later he moved to

Charleston, S. C., where he established a prosperous business as a linen merchant. He took an active part in the Revolution, being a member of Captain Drayton's volunteer company 1775, rising to the rank of Captain. At one time he, with forty other prominent citizens of Charleston, was arrested by the English, and sent to the prison ships at St.ʻAugustine, Fla. He married, March 4, 1776, Sarah, the daughter of Richard and Mary Baker. (Richard Baker died October, 1769, and his wife 1796.) Six children, viz.: *Edward Washington,* John Laurens, Richard Baker, Tucker, Sarah, Mary.

The eldest son, *Edward Washington North,* was born in Charleston, S. C., May 15, 1778, and died March 22, 1843. He was graduated from the University of Pennsylvania May, 1797, and practiced for some years in St. Luke's Parish, S. C. During the War of 1812, he served as surgeon at Forts Moultrie and Johnson. He moved to Charleston 1818, and became one of the most successful physicians of the day. He married, first, March 11, 1802, *Jane Caroline,* the daughter of John Gough, and widow of Ferguson Parker; second, Mrs. Arabella Dart, who died 1840. By first wife, seven children: Edward, *John Gough,* Richard Laurens, James Hayward, Eliza Emily, Anne Jane and Susan Emma.

Their second son, *John Gough North,* a prominent lawyer in Georgetown, S. C., died in 1834. He married, 1827, Jane Gibert Petigru, the daughter of William and Louise (Gibert) Pettigrew, born August 17, 1800, and died November 3, 1863. Four children, viz.: Mary, Louise, Gibert, Albert, and *Jane Caroline,* the eldest, who married *Charles Lockhart Pettigrew,* whose daughter was *Jane North Pettigrew.*

PETTIGREW, OR PETIGRU

The earliest known member of this family is James
Petigru, who left France in the time of Louis XIV., on
account of his religion, and went to England, where he
became an officer in Cromwell's army. After the marriage of his son James to a Scottish lady, he changed
his name to Pettigrew, owing to the great enmity between the English and French. His son, James Pettigrew, was an officer in King William's army at the battle of the Boyne; after peace was declared was given a
tract of three hundred acres in the county of Tyrone.
He married Martha Moore and settled in Ireland,
where his home was called " Crilly House," and here
he lived and died. They had nine children.

One of these, James Pettigrew III., was born in Ireland April, 1718. He is said to have been wild in his
youth, and while preparing for Trinity College, Dublin,
1731, eloped with Mary, the daughter of Captain
George and Rachel (Higginbottom) Cochran, of the
"Grange," Ireland. A famous beauty, she was born
1713, and died October 7, 1786. He is said to have emigrated to America with his family November, 1741, and
to have landed at New Castle, below Philadelphia. Dr.
Benjamin Franklin, whom he came to know, tried in
vain to persuade him to study medicine. He obtained
a tract of three hundred acres of land near the present
Chambersburg, Penn., and lived there until the French
and Indian War, when, shortly after Braddock's defeat,
he sold his land and moved to Lunenburg County, Va.,
removing after a few years to Granville County, N. C.
Toward the end of October, 1768, he again sold his
property, and settled in South Carolina, a few miles
above Abbeville Court House, and lived in this neigh-

Camp near X Creek 3d June 1780

These may certify that the Reverend Charles
Pettigrew a Chap... from the County of Chowan
is hereby discharged from his Tour of Duty he
having procured Lieutenant Carter ... an able
bodied Man in his Room —

By order The Honble Major General Caswell

CERTIFICATE OF HONORABLE DISCHARGE ISSUED TO REV. CHARLES PETTIGREW

borhood until his death. After coming to America he
was "converted," it is said, by Whitfield, and became
an extremely devout Presbyterian. In Granville
County, N. C., he gave the land on which the church
was built, and it was while attending a church meeting
that he contracted the cold from which he died, December 24, 1784. Of their thirteen children, Charles and
William carry down the line of descent.

The elder son, Charles Pettigrew, was born March
20, 1743, at Chambersburg, Penn., and died April·8,
1807. He remained in North Carolina when his parents
moved to South Carolina. He was made master of the
public school at Edenton, N. C., in June, 1773, and
during the winter of 1774 and 1775 he went to England
in order to be admitted to Holy Orders. He was ordained deacon and priest by his Diocesan, the Bishop
of London, and returned at once to North Carolina,
where he was Rector of the church in Edenton, from
1778 to 1784. He took an active part in the Revolution, accompanying the State militia in some of its cam-
paigns. Soon after the war the church in North Carolina was definitely organized, and May 28, 1794. he was
unanimously elected Bishop of the new diocese by its
convention. He died before he could be consecrated,
constant ill health preventing his travelling to Philadelphia. He married, first, October 29, 1778, *Mary*, the
daughter of Colonel John and Sarah Elizabeth (Vail)
Blount, of "Mulberry Hill," who was born 1735, and
died March 16, 1786; second, June 12, 1794, Mary, the
daughter of James Lockhart, of "Scotch Hall." Two
children by first wife.

One of these, *Ebenezer Pettigrew*, was born March
10, 1783, and died July 8, 1848. He was a member of
Congress and of the North Carolina Legislature, each

for one term. He married, May 17, 1815, *Ann Blount,* the daughter of William and Mary (Blount) Shepard, who was born November 16, 1795, and died July 1, 1830.

Their son, *Charles Lockhart Pettigrew,* was born February 21, 1816, and died November 20, 1873. He married, April 20, 1853, *Jane Caroline,* the daughter of John Gough and Jane Gibert (Petigru) North. She was born July 16, 1828, and died March 8, 1887. Their daughter, *Jane North Pettigrew,* married *Stephen Miller,* the son of David Rogerson and Katherine Boykin (Miller) Williams.

Another line from James Pettigrew, the colonist, descended from his youngest son, William Pettigrew, who was born in Lunenburg County, Va., February 26, 1758, and died on his plantations near Abbeville, S. C., January 23, 1837. He came south with his father, and was a soldier in the Revolutionary Army, serving from 1776 to 1783. In his own account of his service he says, he "never was drafted, but always volunteered." At the suggestion of his eldest son, James Louis Pettigrew, the distinguished lawyer of South Carolina, all his children changed the spelling of the family surname to the original French name "Petigru." He married Louise Guy, the daughter of Rev. Jean Louis and Isabeau (Boutiton) Gibert, who was born September 14, 1767, and died September 14, 1826. The line of descent is as follows:

Jane Gibert Petigru, married *John Gough,* the son of Edward Washington and Jane Caroline (Gough) North.

Jane Caroline North, married Charles Lockhart Pettigrew.

Jane North Pettigrew, married *Stephen Miller Williams.*

SERENA CHESNUT WILLIAMS, married Robert Mickle Miles.

(See pp. 6-56, for Williams, Boykin, Miller, Chesnut, Cox, Cantey, Power and other connecting lines.)

BLOUNT

ARMS: *Barry, nebuly of six, or and sable.*
MOTTO: *Lux Tua Via Mea.*

The Blount family[1] of North Carolina is descended from two brothers, Thomas and James, who came to Virginia before 1660, and moved to Chowan Precinct, North Carolina, 1669. (Another brother remained in Virginia.)

CAPTAIN JAMES BLOUNT brought with him a copper-plate of the armorial bearings of his family, which was destroyed by his great-grandson, James B. Shepard, when a candidate on the Democratic ticket for Governor 1850. He was living in Isle of Wight County, Va., 1660, but moving to North Carolina in 1669, became one of the leaders in the colony. He was Captain of the Militia, a member of the Court, and one of the Lords Proprietors' Deputies. His home was " Mulberry Hill," near Edenton, on Albemarle Sound. He married Anne, the daughter of Balthazar Willis, of Ipswich, Mass., and the widow of Robert Roscoe of Roanoke. Children: James, Thomas, JOHN, Ann, and Elizabeth. After James Blount's death, in 1686, his widow married, third, Seth Sothel, Governor of North Carolina, and, fourth, Colonel John Lear of Nansemond County, Va.

[1] In a chart published 1902 by H. M. B. Prescott, the pedigree of the family is traced from Siegfried the Dane, first Count of Guisnes, A. D. 935, and his wife Estrude of Flanders.

JOHN BLOUNT, their third son, was born in Chowan Precinct, September 16, 1669, and died March 17, 1726. He was elected to nearly every office in the colony. A member of the vestry of St. Paul's Parish, Edenton, 1701, he served for several years; a member of the Assembly 1704 and 1711; Justice of the General Court many years, and appointed on the Council as one of the Lords Proprietors' Deputies 1722. He lived and died at "Mulberry Hill," the plantation left him by his father. He was married, June 4, 1695, by Captain John Fendall, to Elizabeth, the daughter of John and Mary (Burton) Davis, of Henrico County, Va., and the granddaughter of John Burton, who died 1687. She was born February 18, 1679, and died 1733. Twelve children, viz.: Mary, Elizabeth, Sarah, Martha, Esther, JOHN, Thomas, James, Ann, Joseph, Rachel, Charles Worth.

COLONEL JOHN BLOUNT II., their eldest son, was born at "Mulberry Hill," May 15, 1706, and died there February 10, 1754. He was Colonel of the Militia; Receiver of the Port of Roanoke; Justice of the Peace 1731, and a Member of the Assembly 1739 and 1740. He married *Sarah Elizabeth,* the daughter of Jeremiah and Mary (Lillington) Vail. Six children, viz.: James, *Frederick,* Wilson, Elizabeth, Martha, and *Mary,* who married Rev. Charles Pettigrew.

Their second son, *Frederick Blount,* was Clerk of the Court of Pasquotauk County, N. C., 1772. He married, April 5, 1769, *Mary,* the daughter of Stephen and Sarah (Swann?) Williams, and widow of Samuel Swann III. Their daughter, *Mary,* married WILLIAM SHEPARD, of Newberne.

VAIL

In 1639, Jeremiah Vail[2] was living in Salem, Mass.
He was a blacksmith by occupation as long as he lived
in this colony, but in 1650, he moved to Gardiner's
Island, off Long Island, where for some years he super-
intended Lieutenant Lion Gardiner's farms. In 1655
he moved to Easthampton, Long Island, and in 1659
to Southold, where he died 1687. He married, first,
Catherine ———; second, May 24, 1660, Mrs. Mary
Paine; third, before 1685, Joyce ———. Six children.

The eldest son of the first marriage, Jeremiah Vail
II., was baptized in Salem, Mass., December 30, 1649,
and died in Southold, Long Island, November 28, 1726.
He was a blacksmith and farmer like his father, and a
noted fox hunter. The name of his first wife is not
known. He married, second, 1691, Ann Hampton, the
widow of Benjamin Moore; she outlived her second husband but one month. Four children.

JEREMIAH VAIL III. is mentioned in his father's will,
as the eldest son, but his younger brother, Thomas, is
made executor and is given the home farm. Jeremiah
is on record March 22, 1697-98, as a mariner, and his
enrollment on the census list that year, with Mary Vail,
is the last record of him on Long Island. Undoubtedly
he is the Jeremiah Vail who came to North Carolina
early in the eighteenth century, settling in Chowan Precinct. In a legal dispute with John Blount, April,
1720, he is referred to as "Jeremiah Vail, mariner."
He was repeatedly selected to serve on the Grand Jury,
and for one year at least, 1727, he was a Member of the
Assembly. He married *Mary*, the daughter of Major
Alexander Lillington and his second wife, Elizabeth

[2] *"Geneal. of some of the Vail Family, descended from Jeremiah Vail,
at Salem Mass., 1639."* New York, 1902.

Cooper; she was born April 22, 1683. A daughter, *Sarah Elizabeth,* married COLONEL JOHN BLOUNT II., and in her will, dated June 6, 1769, she mentions silver spoons marked "S. E. V."

LILLINGTON

ALEXANDER LILLINGTON, the first of the name in America, was born in England 1643, and died in North Carolina September 11, 1697. He was a man of great prominence in the colony, being Major of the Militia, a Member of the Court 1690 to 1694; Deputy-Governor 1693 to 1695 in the absence of the Governor, and President of the Council the year of his death. He married, first, June 11, 1668, Sara, the daughter of Thomas James; second, June 13, 1675, Elizabeth Cooper; third, March 19, 1695, Mrs. Ann Steward. Two children by first wife, and seven children by second wife.

A daughter by the second marriage, *Mary Lillington,* married JEREMIAH VAIL III., and their daughter, *Sarah Elizabeth,* married JOHN BLOUNT II.

WILLIAMS

WILLIAM WILLIAMS, one of the early settlers of Currituck, N. C., was there as early as 1704. His name appears as a member of the vestry of that parish 1715, also as a member of the Assembly, and for some years he was Justice of the Peace. His wife was Mary Tulle, and in his will, written February 2, 1725, and probated January, 1726, he mentions the following children: Thomas, STEPHEN, Tulle, and two married daughters, Jane Brent and Abigail Phillips.

COLONEL STEPHEN WILLIAMS, their second son, died 1767. He served repeatedly on the Commission of the

Peace, and was a Member of the Assembly 1733, 1754, 1760, 1761, 1764 and 1766. In 1754 he was Lieutenant-Colonel of the Currituck Foot. He married Sarah (Swann ?). Their daughter, *Mary*, married, first, Samuel Swann III.; second, *Frederick Blount;* third, 1784, Richard Templeman. A daughter, *Mary*, by the second marriage, married WILLIAM SHEPARD, and their daughter, *Ann Blount*, married *Ebenezer Pettigrew.*

SHEPARD

DAVID SHEPARD settled in Carteret County, N. C., early in the eighteenth century. His name appears on Commissions of the Peace from 1739 to 1750. (David Shepard, Jun., is also named as a Justice of the Peace as early as 1744.) In 1754 he was Major of the Carteret Regiment of Foot. He died late in the year 1774, and in his will mentions three sons, Solomon, JACOB, and Elijah; five married daughters, Sarah Wallis, Rebecca Saunders, Abigail Ward, Wilkins Taylour, Elizabeth Taylor, and several grandchildren. The name of his wife is not known.

JACOB SHEPARD, his second son, was born September 18, 1734, and died June 16, 1773. He was a Member of the Assembly from Carteret 1769, and again the year of his death. He was an engineer and surveyor, and according to tradition he assisted George Washington in surveying the Dismal Swamp Canal. His wife's name was Sara, who afterwards married Mr. Gibbs. They had three children: John, WILLIAM, and Hannah, who married, November 25, 1778, Charles Biddle, of Philadelphia, Vice-President of Pennsylvania 1776.

WILLIAM SHEPARD, the younger son, died 1819. He was commissioned Captain of the tenth regiment of North Carolina Continental Troops, January 20, 1778,

Abraham Shepard, Colonel, and was part owner of the privateers *Snap Dragon* and *Three Sisters*. He was a prominent planter and merchant of Newberne, and owned Shepard's Point, now Morehead. After the Revolution he took an active part in politics, being a strong Federalist, and in 1788 was a Member of the State Legislature. He married, November 12, 1794, Mary, the daughter of Frederick and Mary (Williams) Blount, who was born June 13, 1773, and died October 12, 1864. They had ten children: John Swann, *Ann Blount,* who married *Ebenezer Pettigrew;* William Biddle, Charles B., Mary, Hannah Biddle, Frederick Blount, Penelope Swann, Richard Muse, and James B.

GIBERT

This family is descended from Pierre Gibert and his wife Louise Guy, of Lunès, a village in Languedoc, France. The family belonged to the Huguenot church, and two of the sons, Jean Louis and Etienne, became famous preachers of this faith.

The elder son, Jean Louis Gibert, was born at Lunès, June 29, 1722, and died in New Bordeaux, S. C., early in August, 1773. He determined when quite young to become a pastor in the Huguenot church, and spent three years at the seminary in Lausanne, 1746 to 1749. After his ordination he returned to his own province and took an active part in the work of the church. The times were particularly difficult and the persecutions most intense. He preached ten years, attended synods, built churches and was in constant danger of his life. With the consent of his parish 1761, he went to London to obtain from the British government permission to lead a number of his people to the English possessions in America. After many delays, and through the help of the Archbishop of Canterbury, he embarked on Christmas Day, 1763, with two hundred followers, for South Carolina. There were further delays and the colony did not sail until February 22, 1764. They arrived in Charleston April 14, and were welcomed by all. The land allotted them was near where Abbeville now is, and by the fall of 1764 many houses were erected. The village was called New Bordeaux. The soul of the colony was their pastor, Gibert. He had brought with him a well selected library, and began at once to organize schools for the boys and girls. Unfortunately, he did not live to see the success of his efforts. A monument was erected later to his memory, on which were four inscriptions, two in English, one in French, and one in Latin. He married Isabeau Boutiton (after his death she married Pierre Engivin). They had three children: Joseph, Jeanne, and Louise Guy. The line of descent is as follows:

Louise Guy Gibert, married William Pettigrew.

Jane Gibert Petigru, married *John Gough North.*

Jane Caroline North, married *Charles Lockhart Pettigrew.*

Jane North Pettigrew, married *Stephen Miller Williams.* Their daughter is:

SERENA CHESNUT WILLIAMS MILES,

Member of Chapter I., The Colonial Dames of America.

XXXII
GIBSON

ARMS: *Paly of six gules and vert, a tent argent poled and garnished or, on a chief of the last, a fret between two crescents sable.*

CREST:[1] *An arm embowed in armour garnished or, holding a battle axe sable.*

MOTTO: *"Semper Paratus."*

Three brothers emigrated from the borders of Scotland early in 1700, the tradition being that they were of the clan "Lochiel." One of the three, John Gibson I., settled in St. Mary's County, Md., while his brothers went to Virginia, and later one went to New Orleans. His will was dated 1745. He married Alsie ——.

Their son, John Gibson II., was born in Leonardtown, Md., and died in 1781; his will mentions wife Elizabeth and eight children. His second son:

GIBSON CREST [1]

WILLIAM GIBSON, of "Rose Hill," Baltimore Town, Md., was born in Leonardtown, Md., September 22, 1753, and died April 29, 1832. He is buried with his children and grandchildren in "Old St. Paul's Church Yard." When quite young he came to Baltimore Town and subsequently bought "Rose Hill," which was situated in the suburbs; the house stood at the intersection of Eutaw and Lanvale streets. Appointed a member of the Court of Admiralty in 1776, also the same year one of the signers of Continental Money, and in 1797 one of the electors for the first Mayor of Baltimore, he was chosen "to receive for safe keeping all monies in hands of Commissioners of said Town

[1] Crest on seal and silver in possession of family.

until the Corporation shall further order." [1a]   He was
Vestryman in Old St. Paul's Church for many years.
He married, December 21, 1775, Sarah, daughter of
John and Sarah Morris, of Joppa, Md.

Their eldest son, *John Gibson III.*, of "Chestnut
Hill," Baltimore, was born 1784, and educated at St.
John's College, Annapolis.   He was one of the successful merchants of Baltimore in the early part of the last
century.   When quite young he was chosen Vestryman
of "Old St. Paul's Parish," serving in that capacity for
nearly thirty-five years, and only resigning to become
one of the founders of St. John's Parish, Huntington,
in the immediate neighborhood of his home, "Chestnut
Hill."   To this congregation he rendered very important service and died a member of its Vestry, February
24, 1860.   He married, September 18, 1806, Elizabeth
C., daughter of George II. and Mary (Carr) Grundy,
of "Bolton."   Issue:

George Grundy, married Maria Swift, née Jephson,
of New York.

Mary Carr, married Rev. Richard Clarence Hall.

William Morris, married Mary Hollingsworth.

John.

Charles Crosdale.

Margaret, married Daniel Bowly of "Furley."

Edward James.

Alfred.

Eliza.

Frederick, married Kate Middleton Semmes.

The fourth son and fifth child, *Charles Crosdale Gibson,* married *Priscilla Charlotte,* daughter of Dr. Henry
and Priscilla (Robinson) Boteler, born 1819.   Their
daughter, MARY GRUNDY GIBSON, married Clapham
Murray.

[1a] Griffith's *Annals of Baltimore Town.*

OTHER SONS OF WILLIAM GIBSON

The second son, Professor William Gibson, of Philadelphia, was born 1788. After graduating at Princeton in 1806, he took his medical degree at the University of Edinburgh, 1809, and was the pupil of Sir Charles Bell, the eminent Scotch surgeon. On his return to this country he practiced in Baltimore, and was one of the earliest professors of surgery in the University of Maryland. In the Baltimore Riots of 1812 he rendered essential service. He again visited Europe in 1814, and fought on the side of the allied forces at the Battle of Waterloo, where he was slightly wounded. In 1819 he succeeded Dr. Physick in the chair of surgery in the University of Pennsylvania, where he remained more than thirty years.[2] He was the author of *Principles and Practice of Surgery, Rambles in Europe,* containing sketches of eminent surgeons, and *Lectures on Eminent Belgian Surgeons and Physicians.* At the age of seventy he removed to Newport, and died in 1868. Dr. Gibson married, first, Sarah, daughter of Colonel Samuel Hollingsworth; and second, Sarah Smith, of Loudoun County, Va. He had issue by the first marriage, a son and daughter, and by the second marriage two daughters. His son, Charles Bell Gibson, was born in Baltimore, 1816, and died in Richmond, 1865. He held the position of Surgeon-General of the Confederate States Army. He married Ellen Ayre, of Philadelphia.

The third son of WILLIAM GIBSON, of "Rose Hill," James Gibson, of "Ingleside," was one of the volunteers to defend Baltimore in 1814, and was wounded in the Battle of North Point. He married Emily, daughter of George II. and Mary (Carr) Grundy, of

2 *Cyclo. of Am. Biog.,* Vol. ii, p. 641.

"Bolton," a sister of the wife of *John Gibson III*. They had eight children, but no descendants are living.

GRUNDY

ARMS: *Argent, on a cross engrailed between four lions passant guardant gules, five martlets or.*

CREST: *A demi-leopard rampant guardant sable bezanty.*

The ancestor of the American family, Edmund Grundy, of Chapel House, Bolton Le Moors, Eng., was born 1695. He married Anne Bradshaw. Their son, George Grundy I., of Chapel House, was born 1726,

and died 1810. He married, 1749, Elizabeth, daughter of William By-rom, of Preston, Lancas-tershire, Eng. (1690-1736), who married, 1714, Margaret Pearson (1685-1775).

Their son, George Grundy II., of "Bolton," was born at Chapel House, 1755, and died February 14, 1825. In 1783 he came to reside in Baltimore, where

GEORGE GRUNDY'S BOOK PLATE

his home, adjoining that of William Gibson ("Rose Hill"), called after his old home (Bolton Le Moors), was a facsimile of Chapel House. All the bricks, mantels, doors and windows were brought from England. It had its secret vault, which was placed under the brick pavement in front of the entrance, where, during the Battle of North Point, and bombardment of Fort McHenry, the silver, on which was engraved the Grundy arms and crest, with other valuables, were hidden, and the coach and four stood ready, day and night, to con-

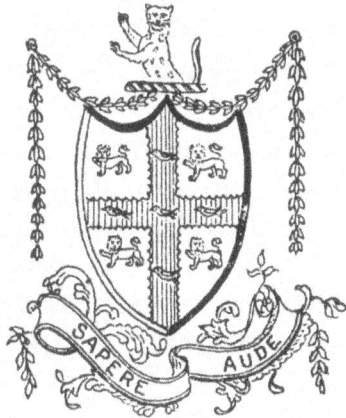

vey the family to a place of safety. The large bow-window at the end of the hall, where all the daughters stood, when married, overlooked a rare and very beautiful horn-beam tree, which Mr. Grundy planted as a small bush, in the year he built " Bolton," 1785, bringing it from Chapel Hill.   There is only one like it in the country, and that is in Cambridge, Mass.   It was at a ball, given at "Bolton," that Prince Jerome Bonaparte met the beautiful Elizabeth Patterson.   "Bolton" is now a name of the past.   The Fifth Regiment Armory is built on its site.   The following extracts are from a letter of Mary (Carr) Grundy, the wife of George Grundy II., to the family at Bolton Le Moors, England:

"Baltimore, May, 1784.   .   .   .   I will continue this letter in part to all, as you will each equally rejoice to hear of our safe arrival, after a passage of 8 weeks and three days.   .   .   .   By what I have seen of Baltimore, I have not a doubt that I shall be very happy and like the place very well, I give it already the preference to New York.   The ladies are very polite, and about 23 or 24 have called, and many more I expect, when they have all been I'll send you a list of their names and those I shall like to keep up an acquaintance with.   I am more fond of my country than I thought I was when with you, could I have yr company here with the rest of my dear friends how much would I give America the preference it deserves, to all the world besides.   .   .   . They are the fondest here of fashions you ever saw, I have had the mantua-maker to take the patterns of my Capes.   Caps have gone out and the hair is tied in a knob at the top.   I was apprehensive if you remember that Mrs. Sayres had made a mistake and not put in my bonnet—whether a wilful one or not I cannot say—

GEORGE GRUNDY

MRS. GEORGE GRUNDY AND DAUGHTER MA
Reproduced from a painting by
C. W. Peale

"BOLTON" IN 1785
Reproduced from a painting

but there was no such thing in the box.   I think it very ungentil in her as I paid 5/6 and cannot replace it here under a great deal of money, gauze and ribbons &ct being very high, but this is a trivial circumstance compared with Mr. Preston's neglect in not sending my china, which they promised faithfully to do, the vessel is now unloaded and no such box is to be found, and unless you have found out the mistake and send it by the first opportunity I shall be at a great loss what to do, as it won't be long in my power to put off having 'tea-company'—to-morrow I shall have some ladies from Phil* old acquaintances, Miss Abbey Biddle, Mrs. Lux &ct—I am under the necessity of having them as they return on Monday. . . ."

In 1780, in New York, George Grundy II. married Mary, daughter of Captain George Carr, of England, and his wife, Mary Marks (or Marx), of Philadelphia (1724-1803). She was born 1763, and died 1797. Issue:

George Carr, married Mary Lawrence Billopp.

Elizabeth C., married *John Gibson III.*, of " Chestnut Hill."

Thomas Byrom, married Mary, daughter of Rev. Dr. Bend, rector of Old St. Paul's Parish.

Sophia, married Colonel Baker Johnson, of " Auburn," Frederick, Md.

Emily, married James Gibson, of " Ingleside."

Mary.

BOTELER

ARMS: *Argent, three escutcheons sable, each charged with a covered cup, or.*

CREST: *A covered cup, or, between a pair of wings endorsed, the dexter arg. sinister az.*[3]

MOTTO: *Dum Spiro Spero.*

The Botelers, of England, from whom those in this

[3] Burke. Arms of Boteler of Eastry.

country descend, are of Norman extraction, and derive their origin (according to the old chronicles), from Rollo himself, the founder of the Norman dynasty. There are many different versions of the Roll of Battle Abbey, in all of which the name of " Boteler " is to be found.[4]

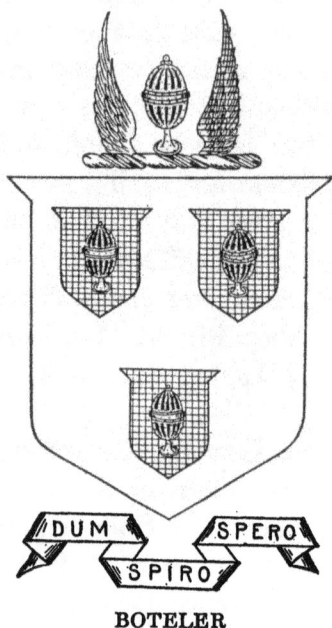

The Botelers, of Eastry, Kent County, Eng., whose descendants settled in Calvert County, Md., are of very ancient standing in Kent County. As far back as the beginning of the fifteenth century, we find Sir John Boteler, of Sandwich, in the County of Kent, Mayor of that corporation (1440-1445), also one of the supporters of the canopy of Queen Margaret, wife of Henry VI., and also one of the Burgesses in Parliament.

BOTELER

The colonist, Edward Boteler II., was a son of Edward Boteler I., of Eastry and came to Maryland in 1669. He died prematurely from grief, on account of the misappropriation of funds by his partner in London. He married Anne, daughter of George and Anne Lingan, who died about 1717.

Their son, Edward Boteler III., was left in the charge of Thomas Lingan, the boy's maternal uncle, to be sent to England. This was not done, and he remained in lower Maryland, marrying Priscilla Lin-

[4] Burke's *Landed Gentry*.

DR. HENRY BOTELER
Reproduced from a painting by his son,
Hon. A. R. Boteler

MRS. ALEXANDER ROBINSON
From a painting by C. W. Peale

ALEXANDER ROBINSON
From a portrait by St. Memin

gan, an aunt of the Revolutionary officer, William Maccubbin Lingan.

Their only son:

CAPTAIN HENRY BOTELER, of Park Hall, Pleasant Valley, Washington County, Md., was born November 15, 1728, and died 1814. "He commanded a Company of Rangers in the French and Indian War, 1757, garrisoned Fort Frederick, and by right of seniority was the Commandant. Was Captain in the Revolutionary War, his Commission dated July 4, 1776." The following is from a letter of Hon. A. R. Boteler, Fountain Rock, Va.:

"Captain Boteler was no less enterprising in peace than patriotic in war. Among the enduring evidences of his public spirit was the opening of the first road from Harper's Ferry, Va., to Frederick, Md., which was not only projected by him, but located and made under his personal supervision. The method he adopted for removing rocks from the road bed along the ragged ridges below Harper's Ferry, at the base of the mountain (which has since become historical as Maryland Heights), was as original and effective as that ascribed to Hannibal, in his famous passage across the Alps. He had large log fires built upon the rocks, which when red hot, were drenched with water from the river, and thus rendered sufficiently pliable to be quarried, without the use of gun powder, that being too precious a commodity to be wasted on engineering operations."

His wife, Sarah Elsby, was the daughter of an Englishman who lived near Brandywine, Del. Her maternal grandmother was one of the Huguenots who came to this country after the "Revocation of Nantes," 1685.

Their son, *Doctor Henry Boteler,* of Fountain Rock, Sheperdstown, W. Va., born 1779, and died 1836, married, 1814, *Priscilla,* daughter of Alexander and Angelica Kauffman (Peale) Robinson, who was born January 8, 1797, and died February 15, 1820. Issue:

Hon. Alexander Robinson, born 1815, married Helen Stockton.

Henry, born 1817, married Nancy Morgan.

Angelica.

Priscilla Charlotte, married *Charles Crosdale Gibson.*

LINGAN

DOMINUS PROVIDEBIT

LINGAN

The Lingans (whose name is spelled equally Lingen and Lingayne in the English records), long held large and valuable possessions in Hereford, Eng., and the name Lingan was notable in the twelfth, thirteenth and fourteenth centuries. The second John of the "De Lingen" race had a grant of free warren 1256, and the third John was knighted at a great solemnity in 1305, before accompanying Edward I. upon his last expedition to Scotland. Sir Ralph was a Member of Parliament for Hereford 1373, during the reign of Edward III., and in 1381, during the reign of Richard II. In the great Cathedral at Hereford are inscriptions to Cecelia, daughter of Sir Henry Lingen, Knight of Sutton, and Alice his Lady, May 9, 1689. In the struggle between Charles I. and his Parliament, in the middle of the seventeenth century, Sir Henry espoused the royal cause and for some time maintained a troop of horse for the King's service. He was subjected to fines and confiscations that greatly reduced his wealth. One amounted to £5000, the highest sum levied upon a commoner, and King Charles failed in any way to remember the loyalty or to compensate the losses.

The Lingans known to be in Calvert County, Md., in 1664, were of Herefordshire descent, and bore the same arms as the English family of Hereford. The annals of the Lingans, of Calvert County, were accidentally destroyed.[5]

HON. GEORGE LINGAN, of Calvert County, Md., was a Commissioner of the Provincial Court of Maryland, 1686, and a Member of the Maryland Assembly from Calvert County, November 14, 1688.[6] His will was probated 1708, and mentions his wife Anne and four children, *Thomas, Anne,* Martha, and Katharine; also sons-in-law, Edward Boteler, Josiah Wilson, and Henry Boteler. Anne, the eldest daughter, married Edward Boteler II., and their son, Edward III., married *Priscilla,* daughter of *Thomas Lingan.*

5 Baltimore *Sun,* by Emily E. Lantz.
6 *Archs. of Md.,* Vol. v, p. 502; Scharf's *Hist. of Md.,* Vol. i, p. 304.

ROBINSON

ARMS: *Vert, on a chevron, or between three bucks trippant, of the last pelletee, as many quarterfoils gules.*

CREST: *A buck trippant, or, pelletee.*

MOTTO: *Solo deo salus.*

" The Robinsons,[7] of Rokeby, are descended from the Robertsons, Baron Struan, of Perthshire, Scotland. William Robinson settled at Kendall in the reign of Henry VIII., and his eldest son, Ralph, became the owner of Rokeby, in the North Riding of Yorkshire, by his marriage with the eldest daughter and co-heiress of James Phillips, of Brignal, near Rokeby." It was of Rokeby Park and the Rokeby Robinsons that Sir Walter Scott wrote his poem *Rokeby,* and to this family belonged Richard Robinson, Archbishop of Armagh, and Primate of Ireland, Baron Rokeby, in the peerages of both England and Ireland, and other dignitaries. In the time of Cromwell, a son of this family went to

---

[7] *Eng. Nat. Dict. of Biog.*

Ireland and settled on their estate in Armagh, to which
Sir Walter Scott alludes in his poem, and the Balti-
more, Louisville, and St. Louis Robinsons are of this
Irish branch.

The first of the line to emigrate, Alexander Robinson, born in the County of Armagh, 1751, came to
America to obtain the release of his brother Arthur, who
was an officer in the British army, and taken prisoner in
the Revolutionary War.   He brought with him a crude
painting of the coat of arms as here described, which, as
is the case with most Irish arms, has "supporters."
After effecting his object, he settled in Baltimore in
1788, and was one of the most successful merchants of
his day, dying August 9, 1845.   He never returned to
his native land.   He married, first, Priscilla (Lyles)
Booth (1760-1790); second, July 15, 1794, *Angelica
Kauffman,* daughter of Charles Willson and Rachel
(Brewer) Peale, who was born December 22, 1775,
and died August 8, 1853.   An interesting story is told
of Angelica Peale.

"When General Washington was on his way to New
York to be inaugurated as first President of the United
States . . . a triumphal arch was erected on both
sides of the (Schuylkill) river, covered with laurel
branches and approached through avenues of ever-
greens.   As Washington passed under the last arch
Angelica Kauffman Peale, daughter of the eminent
artist, and a child of rare beauty, who was concealed in
the foliage, let down a handsomely ornamented civic
crown of laurel, which rested upon the head of the
patriot, while the multitude filled the air with long and
loud huzzas." [8]

Issue, first wife: Lyles Robert (1790-1834), mar-

[8] Lossing's *Hist. of Mt. Vernon.*

ried, November 9, 1813, Catherine W. Goldsborough; from this marriage are descended the Louisville Robinsons.

Issue, second wife:

Alexander (1795-1804).

Priscilla, married *Dr. Henry Boteler,* of Fountain Rock, Va.

Archibald (1798-1848), married, first, Jane S. Rowan; second, Anna Kearsley Mines.

Angelica (1799-1829), married J. Peyton Thompson.

Alverda (1802-1846), married Dr. Horace Waters.

Charlotte Ramsay (1805-1819).

Dr. Alexander Charles (1808-1871), married, first, Rosa Wirt; second, M. Louisa Hall.

Charlotte Ramsay (1819-1886), married Edmund Pendleton, of Virginia.

PEALE

The Rector of Edith Weston, in Rutlandshire, Eng., the Rev. Charles Peale, was heir entail to the Manor Wootton, in Oxfordshire, the estate of Charles Willson, M. D.

His son, Charles Peale, born 1709, and died 1750, was educated for the Church of England, but preferred coming to America, where he settled in Chestertown, Md., 1742. He was master of the county school and received boarding and day scholars in classical studies and surveying, and occasionally officiated in the pulpit. A letter-book of Charles Peale is still in existence, dated 1745 to 1747, written in a manly, well-formed hand and always signed with his monogram. He married, 1740, Margaret Trigg, who died 1791. Issue:

CHARLES WILLSON.

"THE ARTIST'S FAMILY"
By C. W. Peale. Reproduced by
permission from the original

JOHN GIBSON III
Reproduced from a painting by R. Peale

CHARLES WILLSON PEALE
Reproduced from the painting by Benjamin
West

ANGELICA K. PEALE
Reproduced from a painting by
C. W. Peale

James, married and had descendants; he was one of the original members of the Society of the Cincinnati.

Elizabeth, married Captain Digby Polk.

Charlotte, married Colonel Ramsay.

St. George, died unmarried.

CHARLES WILLSON PEALE, born 1741, and died 1827, was known as the "Revolutionary artist," but was twenty-four years of age before he began his career, as the poverty of his widowed mother compelled her to apprentice him to a saddler in his early youth. Peale's first lessons in painting were from Mr. Hesselius, the British artist (who had married Mrs. Henry Woodward, née Mary Young, a lady of fortune, residing in Annapolis), who employed Peale to paint his wife's portrait that he might acquire some knowledge of the proper process of mixing colors. Hearing of the celebrity of Copley, Peale went by sea to Boston to study with him. On his return, his friends were so well assured of his genius that they furnished him with the means of going to London, where he studied under Sir Joshua Reynolds and West. The friends were to be repaid by paintings, on his return, which accounts for the great number of portraits that are still in existence. While abroad, he met Angelica Kauffman, whom he greatly admired, naming his daughter for her.

He commanded a company of volunteers at the battles of Trenton, Princeton, Germantown, and Monmouth, also sharing in the hardships of Valley Forge. In 1777, he was elected a Representative from Philadelphia to the State Legislature; became one of the original members of the Philosophical Society of Philadelphia, and was a naturalist, establishing the first museum and academy of fine arts in America. After the war he inherited "Wootton Manor," in England, but declined the estate and title, preferring to remain in America, having fought for her independence. The last years of his life he had a country home near Germantown, Pa., with a hanging garden, grotto, fountain, and a hospitable table for all his friends. His last painting was a full-length portrait of himself at the age of eighty-three.

He married, first, 1767, *Rachel,* daughter of John IV. and Eleanor (Maccubin) Brewer, of Brewerton, Annapolis, Md., born 1744, and died 1790; issue, ten children; second, 1791, Elizabeth de Peyster; issue, six children; third, a Quakeress, Hannah More.

His daughter by the first marriage, *Angelica Kauffman Peale,* married Alexander Robinson. Their daughter *Priscilla* married *Dr. Henry Boteler,* whose daughter, *Priscilla Charlotte,* married *Charles Crosdale Gibson.*

BREWER

JOHN BREWER I., of Brewerton, Annapolis, Md. (or Bruere, as it was written in Wales, and for several generations in this country), was born in the south of Wales early in the seventeenth century, and died 1667,[9] survived by his wife and three children. He emigrated to Massachusetts, but settled in Virginia, 1645, going to Maryland with the Puritan Colony, 1649, which settled on the present site of Annapolis, naming the town Providence.

In 1659 he patented "Brewerton," South River, Md., and there built a brick residence still in possession of the family. This plantation, with other adjacent farms, contained nearly three thousand acres; he was also an owner of six hundred and forty acres on Wye

[9] *Biog. Cycl. of Rep. Men of Md. and District of Columbia,* p. 65.

River, Talbot County, Md.   He was one of the few
men of that period who adhered to the law of primogeni-
ture, and left a large landed estate in entail.   He was
one of the first Justices of Anne Arundel County
Court, appointed July 12, 1658, by Leonard Calvert,
and with Samuel Chew represented the county in the
House of Burgesses, April 16, 1661.[10]   He married
Elizabeth, whose surname is believed to have been
Heathcote.   She died in 1667, and in her will she
names Rachel, *John,* and William.

Their son, *John Brewer II.,* died in 1690.   He married *Sarah,* daughter of Henry and Sarah (Warner)
Ridgely.

Their son, *John Brewer III.,* married February 14,
1704, *Dinah,* daughter of Fernando and Elizabeth
(Hood) Battee; she was born in 1690.

Their son, *John Brewer IV.,* married *Eleanor,*
daughter of Captain William and Sarah (Westall)
Maccubin.

Their daughter, *Rachel Brewer,* married CHARLES
WILLSON PEALE.

RIDGELY

ARMS: *Argent, on a chevron sable, three mullets pierced of the field.*
CREST: *A buck's head erased, or.*

The founders of the Ridgely family in Maryland were
COLONEL HENRY and William Ridgely, of Anne Arundel County, and Robert, of St. Mary's.   Henry and
William were known to have been brothers, but it is not
yet ascertained whether Robert was related to the fore-
going.[11]   These three men came to the Province of

10 *Archs. of Md., Assembly Proc.,* 1637-64, p. 396.
11 *Family Records* as published in Baltimore *Sun.*   Some of the
Ridgelys of Hampton were descended from both Henry and Robert by
later marriages.

Maryland, 1659, and were living on allotments of land on South River in 1661. The tombs of the family are on Broad Creek, a branch of South River, four miles from Annapolis.

COLONEL HENRY RIDGLEY I., who died in 1710, was Captain in the Maryland Colonial Troops, 1689; Major, 1692; Lieutenant - Colonel, 1 6 9 4; Colonel, 1696; member of the House of Burgesses, 1692 to 1695, and Justice of the court (judge), 1679 to 1697.[12] He married, first, in England, Elizabeth Howard, who came with him to Maryland, and they lived first on Patuxent River, Prince George's County; married, second, *Sarah*, daughter of James and Elizabeth (Harris) Warner; married, third, Mary, widow of Mareen Duvall.

RIDGELY

Issue, by second marriage: Henry II., Charles, Rachel, who married Charles Greenbury, and *Sarah*, who married *John Brewer II.*

HARRIS

WILLIAM HARRIS, with others, had a land grant of eight thousand acres in Charles City County, Va., record dated February 9, 1636.[13] He came with the Puritan Colony to South River, Md., in 1650, where his daughter *Elizabeth* married James Warner, who came

[12] *Archs. of Md.*, Vols. v. viii, xv, xvii, xx, *Council Proc.*
[13] *Va. State Land Recs.*, Book V, fol. 410.

from Virginia, and was on the Severn River in 1651, dying 1673. Their daughter, *Sarah Warner,* married HENRY RIDGELY.

BATTEE

FERNANDO BATTEE, was a resident of South River, Md., and Judge of the County Court (justice) for Anne Arundel County, 1683 to 1694; also Commissioner.[14] He married Elizabeth, daughter of Colonel Thomas Hood. Their daughter *Dinah* married *John Brewer III.*

MACCUBIN

ARMS: *Argent, three crosses crosslet fitches azure.*
CREST: *An arm in armor embowed, grasping a scimiter.*[15]
MOTTO: *Pro rege et patria.*

This name is said to be the Lowland corruption of the Scottish Highland name of "McAlpine."

The colonist of 1659-60, John Maccubin, Gent., came from the Lowlands of Scotland, and was the first of the name to settle in Maryland. He married, first, Susan, daughter of Samuel Howard, and second, Eleanor ——, believed to be Eleanor Carroll, since her will,

MACCUBIN

dated 1705, proved August 4, 1711, was witnessed by Charles and James Carroll, of All-Hallows' Parish.

14 *Archs. of Md.; Proc. of Council,* 1687-93, p. 411.

15 The Maryland family of Maccubin (Maccubbin, Mackbuin) claims descent from Kenneth II, who was the first King of Scotland in 843; Md. Heraldry, Baltimore *Sun,* by Emily E. Lantz.

(After the death of John Maccubin his widow, Eleanor, married John Howard, Sr., but had no issue). Issue, first wife:

John II., married Elizabeth Creagh.

Zachariah, married Susanna Nicholson.

WILLIAM.

Samuel.

Moses.

Sarah, who married William Griffith, is thought by some of the descendants to be the only child of John and Eleanor Maccubin, since the other children are named in the will of Samuel Howard, the father of the first wife, Susan (Howard) Maccubin.

CAPTAIN WILLIAM MACCUBIN, the third child, born 1666, and living 1699, was a Lieutenant, afterwards Captain, in the Colonial Militia of Maryland, and as such participated in various Indian expeditions. He married Sarah, daughter of George and Sarah Westall.

Their daughter, *Eleanor,* married *John Brewer IV.*

Their daughter *Rachel* married CHARLES WILLSON PEALE, and were the ancestors of *Priscilla Charlotte Boteler,* who married *Charles Crosdale Gibson.* Their daughter is:

MARY GRUNDY GIBSON MURRAY,

Member of Chapter I., The Colonial Dames of America.

XXXIII

RIGGS

The descendants of John Riggs of London, Eng., who married Jane Warden, are as follows:

The colonist, John Riggs (1687-1762), married, 1721, Mary, the daughter of Thomas Davis. Two of their sons were SAMUEL and Elisha.

One of the original Virginia settlers on Herring Creek, Thomas Davis was in the Assembly of Virginia in 1619.

LIEUTENANT SAMUEL RIGGS (1740-1814), married, 1767, *Amelia,* the daughter of Philemon and Catherine (Ridgely) Dorsey, and the great-granddaughter of COLONEL EDWARD DORSEY (see pp. 249, 252, 253, 603-604 for Riggs, Dorsey, Ridgely).

Their son, *Thomas Riggs* (1773-1845), married his cousin, *Mary Hammond,* the daughter of Elisha Riggs, (the son of John and Mary [Davis] Riggs), and his wife *Caroline Welsh,* whose mother *Hammatal (Hammond) Welsh,* was the daughter of *John Hammond II.*

Their son, *Samuel Riggs* (1800-1852), married, 1827, Margaret Norris, whose daughter, *Margretta,* born 1836, married *Jacob Hall,* the son of John Pemberton and Mary (Hall) Pleasants, and the grandson of Samuel and Mary (Pemberton) Pleasants.

RIDGELY-DORSEY

COLONEL HENRY RIDGELY I (1645-1710), married second, *Sarah,* the daughter of James and Elizabeth (Harris) Warner.

Their son, *Henry Ridgely II,* married *Catherine,* the daughter of Colonel Nicholas Greenberry.

Colonel Henry Ridgely III, their son, married, 1702, *Elizabeth,* the daughter of Benjamin and Elizabeth (Duvall) Warfield. *Anne Ridgely,* the sister of Henry III, married *Joshua Dorsey.*

Colonel Edward Dorsey, was the son of Edward the emigrant.

His daughter *Anne,* married *John Hammond II,* whose granddaughter *Caroline Welsh,* married Elisha Riggs.

His son *Joshua Dorsey,* married *Anne Ridgely.*

Their son *Philemon Dorsey,* married his cousin, *Catherine,* the daughter of Henry Ridgely III, and their daughter *Amelia,* married Samuel Riggs.

HARRIS-WARFIELD-DUVALL

William Harris, had a grant of eight thousand acres in Charles County, Va., February, 1636. He came to South River, Md., in 1650.[1] His daughter *Elizabeth,* married James Warner, and their daughter *Sarah,* was the second wife of Henry Ridgely I.

Captain Richard Warfield, died 1704. He married Elinor, the daughter of Captain John Browne.

Their son, *Benjamin Warfield,* died 1717. He married *Elizabeth,* the daughter of Captain John Duvall, and their daughter *Elizabeth,* married Henry Ridgely III. (See pp. 82-84, 252, 604-605.)

HAMMOND

Major-General John Hammond, came over with Lord Baltimore and received large grants from him

[1] Va. State *Land Recs.,* Book I, Folio 410.

and the Crown. He held office in Maryland under Queen Anne.[2] (See p. 254).

He married Mary, the daughter of John Howard.

MAJOR CHARLES HAMMOND, their son, President of the Council of Maryland, married *Hannah,* the daughter of CAPTAIN PHILIP HOWARD, who was commissioned to lay out the town of Annapolis, Md.

Their son, *John Hammond II,* married *Anne,* the daughter of COLONEL EDWARD DORSEY.

Their daughter *Hammatal Hammond,* married —— Welsh, whose daughter *Caroline,* married Elisha Riggs. (See pp. 253-254).

PEMBERTON

In 1580, William Pemberton, of Lancastershire, Eng., was born, and died 1642. His son Ralph, born 1610, came to America on the ship *Submission* in 1682, with a party of fifty-two persons.[3] He married, in England, Margaret Seddon.

PHINEAS PEMBERTON, their son, born 1650, and died 1702, came to America with his father and held many important offices in the Colonial Government. In 1683 he was Deputy Register of Bucks County, Penn.; and Register 1684. Of the Provincial Council 1685, for many years he was one of the Assembly, and Master of the Rolls 1696. He married Phoebe Harrison; issue, nine children.

ISRAEL PEMBERTON, their son, born 1684, and died 1754, served for nineteen successive years in the General Assembly of Pennsylvania. He married, as his second wife, Sarah, the daughter of Joseph Kirkbride, who came to Bucks County, Penn., 1681, was Justice

[2] *Am. Hist. Reg.,* February, 1895.
[3] *Friends Miscellany,* Vol. VII, p. 27.

and one of the General Assembly. Their daughter, *Mary Pemberton*, (1738-1821), married, 1762, Samuel Pleasants, of Virginia.

PLEASANTS-HALL

The son of Samuel and Mary (Pemberton) Pleasants, *John Pemberton Pleasants*, died in 1825. He married, second, 1816, *Mary*, the daughter of JACOB HALL, who was Justice of Philadelphia County 1761, 1764 to 1765 and 1770, and Charter Member[4] of the Society of the Cincinnati. Issue, nine children.

Their son, *Jacob Hall Pleasants* (1822-1901), married *Margretta*, the daughter of Samuel and Margaret (Norris) Riggs, whose daughter MARGARET RIGGS, married Josiah Pennington.

MARGARET RIGGS PLEASANTS PENNINGTON,

Member of Chapter I., The Colonial Dames of America.

[4] *Penn. Arch.*, Vol. IX, pp. 729-730.

XXXIV

THEOBALD

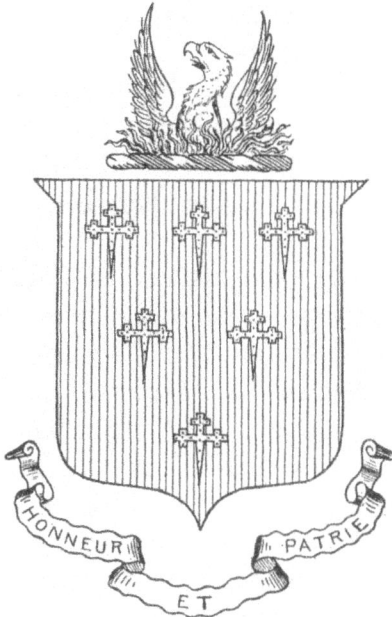

ARMS: *Gules, six crosses crosslet or.*
CREST: *Phoenix with wings expanded, sable proper.*
MOTTO: *Henneur et patrie.*

The colonist, Clement Theobald (pronounced in accordance with English custom " Tibbals "), living in Lower Norfolk County, Va., 1641,[1] went to Maryland, 1654, dying in Charles County 1675. The coat of arms borne by his descendants in America, indicates that he came of the Theobalds of Kent, Eng.[2] He was twice

[1] Probably the first of the name in America as the date of his residence in Virginia was only thirty-four years after the settlement of Jamestown.

[2] *Family Bible,* verified and extended by Dr. Christopher Johnston, Genealogist, Johns Hopkins University.

married, his first wife being Catharine ——, and a son, William, was a sworn attorney of Charles County Court; married second, Mary ——; issue, three sons and three daughters.

The youngest of these sons, John Theobald I., born in Charles County 1666, and died 1713, married Mary ——; issue five children.

His third son, John Theobald II, born in Charles County, was the third husband of *Elizabeth Jenifer, née Mason,* and the widow of Daniel Jenifer; they were married 1729. Issue: Elizabeth, *Samuel,* and Jane.

ROBERT MASON, the father of *Elizabeth Jenifer,* came to Maryland apparently from Virginia, and settled in St. Mary's County. He was alderman 1689, and Burgess 1692, of St. Mary's City; High Sheriff of St. Mary's County, 1692 to 1693, commissioned Justice of the Provincial Court of Maryland, April 16, 1691, and Burgess for St. Mary's County, 1694 to 1696. He died 1701, and his wife, Susanna, 1716. His daughter *Elizabeth,* by her marriage with Daniel Jenifer, became the mother of " Hon. Daniel of St. Thomas Jenifer," President of the Council of Safety of the Province of Maryland 1776.

Their only son, *Samuel Theobald I,* born (probably) in St. Mary's County, where he resided for many years, married Elizabeth Smith, and subsequently removed to what was then Bourbon County, Ky. After the death of his wife, he returned to his old home in St. Mary's County, where he married again, and died at the age of nearly ninety years.

His son, *William Theobald,* born in St. Mary's County, Md., June 16, 1766, continued to reside in Kentucky after the return of his father to Maryland.

He married, at her father's residence, "Libbie Grove," Bourbon County, Ky., November 8, 1789, Mary, the daughter of James and Ann (Davis) Brown; she was born in Virginia, September 25, 1770. Issue, fifteen children, of whom the eldest son was *Samuel Theobald.*

BROWN

One of this family, James Brown, born April 29, 1708, in Middlesex County, Va., died in Culpeper, Va. His wife was Elizabeth Poole. Their son, James Brown II, born April 19, 1740, at Mansfield, Spottsylvania County, Va., was in the Revolution, and died at his residence in Bourbon County, Ky. (afterwards Jefferson County), June 24, 1825. He married, November 15, 1764, in Culpeper County, Va., Ann Davis, who was born April 19, 1746, in Caroline County, Va. Later they removed to Kentucky, and resided at their country seat, "Libbie Grove." Their daughter Mary, married *William Theobald.*[3]

THEOBALD (*Continued*)

The eldest child of William and Mary (Brown) Theobald, *Dr. Samuel Theobald II.,* born at "Libbie Grove," Bourbon County, Ky., December 22, 1790, died at "Blantonia," near Greenville, Miss., August 17, 1867. He received his medical degree at Transylvania University, Lexington, Ky., and for twenty years resided and practised his profession in that town. In the War of 1812, was Judge Advocate upon the staff of Colonel Richard M. Johnston (afterwards Vice-President of the United States), and took part in the battle of the Thames, when the famous Indian

3 Brown *Family Bible.*

chief, Tecumseh, was killed. Colonel Johnston was seriously wounded in this fight, and it fell to the lot of Captain Theobald to assist him from the field, and guide him to where he could receive the attention of the surgeons. Returning to Lexington, after the war, Dr. Theobald married first, April 23, 1816, *Nancy Dorsey,* the daughter of Elisha and Ruth (Burgess) Warfield, who was born at "Sugar Grove," February 13, 1797, and died in Lexington, November 29, 1824; second, Mrs. Harriet B. Blanton, of "Blantonia." Issue, first wife, three children, of whom the eldest was *Elisha Warfield Theobald.*

WARFIELD

CAPTAIN RICHARD WARFIELD, married 1670, Elinor, the daughter of Captain John Browne. (See pp. 82-84).

Their son, *John Warfield,* of Warfield's Plains, South River, Md., who died, 1718, married, 1696, Ruth, the eldest daughter of John and Ruth (Morley) Gaither, and the granddaughter of Joseph Morley.[4]

Their son, *Benjamin Warfield,* of Warfield's Range, married *Rebecca,* the daughter of Judge Nicholas and Sarah (Worthington) Ridgely.

ELISHA WARFIELD, fourth son, a member of the Committee of Observation of Anne Arundel County, Md. during the Revolutionary War, removed to Kentucky in 1790, and settled at "Sugar Grove," near Lexington. He married second, *Ruth,* the daughter of Captain Joseph and Elizabeth (Dorsey) Burgess; issue, fourteen children. *Nancy Dorsey,* the thirteenth child, married Dr. Samuel Theobald.

[4] *Warfields of Maryland, and Founders of Ann Arundel and Howard Counties (Maryland),* both by Joshua Dorsey Warfield.

RIDGELY-WORTHINGTON

COLONEL HENRY RIDGELY, married, Sarah Warner.

HENRY RIDGELY II, married *Catharine,* the daughter of COLONEL NICHOLAS GREENBERRY.

JUDGE NICHOLAS RIDGELY, married *Sarah Worthington.* (See pp. 252-253, 255-257.)

CAPTAIN JOHN WORTHINGTON, married Sarah Howard.

Sarah Worthington, married JUDGE NICHOLAS RIDGELY.

Rebecca Ridgely, married *Benjamin Warfield.*

ELISHA WARFIELD, married *Ruth Burgess.*

Nancy Dorsey Warfield, married Dr. Samuel Theobald.

BURGESS-DORSEY

The ancestry of *Ruth Burgess,* who married Elisha Warfield, is as follows:

COLONEL WILLIAM BURGESS, born 1622, died January 24, 1686. His official career is quaintly set forth on his tombstone, which is still in a state of good preservation.

" He was a member of His Lordship's Deputy Governors; a Justice of ye High Provincial Court; Colon of a regiment of Trained Bands; and sometimes General of all ye Military Forces of this Province."

He married first, Elizabeth, the daughter of Edward Robins.

CAPTAIN EDWARD BURGESS, married *Sarah,* the daughter of COLONEL SAMUEL CHEW, and his wife Anne Ayres, and the granddaughter of JOHN CHEW, the colonist. (See pp. 248-249.)

John Burgess married second 1733, Matilda Sparrow.

CAPTAIN JOSEPH BURGESS, Commander of a company of Elkridge Militia 1776, married *Elizabeth,* the daughter of Michael and Ruth (Todd) Dorsey. Six of their sons were in the Revolution. (See p. 248 for Burgess).

The colonist, Edward Dorsey, settled in Anne Arundel County, Md., in 1650.

COLONEL EDWARD DORSEY (See p. 568), married Sarah, the daughter of Nicholas Wyatt (who came from the neighborhood of Sewall's Point, Va., settled upon the Severn River in Maryland, and died 1673).

John Dorsey, married Honor Elder.

Michael Dorsey, married Ruth Todd.

Elizabeth Dorsey, married CAPTAIN JOSEPH BURGESS.

Ruth Burgess married ELISHA WARFIELD.

Nancy Dorsey Warfield married *Dr. Samuel Theobald.*

THEOBALD *(Continued)*

The eldest child of Samuel and Nancy Dorsey (Warfield) Theobald, *Dr. Elisha Warfield Theobald,* was born at Georgetown, Ky., July 11, 1818, and died at "Blantonia," Miss., March 24, 1851. After graduating in medicine at Transylvania University, he removed to Baltimore, Md. He married, June 7, 1842, *Sarah Frances,* the eldest child of Dr. Nathan Ryno and Julietta Octavia (Penniman) Smith; she was born in Burlington, Vt., May 10, 1822, and died in Baltimore, February 5, 1872. Dr. Theobald practiced his profession in Baltimore until a short time before his death. Issue, five children, of whom the third was *Samuel Theobald III.*

SMITH

The colonist, Henry Smith, of Harghan Hall, near Hingham, Norfolk County, Eng., married Judith Cooper. With their five children they sailed from Ipswich, Eng., in the "good ship *Diligent*," April 26, and landed at Boston, August 10, 1638. The only person on board the *Diligent*, dignified by the title of "Mr.," Henry Smith, brought with him three men and two maid servants and one Thomas Mayer (in what capacity is not stated). Settling at Hingham, Mass., he was one of the first deacons of the church, and Deputy in the Plymouth Council 1641. Removing to Rehoboth, Mass., he died there November 3, 1649. Issue, among others, John, HENRY, and Daniel.[5]

The eldest son, Lieutenant John Smith, commanded the Hingham Fort during King Philip's War, and represented the town in the Plymouth Court for many years. He married Sarah Woodward. His younger brother, Daniel, was magistrate of Rehoboth, and represented that place in the Plymouth Court from 1679 to 1692; also Deputy Governor in 1684, 1690, and 1691, dying April 28, 1692. His wife was Esther Chickering. A brother of these men:

ENSIGN HENRY SMITH, born in England, was one of the original surveyors of the Rehoboth, Attleboro and Taunton purchases from the Indians, and represented Rehoboth in the Plymouth Court. He married Elizabeth Cooper, of Hingham, Eng., who came to America with her parents on the ship *Diligent*.

Their son, *Deacon Henry Smith,* was born Decem-

5 Savage's *Geneal. Hist. of N. E.*
Smith *Family Bible.*
Smith Family of Hingham, Mass., pub. 1889.
Research in Court, Church and Town Records, by Caroll F. Smith.

ber 4, 1673, and died September 4, 1735, married Rebecca Wood (or Atwood).

Their son, *John Smith*, born at Rehoboth April 16, 1717, married second, Elizabeth Hills, a widow, née Ide. They removed to Chester, Windsor County, Vt., where they died.

Their fourth child, *Dr. Nathan Smith*, born at Rehoboth September 30, 1762, and died January 26, 1829, removed with his parents to Vermont in boyhood. Near the close of the Revolutionary War, while not yet arrived at manhood, he joined a body of Vermont Militia stationed on the frontier, to hold in check the hostile Indians, and narrowly escaped being shot by an Indian lying in ambush. When he was about twenty-one years of age, he assisted Dr. Josiah Goodhue, residing in Putney, Vt., to tie an artery at a surgical operation. His deftness elicited commendation from the surgeon, and was the cause of his determination to become a physician. After a year of preparation, he became the pupil of Dr. Goodhue, later attending the Medical School of Harvard University, receiving his degree of M. B. in 1790. Later, in December, 1796, he went abroad to Glasgow, Edinburgh and London. He was elected corresponding Member of the London Medical Society, and shortly after his return to America, the degree of M. D. was conferred upon him by Dartmouth College, where he originated the Medical School in 1797. He was of the first Medical Faculty of Yale, and in 1820 the organizer of the Medical Department of Bowdoin College.

After accepting the professorship of Medicine and Surgery in the newly organized Medical Department of Yale in 1813, Dr. Smith, who had lived in Hanover, N. H., made his home in New Haven, Conn. Here he

HOME OF GEN. JONATHAN CHASE
Cornish, N. H.

DR. JABEZ PENNIMAN
Reproduced from a miniature

"F. B. AE. 23"
Frances Montesque's first
"redcoat" sweetheart

FRANCES MONTESQUE
Aged about nine
Reproduced from a painting by Copley

labored as teacher and practitioner for sixteen years, until his death.

He married first, Elizabeth, the daughter of General Jonathan and Thankful (Sherman) Chase, no issue; second, *Sarah Hall,* daughter of General Jonathan and his second wife Sarah (Hall) Chase. Issue four sons and five daughters.

Their second son, *Dr. Nathan Ryno Smith,* born at Cornish, N. H., May 21, 1797, ånd died at Baltimore, Md., July 3, 1877; was graduated from Yale 1817, and received the degree of M. D. from the same institution 1823. He began to practice in Burlington, Vt. where, in coöperation with his father, he founded the Medical School of the University of Vermont, in which he held the professorship of surgery and anatomy. For two years, 1825 to 1827, he was professor of anatomy in Jefferson Medical College, Philadelphia, which position he relinquished in 1827, to accept the professorship of surgery in the University of Maryland. Becoming a resident of Baltimore, his fame was soon established; the degree of LL.D. was given him by Princeton in 1862. He published several medical works, one a translation from the French. July 26, 1821, he married, at Colchester, Vt., Julietta Octavia, the daughter of Dr. Jabez Penniman, and his wife, Frances (Montesque) Allen; she was born in Burlington, Vt. July 10, 1798; died in Baltimore, Md. April 12, 1883. Issue, nine children; the eldest, *Sarah Frances,* married *Dr. Elisha Warfield Theobald.*

The parents of Jabez Penniman were Jesse and Lois (Wood) Penniman. His supposed descent from James Penniman, the colonist, who married Lydia, the sister of the Rev. John Eliot, Apostle to the Indians, has not been exactly traced. His wife Frances, the daughter of Colonel Monte and Margaret (Schoolcraft) Montesque, had an interesting career, as did her mother, the daughter of Jacobus and Anna Christina (Kemmer) Schoolcraft,[6] of Schoharie, descended from Johann Schoolcraft. Margaret Schoolcraft married at the early age of seventeen, April 6, 1750, Colonel Montesque, an officer of the British army, killed in a battle with the French and Indians. She married second, Crean Brush, a strong loyalist, whom the colonists styled "a virulent tory," who procured the passage of a bill offering a reward of £100 for the apprehension of Ethan Allen, the second husband of Crean Brush's step-daughter, Frances Montesque.[7]

The exact date of Fanny Montesque's first marriage to Captain Buchanan of the British army, is not known. She had been engaged to another British officer, who is known to her great-grandchildren only by the inscription "F.B. AE.23," on the back of his miniature, which she wore many years, and never permitted out of her possession. He was drowned while attempting to cross the Hudson in a small boat during a storm, to pay his court to her. Her husband, Captain Buchanan, was killed within twelve months of their marriage. Thus her early love affairs ended tragically. At twenty-three, with her mother (who had married a third time, Patrick Wall), she went to live in Westminister, Vt., where she met General Ethan Allen, who at first made little progress in his suit, but they were finally married in 1784, and had three children.

October 28, 1792, nearly four years after the death of General Allen, she married Dr. Jabez Penniman,

[6] *Church Records* at Schoharie, N. Y.
[7] See biographical sketch of Crean Brush and an account of Frances Montesque in Hall's *History of Eastern Vermont,* p. 603, et seq.

JUDGE SAMUEL CHASE
Reproduced from a painting by Gilbert Stuart

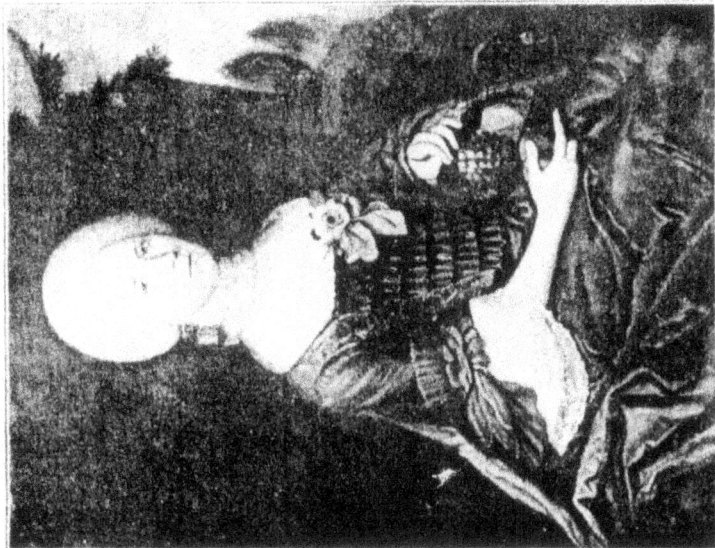

MARGARET SCHOOLCRAFT
Wife of Crean Bush
Reproduced from a painting by Copley

a physician of Colchester, Vt., born September 28, 1764.[8]

Their second daughter, Julietta Octavia, married *Dr. Nathan Ryno Smith.*

CHASE

In the Parish of Chesham, Eng., is recorded the baptism of Thomas Chase, whose son Richard, baptized August 3, 1542, married, 1564, Joan Bishop. Their son Aquila Chase, baptized August 14, 1580, married Sarah ——.

The colonist, Aquila Chase II,[9] baptized in Chesham, 1618, married Anne, the daughter of John Wheeler. He was afterwards of Hampton and Newbury, in New England.

Their son, Moses, Chase, born December 24, 1663, served as Ensign in the Essex, Mass., Regiment. He married Anne Follansbee, in 1684.

Their son, Daniel Chase, born September 20, 1685, married Sarah, the daughter of George March, January 2, 1707.

The eldest of their ten children, Judge Samuel Chase, born in Sutton, Mass., September 28, 1707, died in Cornish, N. H., August 12, 1800. He was Judge of " ye Court of ye County, N. H." When seventy years of age he served in the regiment of his son, Colonel (afterwards General) Chase, at Bennington and Saratoga. At Cornish, he married Mary, the daughter of Samuel Dudley.

GENERAL JONATHAN CHASE, third son, born in Sutton, Mass. December 6, 1732, was an early settler of

[8] Penniman *Family Records.*   Savage's *Dict. N. E. Geneal.*
[9] *A Genealogical Memoir of the Chase family of Chesham, Bucks, Eng., and of Hampton and Newbury in New England,* by George B. Chase.

Cornish, where he died January 14, 1800. He commanded a regiment in the Revolutionary War, and took part in the battles of Bennington and Saratoga, being present at the surrender of Burgoyne. He married second, at Hollis, N. H., October 22, 1770, *Sarah,* the daughter of Rev. David and Elizabeth (Prescott) Hall, who was born December 15 or 17, 1742, and died October 13, 1806. *Sarah Hall,* fifth child, was the second wife of *Dr. Nathan Smith,* and mother of *Dr. Nathan Ryno Smith.*

DUDLEY

The colonist, Francis Dudley, born in England 1640, settled in Concord, Mass., where he married Sarah, the daughter of George Wheeler, of Concord; she died December 12, 1713.

Their third child, Samuel Dudley, was born in Concord, 1682, and died in Douglass, Mass., 1777, where he was first Selectman 1746 and 1747, and a Magistrate. At one time he lived in Sutton, Mass.; it has been inferred that this town was named in compliment to him, it being the earlier name of the Dudleys of Dudley Castle, Eng. He married first, November 1, 1704, Abigail King, who died 1720. Their youngest child Mary, married Judge Samuel Chase.[10]

HALL

In 1630, John Hall, of Coventry, Eng., came to America, and settled in Charlestown, Mass., removing to Barnstable 1640. He went to Yarmouth 1653, where was Selectman 1685, dying July 23, 1696. He married, second, Bethia ———.[11]

---

[10] *History of the Dudley Family,* by Dean Dudley.
[11] *Family Records;* Savage's *Geneal. Dict. of N. E.*

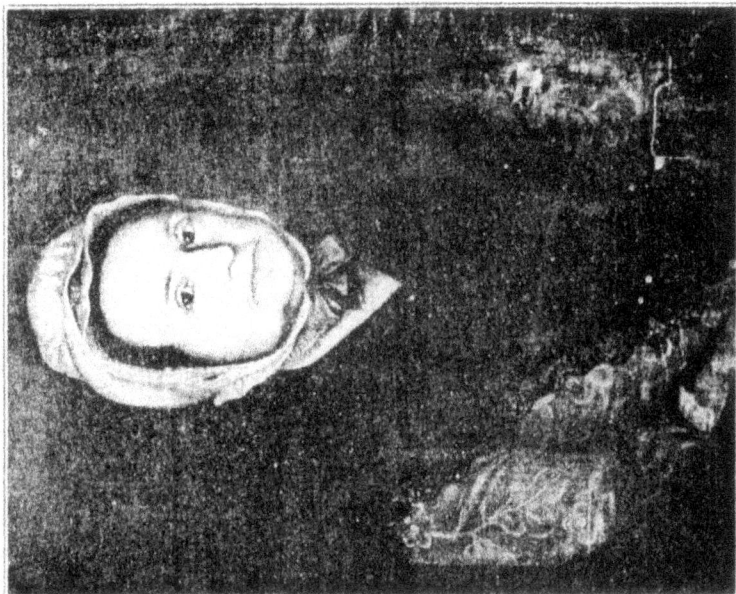

ELIZABETH PRESCOTT
Wife of Rev. David Hall, D.D.

REV. DAVID HALL, D.D.

His son, John Hall II, a deacon of Yarmouth, was born in Charlestown 1637, and died October 14, 1710. He married Priscilla, the daughter of Austin (or Augustine) Bearse, of Barnstable, who came to America from Southampton, Eng., 1638; she was born March 10, 1643, and died March 30, 1710.

JOSEPH HALL, their son, a deacon of Yarmouth, and one of the Selectmen for many years, was born September 29, 1663, and died January 27, 1737. He married first, February 12, 1690, Hannah, the daughter of Rev. John and Margaret (Winslow) Miller.

Their son, *Rev. David Hall,* was born in Yarmouth, August 6, 1704, and died in Sutton, Mass., May 8, 1789. Graduating from Harvard College 1724, and ordained pastor of Sutton October 15, 1729, he held this position until his death. Dartmouth College gave him the honorary degree of D.D. 1777. He was an intimate friend of Dr. Jonathan Edwards, and one of the candidates for the Presidency of Princeton College, when Jonathan Edwards was elected to that office. He married, June 24, 1731, *Elizabeth,* the daughter of Dr. Jonathan and Rebecca (Bulkeley) Prescott, born December 2, 1713, and died August 7, 1803. Their daughter *Sarah,* married GENERAL JONATHAN CHASE.

PRESCOTT

From the ancient Prescotts of Standish, Lancashire, Eng., was descended James Prescott of that place, one of the gentlemen required by order of Queen Elizabeth (1564) to keep in readiness horsemen and armor.

His son, Roger Prescott, of Shevington, Lancashire, married second, August 20, 1568, Ellen Shaw, of Standish.

Their son, Ralph Prescott, baptized 1571, was a resident of Shevington, will proved January 24, 1609. He married Ellen ——.

Their son, John Prescott, of Sowerby, Yorkshire, Eng., landed in Boston 1640, and settled in Watertown, Mass. He married, January 21, 1629, Mary Platts.

CAPTAIN JONATHAN PRESCOTT, their son who died December 5, 1721, removed to Concord, Mass., which he represented in the General Court nine years, and was a Captain of Militia. He married second, December 23, 1675, Elizabeth, the daughter of John Hoar, Esq., an Attorney of Concord; she died September 25, 1687. (He married third, Rebecca Wheeler, the widow of Colonel Peter Bulkeley.)[12]

Their son, *Doctor* and *Major Jonathan Prescott,* born in Concord, April 5, 1677, resided there for many years, practising medicine, and dying, October 28, 1729. The inscription on his gravestone in the Concord cemetery, in a good state of preservation, relates that he was "A gentleman of virtue and merit, an accomplished physician, but excelling in chirurgery." He married, July 9, 1701, *Rebecca,* the only daughter of Colonel Peter and Rebecca (Wheeler) Bulkeley, who was born April 5, 1677, and died October 28, 1729. Their daughter, *Elizabeth,* married *Rev. David Hall,* whose daughter *Sarah,* married GENERAL JONATHAN CHASE.

BULKELEY

The English descent of the Rev. Peter Bulkeley, the founder of Concord, Mass.,[13] is as follows:

[12] Prescott *Memorial,* Part I.
[13] *The Bulkeley Family, or the descendants of Rev. Peter Bulkeley,* by Rev. F. W. Chapman.
   Genealogical Advertiser, Dec., 1898.
   Savage's *Geneal. Dict. of N. E.*

Robert, Lord of the Manor of Bulkeley, in the County Palatine of Cheshire, Eng., one of the barons who, until they attained their end, made life uncomfortable for King John, (who died 1216).

William de Bulkeley.

Robert de Bulkeley II, married a daughter of —— Butler, of Jerosy, Warrington.

William de Bulkeley II, (1302), married Maud, the daughter of Sir John Davenport.

Robert de Bulkeley III, of Eaton, Devonshire, married Agnes ——.

Peter (or Robert IV) de Bulkeley, of Houghton, married Viola, the daughter and heiress of Thomas Bird of Alfraham.

John de Bulkeley, of Houghton, married Ardune, the daughter and heiress of John Filtney, of Woove.

Hugh de Bulkeley, of Woove, married Helen, the daughter of Thomas Wilbraham, of Woove; he died 1450.

Humphrey de Bulkeley, of Woove, married Grissell, the daughter and heiress of John Molton, of Molton.

William de Bulkeley III, of Oakley, married Beatrice, the daughter of William Hill, of Bemsingstall.

Thomas de Bulkeley, of Woove, married Elizabeth, the daughter of Randall Grovenor, of Bellaporte.

Rev. Edward de Bulkeley, D.D. rector of Odell, Eng., married Olyff Irby, of Lincolnshire. Their son:

Rev. Peter Bulkeley, B.D., was born in Bedfordshire, Eng., January 31, 1582 (or 3), and died in Concord, Mass., (of which town he was the founder) March 9, 1659. A distinguished non-conformist minister, he had preached twenty-one years in England, before coming to America, in 1635. His first wife Jane, " a most virtuous gentlewoman," the daughter of Thomas

Allen, of Goldington, Eng., had nine sons and two daughters among them Edward II; his second wife, Grace, the daughter of Sir Richard Chitwood, had four children.

The eldest child, *Rev. Edward Bulkeley II,* born in England 1614, succeeded his father as pastor of the church in Concord, Mass. No record has been found of the date of his marriage or of his wife's name. He died January 4, 1696, at Chelmsford, Eng., but was buried at Concord.

Colonel Peter Bulkeley, M.A., eldest son, was born in Concord, Mass., January 3, 1640, O.S., and died there May 24, 1688. Graduating at Harvard College 1660, he took a second degree, and was chosen a Fellow 1663. He served four years as Deputy for Concord in the General Court, and held the office of Speaker 1676. In September of that year, he was sent to England with William Stoughton, to treat with King Charles II concerning certain charges which had been preferred in England as to the "great independence of the colony in making laws," etc. Appointed Major of the "former regiment of Middlesex" in 1680, and elected to the office of the "First Commissioner in Reserve" 1684, he was appointed by Governor Andros March 3, 1687, one of the Associate Justices of the newly established High Court. Though only forty-seven years old at this time, he appears to have been in poor health and not equal to the duties which his new office imposed, if we can credit the statements of Randolph, who, in writing to England, January, 1688, just before Colonel Bulkeley's death, as to the necessity of sending Judges from that country to Massachussetts, says: "As for Mr. Bulkeley, he is stupefied and drown in melancholy, and almost useless, being seldom with us."

He married, April 16, 1667, Rebecca, the daughter of Lieut. Joseph and Sarah Wheeler (afterwards the third wife of Captain Jonathan Prescott). An only daughter, *Rebecca,* married *Dr. Jonathan Prescott,* whose granddaughter, *Sarah Hall,* married GENERAL JONATHAN CHASE.

THEOBALD *(Continued)*

The eldest son of Elisha Warfield and Sarah Frances (Smith) Theobald, *Samuel Theobald III,* was born in Baltimore, Md., November 12, 1846.   He married, April 30, 1867, CAROLINE DEXTER DEWOLF, born near Bristol, R. I. December 17, 1848, the only child of Francis Le Baron and Caroline Martin (Dexter) DeWolf. (See pp. 701-703 for De Wolf, Dexter, Martin, Colman, Warren, and Bradford). Their second child, CAROLINE DEWOLF, born in Baltimore, May 18, 1870, married Robert Goodloe Harper Pennington, in that city, October 31, 1888.

CAROLINE DEWOLF THEOBALD PENNINGTON,
and her daughter,
CHARLOTTE EMILY PENNINGTON,
Members of Chapter I., The Colonial Dames of America.

XXXV
PITTS

While on a visit to Baltimore, William Pitts of England, stayed over night in a Baltimore County hotel, and in a dream was greatly enamoured of a beautiful " French lady." At breakfast, next morning, seated opposite him at table, was the lady of his dream. He was introduced, and subsequently married her, but history does not give her name.[1]

His son, Thomas Pitts, married Susannah Lusby, and removed to Frederick County, Md.

Their son, Rev. John Pitts (1772-1821), married 1804, *Elizabeth,* the daughter of Nicholas and Anne (Griffith) Hall. He belonged originally to the Church of England, but falling under the influence of the Methodist Church, became a " preacher."

Their son, *Charles Hall Pitts* (1814-1864), is remembered as one of the "gifted lawyers" of Baltimore. He married, June 25, 1844, Elizabeth Reynolds (1825-1855).

Their son, *Charles Hall Pitts II* (1845-1887), married, 1870, Mary Bacôt (1851-1881), the daughter of Samuel J. Person (1823-1869), of Carthage, N. C., and *Mary Bacôt London,* his wife. Their daughter, ALICE DICKINSON, married James Piper.

HALL

CAPTAIN NICHOLAS HALL, was of New Market, Md., his commission as Captain in the Maryland Militia being dated June 10, 1778.[2] He married, 1775, Anne, the

---

[1] Warfield's *Hist. of Anne Arundel County, Md.,* p. 142.
[2] *Archs. of Md.,* Vol XXI, p. 128.

SAMUEL JONES PERSON

MARY BACOT LONDON
Wife of Samuel J. Person

SARAH ELIZABETH LORD
Wife of John Rutherford London

CHARLES HALL PITTS

daughter of Hon. Henry and Ruth (Hammond) Griffith. Their daughter, *Elizabeth,* married Rev. John Pitts.

GRIFFITH

The history of the Griffiths of Wales, forms an exciting review of the feudal splendor of Griffith, Prince of Wales. Their descendants in Maryland fought as valiantly for independence as did their fathers in Wales.

The emigrant, William Griffith, married Sarah, the daughter of John Maccubin, who came from the Lowlands, and claimed descent from the McAlpines of the Highlands, who go back to Kenneth II, first King of Scotland, and Ellinor (Carroll?), his wife.

Their son, Orlando Griffith, married 1717, *Katharine,* the daughter of John and Katharine (Greenbury) Ridgely Howard.

HON. HENRY GRIFFITH, their son, who died 1794, was in the Colonial Assembly from Frederick County, Md., also one of the Committee of Observation, 1777.[3] He married, second, *Ruth,* the daughter of John and Anne (Dorsey) Hammond, whose daughter, *Anne,* married CAPTAIN NICHOLAS HALL.

HAMMOND-DORSEY

MAJOR-GENERAL JOHN HAMMOND, married Mary, the daughter of John Howard, Sr., and the granddaughter of Matthew Howard, the emigrant.[4]

MAJOR CHARLES HAMMOND, their son, married his cousin, *Hannah,* the daughter of Philip and Ruth (Baldwin) Howard.[5]

Their son, *John Hammond,* married *Anne,* the daugh-

---

3 Warfield's *Hist. of Anne Arundel County, Md.,* p. 348.
4 *Year Book Col. Wars.*
5 Warfield's *Hist. of Anne Arundel County, Md.,* p. 222.

ter of COLONEL EDWARD DORSEY and his second wife,
Margaret Larkins.

Their daughter, *Ruth Hammond,* married HON.
HENRY GRIFFITH. (See pp. 250-252 for Hammond
and Dorsey lines.)

HOWARD

Five brothers, Matthew, Cornelius, Samuel, John and
PHILIP, emigrated from England and settled on the
Severn River, Maryland, in 1658.

The elder of these brothers, Matthew Howard (1635-
1694), was the ancestor of the following line:

John Howard I, married Susannah Stevens, whose
daughter, Mary, married JOHN HAMMOND I.

John Howard II, married *Katharine,* the daughter
of COLONEL NICHOLAS GREENBERRY, and the widow of
Henry Ridgely II.

Their daughter, *Katharine Howard,* married Orlando
Griffith, whose son, COLONEL HENRY GRIFFITH, married *Ruth Hammond.*

CAPTAIN PHILIP HOWARD, the youngest of these five
emigrant brothers, died 1701. He was "one of his Majesty's Justices" 1694, and one of the Commissioners to
lay out Annapolis, Md. He married Ruth, the daughter of John Baldwin, of Anne Arundel County, Md.

Their daughter, *Hannah,* married MAJOR CHARLES
HAMMOND, whose son *John* married *Anne,* the daugh-
ter of COLONEL EDWARD DORSEY,[6] and their daughter
Ruth married HON. HENRY GRIFFITH.

LONDON

ARMS: *Argent, three cross crosslets between two bendlets gules.*

In 1664, Sir Robert London was knighted by King

[6] *Archs* of Md.

Md. Society of Colonial Dames.

Charles II, for services to Charles I. His grandson, John London, who died 1764, married, 1740, Mary Walliston, who died 1779.

JOHN LONDON, their son, of Al-bye, Norfolk County, Eng., born 1747, and died 1816, came to North Carolina about 1767, becoming Private Secretary to Governor William Tryon 1769, Secretary to the Province, and Clerk of the Crown for New Hanover County, N. C., 1770.[7] He married, 1785, Peggy (Marsden) Chivers.

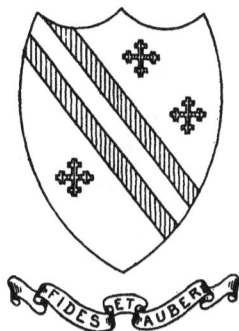

LONDON

Their son, *John Rutherford London* (1786-1832), married, 1813, *Sarah Elizabeth,* the daughter of John Quince and Elizabeth S. (Bradley) Lord, whose daughter, *Mary Bacôt,* married Samuel J. Person.

LORD

The original emigrants of this family came to Dorchester, Mass., about 1630, one of whom, Thomas Lord, born in England, settled in Newtown (later Cambridge), and in 1636 is named as " one of the original proprietors and settlers of Hartford, Conn." His wife was Dorothy ⁓⁓(1589-1676).

The Lords of North Carolina are undoubtedly a branch of the New England family. They came to North Carolina " by way of South Carolina," and it is believed that they formed a part of the Dorchester Colony from Massachusetts, that settled in South Carolina 1696. Their pastor was the Rev. Joseph Lord, whose death was recorded on a simple monumental stone still

---

[7] *Col. Recs. of N. C.,* Vol. VIII, pp. 85, 142, 254.

in existence near Summerfield in that state. In 1752, these colonists moved in a body to Georgia, and the South Carolina records say that " some of them went into North Carolina."

It was at an earlier date than this, however, October 19, 1739, that William Lord, of North Carolina, the first of whom we have authentic knowledge, settled on Cape Fear River, and was a large planter in Brunswick County,[8] where he died 1748. He married, about 1728, Margaret, the daughter of James and Margaret Espey.

COLONEL WILLIAM LORD II (1732-1780), their son, was also a large planter in Brunswick County, he and his father residing there until the beginning of the Revolutionary War, when they removed to Wilmington for greater security and protection. The town of Brunswick was abandoned, and now only the ruins of the beautiful church of St. Philip and its surrounding burial-ground are left to mark the site of the town which had been the home of the Royal Governors, Tryon and Dobbs. " In that churchyard lie the remains of the Lords who dwelt there. Their gravestones still remain, but of the early colonists no memorials exist." William Lord represented Brunswick in the Legislature 1765 to 1777; was High Sheriff 1771; on the Committee of Safety June 20, 1775; on the Provincial Council at Halifax, which framed the State Constitution, April, 1775, and Lieutenant-Colonel of the North Carolina Regiment, June, 1776.[9] He married, July 13, 1758, his cousin, Sarah Espey.

Their son, *John Quince Lord,* married, 1792, Elizabeth S., the daughter of Richard and Elizabeth (Shar-

[8] *Family Records; New Hanover County Records,* Vol. A. B., p. 283.
[9] *Col. Recs. of North Carolina,* Vol. IX, p. 574, Vol. Xa, p. 622, etc.

ples) Bradley, and their daughter, *Sarah Elizabeth,* married *John Rutherford London.*

SHARPLES

Among the treasured family heirlooms, is a quaint old silver "' tankard," marked " J. S. J." (being the initials of John and Jane Sharples), with the coat of arms, consisting of a shield and three stags stalking a cup.[10]

The colonist, John Sharples (1621-1685), was the son of Jeffrey Sharples and his wife Margaret Ashley, of Winbunbury, Chester County, England. He emigrated in 1682, just two months before William Penn, and settled on Ridley Creek, near Chester, Pa., with his wife and seven children.

" They purchased from William Penn one thousand acres of land, and having felled a large tree, took shelter among the boughs thereof for about six weeks, in which time they built a cabin against a rock that answered for their chimney back, and also contained the date of the year (1682) when the cabin was built. Here the family lived twenty years. The original grant is still preserved, bearing the autograph and seal of the illustrious Penn."

Elected to the first Pennsylvania Assembly, John Sharples declined the office, being a Quaker. In 1882, his descendants celebrated the two hundredth anniversary of his arrival in Chester, Pa. They came from nearly every state in the Union and numbered three thousand eight hundred. He married, 1662, Jane Moore.

---

10 *Family Recs.*

Sharples Hist., comp. by Gilbert Cope, of North Chester, Pa.

Their son, John Sharples II, married, 1696, Hannah Pennell.

Their son, John Sharples III, married Elizabeth Ashbridge, whose daughter Elizabeth married, 1755, Richard Bradley.

Their daughter, Elizabeth S. Bradley, married *John Quince Lord,* whose daughter, *Sarah Elizabeth,* married *John Rutherford London.*

Their daughter, *Mary Bacôt London,* married Samuel J. Person, whose daughter, *Mary Bacôt,* married *Charles Hall Pitts II.*

Their daughter is:

ALICE DICKINSON PITTS PIPER,

Member of Chapter I., The Colonial Dames of America.

XXXVI
DU BOIS

ARMS: *Argent, a lion rampant, sable, armed and langued gules.*
CREST: *Between two tree stumps, vert, the lion of the shield.*
MOTTO: *Tiens ta foy.*

Another coat of arms entitled "Original Du Bois Arms"[2] is described as "Armes d'or, â l'aigle éployé de sable onglé, becqué de gueules."

The name Du Bois is one of the oldest in France, and exists also in Flanders and England. Père Anseline and Dufourney in their great work, *"Maison Royale de France,"* speak of the family Du Bois as the "Grand Masters of the Forests of France." Some authors trace the name to Neustria, a part of France afterwards known as Normandy, where it existed before Rollo invaded that province, and became the first Duke of Normandy. As regards the orthography of this ancient name,—it is universally admitted in France that the prefix de, de la or du is a badge of noble extraction and the name is seldom found in books of Heraldry written otherwise than with a small d and a capital B.

The progenitors of this line in New Netherlands, Louis and Jacques, sons of Chretien du Bois, wrote their name in this manner. Louis du Bois, born at Wicres, near Lille in Artois, France, 1626, migrated to Man-

DU BOIS

---

[1] *America Heraldica.*

[2] *Du Bois Reunion,* pp. 41, 44, 97, and *Records* in possession of the family.

heim in the Palatinate of the Rhine, Germany, to escape religious persecution. He married, October 10, 1655, Catherine Blanshan or Blanjean. They emigrated to America 1660, with their two sons, Abraham and Isaac. Louis du Bois died 1696, and his wife Catherine survived him several years. The line of descent after Chretien and Louis du Bois is as follows:

Abraham, 1657-1731; married March 6, 1681, Margaret Doios.

Abraham II, died 1758; married October 12, 1717, Marie la Siliere.

Abraham III, died 1792; married October 28, 1747, in Somerset County, N. J., Jannettie Van Dike.

Abraham IV, died 1807; married May 2, 1776 (first wife), Elizabeth Cheesman.

Nicholas died 1819; married May 12, 1808, Agnes McKim, who died 1856.

Edmund James, 1815-1862; married, October 19, 1848, *Mary Ladson Chiffelle.*

CHARLOTTE EMILY DuBois married George Harris Sargeant.

McKIM

The McKims of Maryland descend from John McKim, born in Londonderry, Ireland, 1670.

THOMAS McKIM, the immigrant (1710-1784), a son of John by a second marriage, settled in Philadelphia, October 3, 1734, and was Justice of New Castle County Court, 1774.[3]   His wife was Agnes McMorry, a widow, whom he married April 3, 1739.

ALEXANDER McKIM (1748-1832), their son, Delegate to the Maryland Assembly 1778, one of the Baltimore Town Council 1797, and Commissioner 1805, was

[3] Scharf's *Hist. of Baltimore and Maryland*, p. 475, and Atkins' *Gen. Am. Reg. and Cal.*

elected to Congress, February 8, 1814. When General Lafayette visited Baltimore after the Revolutionary War, "The Mayor introduced him to Alexander Mc-Kim, William Patterson, Samuel Hollingsworth and Nathaniel Levy as a small remnant of that gallant, and patriotic troop, the First Baltimore Cavalry, who voluntarily repaired to the standard of La Fayette on his call upon Maryland for soldiers, and fought under him in Virginia during the campaign of 1781." [4]   Alexander McKim married July 20, 1785, Catherine Sarah Davy, and their daughter *Agnes* married Nicholas du Bois.

CHIFFELLE

The colonist, Henry Francis Chiffelle (1704-1758), born in Switzerland, came from England to Charleston, S. C., 1734. Before his departure, he was ordained a minister of the Church of England by the Bishop of London. The first rector of the newly settled parish of St. Peter's, Purysborough, he officiated there until his death.[5] He married in this province, Marguaritte, the daughter of Abraham Erhardt, a native of Switzerland.

PHILOTHEOS CHIFFELLE (1753-1794), their son, was a Delegate to the Provincial Congress from Purysborough, S. C., 1775.[6] He married *Rebecca,* the daughter of Thomas and Rebecca (Holman) Hutchinson.

Their son, *Thomas Philotheos Chiffelle,* married *Henrietta Columbia,* the daughter of James and Judith (Smith) Ladson, whose daughter, *Mary Ladson Chiffelle,* married Edmund James du Bois.

---

4 Scharf's *Chronicles of Baltimore,* pp. 276, 296, 414.
5 *Bible* of the Chiffelle family.
6 *Recs. of South Carolina,* Vol. XXVI, p. 123.

HUTCHINSON

Some of the descendants of John Hutchinson, the colonist, are as follows:

JOHN HUTCHINSON II, married Anne Holland.

COLONEL THOMAS HUTCHINSON, married *Rebecca,* the daughter of William and Ruth Holman, and the granddaughter of THOMAS HOLMAN.

Rebecca Hutchinson, married *Philotheos Chiffelle.* (See pp. 394-396 for Hutchinson and Holman.)

LADSON

JOHN LADSON, the colonist of 1679,[7] married *Mary,* the daughter of COLONEL JAMES STANYARNE, whose son, *William Ladson* (1686-1739), married Martha Elams.[8]

CAPTAIN THOMAS LADSON, their son, was a Chaplain, also in the South Carolina Assembly of 1721.[9] He married Mary Graves, and their son *William,* who died 1755, married *Anne,* the daughter of COLONEL JOHN GIBBES. She had the following line of descent (see pp. 377, 381-387):

COLONEL JOHN GODFREY.

Mary Godfrey, married DOCTOR HENRY WOODWARD.

COLONEL JOHN WOODWARD, married Elizabeth Stanyarne.

Mary Woodward, married COLONEL JOHN GIBBES.

Anne Gibbes, married William Ladson.

JAMES LADSON, William's son, was a Major in the Continental Army 1775, also Lieutenant-Governor of South Carolina. His original commission on parchment, in the possession of the family, is as follows:

[7] McCready's *Hist. of S. C.,* p. 239.

[8] Ladson *Bible.*

[9] *State Records of S. C.,* Vol. II, p. 117; III, p. 543.

MAJOR JAMES LADSON

JUDITH SMITH
Wife of Maj. James Ladson

NICHOLAS DU BOIS

BENJAMIN SMITH

WILLIAM LADSON

"James Ladson, gentleman, made 1st Lieut. in the
First Regiment and to rank as 2d Lieut. in the Army of
the Provincial Service, June 17th, 1775. He was also
Captain in the Continental Regiment raised by S. C.
for the defence of American Liberty, 1775." [10]

Major Ladson married *Judith,* the daughter of Benjamin and Mary (Wragg) Smith. Their daughter,
Henrietta Columbia, married *Thomas Philotheos Chiffelle.*

WRAGG

JOSEPH WRAGG was one of the Council of South Carolina 1731. He married Judith, the daughter of James
and Marie (Dugué) Dubose, and their daughter *Mary*
married BENJAMIN SMITH, whose daughter, *Judith,*
married MAJOR JAMES LADSON.[11] Benjamin Smith had
the following line of descent:

GOVERNOR THOMAS SMITH I, Landgrave of South
Carolina.

THOMAS SMITH II, the second Landgrave.

Sabina Smith, married THOMAS SMITH III, a son of
William and Elizabeth (Schenking) Smith.

BENJAMIN SMITH, married *Mary Wragg.*

He also had the following line of descent:

Robert Yeamans, of Bristol, Eng.

GOVERNOR SIR JOHN YEAMANS, of South Carolina.

Margaret Yeamans, married GOVERNOR JAMES
MOORE.

Elizabeth Moore, married COLONEL BERNARD SCHEN-
KING.

Elizabeth Schenking, married William Smith.

THOMAS SMITH III, married *Sabina,* the daughter
of THOMAS SMITH II.

10 Family *Records.*
11 Ladson *Papers,* by Ramsey, Vol. I, p. 104.

BENJAMIN SMITH, married *Mary Wragg*. (See pp. 387-392, 398-400.)

DUBOSE

An ancestor, Andrea Dubose, married Marie de Stoade. Their son, James Dubose, married Marie, the daughter of Jacques and Marianne (Fleury) Duguè, whose daughter Judith married JOSEPH WRAGG. Their daughter:

Mary Wragg, married BENJAMIN SMITH.

Judith Smith, married JAMES LADSON.

Henrietta Columbia Ladson married *Thomas Philotheos Chiffelle.*

Mary Ladson Chiffelle, married *Edmund James Dubois,* whose daughter is:

CHARLOTTE EMILY DUBOIS SARGEANT,

Member of Chapter I., The Colonial Dames of America.

XXXVII
FAIRFAX

ARMS: *Argent, three bars gemelles gules, surmounted by a lion rampant sable.*
CREST: *A lion passant guardant sable.*
MOTTO: *Fare fac.*

The Fairfaxes, said to be of Saxon stock, at the time of the Conquest, were seated at Towcester (or Torcester) in Northumberland. The name is of Saxon origin, from two words meaning *fair hair.* The play upon the words in the family motto, "Fare fac," is referred to in several books on Heraldry. The line of descent is as follows: Henry Fairfax; John Fairfax; Richard de Fairfax, in 1204 possessed the manor of Askham in Yorkshire, and other lands.

FAIRFAX

William Fairfax, son and heir, living in 1212-13, married Alice, the daughter and heiress of Nicholas de Bugthorpe.

William, son and heir, High Bailiff of York, 1249, bought the manor of Walton; married Mary, the widow of Walter Flower.

Thomas, son and heir, living 1284, married Anne, the daughter and heiress of Henry de Sezevaux, Mayor of York. Issue, three children, of whom:

John, living 1312, married Clara, the daughter and co-heiress of Roger Brus, of Walton.

Thomas, their son and heir, married Margaret, the daughter of John Malbis. Issue, three children, of whom:

William, married Ellen, the daughter of John Rou-cliffe, of Roucliffe. Issue, five children, of whom:

Thomas, living 1350, married Elizabeth, the daughter of Sir Ivo Etting (or Etton) of Gilling. Issue, five children, of whom:

William, married Constance, the sister and co-heiress of Peter, fourth Baron de Mauley (the present Lord Fairfax is eldest co-heir to this Barony, created in 1295). Issue, three sons, of whom:

Thomas, living between 1385 and 1396, married Margaret, the widow of Sir Robert Roucliffe, Knt., and the sister and heiress of Richard Friston of Marston. Issue, six children, of whom:

Richard, living between 1400 and 1430, married Eustace, the daughter and heiress of John Carthorp by his wife Elisabeth, the daughter and co-heiress of William Ergham.[1] Issue, nine children, of whom:

Sir Guy appointed Judge of the Court of King's Bench, September 29, 1478, built the Castle of Steeton, married Margaret, the daughter of Sir William Rither, of Rither, and died 1495. Issue, six children, of whom:

Sir William, appointed a Judge of the Court of Common Pleas, May 21, 1510, married Elizabeth, the sister of Thomas Manners, first Earl of Rutland, and the granddaughter of Anne, Duchess of Exeter, the sister of Edward IV; died 1514-15. Issue, five children, of whom:

Sir William, High Sheriff of York in the reign of Henry VIII, married 1518, Isabel Thwaites, who brought him the manor of Denton and Askwith in Wharfedale, Bishop Hill, and Davy Hall within the walls of York; he joined the "Pilgrimage of Grace," but appears to have been pardoned for his share in that

[1] Phillips *Mss. Argum.*

THE THIRD LORD FAIRFAX

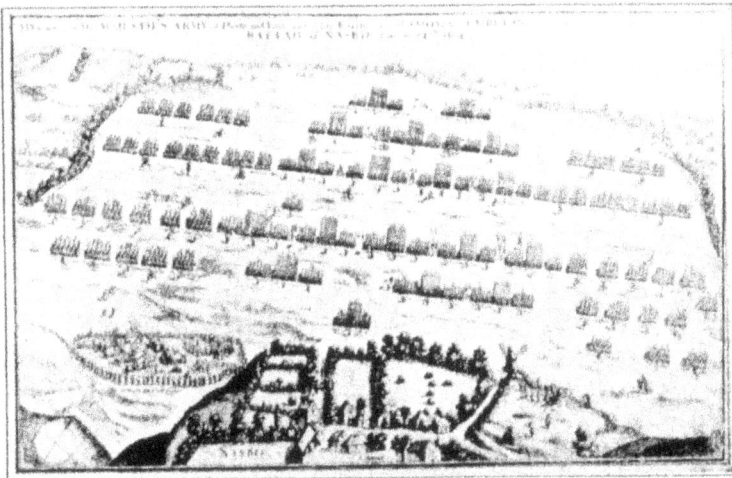

BATTLE OF NASBY, JUNE 14, 1695
In which Sir Thomas Fairfax commanded the Parliamentary forces

outbreak, and died October 31, 1557. Issue, eleven children,[2] of whom:

Thomas, Sheriff of Yorkshire, 1571, knighted by Queen Elizabeth 1576, married Dorothy, the daughter of George Gale, of Askham Grange; died 1599. Issue, three children, of whom:

Thomas, first Baron Fairfax, born 1560, fought in the Low Country Wars, and was knighted by Lord Essex for gallant conduct before Rouen. He served Elizabeth as a diplomatist, was one of the Council of the North under the Presidency of Lord Sheffield, from 1602 to 1619, and was created Baron of Cameron in the peerage of Scotland, October 18, 1627; married, 1582, Ellen, the daughter of Robert Aske of Aughton, and died May 1, 1640. Issue, thirteen children: i. Ferdinando; ii. Henry, a clergyman; iii. William, a soldier in the Low Country Wars, killed at the siege of Frankenthal, 1621; iv. Charles, a lawyer, the antiquary who compiled the pedigree and left a large collection of manuscripts; v. John, killed with his brother William in 1621; vi. Peregrine, Secretary to the Ambassador at Paris, and killed at the siege of Montauban in 1621; vii. Thomas, a merchant adventurer, died at Scandaroon, in the same fatal year; viii. Dorothy, married Sir William Constable; ix. Anne, married Sir Godfrey Wentworth; x. Mary, and three others.

The eldest son, Ferdinando, succeeded his father as second Lord Fairfax; born March 29, 1584; fought on the side of the Parliament in the Civil War; married first in 1607, Lady Mary Sheffield, the daughter of the first Earl of Mulgrave; married second, in September, 1646, Rhoda, the daughter of Mr. Chapman, of Lon-

---

[2] One son was Gabriel, the ancestor of the Fairfaxes of Steeton, still residing at Poilbrough in Yorkshire.

644 ANCESTRAL RECORDS AND PORTRAITS

don, and widow of Thomas Hussey (by whom he had a daughter, Ursula, who married William Cartwright of Aynho, and had issue: i. William; ii. Rhoda, who married Lord Henry Cavendish). Ferdinando, second Lord, died March 14, 1647-48, and left issue by his first wife: i. Thomas, third Baron of Cameron; ii. Charles, a Colonel in the Parliamentary Army, mortally wounded at Marston Moor in 1644, died s. p.; iii. a son, died; iv. Ursula; v. Ellen, born 1610, married Sir William Selby of Twizell; vi. Frances, born 1612, married Thomas Widdrington of York; vii. Elizabeth, born 1614, married Sir William Craven, of Lenchwicke; viii. Mary, born 1616, married Henry Arthington; ix. Dorothy, born 1617, married Edward Hutton, of Poppleton.

The eldest son, Thomas, born January 16, 1611-12, succeeded his father as third Lord Fairfax and was the great Parliamentary General of the Civil War, and largely instrumental in restoring Charles II, who rode into London on a magnificent charger presented to him by Lord Fairfax, from his famous stud at Nunappleton. He is said to have saved the Bodleian Library at Oxford from destruction by the Roundheads.[3] He married, June 20, 1637, Anne, the daughter and co-heiress of Lord Vere, of Tilbury, who died October 16, 1665. He died November 12, 1671, leaving an only daughter, Mary, born July 30, 1638, who married, September 15, 1657, George Villiers, second Duke of Buckingham; she died s. p. October 20, 1704, and the estates of the family were inherited by the heir of line.

The second son of the first Lord Fairfax, Rev. Henry Fairfax, born 1588, was Rector of Ashton-under-Lyne,

[3] For his life, see the *Biography of Sir Clements Markham*, and any writers on the history of the period.

1627; Rector of Newton Kyme and Bolton Percy; inherited Oglethorpe, and died 1665; married Mary, the daughter of Sir Henry Cholmley, and died December 24, 1649. He was buried under the altar of the church at Bolton Percy, where he remained the Rector undisturbed by Cavaliers or Roundheads. Through Mary Cholmley the Fairfax family is descended (through the Percys, Nevilles and Cliffords) from the Plantaganets, the Saxon Kings, the Scottish Kings from Kenneth I, the Dukes of Normandy, Counts of Flanders, and the French kings back to Pepin.[4] Issue: i. Henry; ii. Bryan, born October 6, 1633, married, April 22, 1675, Charlotte, the only daughter and heiress of Sir Edmund Cary, by Anne, sister of the Earl of Macclesfield, who died November 4, 1709; her husband died September 23, 1711. (Bryan Fairfax's issue were: i. Bryan; ii. Ferdinando; iii. Charles, M. A. Christ Church, Oxford, 1712; all died s. p.)

The eldest son, Henry, fourth Baron of Cameron, born at Whitby, December 30, 1631, and died April, 1688, married Frances, the daughter of Sir Robert Barwicke, of Tolston. Issue: i. Thomas; ii. Henry (q. v.); iii. Bryan, Commissioner of Customs, died January 9, 1747-48; iv. Barwicke; v. Dorothy, married first, Robert Stapleton of Wighill; second, Bennctt Sherrard of Whissenden; vi. Frances; vii. Anne; viii. Ursula; ix. Mary.

The eldest son, Thomas, fifth Lord Fairfax, who took an active part in the Revolution of 1688, and the accession of William and Mary to the throne of England, married Catherine, the daughter and heiress of Thomas, Lord Colepepper, of Thoresway, by Margaret, the daughter of Jean de Hesse, by whom he obtained the

4 See *pedigree* compiled by Wilson Miles Cary.

estate of Leeds Castle in Kent, and over five million
acres of land in Virginia.   Lord Fairfax died 1709-10.
Issue: i. Thomas, the sixth Lord Fairfax, born 1690,
obliged to alienate Denton Hall and the Yorkshire
property in order to save Leeds Castle and the Kent
estates, removed to America in 1747, alienated his English estates in favor of his brother Robert, and built
Belvoir and Greenway Court in Virginia.   He is said
to have met with a disappointment in love which pre-
vented his marrying.   He was a contributor to the
Spectator and the friend and patron of Washington.
His death occurred at Greenway Court 1781;   ii.
Henry Colepepper, died October 14, 1734;   iii. Margaret, married Rev. David Wilkins, and died s. p.;   iv.
Frances, born 1703, married Denny Martin, and died
December 13, 1791 (issue: i. Denny, a clergyman; ii.
Philip, a General in the army; each of these brothers
Martin assumed the name of Fairfax, and inherited in
succession the English estates of the family);   v. Robert, born 1706, succeeded as seventh Lord Fairfax, was
a major in the Life Guards, M. P. for Kent in 1754
and 1761; married first, April 25, 1741, Martha, the
daughter and co-heiress of Anthony Collins, of Bad-
dow; she died 1744 (leaving a son who died in 1747);
married second, 1749, a daughter of Thomas Best, of
Chatham, who died s. p. 1750; and Lord Fairfax died
s. p. July 15, 1793, leaving his English estates by will
to his nephew, Rev. Denny Martin.

The second son of the fourth Baron Cameron, Henry
Fairfax, Sheriff of Yorkshire 1691, married Anne, the
daughter and co-heiress of Richard Harrison, and died
1708.   Issue, seven children, of whom:

WILLIAM FAIRFAX, born 1691 at Newton Kyme, was
Virginia agent for his cousin, the sixth Lord Fairfax.

LEEDS CASTLE
The home of the sixth Lord Fairfax
before he came to Virginia

BOLTON PERCY CHURCH

GILLING CASTLE
West side of the Great Chamber

GILLING CASTLE
South and east elevation

He married first, 1723, Sarah, the daughter of Major Walker of the Bahamas; second in Salem, Mass., September 3, 1757, Deborah Clarke. He was Collector of Customs in Salem as well as of the Potomac River; also County Lieutenant and President of the King's Council in Virginia. Issue by first marriage: i. George William, born 1724, married Sarah Cary and died s. p. at Bath, April 3, 1787; ii. Thomas, entered the Navy and was killed on the *Harwich* in a sea fight in the West Indies, under Captain Carteret; iii. Sarah, married Major John Carlyle of Alexandria, and had a daughter who married William Herbert; iv. Anne, born at Salem, Mass., married first, July 19, 1743, Major Lawrence Washington of Mount Vernon, eldest brother of George Washington (issue, four children, who died young); second, Colonel George Lee, before 1756 (issue, three sons). Issue of William Fairfax, by second marriage: v. William Henry, Lieutenant 28th Regiment of Regulars; died s. p. of wounds received in the siege of Quebec 1759; vi. Hannah, married, 1764, Warner Washington; vii. *Bryan.*

The youngest son, *Bryan Fairfax*, eighth Baron Cameron,[5] who was born 1737, married first, Elizabeth, the youngest daughter of Wilson Cary; he was Rector of Christ Church where Washington worshipped in Alexandria, and died at Mount Eagle, Va., 1802. Issue: i. Thomas; ii. Ferdinando; iii. Elizabeth, who married David Griffith. Bryan Fairfax married a second wife, and had issue a daughter Anne, who married Charles Catlett.

The eldest son, *Thomas Fairfax*, ninth Baron of Cameron, was born 1762 and died 1846 at Vaucluse, Va. He married first, Mary Aylett; second, Louisa Wash-

[5] Claim to title recognized by the House of Lords, 1800.

ington; third, Margaret, the daughter of William Herbert. Issue, only by third wife: i. *Albert;* ii. Henry, born May 4, 1804, married 1827 Ann Caroline, daughter of John C. Herbert; iii. Orlando, born 1809, married 1829, Mary R. Cary; iv. Raymond, died 1843; v. Eugenia, married first, Edgar Mason; second, Charles K. Hyde; vi. Ethelbert, died 1827; vii. Aurelia, married 1857, Colonel James W. Irwin; viii. Lavinia, died 1822; ix. Monimia, married November 15, 1828, Archibald, the son of Wilson Jefferson and Virginia (Randolph) Cary (issue: i. Constance, married Burton Harrison, Esq.; ii. Clarence); x. Reginald, died 1862.

The eldest son, *Albert Fairfax,* married, April 8, 1828, Caroline Eliza, the daughter of Richard and Eliza (Warfield) Snowden, and died in the lifetime of his father; his widow married, March 1, 1838, Captain Sanders, but had issue by her first husband only; viz.: i. Charles Snowden Fairfax, tenth Baron of Cameron, born 1829, married, 1855, Ada, the daughter of Joseph S. Benham of Cincinnati, O.; emigrated to California 1851; was Speaker of the House of Delegates 1854; died in Baltimore 1869; his widow died 1888; ii. *John Contee.*

The eleventh Baron of Cameron, *John Contee Fairfax,* was born 1830, and married, 1857, Mary, the daughter of Colonel Edmund Kirby, U. S. A., and died September 28, 1900. Issue: Albert Kirby, twelfth

ᵒ Authorities. *The Fairfax Mss.* from the collection of Sir F. Philips; Sir Clement Markham's *Life of Lord Fairfax;* The Fairfax *Cororrespondence; Arcana Fairfaxiana Manuscripta,* by George Weddell; *Lower Wharfdale,* by H. Speight; *Pedigree,* compiled by Wilson Miles Cary; *The Encyclo. Brittanica,* ninth edition; Family *Papers; Leeds Castle,* by C. Wykeham Martin, M. P., F. S. A.; *The Thomas Book; The Fairfax Pedigree,* by Joseph Foster, M. A. Oxon; *Blazoned Parchment Pedigree of Fairfax,* from Phillips *Collection,* etc.

"NUNAPPLETON,"
For many generations the home of the Fairfax family, Yorkshire, England

HOME OF LORD FAIRFAX
Northampton, Prince George's Co., Va.

Baron of Cameron; ii. Charles Edmund; iii. Caroline; iv. JOSEPHINE, married, 1892, Tunstall Smith; v. Mary Cecilia; vi. Frances Marvin, married, 1903, Lowndes Rhett.[6]

JOSEPHINE FAIRFAX SMITH,
Member of Chapter I., The Colonial Dames of America.

XXXVIII
BIRD

The colonist, William Bird, was born in England 1707, and died November 16, 1762. He came to Berks County, Pa., before 1729, in which year he obtained land along "Hay Creek," in Robinson township. The iron business in this region was first started by him in 1740, by the erection of a forge on Hay Creek near the Schuylkill. In 1750 he laid out a town below the forge, towards the river and called it "Birdsboro." In 1751 he erected, within the limits of the town plan, a fine two-story, cut-stone mansion house. This building is still standing in good condition. For a long time it was a hotel, the "Birdsboro House." It is a notable example of the architecture of that period, and was the gathering place of the most prominent people of the time. Taking up additional tracts of land by means of warrant and survey, William Bird secured three thousand acres, by the year 1756. Three years later he built the furnace in Union township, and a year later the one in lower Heidelburg township. These enterprises were carried on by him until his death, and later, first by his son, Mark Bird, and then until 1794 by his widow, who leased the property, the final results being the large and rich modern iron industry in Birdsboro.

Not only as a business man did William Bird[1] establish lasting activities, but as a churchman he founded and strengthened St. Mary's Church, a mission of the Church of England, the first to be established in 1762 in Reading, and St. Gabriel's Church in Morlatton, now

[1] *Penn. Hist. Mag.,* Vol. viii, p. 56.

RESIDENCE OF WILLIAM BIRD I
Birdsboro, Pa., built 1750

SILVER OWNED BY COL. WILLIAM BIRD
Intricate cyphers on the bottom of each of these pieces indicate initials of
William and Brigitta Bird

Douglassville. He also gave a helping hand to the church, built in 1753, by the Swedish Lutherans, which was afterwards merged into the Episcopal congregation. The *Pennsylvania Gazette,* November 26, 1761, gave the following obituary notice:

"Philadelphia, November 26. Last week departed this Life of a Appoplectic Fit at the Town of Reading in Berks County William Bird Esq. one of His Majesty's Justices of the Peace for that County, a Gentleman who by his Industry, had acquired with great Reputation a very considerable Fortune, and a man of Strict Honor and Integrity. In him only dwelt the Amiable Graces of an Affectionate Husband, a tender loving Parent, a Kind Master and a sincere Friend; loved his country, and was ever pleased to do a Kind Office to any who needed it. He lived in Charity with all Men, was highly esteemed, and his death was sincerely lamented."

The marriage of William Bird to Brigetta, the fourth child of Marcus and Margaret (Jones) Huling, was solemnized by the Rev. Alexander Murray, October 28, 1735. They are buried at St. Gabriel's Church, Douglassville, where also are the records of the Bird and Huling families. Issue, six children, four recorded as follows:

The eldest son, Marcus, was a member of the Committee of Safety of Berks County, and Lieutenant-Colonel of Pennsylvania troops during the Revolution; he married Mary Ross, the sister of the signer.

Rachel married James Wilson, Signer from Pennsylvania, member of Congress, Delegate to the Constitutional Convention, 1787, and appointed Justice of the United States Supreme Court at its formation, by Washington, holding that office until his death.

Mary, married George Ross, the third son of the signer.

WILLIAM II.

HULING

The Hulings came from France, and several branches belonged to the nobility. A large number of this name were of the Protestant faith, and fled to many lands during the Huguenot persecution.[2] William and Abraham Huling, who came to New Jersey in 1674, were of those who fled to England. Ambrose Hulin emigrated to South Carolina. The name is sometimes spelled Hewling.

The ancestor of the so-called " Swedish branch " of the family was Marquis Jean Paul Frederick de Hulingues, a Huguenot nobleman of the Province of Bearn and attached to the Court of Henry of Navarre. He was in Paris, at the time of the massacre of St. Bartholomew (1572), but escaped with his betrothed, Isabella du Portal, a lady in waiting to Catherine de Medici. Fleeing to Dieppe, they were married there, and taking a vessel put to sea, but adverse winds carrying them beyond their destination, they settled in Sweden. The Marquis had but one son. A grandson, Lars (i. e. Lawrence) Huling, who came with the Swedish emigrants to the Delaware, prior to 1640, had two sons, Lars and Marcus. The Hulings of America descend from Marcus, son of Lars Huling, born in 1687 (not the son of Marcus, brother of Lars, as stated in the *Memorial of the Huguenots*), who was known in Morlatton, now Douglassville, as early as 1720, and married Margaret, daughter of Mons Jones.

[4] *Memorial of the Huguenots* in America, by Rev. A. Stapleton, published 1900.

Owing to trouble with the Indians, Marcus Huling and two others were commissioned by Governor Patrick Gordon, about 1728, to preserve the peace in the then remote Swedish settlement of Manatawny (Morlatton).[3] The Swedish settlement of Morlatton, the early home of the Bird, Huling and Jones families, although only about sixty miles from Philadelphia, was so inaccessible, for lack of roads, that upon the occasion of the wedding of Magdalene Huling, the daughter of Marcus, to Mathias Holstein, of "Swedes Ford," near Norristown, the bride, with her entire retinue, made the journey thither in canoes, a distance of about forty miles.[4] Huling was a noted Indian fighter. During one of his encounters with them he was obliged to jump over the crest of the "Blue Hill," a precipitous part of the country, landing ninety feet below; from this point he jumped forty feet more and reached the bank of the river with a dislocated shoulder. This is known in local history as the "big jump." In 1735 he lived on Duncan's Island, fourteen miles from Harrisburg.[5] At one time he owned the island, which was called by his name. In 1757 he went to Fort Pitt, where he is said to have acquired the point of land on which Pittsburg now stands, but sold it for £200. He was severely wounded in a fight with the Indians, and returned to Duncan's Island, dying April 2, 1757, and was buried at St. Gabriel's Church, Douglassville. Brigetta, fourth child of Marcus Huling, married WILLIAM BIRD.

JONES

The colonist, Mounce (or Mons, Moses) Jones, died

---

[3] *Commemoration Service,* St. Gabriel's Church, 1901.
[4] Watson's *Annals of Philadelphia and Penn.*
[5] *Hist. West. Branch Susquehanna,* p. 148.

1727; married Ingeborge ——; lived in Pennsylvania
before 1704, he, and other Swedes, receiving that year
grants of land, from three hundred to twelve hundred
acres each, in what is now Amity, and part of Douglass
township, Berks County. The region was known as
the Swedish settlement of "Manatawny." Mons Jones
built the quaint old stone house in Morlatton, now
Douglassville, Berks County, still standing near the
Schuylkill bridge; its date-stone (1716) contains the
initials of Mons Jones and of his wife Ingeborge. So
substantial were its walls that it was the place of defence
against Indian incursions, and it is believed to have been
originally surrounded by a wall and supplied with some
of the appointments of a fort. Mons Jones had a large
family and many of his descendants live in Berks and
adjoining counties of Pennsylvania. His daughter
Margaret married Marcus Huling.

BIRD (Continued)

WILLIAM BIRD II., the youngest son of William and
Brigetta (Huling) Bird (1757-1812), was Second-
Lieutenant in the Pennsylvania troops, March, 1776.[6]
He married, first, Julianna Wood, of Reading, Pa., and
second, 1781, Catherine, the daughter of John and
Jemima (Shaw) Dalton, the mother of his children.
She was born in Alexandria, Va., 1763, and died at
"The Aviary," 1822. William Bird moved to Alexan-
dria 1780, and in 1796 went to Warren County, Ga.,
settling at the "Shoals of the Ogeechee," where he es-
tablished iron works, among the first in Georgia. His
home was called "The Aviary." Issue, twelve children,
most of them being represented by descendants in the
Southern States.

6 Penn. Arch. (second series), Vol. x, p. 109.

At " The Aviary " was born in 1814 his distinguished grandson, William L. Yancey, the son of his eldest daughter, Caroline, who married Hon. Benjamin C. Yancey, of South Carolina.

His third daughter, Louisa Bird, married Captain Robert Cunningham, of South Carolina, and it was her daughter, Ann Pamela Cunningham, who organized the "Mount Vernon Ladies Association," 1853, and devoted her life to its work.

One of his sons was *James Wilson Bird.*

DALTON

Records in the Dalton family Bible, formerly belonging to Catherine Dalton, but destroyed during the Civil War, carried the pedigree back to a younger branch of a family of which Sir John Dalton was the head, and long established in England. Investigations by Hon. William L. Yancey, a grandson of Catherine Dalton, who was familiar with this Dalton Bible, and later research by others of the family, substantially ratifies these Bible records and show that John Dalton, first of the name in America, was of the younger branch of the Dalton family, of York County, Eng., and that the elder line had become extinct during the life of John Dalton, the colonist.

The head of the Daltons of Hanxwell, County York, was Colonel John Dalton, fifth in descent from John Dalton, who was settled at Kingston-upon-Hull, 1458, and was a son of Sir William, who was knighted in 1629; died 1649, and was buried in York Minster. Colonel John Dalton married Hon. Dorothy, the daughter of Sir Conyers Darcy (Lord Darcy), under whom Dalton was Lieutenant-Colonel, and was wounded July 5, 1643, while conducting Queen Henrietta Maria from

Bridlington to Oxford. He died of his wound July, 1644, and is buried at York Minster. The elder line of his descendants became extinct in 1792, upon the death of Francis, his great-grandson, and the title reverted to a descendant of one of the younger sons of Colonel John Dalton.

The colonist, John Dalton, one of several brothers, had settled in Westmoreland County, Va., before 1722, although coming to this country in the period between 1685 and 1690, going first to Gloucester County.

His son, John Dalton, born 1722, died in Alexandria, Va., 1777. He removed to Alexandria, then Belhaven, in 1755, and was one of the founders of the town, and one of the first trustees. He was a vestryman of " Old Christ Church,[7] serving with George Washington, John Shaw and Thomas Carlyle. The latter was his partner, and after his death, the guardian of his two daughters,[8] who lived with Thomas Carlyle, whose residence was the " Braddock House." John Dalton's residence is now the " Home for Aged Men." He was a member of the Committee of Correspondence for Alexandria, 1775. Washington[9] wrote of him as " Captain." He married in December, 1749, Jemima, the daughter of Thomas and Jane Shaw, of Alexandria, born April 4, 1730, and died December 3, 1765.

Their daughter, Jenny Dalton, married William Herbert. They have no descendants living. Two of their grandchildren were taken suddenly ill while on a visit to Mt. Vernon, and died there. Both were quite young, and the last of their family. Their father was Noblett Herbert, who married, 1819, at Mt. Vernon, Mary Lee

---

[7] Mead's *Old Churches,* Vol. ii, p. 270.

[8] Slaughter's *Truro Parish.*

[9] Ford's *Letters of Washington,* Vol. ii.

Washington (who died 1827), the fourth child of Corbin Washington, the son of John Augustine Washington, who was the son of Augustine Washington and Mary Ball.

The only other surviving child, Catherine Dalton, married, 1781, WILLIAM BIRD II., the wedding taking place at "Cameron," near Alexandria, as stated in the Family Bible.

SHAW

The Shaws were very early represented in this country by John Shaw, who came to Lancaster County, Va., in 1705, as surgeon to Captain Robert Tayloe, of London, the brother of the second William Tayloe, of Richmond County. Of this voyage Mr. Joseph Tayloe wrote: "Mr. John Shaw was ye Chy[n] of ye Cabin—ye most Inteligible Gent on board ye Ship."

Their son, William Shaw, moved from Westmoreland County to Alexandria. His wife, Eleanor ——, died there 1774.

Their son, Thomas Shaw, was born in Westmoreland County, and moved to Alexandria with his father. He was a member of the Vestry of Christ Church, 1765.[10] He married Jane ——, who died 1768. He died in 1777. Their daughter, Jemima Shaw, married John Dalton, of Alexandria, Va.

BIRD (*Continued*)

One of the sons of William and Catherine (Dalton) Bird, *James Wilson Bird,* was born in Alexandria, Va., 1787, and died 1868, near Sparta, Ga. He married, February 1, 1820 Frances Pamela, the daughter of

[10] Mead's *Old Virginia Churches,* Vol. ii, p. 268. Slaughter's *Truro Parish.*

John and Philoclea (Edgeworth) Casey, born 1789, and died 1855, then living in Savannah, Ga. Their son was *William Edgeworth Bird.*

CASEY

A young surgeon of Edgeworthtown, Ireland, John Casey, married Philoclea Edgeworth, and moved with his family to Prince George County, Md., where he appears in the census of 1790. Later he lived in Georgetown, Md., where he died, 1794. Evidently he was in close touch with the Catholic Church, as Henry Rozier and the Rev. Nottley Young were his executors, and his will was witnessed by Rev. Robert Molyneux, an early president of Georgetown College. Issue, four children.

The only daughter, Frances Pamela, born 1789, lived under the care of her guardian, Henry Rozier, at Notley Hall, on the Potomac, until she moved to Savannah, Ga., to live with her brother, Dr. John Casey, whose wife was a daughter of the distinguished jurist, Judge John McPherson Berrien. Here she married *James Wilson Bird.*

EDGEWORTH

Family tradition tells of the treasonable effort of Sir Edward Tyrrell against Henry II. of England. His property was confiscated, but restored to his daughter, Caroline Tyrrell, upon her marriage with one in favor, Robert, son of John Edgeworth.

From them was descended Roger, a monk, whom we find at Edgeworth,[11] now Edgeware, Middlesex, in the time of Henry VIII., who followed in the footsteps of his sovereign, renounced his faith and married.

---

[11] *Mem. R. L. Edgeworth* (father of Maria E.)

During the reign of Elizabeth, his sons Edward and Francis went to Ireland. The eldest, Edward, was made Bishop of Down and Connor, and dying without issue in 1593, left his brother Francis, clerk of Hanapor, in 1619, who was the founder of the family in Ireland. Francis married Jane, daughter of Sir Edmund Tuite, knight of Sonna in the County of Westmeath.

Their son, John, married the daughter of Sir Hugh Cullum, of Derbyshire. He was a captain.

Their only child, John Edgeworth, married —— Bridgeman. He was knighted by Charles II., and his first son was Francis; his fifth son, Essex, was the father of Abbé Edgeworth, who attended Louis XVI. on the scaffold. Lady Edgeworth, widow of Sir John, lived at her husband's castle of Lissard, Ireland, dying when ninety years old.

In direct descent from Sir John was Philoclea Edgeworth, who married John Casey, of Edgeworthtown, Ire., in County Longford, and shortly after moved to America with her husband and settled in Prince George County, Md. She died, leaving four children: John, Thomas, Francis P. M. and one daughter, Frances Pamela, three months' old. Another daughter, Philoclea, died some time before her mother.

The authoress, Maria Edgeworth, in a letter to Mrs. Victor Smith's great-aunt, says: "We all without doubt, descend from one common great-great-grandfather; and whether there be two or three great-grandfathers between us and the common stock, Sir John, I do not know, but indisputably I am your kinswoman, Maria Edgeworth."

The youngest child of John and Philoclea (Edgeworth) Casey, Frances Pamela Casey, married *James Wilson Bird.*

BIRD (*Continued*)

A son of James Wilson and Frances Pamela (Casey) Bird, *William Edgeworth Bird,* born July 21, 1825, and died January 11, 1867, resided in Hancock County, Ga. He was Captain of Company E, 15th Georgia Volunteers, C. S. A.; later Major on the staff of Major-General Benning, and was wounded at the second battle of Manassas. He married, February 24, 1848, SARAH C. BAXTER, the daughter of Thomas W. and Mary (Wiley) Baxter, of Athens, Ga., born March 26, 1828. Issue:

SAIDA BIRD, married, November 16, 1871, Victor Smith. (See Baxter, Harris, Alexander, Shelby, Wiley, Jack, Barnett, and Spratt lines.)

Wilson Edgeworth Bird, married IMOGEN REID.

SAIDA BIRD SMITH,

SALLIE BIRD,

Members of Chapter I., The Colonial Dames of America.

XXXIX

WILLIAMS

ARMS: *Gules a chevron ermine between three Saracens' heads affrontee couped at the shoulders proper.*

CREST: *A Saracen's head as in the arms.*

MOTTO: *Heb dduw heb dyn duw a digon.*

The immediate ancestors of the Williams family were for many generations settled at Great Yarmouth, County of Norfolk, Eng., where they are frequently mentioned in the local records.[1]

Of this family, Stephen Williams, buried at Great Yarmouth, September 19, 1625, married, 1605, at St. Nicholas Church, Margaret, the daughter of Nicholas and Winifred Cooke, of North Repps, Norfolk. Margaret died 1625; she was sister and devisee of Thomas Cooke, of Great Yarmouth, whose will is dated November 3, 1623.

Their son, Robert Williams, was baptized in Yar-

[1] Family tradition places their origin in Wales.

mouth, December 10, 1608, and died in Roxbury, Mass., September 1, 1693. Robert removed to Norwich, England, and was Freeman of that town, 1630, and warden of his guild, 1635. He came to New England in the ship *John and Dorothy*, of Ipswich, 1637, settled in Roxbury, and became Freeman the following year. In 1644 he was a member of the Ancient and Honorable Artillery Company. He was accompanied to New England by his brother Nicholas, who died in Roxbury at Robert's home, August 27, 1672.

He married, first, Elizabeth Stalhan; second, Margaret, the widow of John Fearing. Issue, among others, first wife:

CAPTAIN STEPHEN WILLIAMS,[2] born 1640, and died 1720, was Captain of a Troop of Horse, serving " at the Eastward," 1704 and 1705, and from 1707 to 1712, was Captain of the " Red Troop of Horse," in command of the frontier. In the summer of 1710, his troop served as a guard to Colonel Schuyler and the Maqua Indians.

He married, 1666, Sarah, the daughter of Joseph and Mary (Thompson) Wise. She was born 1647, and died 1728.

Their son, *Ensign Joseph Williams*, was born 1682, and died 1720; married, 1706, Abigail, the daughter of John and Mary (Torrey) Davis, born 1687, and died 1771. Their son:

COLONEL JOSEPH[3] WILLIAMS, was born 1708, and died 1798. He rendered important services to his country, both military and civil. He served as Colonel of a regiment, in the Mohawk War of 1755, and later in the Canadian campaign. As Representative for his native

---

[2] Year Book of *Colonial Wars*, 1897-1898, p. 580.
[3] *Ibid*, p. 580.

ELIZABETH BORDLEY HAWKINS
Wife of George Williams of Baltimore

JOSEPH WILLIAMS
From a painting by Gilbert Stuart

GRAVEYARD AT LONG GREEN, BALTIMORE COUNTY, MD.
Showing the tombs of James and Elizabeth Gitting

town of Roxbury, 1765, he urged the repeal of the
Stamp Act, and in March, 1770, was chairman of the
committee that waited on Governor Hutchinson, after
the "Boston Massacre," to demand the withdrawal of
the British troops from Boston. In March, 1775, he
was muster master of the Minute Men, for the town of
Roxbury, and two months later one of the officers of
the "Main Guard," encamped at Cambridge.

He married, March 23, 1732, *Martha*, the daughter
of Henry and Martha (Deming) Howell, born 1713,
and died 1766.   Their son was *Joseph*.

HOWELL

ARMS: *Gules, three towers triple turreted argent.*

The manor of Westbury, in the Parish of Marsh Gibbon, Bucks County, Eng., was purchased, in 1536, by
William Howell, who died November 30, 1557.   He
had issue, by second wife, Anne Dyer, a son Henry,
who became possessed of the manor, by the terms of his
father's will, and was buried July 20, 1625.   His son:

EDWARD HOWELL, was baptized at Marsh Gibbon,
July 22, 1584, and sold Westbury in June, 1639.   He
came to New England, where he was made Freeman in
Boston, March 14, 1639-40, and lived for a time at
Lynn, but soon removed to Southampton, L. I., then a
part of Connecticut.   He was Governor's Assistant,
1647 to 1653, and died 1656.   His wife Frances was
buried at Marsh Gibbon, July 2, 1630, nine years before his departure for America.   Their son:

MAJOR JOHN HOWELL, of Southampton, born 1624,
and died 1696, was Deputy, 1662 to 1664, commanded a detachment against the Dutch, 1673 to 1674,
and was Major of Horse, 1684.   His tombstone, at

Southampton, bears the family arms. He married Susanna ——.

Their son *John* (1648-1696) married, 1673, Martha, the daughter of John and Ann White.

Their son *Henry* (1685-1754) married *Martha,* the daughter of David and Mary Deming.

DEMING-TREAT

JOHN DEMING (1610-1705), of Wethersfield, Conn., a Deputy, 1649 to 1661, and one of the patentees of Connecticut, named in the Royal Charter of 1662, married *Honour,* the daughter of Richard and Alice (Gaylord) Treat.

Their son *David* married Mary ——, whose daughter *Martha* married Henry Howell.

RICHARD TREAT, of Wethersfield (1584-1669), was Deputy, 1637 to 1638; Assistant, 1658 to 1665, and a Member of Governor Winthrop's Council, 1663 to 1665. He was also one of the patentees of Connecticut, 1662. He married Alice Gaylord.

Their daughter *Honour* married JOHN DEMING, whose daughter, *Martha Deming,* married Henry Howell.

WILLIAMS (*Continued*)

One of the participants in the Battle of Lexington was *Joseph Williams,* son of Colonel Joseph and Martha (Howell) Williams. He was born 1738 and died 1822. He was a Sergeant in the 2d Company of Roxbury, Mass. During the Revolution he was a Member of the Committee of Correspondence and Safety of Roxbury.

In 1763 he married his cousin *Susanna,* the daughter of Benjamin and Mary (Williams) May. She was born 1741, and died 1782. Their son was *George.*

MAY

ARMS: *Gules, a fess between eight billets, or.*
CREST: *Out of a ducal coronet or, a leopard's head couped proper.*

The colonist, John May, was born in England, 1590, and settled in Roxbury, Mass., where he died April 28, 1670. He was a member of the church there under the ministry of the Apostle Eliot; became Freeman 1641; in 1647 was a Member of the Roxbury Military Company. His first wife, whose name is not recorded, died in 1651.

Their son, John II. (1631-1671), married Sarah Brewer.

Their son, John III. (1663-1730); married Prudence, the daughter of John and Prudence (Robinson) Bridge; born 1664; died 1723.

Their son Benjamin (1708-1774) married, first, 1737, *Mary*, the daughter of Stephen and Mary (Capen) Williams, and the granddaughter of Captain Stephen and Sarah (Wise) Williams; second, Abigail (1724-1799), the widow of John Gore. Daughter, first wife:

Susanna, married her cousin, *Joseph Williams.* Daughter, second wife:

Abigail (1754-1783), married Cumberland Dugan (1747-1836), of Baltimore, and they are buried in Westminster Church.

Their daughter, Margaret Dugan, married *William Rogers Smith.*

Their daughter, *Eleanor Addison Smith*, married *John Sterett Gittings.*

CAPEN

The first New England ancestor of *Mary (Capen) Williams*, was Bernard Capen, born 1562, who came to New England before 1636, settling at Dorchester,

Mass., where he died November 8, 1638; married, 1596, June, the daughter of Oliver Purchis, born 1578, and died 1653.

Their son, Captain John Capen (1613-1692), was a Member of the Ancient and Honorable Artillery Company, 1646; Deputy for Dorchester, 1671, 1673, and 1678, and Captain of the Militia, 1683; married, 1647, *Mary* (1631-1704), the daughter of SAMUEL BASS,[4] of Braintree Mass., who was Deputy, 1641 and later.

Their son *Samuel* (1648-1733) married, 1673, Susanna, the daughter of Edward Payson, born 1655, died 1737.

Their daughter *Mary*, born 1679, married Stephen Williams, of Roxbury.

Their daughter, *Mary Williams* (1714-1750), was the first wife of Benjamin May.

Their daughter, *Susanna May*, married *Joseph Williams*.

WILLIAMS (*Continued*)

One of the sons of Joseph and Susanna Williams, *George Williams*, was born 1778, and died 1852. He settled in Baltimore, Md., and married, June 1, 1815, Elizabeth Bordley, the daughter of Matthew and Sarah (Bordley) Hawkins. Their son was *George Hawkins Williams*.

HAWKINS

The ancestor of this family, Thomas Hawkins, settled at Nominy, Westmoreland County, Va., and later removed to Maryland, where he purchased from Governor Thomas Green, 1650, Poplar Island, then containing a thousand acres.

He married Elizabeth, the widow of Daniel Stipping,

---

[4] *Col. Recs. of Mass.*, Vols. i, ii, iii.

of Virginia, and died October 12, 1656. (His widow married, third, Seth Foster, of Talbot County, and had two daughters; the elder married, first, Colonel Vincent Lowe, brother of Jane Lowe, the wife of Charles, Lord Baltimore; and second, Colonel William Coursey.) Thomas Hawkins and his wife Elizabeth had issue, two sons: Thomas II., died in 1677, leaving no male issue. The second son:

COLONEL JOHN HAWKINS (1655-1717), of Queen Anne County, acquired extensive landed estates and was ·prominent in public affairs. In 1694 he was a County Commissioner for Talbot County, Justice of the Provincial Court of Maryland, 1698, and represented Queen Anne County in the Assembly, 1714 to 1717.

A communion service of silver, presented by him to St. Paul's Church, Centreville, is still used in that church. The tankard bears the inscription: "The Gift of Colonel John Hawkins, 1717," while on the chalice is inscribed: "The Gift of Collonell John Hawkins of Chester River in Maryland 1716." Ernault Hawkins, the son of Colonel John, completed the service by the gift of a patten on which is inscribed: "The Gift of Ernault Hawkins."

The first wife of John Hawkins was Frances, the daughter of Roger Gross, of Anne Arundel County.

Their son *John* (1681-1745), by his first wife, Elizabeth (living in 1713), had three sons and two daughters.

One son, *Matthew,* married, July 25, 1746, Frances, the daughter of James and Frances Gould.

Their son, *Matthew II.,* removed to Harford County, on the other side of the Bay, and died there 1813. He married *Sarah* (died 1805), the daughter of *Doctor William Bordley,* of Chestertown.

Their daughter, *Elizabeth Bordley Hawkins,* who died 1850, married, June 1, 1815, *George Williams,* of Baltimore.

BORDLEY

Two of the sons of the Rev. Stephen Bordley, Prebendary of St. Paul's, London, Stephen and Thomas, came to Maryland in 1694. The younger son, Thomas, then about twelve years old, eventually settled at Annapolis, rose to distinction as a lawyer, and was Attorney-General of the Province in 1715. He was twice married, and died 1726, leaving a numerous progeny. One of his sons, John Beale Bordley, was a Justice of the Provincial Court in 1766.

The elder son of the Prebendary, the Rev. Stephen Bordley, was inducted Rector of St. Paul's Parish, Kent County, June 23, 1697, and continued to officiate until his death, some twelve years later. He was buried August 25, 1709. He married, October 14, 1700, Anne, the daughter of Colonel John Hynson, the son of Thomas Hynson. Issue, three daughters and two sons, Thomas and Stephen.

Their elder son, Thomas Bordley (1704-1752), married, second, December 21, 1731, *Anne* (born 1707), the granddaughter of MICHAEL MILLER.

Their son, *Doctor William Bordley,* of Chestertown (1741-1784), was an active patriot in the Revolution and a zealous member of the County Committee; in 1777 he was commissioned Colonel of the 13th Battalion of Kent County. By his first wife, Elizabeth, the widow of John Tilden, he had issue:

Thomas.

Sarah, married *Matthew Hawkins.*

Elizabeth.

HYNSON

The Hynsons were represented in Virginia and Maryland, by Thomas Hynson (1620-1667), who was in Isle of Wight County, Va., 1646, and went to Maryland, 1651. He was Clerk of Kent County, 1652-53; County Commissioner, 1652 to 1656; High Sheriff, 1655 to 1656; Member of the Assembly, 1654, 1659 to 1660.

His son, Colonel John Hynson, died 1705. He was a Member of the Maryland Assembly, 1681 to 1683, 1694 to 1697, 1701 to 1704, and Colonel of the County Militia, 1694. His daughter Anne married Rev. Stephen Bordley.

MILLER

MICHAEL MILLER (1644-1699), was High Sheriff of Kent County, 1678, 1681 to 1682; in 1690 was one of the Committee of Twenty for regulating affairs in Maryland; a Member of the Assembly, 1678 to 1699.[5]

His son, *Arthur Miller,* had a daughter *Anne,* who married Thomas Bordley.

WILLIAMS (*Continued*)

A son of George and Elizabeth Bordley (Hawkins) Williams, *George Hawkins Williams,* of Baltimore, born 1818, and died 1889, married, June 3, 1843, Eleanor Addison, the daughter of John Sterett and Eleanor Addison (Smith) Gittings. Issue:

John Sterett Gittings, died young.

George May, died unmarried.

Eleanor Addison, married Dr. Thomas Marean Chatard.

ELIZABETH HAWKINS, married Dr. Robert Brown

5 *Old Kent,* p. 301.

Morison. Issue: ELEANOR ADDISON, who married Randolph Barton, Jr., and SIDNEY B.

Charlotte Ritchie, died young.

REBECCA NICHOLS, married Dr. William Travers Howard.

CHARLOTTE CARTER RITCHIE, married Dr. Walter Prescott Smith.

William Smith Gittings, married Julia Bell Deford.

GITTINGS

The first American ancestor of this family, Thomas Gittings, of Baltimore County, Md., was born 1682, and died 1760. He married, first, 1719, Elizabeth, born 1703; the daughter of Abraham Redgrave, of Kent County; and second, 1734, Mary, daughter of James Lee and widow of James Lynch, of Baltimore County. The eldest son, second wife:

JAMES GITTINGS, of Long Green, born 1736, and died 1823, was a Member of the Baltimore County Committee, 1774 to 1775; Captain in the County Militia, 1775, Major, 1776, and Member of the Legislature, 1789. He married *Elizabeth,* the daughter of GEORGE BUCHANAN (1698-1750), of the Buchanans, of Auchentorlie, in Scotland, one of the commissioners for laying out Baltimore, 1729, and a Member of the Assembly, 1745 to 1750.

Their son, *James II.,* born 1769, died 1819, married *Harriet,* the daughter of John and Deborah (Ridgely) Sterett.

Their son, *John Sterett,* born 1798, died 1879, married, April 5, 1821, *Eleanor Addison,* the daughter of William Rogers and Margaret (Dugan) Smith; she was born 1799, and died 1848.

Their daughter, *Eleanor Addison* (1824-1881), married *George Hawkins Williams,* of Baltimore.

STERETT

JAMES STERETT, died in 1796. His son:

JOHN STERETT, died January 1, 1787. He was a Member of the Legislature from Baltimore County, 1783 to 1785. He married *Deborah,* the daughter of John and Mary (Dorsey) Ridgely, who died in 1786. Their daughter *Harriet* married *James Gittings II.*

ADDISON-TASKER

COLONEL JOHN ADDISON,[6] came to Maryland before 1678, and settled in Charles County, of which he was one of the Justices, 1689. At the formation of Prince George's County, 1695, his estates were included in that county. He was a Member of the Council of Maryland from 1692 until his death, in 1706; Chancellor and Keeper of the Great Seal, from December, 1696, until January, 1699; commissioned, August 14, 1695, Colonel of the Militia of Prince George's County. He married 1678, Rebecca, the daughter of the Rev. William Wilkinson, one of the first Anglican clergymen who settled in Maryland, and the widow of Thomas Dent, Esq.

COLONEL THOMAS ADDISON, their only son, born 1679, and died 1727, like his father, was a Member of the Council, serving from 1721 until 1727. He was twice married, first, 1701, to *Elizabeth,* the daughter of Captain Thomas and Eleanor (Brooke) Tasker; second, to Eleanor, the daughter of Colonel Walter and Rachel (Hall) Smith. Issue, first wife: two daughters, one of whom, *Eleanor,* born 1705, married

[6] On the authority of letters seen by Rev. Jonathan Boucher, who married a great-granddaughter of the immigrant, it is stated that Colonel John was uncle of the celebrated Joseph Addison, and brother of the Dean of Litchfield, Launcelot Addison.

four times, her second husband being RICHARD SMITH III.

CAPTAIN THOMAS TASKER, was a Burgess, 1692 to 1698, and of the Council, 1698 to 1700, in which latter year he died; married *Eleanor,* the daughter of Colonel Thomas and Barbara (Dent) Brooke.

Their daughter *Elizabeth* married COLONEL THOMAS ADDISON.

SMITH

ARMS: *Per chevron argent and sable; three anvils counterchanged.*
CREST: *Out of a mural crown or, an ostrich head argent, in its beak a horseshoe of the first.*

RICHARD SMITH,[7] came to Maryland, February, 1649, and settled on St. Leonard's Creek, Calvert County. His wife Eleanor arrived in August, 1651. He was a lawyer, and frequently appears in the records of the Provincial Court. He was commissioned Attorney-General of the Province, 1657, holding office under Fendall's administration, until 1660, and was a Member of the Assembly from 1661 to 1667. He was living in 1684. Issue: Richard and Walter.

The elder son, Captain Richard Smith, died in 1714. He was Captain of a company of Militia in Calvert County, and for his opposition to the revolutionsts, 1689, was imprisoned for some time. In 1693 to 1694 he was Surveyor-General of the Province.

He married, first, Elizabeth, the youngest daughter of Robert Brooke, of De la Brooke Manor and Brooke Place, who was born 1655; second, July 13, 1686, Barbara, the daughter of Henry Morgan, of Kent County, and the widow of John Rousby, of Calvert County; third, Maria Johanna, the widow of Colonel Lowther, and the daughter of Charles Somerset, Esq., the third

[7] *Archs. of Md.*

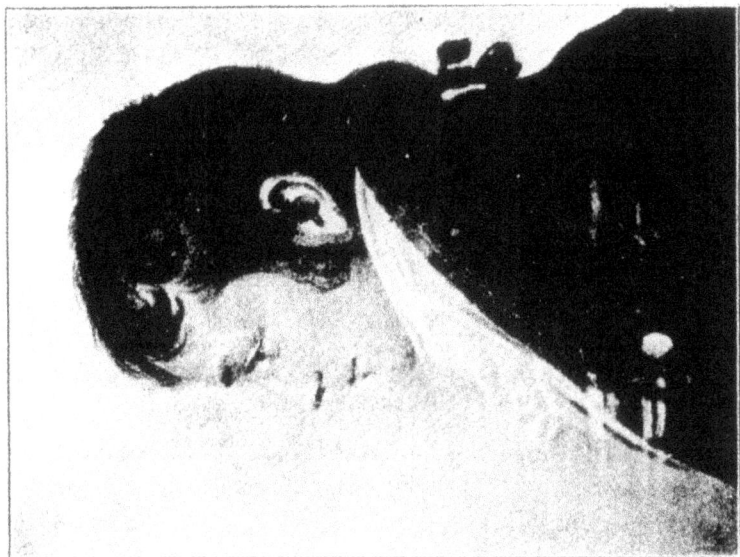

JOHN ADDISON SMITH

ELEANOR ADDISON
Wife of Richard Smith III

son of Lord John Somerset, who was the son of the first Marquis of Worcester.

COLONEL WALTER SMITH,[8] the younger son of Richard Smith, Sr., was a Member of the Assembly for Calvert County, 1696 to 1704, 1708 to 1711, and made Presiding Justice of Calvert County Court, May 10, 1699. He was Captain 1689, Major 1695, and Colonel 1706, in the Calvert County Militia, dying in 1711. He seems to have had Jacobite tendencies, for July, 1698, he was required to give security to appear at the next Provincial Court for drinking King James' health.

He married, 1686, *Rachel* (who died October 28, 1730), the daughter of RICHARD HALL,[9] who arrived in Maryland before 1663, with his wife Elizabeth, died in 1688, and was Burgess for Calvert County, 1666 to 1670, 1674 to 1685.

RICHARD SMITH III,[10] son of Walter, was High Sheriff of Calvert County, 1728. He lived at Lower Marlboro, and died 1732, having married, as her second husband, *Eleanor,* the daughter of Colonel Thomas and Elizabeth (Tasker) Addison. She was born March 20, 1705, and married four times, viz.: First, Bennett Lowe; second, RICHARD SMITH III.; third, Captain Posthumus Thornton; fourth, Corbin Lee.

A son of Richard and Eleanor (Addison) Smith, *Captain John Addison Smith,* of Baltimore, who died May 8, 1776, married, October 17, 1765, Sarah, the daughter of William and Sarah Rogers (she married, second, John Merryman).

Their son, *William Rogers Smith,* of Baltimore, was

8 *Ibid.*
9 *Ibid.*
10 *Ibid.*

born November 25, 1774; died June 10, 1818; married, October 2, 1798, Margaret, the daughter of Cumberland and Abigail (May) Dugan. She was born April 13, 1780, and is buried in Old St. Paul's Church Yard.

Their daughter, *Eleanor Addison,* married *John Sterett,* the son of James and Harriet (Sterett) Gittings.

ROGERS

The immediate ancestors of William Rogers, of Baltimore, who died in June, 1761, were Nicholas Rogers, of Maryland, his grandfather, who died 1690, and Nicholas Rogers II., his father, who died 1720.

His daughter Sarah, married *Captain John Addison,* the son of RICHARD SMITH.

RIDGELY

ROBERT RIDGELY, came to Maryland about 1660, and settled at St. Inigoes, in St. Mary's County. He soon became a man of note, acquiring a considerable law practice, and in 1665 was Clerk of the Council. He qualified as Clerk of the Provincial Court, January 19, 1670-71, and on June 5, 1671, he was commissioned Chief Clerk to the Secretary, Register and Examiner of the High Court of Chancery, as the Deputy of Sir William Talbot, then about to leave the Province. Robert Ridgely died in 1681, leaving a handsome estate to his wife Martha and their four children.

Their second son, *Charles Ridgely,* who died in 1705, was a minor at the date of his father's death; married *Deborah,* the daughter of COLONEL JOHN DORSEY (see pp. 249-251). Deborah Dorsey, married second, Richard Clagett, and was the grandmother of the Right Rev. Thomas John Clagett, the first Episcopal bishop of Maryland.

COLONEL CHARLES RIDGELY (1702-1772), son of Charles and Deborah Ridgely, removed to Baltimore County, where he acquired, in 1745, the Hampton estate, then called "Northampton." He was County Commissioner, 1741 to 1754, and represented his county in the Assembly, 1751 to 1754. His wife, Rachel Howard, who died 1750, was the daughter of John Howard, of Timberneck, son of John Howard of Anne Arundel County.

JOHN RIDGELY (1723-1771), their son, was County Commissioner, 1750 to 1756, and a Member of the Assembly, 1768. He married *Mary Dorsey* (1725-1786), daughter of *Caleb* and granddaughter of COLONEL JOHN DORSEY (see Dorsey), and their daughter *Deborah* married JOHN STERETT, whose daughter, *Harriet,* married *James Gittings.*

Their son, *John Sterett Gittings,* married *Eleanor Addison Smith,* whose daughter, *Eleanor Addison Gittings,* married *George Hawkins Williams.*

CHARLOTTE CARTER RITCHIE WILLIAMS SMITH,
ELIZABETH HAWKINS WILLIAMS MORISON,
ELEANOR ADDISON MORISON BARTON,
SYDNEY B. MORISON,
REBECCA NICHOLS WILLIAMS HOWARD,
Members of Chapter I., The Colonial Dames of America.

XL

STEELE

ARMS: *Argent, a bend chequy sable and ermine between two lions' heads erased gules, on a chief azure three billets or.*
CREST: *A lion's head erased gules.*
MOTTO: *Prudentia et animis.*

The Steeles are descended from John Steele, of White Haven, Cumberland County, Eng., who married Dorothy, the daughter of Sir John Ponsonby of Hale Hall, Cumberland County, whose family dates from the time of William the Conqueror. They had four children: HENRY, Peter, Isaac, Isabella.

HENRY STEELE, who died February 5, 1782, and is buried at the family place "Weston," Dorchester County, Md., came to America in 1752 and settled near Vienna, Md. He was a man of refinement, and learning, who owned large tracts of land in Dorchester County, viz.: The Nanticoke Plantation, The Forest, Indian Town, Chickininconico, also a large number of slaves. He held many offices in the Province of Maryland, being Justice 1759, Burgess 1763 to 1770, in the first General Assembly of the State of Maryland 1777, and represented Dorchester County at the Convention at Annapolis June 22, 1774. He married in 1756, *Anne,* the daughter of James. and Anne (Rider) Billings. MAJOR JAMES BILLINGS, who died 1749, held the office of Justice 1743 to 1744.[1] His wife Anne, was the daughter of John and Anne (Hicks) Rider. Issue of Henry and Anne Steele, four children, viz.: *James,* Henry, Isaac, and Peter.

Their eldest son, *James Steele,* born at "Weston," Dorchester County, Md., January 17, 1760, and died September 16, 1836, on his way home from Bedford Springs, is buried in Annapolis. Obtaining his education at Wilmington Academy, Delaware, he moved to Cambridge, Md., where he owned several thousand acres of land, which " he divided among his children during his life," also a large number of slaves.[2] Some years later he moved to Annapolis, and the Steele house of that day, is still standing there. He married *Mary,* the daughter of John Rider and Sarah (Maynadier) Nevett (she married second Dr. James Murray of Annapolis). Issue, ten children, viz.: John, James, *Isaac Nevett,* Charles Hutchins, Henry Maynadier, Anne, Sarah, Catharine, Isabel and Mary Campbell.

Their third son, *Isaac Nevett Steele,* born in Cambridge, Dorchester County, April 25, 1809, and died April 10, 1891, is buried at Greenmount, Baltimore. He went to St. John's College, Annapolis, and afterwards to Trinity College, Hartford. At eighteen years of age, he began the study of law, receiving the degree

[1] Jones' *Hist. of Dorchester County,* p. 422.
[2] *Land Records of Cambridge, Md.*

of LL. D., July 31, 1827, came to the bar in 1830, rose rapidly, and in 1839 was appointed Deputy for the Attorney-General of Maryland, which office he held until 1849. In that year he accepted a position of Charge d'Affaires to Venezuela. While there he narrowly escaped death from robbers who broke into the house, hoping to find money, which it was customary for persons to deposit with the diplomatic representatives of their respective nationalities. While in Venezuela, Mr. Steele gained much credit for having secured the settlement of heavy claims on the part of citizens of the United States, which had been postponed so long as to be regarded as hopeless. On his return home in 1853, he resumed the practice of law, to which he devoted himself until his death. At one time Chairman of the Whig State Central Committee, in 1880 was Democratic Presidential Elector of Maryland. There were few cases before the Maryland Courts, involving great principles or large interests, in which Mr. Steele was not counsel, and he ranks among the leaders of the American bar. He married at Washington, January 22, 1849, *Rosa Landonia*, the daughter of *Hon. John Nelson*, of Maryland. They had eight children, as follows:

James Nevett, married Helen Hudson Aldrich.

Mary.

John Nelson, married Mary Alricks Pegram.

Charles, married Nannie French.

ROSA NELSON.

KATE NEVETT.

Samuel Tagart, married Mary Thompson.

Henry Maynadier, married Margaret Hollins McKim.

RIDER

In 1687, John Rider, Esq., of England, and his wife

Dorothy, the daughter of COLONEL CHARLES HUT-
CHINS, died on the voyage to America, leaving their
son, *John Rider II* (1686-1739), to his maternal grand-
father, who left him large and valuable tracts of land in
Dorchester County, Md., including the family home
" Weston."

In his will, dated February 15, 1737, *Colonel John
Rider II,* divided his property among his three daughters, viz.: Sarah Nevett, *Anne Billings,* and Dorothy
Henry. Colonel and Commander of all the Militia,
Horse and Foot, in Dorchester County, he was also Justice 1708 to 1720, Commissioner of Schools 1723, Judge
1725, and in the Assembly 1729.[3] His commission was
issued by " Samuel Ogle, Esq., Governor, & Commander-in-chief in & over the Province of Maryland &
the Territory thereto belonging. . . . Given at the
City of Annapolis, August 8th. The eighteenth year
of his Lordships, the Lord proprietor, Dominion Anno-
Domini 1732." He married, January 23, 1705, *Anne,*
the daughter of COLONEL THOMAS HICKS, of Dorchester County, Md., and their daughter, *Anne,* married
MAJOR JAMES BILLINGS, whose daughter *Anne,* married HENRY STEELE.

HUTCHINS-HICKS

COLONEL CHARLES HUTCHINS, who died 1699, came
from England and settled in Vienna, Dorchester
County, Md., 1665, where he built " Weston House,"
which is still standing. Justice 1674 to 1691, Burgess
1690 to 1695, and for many years one of the Council of
their Majesties, King William and Queen Mary, for
the Maryland Colony, he was also Colonel of the Militia, and commissioned to treat with the Indians. In

---

[3] Jones' *Hist. of Dorchester County, Md.*
Life and Letters of Gov. John Henry of Maryland.

those days there was direct trade between Vienna and England, and the ship, in which his only daughter *Dorothy*, whom he had sent to England to be educated, was expected, anchored in the Nanticoke River, at the foot of his lawn. Instead of his daughter, however, he received her miniature, and a letter informing him she was engaged to John Rider. Colonel Hutchins, disappointed and angry, threw the miniature into the fire—fortunately it was rescued, and is now in the possession of one of his descendants. Dorothy Hutchins married in England 1685, John Rider, a man of culture and position. They both died on the voyage to America 1687, leaving their young son, *John*, to Colonel Hutchins, who brought him up and left him all his property.[4] *John Rider* married *Anne*, the daughter of COLONEL THOMAS HICKS (1659-1722), who came from Whitehaven, Cumberland County, Eng., and settled in Dorchester County, Md., holding offices under the Colonial Government, being Justice 1692 to 1722, and Burgess 1694 to 1697.[5] The name of his wife is not known.

His daughter *Anne*, married *John Rider II*, whose daughter *Anne* married JAMES BILLINGS, and their daughter, *Anne Billings*, married HENRY STEELE.

NEVETT-MAYNADIER

RICHARD NEVETT, a Burgess of Dorchester County, Md., 1638, was one of the Committee of Safety of the Colony in St. Mary's, September 13, 1642.[6]

THOMAS NEVETT, his son, was born in Cambridge, Dorchester County, Md., 1669, died there February 10, 1748, and is buried in Christ Church graveyard. He

[4] *Ibid.*
[5] History of Dorchester County.
[6] *Proceedings and Acts of Maryland.*

owned large estates and held offices under the Colonial Government, being Justice 1732 to 1748, and Judge of the Provincial Court 1742.[7]   He married *Sarah*, the daughter of John and Anne (Hicks) Rider.

Their son, *John Rider Nevett*, born 1746, was on board a sailing packet, going to Annapolis to serve as a juror, when the boat capsized in a violent storm near Cambridge, and he was drowned, April 13, 1772.   An attempt at rescue was made, and Mr. Nevett tried to cling to the vessel until the women and children were saved, but became exhausted and lost his hold; is buried in Christ Church graveyard, Cambridge.   He married *Sarah*, the daughter of Daniel and Mary (Murray) Maynadier.   (She married second, Dr. James Murray of Annapolis.)   Their daughter *Mary* married *James Steele*.

A Huguenot minister, Rev. Daniel Maynadier, expelled under the Edict of Nantes, fled from Languedoc, France, to Annapolis, Md.   Two of his brothers started with him, one going to Ireland, the other to the West Indies.[8]   He married Mrs. Parrott.

Their son, Daniel Maynadier II, married *Mary*, the daughter of William and Sarah (Ennalls) Murray.   Issue, eight children, of whom the fourth, *Sarah*, married at the age of sixteen, *John Rider Nevett*.   (See pp. 146-148, for Maynadier, Murray, Ennalls.)

MURRAY-ENNALLS

DR. WILLIAM VANS MURRAY (1692-1759), the son of William and Mary (Vans) Murray, was the young-

---

[7] Jones *Hist of Dorchester County*, p. 521.

Assembly and Proceedings of Maryland, pp. 30-109, 170, 173-177, 1640 to 1646.

[8] Harrison's *Annals of Talbot County, Md.*

est child of a family of seventeen.   He married *Sarah,*
the daughter of Henry and Mary (Hooper) Ennalls.
Issue, seven children, of whom *Mary,* the fifth child,
married Rev. Daniel Maynadier II, and their daughter *Sarah,* married *John Rider Nevett.*

BARTHOLOMEW ENNALS (1648-1688), married Mrs.
Mary Heyward.

COLONEL HENRY ENNALLS, his son, married *Mary,*
the daughter of Henry and Elizabeth (Denwood)
Hooper and they are buried at Eldon, near Cambridge.
The inscription on their tomb says:
"Here lies the bodies of Henry Ennalls and his wife
Mary.   He departed this life in 1734 and she departed
this life ye 27th July, 1745."

Their daughter *Sarah,* born September 14, 1697, died
1742, married WILLIAM VANS MURRAY.

HOOPER-DENWOOD

CAPTAIN HENRY HOOPER I, emigrated from England
with his wife Sarah and son Henry, settling in Calvert
County, Md., 1651.   They brought over many settlers
with them.   December 20, 1667, the family moved to
Dorchester County, Md., as that year one hundred acres
were surveyed on Hooper's Island, near Hungar River,
for Henry Hooper.[9]   Subsequently by grants they acquired many thousand acres.

HENRY HOOPER II, their son, lived in 1684 on Hooper's Island.   The rent rolls of Dorchester County, Md.,
show that he had surveyed August 12, 1669, "Hooper's
Lot" and other estates.[10]   He married first, *Elizabeth,*
the daughter of LEVIN DENWOOD I.   Their daughter

9 *Land Records of Annapolis.*
10 *Archs. of Md.,* Vol. IX, p. 52.

DR. WILLIAM VANS MURRAY

JAMES STEELE

MARY DE HONEYWOOD

ISAAC NEVETT STEELE

Mary married HENRY ENNALLS. (See pp. 148-149, for Hooper and Denwood.)

NELSON

ARMS: *Argent, a cross flory azure over all a bend gules.*
CREST: *A dexter arm erect holding a tilting spear all proper.*

Prior to 1694, John Nelson came from England and settled in Frederick County, western Maryland. The old Queen Anne service of silver belonging to him is still in the possession of his descendants. It is recorded that "'Dumfries' was surveyed July 10,[11] 1694, for John Nelson, lying in the fork of the Eastern branch of the Potomac River," also other large tracts of land in Ohio and Virginia. He married, and his wife married second, Edward Packwood.

His son, Arthur Nelson, had

NELSON

ten tracts of land surveyed for him, among them, "Arthur's Seat," in 1720; "Token of Love," and "Point of Rocks," in 1722, all lying near the Potomac River, western Maryland.[12]

ARTHUR NELSON II., his son, was living in 1774 at "Point of Rocks" homestead. He was an ardent patriot and one of the Committee of Safety of Maryland; appointed, November 18, 1774, one of the Committee to represent Frederick County to carry into execution the association agreed on by the Continental Congress.[13]

11 *Rent Roll of Lord Baltimore.*
12 *Ibid.*
13 *American Monthly Mag.*, October, 1893, p. 399.
    Scharf's *Hist. of Maryland*, Vol. II, p. 164.

The name of his wife is not known. He had four children, viz.: John, married Louisa Fairfax, of Virginia; Sally, married Colonel Luckett; Jane, married Mr. Waters, of Georgetown, and ROGER.

GENERAL ROGER NELSON, the youngest son, was born in 1760 at the Nelson homestead, " Point of Rocks," Frederick County, Md., died in Frederick, June 7, 1815, and is buried in All-Saints' Church graveyard. At the age of sixteen he joined Colonel William Washington's troop of horse, then acting in Charleston, S. C. With the other Continentals he engaged in the defence of Charleston, and after its surrender, underwent great hardships for several months, in the British prison ships in the harbor. He entered the Maryland Line with the rank of Lieutenant, July 15, 1780, served until the close of the war 1783, when he was made Brigadier-General, and received several wounds at the Battle of Camden. After the war he studied law and practised with success. For several years he was in the Legislature of Maryland, and U. S. Representative from 1804 to 1810; also Judge of the Upper District of Maryland, 1810 to 1815.[14] He married in 1777, *Mary Brooke*, the daughter of Joseph and Katharine (Murdock) Sim. They had four children: Arthur, born 1788, Katharine Murdock, born 1790, Joseph, born 1792, and *John.*

The youngest son, *John Nelson,* was born in Frederick, Md., 1794, died in Baltimore, January 8, 1860, and is buried at Greenmount. Graduating from William and Mary College with honors, and later Representative from Maryland in Congress 1821 to 1823, he received

14 McSherry's *Hist. of Maryland.*
    Fifth Regiment.
    Lamnan's *Biog. Annals of Government of United States.*

the appointment of Minister to Naples 1831; was Attorney-General of the United States under President Jackson 1844. The College of New Jersey conferred upon him the degree of A. M. His name is associated with several of the "most famous successes that the annals of the law record." [15] He married at Washington, November 18, 1816, *Frances Harriet,* the daughter of William Ward and Mary (Bond) Burrows, who was born June 14, 1798, and died in Baltimore, Md., April 28, 1836. They had ten children, five of whom died young: the others are: William Burrows, Mary Sim, Anne Cecelia, John Lawrence, and *Rosa Landonia,* who married *Isaac Nevett Steele.*

SIM

Implicated in the Scottish rebellion of 1715, Dr. Patrick Sim fled from Scotland, where he possessed the estate of "Kilcairn," which was confiscated. He settled in Prince George's County, Md., where he married, 1718, *Mary,* the daughter of Thomas and Barbara (Dent) Brooke, of Brookefield Manor. She died in 1758 and her will, dated February 16, and proved March 31, 1758, mentions the following children:

JOSEPH.

Walter, died unmarried.

Barbara, married Dr. Clement Smith.

Christian, married Thomas Lee.

COLONEL JOSEPH SIM, was born in Prince George's County, Md., and died November 27, 1793. Justice of the Supreme Court, and one of the famous Assembly held at Annapolis, June 22, 1774, which denounced the English bill closing the Port of Boston, he represented his County in the Convention of June 15, 1775, which

[15] Scharf's *Chronicles of Baltimore.*

met at Annapolis, and which framed the Constitution,
known as the Association of the Freemen of Maryland. Serving in the Convention of Maryland which
governed the Province during the Revolution, and one
of the first Privy Council under the state Government
in 1777, he was also one of the General Assembly of
1780.[16] He married first, *Katharine,* the daughter of
William and Anne (Addison) Murdock. Four children; Patrick, Thomas, Anthony, and *Mary Brooke,*
who married ROGER NELSON.

BROOKE

The descendants of Richard Brooke of Whitchurch,
Southampton, Eng., and his wife Elizabeth Twynne,
in this line, are as follows:

Thomas Brooke, married Susan, the daughter of Sir
Thomas Forster.

GOVERNOR ROBERT BROOKE, married first, Mary, the
daughter of Thomas Baker of Battel, Sussex, and his
wife Mary Engham, the granddaughter of Robert de
Honeywood.

Thomas Brooke I., married Elinor Hatton.

Thomas Brooke II., married *Barbara,* the daughter
of THOMAS DENT and his wife Rebecca Wilkinson.

Mary Brooke, married Patrick Sim. (See pp. 553-
561, for Brooke, Forster, and connecting lines).

DE HONEYWOOD-BAKER

A younger son of John de Honeywood, of " Honeywood," Robert de Honeywood, of " Charing Kent "
and " Marks Hall," Essex, married Mary (1527-1620),
the daughter and heiress of Robert Waters, of Lenham,
Kent County, Eng., when she was sixteen years of
age. She lived in the reigns of Henry VIII, Edward

16 *American Monthly,* October, 1893, p. 399.

VI, Mary, Elizabeth, and seventeen years in the reign of James I. Her grandson, Dr. Michael de Honeywood, Dean of Lincoln Cathedral, stated that he was at a dinner party given by her to two hundred of her descendants. Her daughter, Priscilla de Honeywood, married, 1567, Sir Thomas Engham, Knight of Goodweston.

Their daughter, Mary Engham, married Thomas Baker, of Battel, Sussex, whose daughter Mary, married ROBERT BROOKE.

MURDOCK

WILLIAM MURDOCK was born in Prince George's County, Md. In 1756 he was appointed Commissioner to disburse the state fund for protection against the hostile Indians; also the state fund for the expedition against Fort Duquesne. In the House of Delegates 1765 to 1776, he represented Maryland in the Stamp Act Congress of National Deputies, which met at New York in October, 1765; on the Committee to draw up and report a vote of thanks to those members of the British Parliament who had defended the rights of the Colonists, and in 1768, was appointed on a Committee to draft a petition to the King, remonstrating against the imposition of taxes on imported articles.[17]   He married *Anne,* the daughter of Thomas and Elinor (Smith) Addison; she died in 1769, and their daughter, *Katharine,* married JOSEPH SIM.

SMITH-ADDISON

RICHARD SMITH, of "Hallscroft," Calvert County, Md., was a large land-owner, rights for himself and wife Ellinor being entered in 1649 and 1651. The rec-

---

[17] McSherry's *Hist. of Maryland.*
Votes and Proceedings of Assembly of Maryland, 1765, 1766, 1768.

ords of Calvert County show that he purchased August
4, 1658, " one hundred acres of land on the right side
of St. Leonard's Creek, with one dwelling-house, one
servants' quarter, one orchard, and three tobacco
houses." He also purchased " Hallscroft," seven hundred acres of land, February 7, 1675. This, with his
rights, " making an estate of one thousand acres." Issue: Richard and WALTER.

COLONEL WALTER SMITH, the youngest son of Richard, signed the " Declaration against choosing Burgesses," August 20, 1689, also the addresses of the Protestant inhabitants of Calvert County. He had " Hallscroft " surveyed May 1, 1695, for a surplusage of nine
hundred and seventy-two acres, making the whole estate one thousand six hundred and seventy-two acres,
and May 10, had a grant of five hundred acres in Baltimore County, called " Bear Neck." He was Vestryman of All Saints' Parish, Calvert County, from 1696
until his death, the last vestry meeting which he attended
being April 2, 1711. His will was proved June 4, 1711,
by his wife *Rachel*, the daughter of RICHARD HALL, and
her will was proved February 3, 1731. Issue: Walter,
Lucy, *Ellinor*, Anne, Rebecca, who married Daniel
Dulany, Sr., Elizabeth, who married Rev. Mr. Battle,
Richard, and Mary.

Their third child, *Ellinor Smith*, married COLONEL
THOMAS ADDISON (1679-1729), the son of COLONEL
JOHN ADDISON and his wife Rebecca (Wilkinson)
Dent. Four hundred acres of land were laid out for
John Addison in St. Mary's County, April 17, 1680.
The Council, October 18, 1697, ordered a fort built on
his land, and he was placed in command of Baltimore

County and the shores of the Potomac River, March
30, 1698. His granddaughter, *Anne Addison*, the
daughter of Thomas and Ellinor (Smith) Addison,
married William Murdock, of Prince George's County,
Md. (See pp. 671-672 for Smith and Addison lines.)

BURROWS

ARMS: *Azure, three fleur-de-lis ermine.*
CREST: *An eagle with wings extended, ermine.*

The first of his name in America, William Burrows,
was born at St. Olive's Parish, Southwark, Great Britain, December 19, 1725. He settled in St. John's Parish, Berkeley County, Province of South Carolina.
There he married, April 20, 1749, Mary Ward, who was
born October 11, 1728, in St. John's Parish. Their
children were: William Ward, Sarah, John, and Neigh-
lor.

Their eldest son, William Ward Burrows, born January 16, 1758, in South Carolina, was made Commandant
of the Marine Corps, July 12, 1798, Lieutenant-Colonel
in 1800, and was the first Commandant of the Washington Navy Yard. He moved to Philadelphia, and on
September 13, 1783, married *Mary*, the daughter of DR.
THOMAS BOND, JR.[19] Their children were:

Sarah.

William, born October 6, 1785, and died at sea, September 16, 1813, from a wound received in action with
the British brig *Boxer*, was buried at Portland, Me.
Congress awarded a gold medal to his family for his
bravery.

Ann Elizabeth.

Frances Harriet, married *John Nelson*. Their
daughter, *Rosa Landonia*, married *Isaac Nevett Steele*.

[19] *Taken from Family Bible* of William Ward Burrows, now owned by
Alex. Neill.

BOND

The Bonds are descended from Jonas Bond, who married Rosa Wood, Bury St. Edwards, Eng.

Their son, Thomas Bond, died 1658, married Elizabeth ——, and was the father of Thomas II, who emigrated to Maryland in 1645, and settled in Calvert County.

His son, Richard Bond, was born in Calvert County, Md., and died November 16, 1719. He married, 1702, in a Quaker Meeting-house at West River, Md., Elizabeth, the daughter of John and Elizabeth (Smith) Benson, and the widow of Benjamin Chew. Their children were: Richard, born 1705, Sarah, Thomas, John, Benson, and Phineous.

Their second son, Thomas Bond (1712-1784), received a medical education abroad, returned to America and settled in Philadelphia in 1734, where he was an eminent physician, giving the first clinical lecture in America. He was one of the founders of the Penn Hospital 1751, one of the original trustees of the University of Pennsylvania, and instrumental in its incorporation 1754. He married Sarah Venables, of Philadelphia.

DR. THOMAS BOND, JR., their son, born in Philadelphia 1735, studied medicine with his father. In 1776 he became surgeon of the " Flying Camp," organized for the purpose of resisting the advance of the British army. The troop joined General Washington's forces at the time of the capture of Fort Washington, and participated in the retreat which ended in the battles of Princeton and Trenton. In 1779 became Assistant Surgeon of the Philadelphia City troop, and appointed Medical Purveyor of the army 1781, by the Continental Con-

gress, serving through the entire war.   In 1793 he made
a visit to Morgantown, Va., died there, and was buried
in the Presbyterian Church.   One hundred and eight
years afterwards a contractor, who was tearing down
the old church, unearthed the tomb of Dr. Bond, and
the brass plate on the coffin bore the following inscription: " Thomas Bond, Jr., of Philadelphia, died July
17th, 1793." [20]   His remains were brought to Philadelphia in 1901, and are buried in Christ Church graveyard.   He married Anne Morgan; their daughter,
Mary, married William Ward Burrows.

SMITH-BENSON

The progenitor of this Smith line, Nathan Smith,
of Calvert County, Md., was the father of Thomas, who
married Alice ——.[21]

Their daughter, Elizabeth, married John Benson, of
Calvert County.

Their daughter, Elizabeth Benson, married, first,
Benjamin Chew, second Richard Bond; their son,
Thomas Bond, and his wife, Sarah Venables, were the
parents of THOMAS BOND II, who married Anne Morgan.

Their daughter, *Mary,* married William Ward Bur-
rows, and their daughter, *Frances Harriet,* married
John Nelson, whose daughter, *Rosa Landonia,* married
Isaac Nevett Steele.   Their daughters are:

ROSA NELSON STEELE,

KATE NEVETT STEELE,

Members of Chapter I., The Colonial Dames of
America.

20 *Records of Philadelphia City Troops.*
21 Md. *Cal. of Wills,* Vol. I, p. 163.

XLI

TILDEN, OR TYLDEN

ARMS: *A saltier between four pheons.*
CREST: *A battle ax with a serpent twisted around it.*
MOTTO: *" Truth and Liberty."*

The Tyldens of " Milsted Manor " have been seated
in Kent for many centuries. One possessed Milsted,
another moved to Sussex, and a third, emigrating to
America, founded the large family of Tildens. In the
reign of Edward III, William Tylden paid aid for
lands in Kent, when the Black Prince was knighted.

JOSEPH TYLDEN I, born in England before 1600, was
one of the forty-two " adventurers " of the Plymouth
Colony, 1620.[1]

His son, *Nathaniel Tilden,* one of the founders of
Scituate, Mass., came to the Colony before 1628. He
married, in England, *Lydia,* the daughter of Thomas
and Elizabeth Bourne.[2]

ENSIGN JOSEPH TILDEN II., their son, born in England, was Ensign in the Colonial Militia 1652. He
married in England, 1648, Elizabeth, the daughter of
John and Elise de Twysden of " Royden Hall," Kent.
Sir William Twysden, first Baronet, was one of the
gentlemen who escorted James VI of Scotland to London, when he took possession of the British Crown.
Adam de Twysden possessed estate of Twysenden in
Kent, in the time of Edward I.

Their daughter, *Rebecca Tilden,* born 1665, married,

[1] Arbor's *Story of the Pilgrim Fathers.*
  Savage's *Geneal. Dic.*
[2] Deane's *Hist. of Scituate.*

1678, LIEUTENANT JAMES BRIGGS, the son of Walter
and Mary (Watson) Briggs, born in Scituate, Mass.,
1647-48. He was in the Colonial Militia, and served
in King Philip's War, 1675-1676, as did his father,
Walter Briggs. Their daughter, *Mary,* married *Josiah
Litchfield II.*

BOURNE

THOMAS BOURNE of Tenderten, Kent, of the same
family as Rear-Admiral Nehemiah Bourne, who commanded the Parliamentary forces, was born in England
1601, and died in Marshfield, Mass., 1684. A Deputy
from Marshfield 1642, he was Assistant to Governor
Winslow, 1642 to 1646. He married Elizabeth ——.
One of their daughters married John Bradford, a son
of the Governor, and another daughter married Josiah
Winslow, a brother of Governor Edward Winslow.
Their daughter, *Lydia,* married *Nathaniel Tilden.*

LITCHFIELD

ARMS: *Per cheveron sable and argent in chief, three leopard's faces.*
CREST: *An arm in armour embossed, in hand a sword ppr.*
MOTTO: *" Semper pugnare paratus."*

One of this family, Lawrence Litchfield,[3] married
Judith, the daughter of William Dennis.

Their son, Josiah Litchfield I, married 1671, *Sarah,*
the daughter of REV. NICHOLAS BAKER, of Kent, Eng.,
a graduate of St. John College, Cambridge, 1631-32,
and A. M. 1635; Representative to the General Court
from Hingham, Mass., 1636 to 1638, and first Deputy
from Hingham.[4]

Their son, *Josiah Litchfield II.,* born in Scituate,

3 *The Litchfield Family in America.*
4 *Hist. of Hingham.*

Mass., January 10, 1677, married *Mary,* the daughter of LIEUTENANT JAMES BRIGGS; she was born May 14, 1682.

JOSIAH LITCHFIELD III., their son, one of the Committee of Eleven, on Correspondence, Inspection and Safety, in Scituate, March 17, 1777, married *Abigail,* the daughter of David and Susanna (Vinton) Studley. This line of Studleys were descended from GOVERNOR THOMAS HINCKLEY.

Their daughter, *Lucy Studley Litchfield,* born April 20, 1760, married December 22, 1784, John, the son of John Doane. Their daughter, *Nancy Litchfield Doane,* married William Wentworth Hailey.[5]

The elder Doane (1590-1675), born in Eastham, Cape Cod, a Deputy to the General Court 1633, was with Captain Miles Standish and William Bradford on the Board of Assistants to Governor Winslow.

HINCKLEY-STUDLEY

GOVERNOR THOMAS HINCKLEY, born in England 1618, the son of Samuel Hinckley, was Representative 1647, Assistant of the Colony of Maryland, the first Deputy-Governor 1680, and Governor 1681 to 1692. His daughter, *Mary,* married John Weyborn and their descendants are as follows:

Elizabeth Weyborn married John Merritt.

Mary Merritt, born 1668, married, 1683, Benjamin Studley, who was born in England, 1661.

Studley is an old English name found in Kent and Yorkshire, the seat of the family being "Studley Park," near where are the ruins of the celebrated Fountain Abbey and Lord Ripon's estate, Studley Royal.

5 *The Doane Genealogy.*
Swift's *Barnstable Families.*

David Studley, the son of Benjamin, was born January 18, 1696; married, November 12, 1717, Susanna, the daughter of Blaise and Lydia (Hayden) Vinton. Blaise Vinton was the son of John and Ann Vinton, and his wife was a daughter of John and Hannah (Ames) Hayden, of Braintree.

Abigail Studley married *Josiah Litchfield III.*

HAYLEY

The Hayleys are believed to have been originally Hawleys. After the American Revolution, an effort was made by the estate of Lord Hawley (extinct Irish peerage) to find the descendants of two sons of a former peer who had come to the colony of Massachusetts, and it is said that one of the Hayley family, Sylvestre by name, was paid an annuity by the estate of the widow of Lord Hawley, during his lifetime.[6]

The Hayleys claim descent from Robert Cecil, Lord Burleigh, Queen Elizabeth's famous Premier. Robert Cecil is a frequently recurring name in the Hayley family, and Salisbury Hayley possessed an old seal with the Cecil (Salisbury) coat of arms engraved on it.

The first of the name in New England, Andrew Hayley, had a land grant near Kittery in 1660, which is in possession of a branch of the family, and the house built by him is yet standing. He married Deborah, the daughter of Gowan Wilson, who founded the town of Kittery, Me.[7]

Their son, Andrew Hayley II, married Elizabeth,

6 *The Hayley Genealogy.*
7 Baylies' *New Plymouth.*
  History of Hingham.
  American Ancestry.
  Memoirs of the Plymouth Colony.

the daughter of Humphrey and Elizabeth (Champernon) Scammon. Humphrey Scammon was the son of Admiral Scammon, Royal Navy.

Their son, John Hayley, married Margaret Bryar.

Their son, Robert Cecil Hayley, married September 10, 1772, Elizabeth Parker.

Their son, William Wentworth Hayley, married at Rye, N. H., September 15, 1807, *Nancy Litchfield Doane*, who was born March 27, 1787.

Their son, *Salisbury Hayley*, was born near Kittery, Me. Graduating from Bowdoin College, he studied medicine and later law; was admitted to the bar at Los Angeles, Cal., in December, 1868. He married, at St. Augustine, Fla., 1841, Maria de Burgos (1821-1848), the daughter of Guiseppe Martinelli, and his wife Heronima Pozzo di Borgo. The mother of Giuseppe Martinelli was one of the Gustiniani family of Venice, and his wife the daughter of Pedro Jose Pozzo di Borgo and his wife Maria de Velasquez, was born near Ajaccio, Corsica; he himself was educated at Brienne and emigrated to Augustine, Fla., during the Spanish possession. With others loyal to Spain, he loaned money to the Spanish King, Ferdinand VII, to carry on the war against Napoleon, and a claim, known as the McIntosh claim, is held by the heirs of Pozzo di Borgo and others. Their daughter, *Ellen Salisbury*, married *Yates Stirling*, descended from MAJOR THOMAS YATES.

The Pozzo di Borgo have been long known in the annals of Corsica.[3] In the sixteeth century they distinguished themselves in the service of Venice, and the Corsican poet, Biagino de Luca, eulogizes in his epic poem, ' Ornano Maro," several Pozzo di Borgo, and predicts immortal glory to their race. Originally, as

[3] *Wanderings in Corsica; Corsican Families.*

CHARLES FREDERICK VON MEYERS
From an 18th century miniature

SALISBURY HAYLEY
Reproduced from a miniature, 1835

JACOB WALSH, JR.

it is supposed, from Burgos, Castile, Spain, they were ennobled in the fifth century. Tradition says that one who defended a pass near Burgos against the Goths, was made hidalgo, and allowed to bear the name Del Paso de Burgos (of the Pass of Burgos).

YATES

CAPTAIN THOMAS YATES, born in England, and died at his country seat " Springfield," near Baltimore Town, October 15, 1815, served throughout the War of the Revolution. June 19, 1776, a Lieutenant in Captain MacCubbin's Company; August 5, 1776, promoted to Captain; served under General Lafayette at Yorktown, and present at the surrender of Lord Cornwallis. He was Captain of the 3d Company, 4th Battalion, in Brig-Gen. Smallwood's Brigade of Regulars, March 27, 1777. (Other officers were Colonel Josias Carrol Hall, Lieut.-Col. Samuel Smith, Major John Eager Howard.) He married Mary, the daughter of Charles Frederick and Mathilda (Jarrold) Myers (von Myers); she died at " Springfield," November 30, 1796.

Their daughter, *Margaret Yates,* married in Baltimore, June 24, 1802, Jacob, the son of Jacob Walsh; she died April 25, 1824. One of their sons, Thomas Yates Walsh, was Congressman from the Fourth District of Maryland, and a noted wit and speaker. Their daughter, *Elizabeth Ann,* married Archibald Stirling.

Through her father's line, the von Myers, Mary Myers Yates was descended (through his daughter Sarah) from William the Silent, Prince of Orange, and his fourth wife, Marie Louise de Chatillon, the daughter of Gaspar de Coligny, Admiral of France, the son of Gaspar de Coligny, Marshal of France, and Louise de Montmorency. Mathilda Jarrold was the daughter of Captain Jarrold of the Royal Navy.

STIRLING

ARMS: *Argent, on a bend engrailed azure, between two roses one in chief and the other in base, gules, three buckles or.*
CREST: *A stag's head issuing from a ducal coronet.*
MOTTO: *" Gang forward."* [9]

The colonist, James Stirling, born near Stirling, Scotland, 1752, died at his country seat, near Baltimore, June 25, 1820. Of the Scotch family of Stirling, of Kier and Cadder (Cawdor), he came to the colonies about 1774. The origin of the family is variously attributed to Henry de Strevelin, the youngest son of David, Earl of Huntington, the brother of King William the Lion, and by later investigators to Walter de Strieulyng, born about 1100.[10] The estate of the head of the house is Keir, near Stirling, a beautiful and historical place, dating back to the twelfth century. James Stirling received a testimonial from General Greene " for bravery at Yorktown," where he fought for his adopted country. He married Elizabeth, the daughter of Judge Andrew Gibson, of Carlisle, Pa.

STIRLING

[9] As shown on old letters and papers belonging to James Stirling from an impression in wax. Over fifty arms have been granted to the Stirling family and nearly all carry the three buckles on the shield and give this motto.

[10] Fraser's *Stirlings of Kier* and their *Family Papers.*
Sterling Genealogy, by Albert M. Sterling.

Their son, Archibald Stirling, born July, 1798, in Baltimore, Md., and died there February, 1888, was a founder of the Savings Bank of Baltimore. For many years, until the time of his death at the age of ninety, he was its President. He married *Elizabeth Ann*, the daughter of Jacob and Margaret (Yates) Walsh; she was born in December, 1809, and died at " Snowdoun," their country place, near Baltimore, in September, 1859.

Their son, *Rear-Admiral Yates Stirling* (retired), was born in Baltimore, Md., May 6, 1843. Appointed to the United States Naval Academy, as Acting Midshipman upon recommendation of Hon. Henry Winter Davis, Representative of the Fourth District, Maryland, he entered the Academy September 27, 1860, graduating May 28, 1863, and being commissioned an Ensign on the same day. He served in the Civil War on sloop-of-war *Shenandoah,* North Atlantic Blockading Squadron. In April, 1864, he was temporarily detached from the *Shenandoah,* while that vessel was under repairs, in consequence of damage received in a cyclone, and served until June, 1864, on flagship *Minnesota,* on staff of Rear-Admiral S. P. Lee, and on monitor *Onandago,* on James River, during General Grant's advance upon Richmond; in both attacks on Fort Fisher; promoted to Master, November 10, 1865; Lieutenant, November 10, 1866; Lieutenant-Commander, March 12, 1868; and served in various ships and stations. Promoted to Commander, November 26, 1880; stationed at Washington Navy Yard 1882-1884; commanded the *Iroquois,* Pacific Station, 1884 to 1886; commanded Receiving Ship *Dale,* 1887-1890; commanded *Dolphin,* 1890-1891; on the Examining and Retiring Board, 1891-1892; Light House Inspector, Baltimore, Md., 1892 to 1894; promoted to

Captain, September 16, 1894; commanded the *Newark,* South Atlantic Squadron, 1895-1896; commanded *Lancaster,* and also the naval force on South Atlantic Station, 1896-1897; Member Light House Board, 1898-1900; commanded Naval Station San Juan, Puerto Rico; promoted to Rear-Admiral, June 8, 1902; Commandant Puget Sound Navy Yard, 1902 to 1903; commanded Phillipine Squadron, Asiatic Fleet, 1903 to 1904; commanded Asiatic Fleet, 1904 to 1905. Retired, May 6, 1905, upon reaching the age of sixty-two years.

He married, August 29, 1867, *Ellen Salisbury,* the daughter of Salisbury and Maria de Burgos (Martinelli) Hayley. Their daughter is:

HELEN STIRLING,

Member of Chapter I., The Colonial Dames of America.

XLII

DE WOLF

There seems to be good warrant for the claim that the first De Wolf who came to America was a younger son of one of the Barons de Wolff of the Livonian family, which is an offshoot of the Saxon branch.

The legend of the origin of the name of " de Wolf," which is practically the same in every country in which there are representatives of the family, is that Louis de Saint-Etienne, of the French noble family of that name, was one of the attendants of King Charles V., of France, on a hunting expedition. During the chase, a wolf cub crossed the King's path. Charles threw his lance, wounding the cub, and breaking the weapon against a tree. An enormous she-wolf, seeing her offspring

DE WOLF

wounded, rushed from her hiding-place upon the King, who had only his hunting knife with which to defend himself. At this moment, Louis de Saint-Etienne sprang between the savage beast and the King, dispatching it with his sword, for which act of bravery the King knighted him, dubbing him " de Loup." · And so originated the noble French family of that name.

His grandson, Emile de Loup, accompanying the Princess Mathilda to Germany at the time of her marriage to the eldest son of Frederick, Elector and Duke

of Saxony, in 1423 became a favorite at the Saxon
Court, and was created a Baron in 1427. He then
changed his name from the French to the German, and
was known thereafter as " de Wolf." His direct descendant, Maximillian de Wolf, founded the Belgian
branch of the family, and from him, also, descended the
de Wolfs of Holland, Prussia and Livonia.

The first known ancestor of the family in America,
Balthasar De Wolf, is mentioned in the court records
of Hartford, Conn., March 5, 1656. He was chosen
" Committee of the town " 1677, and was living in
1695. He married Alice ——, who was living in 1687.

Their eldest child, Edward De Wolf, was born 1646,
and died 1712. He and his brother Stephen, " were of
the Connecticut Volunteers," in King Philip's War.
He married Rebecca ——.

Their son, Charles De Wolf, was born September 18,
1673, and died December 5, 1731. He lived in Glastonbury and Middletown, Conn., and married Prudence
White.

Their son, Charles De Wolf II., born in Lyme, Conn.,
1695, emigrated to Gaudaloupe and married, March
31, 1717, Margaret Potter. He continued to reside
there until his death in 1731.

Their fourth child, Mark Antony De Wolf, was born
in Gaudaloupe, November 8, 1726, and died November
9, 1793. When about seventeen years of age he accompanied Captain Simeon Potter in one of his ships to
Bristol, R. I., and shortly afterwards, August 25, 1744,
married Abigail, the daughter of Hopestill and Lydia
Potter and a sister of Captain Simeon Potter. She was
born February 2, 1726. Within a few months of his
marriage, war between England and France having
been declared, he sailed on the privateer *Prince Charles*

of Lorraine, under the command of his brother-in-law,
Captain Potter. In 1773, this same intrepid Captain
Potter commanded the Bristol Contingent of the
" fleet " of nine long-boats which captured and burned
the *Gaspée*. Having had enough of privateering,
Mark Antony returned to Rhode Island, purchased a
farm near Bristol, and settled down to a quiet life.

One of his sons, Hon. James De Wolf, born in Bristol,
R. I., March 18, 1764, and died there December 21,
1837, inherited his father's earlier fondness for a " stren-
uous life," deserting the farm when only a boy, joined
his uncle " Sim " Potter and became a privateersman.
While so engaged and preying upon British commerce,
he was twice captured. Later, he became famous as
an owner of privateers and slavers, and accumulated
a large fortune for that time. His most famous vessel the *Yankee* is said to have netted " a round million
of dollars in prize money." With grim humor he re-
named the British ship *Shannon* which he captured and
converted into a privateer the *Balance,* and another privateer that soon followed her he named the *Remittance*.
It has been said that he was the only American who
collected his own " French claims." His communica-
tion to the Government at Washington asking for a
" letter of Marque and Reprisal " for the *Yankee,* which
was written only eleven days after war with England
had been declared by President Madison, is of sufficient
historical interest to warrant its reproduction:

" BRISTOL, R. I., 30th June, 1812.
" To Hon. William Eustis, Secretary of War:—Sir:
I have purchased and now ready for sea, an armed Brig
(one of the most suitable in this country for a Privateer) of one hundred and sixty tons burthen, mounting

eighteen guns, and carries one hundred and twenty men, called the *Yankee,* commanded by Oliver Wilson. Being desirous that she should be on her cruise as soon as possible, I beg you will cause a commission to be forwarded as soon as practicable to the Collector of the District, that this vessel may not be detained. I am very respectfully, Sir, Your obedient servant, James De Wolf."

Within less than two weeks, on July 13, the desired commission was issued, and without loss of time the *Yankee* put to sea. One of her first captures, made off the coast of Nova Scotia, August 1, was the fine ship *Royal Bounty,* more than four times as large as the *Yankee,* and carrying ten guns. The *Bounty* put up a stiff fight, but was soon compelled to strike her colors. It is said that in her first cruise, of less than three months, the *Yankee* captured ten prizes, took or destroyed nearly half a million dollars' worth of property, and paid for herself many times over. For thirty years James De Wolf represented Bristol in the State Legislature, and for two years acted as Presiding Officer of the Lower House. In 1821 he represented Rhode Island in the United States Senate, but finding his duties there interfered with the oversight of his increasing business interests at home, he resigned his seat in the Senate before the expiration of his term. He married, January 7, 1790 *Nancy* (or *Ann*), the daughter of William and Mary (Le Baron) Bradford; she was born August 6, 1770, and died in Bristol, R. I., January 2, 1838. Their son was *Mark Antony De Wolf II.*[1]

[1] *Family Bible.*
  "The De Wolfs," by Rev. Calbraith B. Perry, D. D.
  The Hist. of the Town of Bristol, R. I., by W. H. Munro.
  The Pilgrim Fathers of New England, by John Brown, D. D.

AMEY BROWN
Wife of Lieut. Sylvanus Martin

CAPT. MARK ANTONY DE WOLF

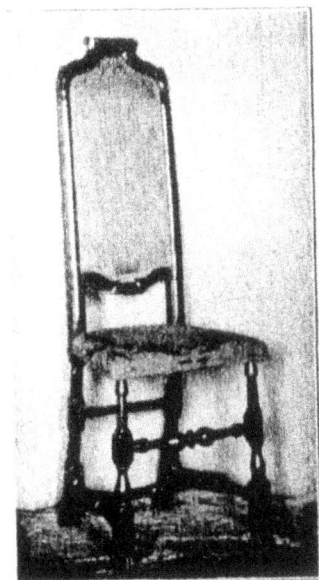

Gov. WILLIAM BRADFORD CHAIR

NANCY BRADFORD
Wife of James De Wolf.
Reproduction of a miniature

BRADFORD

A native of Austerfield, Yorkshire, Eng., William Bradford is the first of the family of whom we have record. The date of his birth is not known, but he died in Austerfield, and was buried January 10, 1595. His son, William Bradford II., married, 1584, Alice Hanson.

WILLIAM BRADFORD III., of *Mayflower* fame, their son, was born in March, 1588, and died May 9, 1657. He lived in Austerfield. At the age of seventeen, however, he went to Scrooby, and became an associate of Brewster, who was the head of what was called the "Separatist Church." The "Separatists" tried to leave England in a body, but, failing in this attempt, they left in small boats, going first to Amsterdam and later to Leyden, where they remained for eleven years. At the end of this time they concluded to emigrate to America, and sailed from Delf in the ship *Speedwell,* having arranged to meet the *Mayflower,* on board of which were a number of their co-religionists, at Southampton. The *Speedwell* proved unseaworthy, and such of her passengers as had not lost heart, were transferred at Plymouth to the *Mayflower,* many of those who had originally embarked on the *Mayflower* having also become disheartened, and returned to their homes, preferring, it would seem, persecution to seasickness. The *Mayflower* sailed from Plymouth, September 16, 1620, with one hundred and two emigrants on board, William Bradford, Miles Standish, and John Carver being the leaders of the company. On the death of John Carver, the first Governor of Plymouth Colony, William Bradford succeeded him, and twice subsequently was elected Plymouth's Governor. Dorothy May, of Wisbeck,

Bradford's first wife, whom he had married at Leyden, November 26, 1613, was drowned from the *Mayflower*, while she was at anchor in Plymouth Bay, before the ship's company had landed. Three years afterwards he married Alice Carpenter, the widow of Constant Southworth, who, tradition says, was in love with him before he left England; she died 1670.

WILLIAM BRADFORD IV., their son, born in Plymouth, June 17, 1624, and died February.20, 1703, second in command to Miles Standish, commanded the Plymouth forces in King Philip's War, having the rank of Major, and receiving a serious wound. He was Deputy-Governor of Plymouth from 1682 to 1686, 1689 to 1691, and in the last named year one of the Council of Massachusetts. He married Alice Richards.

MAJOR JOHN BRADFORD, their son, born February 20, 1653, was a Major of the Plymouth forces, and the first Deputy from Plymouth to the General Court of Massachusetts 1689. He married, February 5, 1674, Mercy Warren.

Their son, *Samuel Bradford,* born December 23, 1683, and died March 26, 1740, lived in Plympton, and was a Lieutenant of the Plympton Battery. He married, October 21, 1714, Sarah Gray.

GOVERNOR WILLIAM BRADFORD V., their son, born November 8, 1728, and died in Bristol, R. I., July 6, 1808, was a physician and practised his profession in Warren, R. I., 1751. He removed soon after to Bristol, where he practised law, having abandoned medicine. He was Rhode Island's last Deputy-Governor under the Crown, the first Governor under the Continental Congress, and from 1792 to 1797 representing the State in the United States Senate. He married, 1751, Mary, the daughter of Dr. Lazarus and Lydia (Bartlett) Le

Baron; she was born 1731, and died October 2, 1775; their daughter, *Nancy,* married Hon. James De Wolf.[2]

LE BARON

The "Nameless Nobleman" of Jane Austen's novel, Dr. Francis Le Baron, was born in Provence, France, in 1668, and died August 8, 1704. From early childhood he had been brought up as the foster-son of Dr. Louis Pictou, a physician of Bordeaux, to whom his father had confided him, with the injunction that he be raised a good Catholic, always wear a gold cross which hung about his neck, and be buried with it. His real name and identity, though known to Dr. Pictou and, before his death, revealed to Francis, have remained a mystery to this day. There is some ground for the belief that it was "de Montarnaud," but if such were the case, he never revealed it, and, it is said, would laughingly reply to the too curious that he was "Baron de rien de tout." Through the influence of his foster-father, who bequeathed to him such property as he possessed, he became a physician. With a portion of this inheritance, he fitted out a privateer, which he called *L'Angle,* for the purpose of preying upon the commerce of England, that country and France being then at war. In 1694, this ship, of which Dr. Le Baron was acting as surgeon, was wrecked in Buzzard's Bay, Mass. The ship's company succeeded in reaching Falmouth in small boats, where they were all promptly made prisoners by the hostile inhabitants, with the exception of Dr. Le Baron. He managed to escape capture, and making his way inland, came to the house of a colonist named Wilder. Only the colonist's daughter was at home at the time. To her he told of his plight, and, whether or not it was love at first sight, she offered him shelter, and with the connivance of her parents, kept him in hiding for some time. Perhaps because the colonists were greatly in need of a physician, he was ultimately paroled and became a medical practitioner in Plymouth. A year later, in 1695, Mary Wilder became his wife. She was born in Hingham, Mass., April 7, 1668, and died September 25, 1737.

Their third child, Dr. Lazarus Le Baron, who was born December 26, 1698, married, first, May 16, 1720, *Lydia Bartlett* (a granddaughter of Lieutenant Francis Griswold, and a great-great-granddaughter of RICHARD WARREN, one of the *Mayflower* pilgrims); second, Lydia (Bradford) Cushman. Issue, first wife: *Mary,* who married WILLIAM BRADFORD V, of Bristol, R. I.[3]

DE WOLF (*Continued*)

The fourth son of Hon. James and Nancy Bradford) De Wolf, *Mark Antony De Wolf II,* was born in Bristol, R. I., September 28, 1797, and died there in March, 1851. He married in Providence, R. I., October 10, 1821, *Sophie Catherine Virginia,* the daughter of Pierre Leon and Bridget (Colman) De Chappotin; she was born in Brookfield, N. H., July 8, 1802, and died in Baltimore, Md., January 10, 1879. *Their son was Francis Le Baron De Wolf.*

[3] *Ibid.*

Descendants of Francis Le Baron, compiled by Mary Le Baron Stockwell.

DE CHAPPOTIN

The ancestors of Pierre Leon De Chappotin were from Nantes, France. He was born in the Island of San Domingo, baptized there, October 10, 1768, and his parents were Denis and Mary (Francis) De Chappotin. He came to America at the outbreak of the Revolution in San Domingo, 1791. He married *Bridget* (born December 7, 1775), the daughter of Dudley and Mary (Jones) Colman.

COLMAN

COLONEL DUDLEY COLMAN, born August 13, 1745, and died in Dover, N. H., November 16, 1797. As Lieutenant-Colonel of the regiment of Massachusetts troops, commanded by Colonel Edward Wiggleworth, commissioned by the Provincial Congress, June 24, 1776, he saw much service in the Revolutionary War. He married Mary Jones. Issue, among others:

Henry, who spent many years in England, dying at Islington, August 17, 1849. He was the author of several works upon European Agriculture, and was an intimate friend of Lady Byron, who erected a handsome monument over his grave in Kensal Green.

Bridget, who married Pierre Leon De Chappotin.

DE WOLF (*Continued*)

The third son of Mark Antony and Sophie Catherine Virginia De Wolf, *Francis Le Baron De Wolf,* was born in Bristol, R. I., October 12, 1826, and died there, June 4, 1861. He married, first, 1848, in Providence, R. I., Caroline Martin, the daughter of Samuel and Amey (Martin) Dexter, of Providence, R. I.; she was born April 2, 1823, and died in Bristol, R. I., December 27, 1848. Issue:

CAROLINE DEXTER, who was born in Bristol, R. I., December 17, 1848, married in St. Michael's Church, Bristol, April 30, 1867, Dr. Samuel Theobald, of Baltimore, Md., whose daughter, CAROLINE DE WOLF, married Robert Goodloe Harper Pennington.

DEXTER

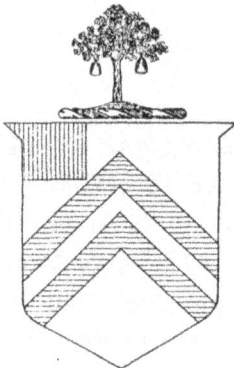

DEXTER

All the Irish Dexters were descended from Richard de Excester, Governor and Lord Justice of Ireland, who died in 1269. The family probably emigrated to Ireland from Devonshire, Eng., as the name implies that they lived in or near the cathedral town of Exeter. At the time of the Irish massacre of the Protestants, October 27, 1641, Richard Dexter, of Slane, County Meath, one of the descendants of Richard, with his wife Bridget and their children, fled to England, shortly afterwards emigrating to America. The exact date of his arrival is not known, but he was living in Boston prior to February 28, 1642. He settled at Charlestown, Mystic side, and later removed to Malden, Mass., where he had purchased a farm. He died in Charlestown, Mass., 1680.

Their son, John Dexter, born in Ireland 1639, and died in Malden, December 8, 1677, married Sarah ——.

JOHN DEXTER II., their son, was born August 21, 1671, and died November 14, 1722. He was "Captain of a company of foot under George I " and "Deacon " at the time of his death, and for a number of years was Selectman of the town of Malden. He married Winnifred, the daughter of Samuel and Rebecca (Crawford) Sprague; she was born in Malden, Mass., December 31, 1673, and died there December 5, 1752.

Their son, the *Rev. Samuel Dexter*, born in Malden, Mass., October 23, 1700, and died January 29, 1755, in Dedham, Mass., was graduated from Harvard College 1720, and ordained Minister of the First Church in Dedham, May 6, 1724. He married in Boston, July 9, 1724, Catharina, the daughter of Samuel and Maria Catharina (Smith) Mears; she was born September 25, 1701, and died in Dedham, June 10, 1797.

SAMUEL DEXTER II., their son, born in Dedham, Mass., March 16, 1725, and died in Mendon, Mass., June 10, 1810, was Representative from Dedham to the General Court from 1764 to 1768, and elected to the Council each year from 1766 to 1774. He married, June 28, 1748, in Boston, Hannah, the daughter of Andrew and Mary (Germaine) Sigourney.

Their second son, *Andrew Dexter*, born in Boston, Mass., May 4, 1751, and died in Athens, N. Y., November 12, 1816, married in Woodstock, Conn., May 5, 1778, Mary, the daughter of Simon and Mary (Richardson) Newton; she was born in Newport, R. I., November 20, 1757, and died September 13, 1825.

Their second child, *Samuel Dexter III.*, born in Boston, Mass., July 5, 1781, was graduated from Brown University 1801, and was a resident of Providence, R. I. where he died February 26, 1862. Unlike his forbears, who were little given to multi-marriages, he had four wives. His third wife, *Amey Martin,* whom he married in Providence, R. I., September 10, 1821, was the daughter of Joseph and Abby Brown Martin, and was born in Providence, May 9, 1805, where she died September 7, 1826. Their daughter, *Caroline Martin,* married *Francis Le Baron De Wolf.*[4]

MARTIN

The colonist, Richard Martin of Badcombe, Somersetshire, Eng., arrived in America 1663, to take possession of property left him by his brother Robert of Rehoboth, Mass., who came here in 1635. Richard Martin died in Rehoboth, March 2, 1694.[5]

His son, John Martin, born in England, 1633, and died in Rehoboth, March 21, 1713, where he settled when he emigrated with his father, was surveyor of highways there from 1673 to 1685.

His third son, Ephraim Martin, was born in Rehoboth, February 7, 1676, and died there June 25, 1734.

His eldest son, Edward Martin, was born in Rehoboth, October 22, 1700, and died there June 2, 1745.

CAPTAIN SYLVANUS MARTIN, his only son, was born in Rehoboth, July 17, 1727, and died there August 13, 1782. He commanded a company of Massachusetts

[4] *Family Bible.*
[5] *Ibid.*

Family Records including two military commissions from Governor Trumbull last Colonial Governor of Connecticut and first American Governor of Connecticut.

troops in the Revolutionary War, was Justice of the Peace, one of the Committee of Safety, and a Selectman of Rehoboth. He married, February 20, 1746, Martha Wheeler.

LIEUTENANT SYLVANUS MARTIN, JR., their son, born in Rehoboth, March 19, 1748, and died in Providence, R. I., November 25, 1818, was Lieutenant and afterwards Captain of Connecticut troops during the Revolution. He married Amey, the daughter of William and Susanna (Dexter) Brown; she was born November 6, 1749.

Their daughter, *Abby Brown Martin*, born November 2, 1775, married her fourth cousin, Joseph S. Martin, whose daughter, *Amey*, married *Samuel Dexter III*.

Their daughter, *Caroline Martin Dexter*, married *Francis Le Baron De Wolf*, whose daughter is:

CAROLINE DEXTER DE WOLF THEOBALD,
        her daughter,
CAROLINE DE WOLF THEOBALD PENNINGTON,
        and her granddaughter,
CHARLOTTE EMILY PENNINGTON,
Members of Chapter I., The Colonial Dames of America.

XLIII

THOMAS

VIRTUS ✦ INVICTA ✦ GLORIOSA

During the reign of Queen Anne of England, two brothers, James and Samuel Thomas, emigrated from Wales, were among the first settlers of Kent County, Md., and possessed of landed property. One was said to be a Whig, the other a Tory, but they lived in fraternal affection and friendship. James Thomas, born in Wales or West England, married first an English lady, who came to America with him, and second, Elizabeth Hacket, born in Maryland, her parents being of English descent. The property of Samuel (a Colonel of Militia) who died without children, descended by his will to two nephews.

One of these nephews, James Thomas II., born in Kent County, Md., married Elizabeth Bellicum (who married second, Mr. Farrell); she was born in Cecil (or New Castle) County, her father, a colonist from

Holland, being one of the first settlers on the Delaware, and evidently a large land owner. Elizabeth and one of her brothers, Christopher Bellicum, held landed property in Kent County, Md.

DR. PHILIP THOMAS,[1] their son, was born near Chestertown, Kent County, Md., June 11, 1747, and died in Fredericktown, Md., April 25, 1815. Appointed by the inhabitants of Frederick County a Delegate to attend the General Congress at Annapolis,[2] June 22, 1774, when resolutions condemning the blockading of the port of Boston were passed, he also represented the county, November 18, 1774, in carrying into execution the association agreed on by the American Continental Congress.[3] January 24, 1775, being directed to promote subscriptions for the purchase of arms and ammunition, he was placed on the Committee of Observation for Frederick County, remaining a member during its entire existence. Delegated to represent the county[4] at any Provincial Convention[5] to be held at the City of Annapolis before October, 1775,[6] he served also on the Committee of Correspondence,[7] and was County Lieutenant-Colonel during the greater portion of the Revolutionary War.[8] He was sent as a Delegate to the House of Delegates, November 10, 1777,[9] and June 16, 1779,[10] became Justice of the Peace. Further responsi-

[1] *Hist. of Maryland*, by J. Thomas Scharf; Scharf's *Chronicles of Baltimore, etc.*

[2] *Am. Arch.*, Series 4, Vol. I, pp. 433-438.

[3] *Ibid.*, p. 986.

[4] *Ibid.*, p. 1173, Vol. II, p. 1044.

[5] *Ibid.*, Series 5, Vol. III, p. 1288.

[6] *Ibid.*, p. 1173.

[7] *Ibid.*, pp. 433, 986, 1173; Vol. II, p. 1044; Series 5, Vol. II, p. 298.

[8] See *Correspondence Governor and Council of Maryland.* Also small volume of *Governor and Council*, pp. 111, 117, 159.

[9] *Jour.* of House of Delegates p. 22.

[10] Landsman's *Dict.* of Congress.

bilities were soon laid upon him for at the June session, General Assembly of 1780, an act was passed "to encourage raising a voluntary troop of Light-Horse in Baltimore Town and each County of this State." This act provided that any number of Militiamen, not exceeding forty-five, and not under fifteen years of age, in Baltimore Town or in any of the counties of the state, were authorized to form themselves into a troop of horse. The officers when in service were to have the same rations, pay and forage as was allowed to the Continental Horse; the companies were to be under the militia rules and in case of invasion were to serve under the direction of the Governor in any part of the state. The records of this office show that February 3, 1781, commission was issued to Philip Thomas appointing him Captain, and John Ross Key, Lieutenant, of a Troop of Horse, called the Frederick Light Dragoons. Dr. Thomas did not remain long in command, for on the 20th of the same month, he was made Lieutenant-Colonel, to fill the vacancy caused by the resignation of Colonel Baker Johnson, the brother of Governor Thomas Johnson, and John Ross Key succeeded him as Captain.

By virtue of Dr. Thomas' appointment the entire militia of the county was under his supervision with power to call them into action at all times and to do everything in his discretion for defending and strengthening the county. He supervised and directed the raising, arming and equipping of all the soldiers sent from Frederick County to the armies, from February, 1781 to the close of the war. The proceedings of the "Council of Safety" record:

"Monday, June 4th, 1781, That the Lieutenant of Frederick County immediately arm equip and march 500 militia of his command under proper officers to

JANE COXTEE HANSON
Wife of Dr. Philip Thomas

DR. PHILIP THOMAS

Georgetown in Montgomery County and there to remain till the Board otherwise direct."

This order was occasioned by the movement of the armies towards Yorktown, with the view of capturing the British Army under Lord Cornwallis. The Lieutenants of the various counties were ordered to facilitate the march of Generals Lafayette and Wayne through Maryland, to seize all the salt and fresh meats in their districts, and to impress all vessels, wagons, teams, drivers, etc,, for the transportation of troops, cannon, stores, etc. General Anthony Wayne passed through Frederick, May 31, 1781, to join Lafayette in Virginia, and Colonel Thomas ordered five hundred militia to be sent to the same command, which was retreating through Virginia towards Maryland. The Frederick Light Dragoons, then commanded by John Ross Key, crossed the Potomac on the 18th of June, and joined Lafayette in the surrender of Cornwallis at Yorktown.

When Washington was marching to Yorktown, his army was suffering greatly for the want of food. In this pressing emergency, Philip Thomas, the untiring commander, besides recruiting Washington's army with nearly a regiment of men, forwarded an immense quantity of flour and other provisions, and five hundred cattle, to Georgetown, from which point it was hauled to the army. After the surrender of Cornwallis, Colonel Thomas took a conspicuous part in the removal of the prisoners to Maryland and finally sent them to Lancaster, Penn. During all this trying period his bold demeanor and unwavering confidence infused hope and courage into many wavering hearts. His patriotic exertions in support of the cause often received the grateful acknowledgment of the leading generals and statesmen of the time.[11] He was elector for General Washington to the first Presidency of the United States, and was appointed by him supervisor of distilleries.

About 1770, Dr. Thomas removed to Fredericktown, Md., where he was married, February 18, 1773, by the Rev. Daniel McKennon, to *Jane Contee,* the daughter of John and Jane (Contee) Hanson, who was born in Charles County, Md., February, 1747, and died in Frederick, Md., June 17, 1781. Issue:

Catherine Hanson, born October 15, 1775; married Dr. Ashton Alexander, a celebrated physician of Baltimore. Issue: Ashton, George, who married Miss Levering, and Elizabeth, who married John, the son of Chief Justice Marshall.

Rebecca Bellicum, born February 8, 1777, married Judge Alexander Contee Magruder. Issue: Rebecca Thomas, married Major Scott, U. S. A.; Jane, married James Biays, John Hanson Thomas, and Philip.

John Hanson.

HANSON

The Maryland Hansons are descended from Roger de Rastric, who was seated at Rastric, Parish of Halifax, York County, Eng., in the year 1251. The name of Rastric continued through four generations until the year 1330, when John de Rastric assumed the surname of Hanson (a diminutive of Henry's son), and signed his name John Hanson to a deed in 1337. He married Alice, the daughter of Henry de Woodhouse (granddaughter, and heiress of Alexander de Woodhouse

---

[11] *Land and Historical Records* in the Land Office and State Library at Annapolis, Md.

JOHN HANSON
From the painting in Independence Hall,
Philadelphia

ELIZABETH MARSHALL.
Wife of Rawleigh Colston

whose wife was Beatrice, the daughter and heiress of Thomas de Toothill). Their descendants are as follows:

John of Woodhouse, the first of a line of four John Hansons in direct descent, married Cicely de Windebank.

John, married Cicely, the daughter of John Ravenshaw.

John of Woodhouse, married Catherine, the daughter of John Brooke (whose wife was a great-grandchild of Thomas Beaumont of Whitely).

John, married Agnes, the eldest daughter of John Savile, Esq., of New Hall, and his wife Margery (the daughter of John Gledhill); issue, among others:

HANSON

Thomas of Rastric, third son, who married Janet, the daughter of John Gledhill of Little-even, in Barkisland; issue among others:

John of London, third son, married Frances, the daughter of John Prichard; issue, three sons, of whom the eldest:

Colonel John, while taking a summer tour in Sweden, fell in love with and married a Swedish lady, who was closely connected in friendship with the Royal family. They died early, leaving a son:

Colonel John Hanson, who was reared in familiar intimacy with Gustavus Adolphus, then a youth about the same age. He entered the army at a suitable time,

served with credit, rose to the rank of Colonel, became
a trusted officer, and was always retained near the royal
person in action. While defending and attempting to
shield the King, he was slain in battle with Gustavus
Adolphus, at Lutzen, November 16, 1632. He left four
sons: Andrew, Randal or Randolph, William and
JOHN, all of whom were taken under the immediate protection of the Royal family of Sweden. In August,
1642, Queen Christina placed them in the special care
of Lieut.-Colonel John Printz, Governor of New
Sweden, with whom they came to the Delaware, and remained there on Tinicum Island until the year 1653,
when they came to Kent Island, Md.[12]

JOHN HANSON, the youngest of the four sons of Colonel John Hanson, of the Swedish Army, was born in
Sweden about 1630. After a short sojourn on Kent
Island, he finally settled in Charles County about
1655-6 where he died 1713. He married *Mary,* the
daughter of THOMAS HUSSEY, who was Justice for
Charles County, Md., 1672.[13]

COLONEL SAMUEL HANSON, second son, born in
Charles County, Md., 1685, and died 1740, was Burgess
for Charles County 1716 to 1728, Commissary 1734,
and Clerk of the Provincial Court 1739.[14] He married
Elizabeth (1689-1764), the daughter of COLONEL WAL-
TER STORY (1666-1726, the son of Walter Story a set-
tler, and Elizabeth his wife), a Magistrate for Charles
County, 1696.[15] Among their children were two sons,
Walter and JOHN.

The elder, Judge Walter Hanson, of " Harwood "

12 Hanson's *Old Kent,* pp. 110, 112.
13 *Md. Arch., P. C.,* 1671-1681, p. 72.
14 Hanson's *Old Kent,* p. 114.
15 *Arch. of Md.,* Vol. XX, p. 543.

(1711-1794), was High Sheriff of Charles County, 1739; Justice, 1741 to 1786; one of the Quorum from 1749, and Presiding Justice 1778.[16] He married Elizabeth, the daughter of William Hoskins.

HON. JOHN HANSON, of "Mulberry Grove," Charles County, was born there 1715, and died at "Oxen Hill," Prince George's County, Md., November 22, 1783. Long before the American Revolution he took an active part in the affairs of the Province of Maryland, and wielded strong influence in the administration of colonial affairs. He represented Charles County in the Lower House of Assembly in the years 1757, 1758, 1765, 1766, 1768, and in the political discussions which took place during these exciting years in relation to the oppression of the Mother Country, he took a leading and distinguished part, and soon ranked with the Chases, the Tilghmans and the Carrolls, in the regard of his fellow citizens. Out of the disputes which took place between the two houses of Assembly from 1757 to 1768, parties were formed, and the Lower House of Assembly, being composed of the representatives of the people in the Province, drew to its body the ablest men in Maryland.[17] John Hanson was one of the strongest advocates of the non-importation system, and among the first to sign the agreement, June 22, 1769, "neither to import nor to purchase any article then taxed, or which should thereafter be taxed by Parliament, for the purpose of revenue." In October following, their patriotism was put to the test. Several packages of goods were landed in Charles County contrary to the terms of the non-importation association, and openly and without fear

16 *Record of Commission Book of Charles County.*
17 Maryland *Senate and House Journals.*

of detention or punishment, the association of the
county, under the leadership of Hanson, compelled the
owners to reship the goods to England.[18]

From the close of the French and Indian War, Frederick County assumed importance as a region of uncommon productiveness, attracted a large number of prominent persons from other portions of the province and
Pennsylvania, and became a favorite section with emigrants from Germany, Switzerland and Great Britain.
Repairing thither in 1773, John Hanson led the people
to become practically a unit in their devotion to the
principles of the Revolution. Almost immediately upon his arrival in Frederick, his counsel was sought by
the people and his associates. The passage of the "Boston Port Bill," in 1774, roused the people of Maryland.
At a meeting of the citizens of Frederick, held at the
Courthouse, June 20, 1774, John Hanson presided.[19]
Philip Thomas, John Hanson, and his son, Alexander
Contee Hanson, were appointed Delegates to the
"General Congress at Annapolis." They were also
chosen members of the Committee of Observation, John
Hanson, Chairman, which position he held until it was
abolished by the establishment of the State govern-
ment.[20]

Shortly after assuming the duties of his office he sent
£200 sterling for the relief of the poor of Boston, which
was acknowledged by Samuel Adams of that city.
"The General Congress" or Convention of Maryland,
assembled at Annapolis June 22, and adjourned June

[18] McMahon's *Hist of Maryland.*
[19] *Am. Arch.,* Series 4, Vol. I, p. 433.
   Ibid., p. 1173.
[20] *Ibid.,* 433, 986, 1173; Vol. II, p. 1044; Vol. III, p. 1660; Vol. IV, pp.
480, 711; Vol. V, pp. 47, 171, 495, 942, 1067, 1554; Series 5, Vol. I, pp. 251
326, 569, 594, 757, 831, 1134, 1190; Vol. II, p. 296.

STATUE OF JOHN HANSON
"President of United States in Congress assembled."   Erected by the State
of Maryland in Statuary Hall at the Capitol, Washington

25, 1774. John Hanson as Delegate from Frederick County, assisted in the adoption of a series of non-importation resolutions [21] of the strongest character. The citizens of Frederick in 1774 and 1775, formed new Committees. John Hanson, as Chairman, representing them, was also a Delegate in the Provincial Convention at Annapolis, October, 1775. Became Treasurer of Frederick County, June 21, 1775.[22]

The Maryland Delegates in Congress required of the county two companies of expert riflemen to join the army at Boston. These were organized at once, and marched from Frederick July 18, 1775, less than thirty days after John Hanson called for them. They arrived at Cambridge, Mass., August 9, 1775, making the long journey over difficult roads in twenty-two days without the loss of a man. These were the first troops from the south to join Washington. In the proceedings of the convention of Maryland, which assembled July 26, 1775, John Hanson's boldness in advocating and advancing sentiments which might prove disastrous to him afterwards, alarmed even his friends, but he knew no fear and was prepared to take the consequences. The Convention issued its Declaration of Independence [23] known as the "Association of the Freemen of Maryland." At a meeting of the inhabitants of the middle district of Frederick County, held at the Courthouse in Frederick Town, September 12, 1775, John Hanson was placed on the Committee of Observation according to the resolution of the Convention of Maryland. December 26, 1775, he was appointed by the Provincial Convention on the committee to establish a gunlock

21 *Ibid.*, pp. 433, 986; Vol. II, p. 1044.
22 *Ibid.*, Vol. II, p. 1044.
23 *Ibid.*, Vol. III, pp. 100, 132.

manufactory at Frederick.[24]   He also filled positions on various other important committees.

During his Chairmanship of the Committee of Observation, the formidable Tory conspiracy of Lord Dunmore, Dr. John Connolly, Allen Cameron, Dr. John Smith and White Eyes, an Indian Chief, was discovered and frustrated.[25]   John Hanson had the people of Frederick County on the alert and to their vigilance was due the discovery and frustration of this well-conceived plot.

January 20, 1776, John Hanson was appointed by the Maryland Council of Safety on a committee to collect silver and gold from the inhabitants of Frederick County, for the benefit of the popular cause.[26]   October 9, 1776, he was on a commission which proceeded to the camps of the Maryland troops to reorganize those already in service upon the new footing, and to induce as many as possible to enlist for the war.[27]   The Commission were directed to act under the advice of Washington in appointing the officers of the new battalions. Hanson was tendered the nomination of Delegate to the first State Legislature, but could not accept because of his other important work.   Prevailed upon, however, to accept a seat in the General Assembly at the sessions of 1779, 1780 and 1781, he led in the support of all measures of the popular cause.   In the Congress of 1780, notwithstanding all the States had ratified the Articles of Confederation excepting Maryland, she renewed her previous instructions to the delegates not to sign unless provision was made towards settling the question of the western lands.   Elected a delegate John

[24] Ibid., pp. 99, 117; Vol. IV, pp. 58, 725; Vol. V, pp. 485, 537, 1523.

[25] Ibid., pp. 1660, 1661, 1662; Ibid., pp. 155, 201, 218, 453, 479, 480, 508, 615, 616, 891, 892, 955, 959.

[26] Ibid., p. 1044.

[27] Ibid., Series 5, Vol. III, pp. 121, 673, 674, 1054.

Hanson made great efforts to remove the impediment, and with the aid of his colleagues succeeded in effecting a compromise. January 29, 1781, Maryland passed " an act to empower the Delegates of this State in Congress to subscribe and ratify the Articles of Confederation." March 1, was assigned as the time for completing the Confederation, and on that day John Hanson, with Daniel Carroll, signed the Articles and the Union of the states was complete.

After his entrance to Congress, November 5, 1781, John Hanson was elected President. General Washington was presented to that body November 28, 1781. After the surrender of Cornwallis at Yorktown, Washington returned to his home at Mount Vernon, where he remained several weeks, and then set out for Philadelphia. Being attended by two members he made his appearance in Old Independence Hall, and was introduced to Congress. President Hanson greeted him with an address.

It appears by the minutes of the proceedings, April 15, 1782, that President Hanson was rendered unable by sickness to discharge the functions of his place as President in Congress, and it was resolved "that one of the members present be chosen by ballot to act as chairman for the purpose of keeping order in the house, but that all official papers shall nevertheless be signed and authenticated by the President as heretofore." His term of office expired November 4, 1782, and a resolution of thanks was passed by Congress. Failing health compelled him to decline reelection as a delegate to Congress, and he decided to withdraw from public life after having served his state and country continuously from 1757 to 1783.[28]

28 *Hist. of Maryland*, by J. Thomas Scharf.

He married *Jane,* the daughter of Alexander and
Jane (Brooke) Contee; she was born in Prince George's
County, Md., September 17, 1728, and died in Fred-
erick, Md., February 21, 1812. Their daughter, *Jane
Contee,* married DR. PHILIP THOMAS, whose son was
John Hanson Thomas.

CONTEE

During the reign of Louis XIV of France, the Protestant De Contee family of Rochelle, emigrated to
England. In the French Heraldic work called " La
France Genealogigue "
the name is written " De
Contee of Rochelle," and
the title of " Viscount "
is attached. It also ap-
pears that there are three
other families of Contee
and Conte in France, all
evidently having the same
origin. Marquis of Gra-
viers, Count de Noirant
of Normandy, and Baron

CONTEE

de Conte of Orange, all have the same arms. Adolp de
Contee was High Sheriff of London and Middlesex
1643. The motto under his arms in Guild Hall, London, is " Pour Dieu et mon Roi."

The first Contee from whom it is possible to trace,
Peter Contee, of Barnstable, Devonshire, Eng., married
Catherine ———. His father's name is not known, but
his mother was Grace Contee, and he had a brother
John.

ALEXANDER CONTEE, their son, born in England
1691, was " baptized ye 22nd day of April, 1693," and

died in Maryland 1740. He emigrated to America with his uncle, the Hon. Colonel John Contee (subsequently a member of the Council of State 1707 to 1708), and settled in Prince George's County, Md. He was Clerk of that county, and Burgess 1724. His will, dated 1739 and proved 1741, displays the strongly marked individuality of the testator, and is remarkable for beauty of style. In it much silver plate is bequeathed, including a silver punch bowl; extensive real estate is disposed of, "Buck's Range," a tract in Baltimore County, being given to his daughter *Jane*. His personal estate included negroes and many pounds sterling.[29] He desired to be buried according to the service of the English church, and gave a guinea respectively to the rector of St. Paul's, in Prince George's and Port Tobacco Parish in Charles County, with the request to preach a funeral sermon on "Ye Folly and Danger of ye Deathbed Repentance." A small tea-service with a muffineer and waiter, all bearing the family arms and the Tower of London Stamp for the year 1734, which belonged to Alexander Contee, has descended through five generations to the present owner, Douglas H. Thomas. The punch bowl mentioned in Alexander Contee's will descended through another branch of the family, for one hundred and thirty-six years, but in 1876, also passed into the possession of Mr. Thomas.[30] Alexander Contee married *Jane,* born in Prince George's County, Md., the daughter of Colonel Thomas and Barbara (Dent) Brooke, whose daughter *Jane,* married JOHN HANSON.

BROOKE

ROBERT BROOKE, ESQ., of De la Brooke Manor (1602-1655), married first Mary Baker.

29 *Liber D. D.,* No. 1, p. 347.
30 Hanson's *Old Kent,* p. 383.

MAJOR THOMAS BROOKE (1632-1676), second son, married Eleanor (1642-1725), the daughter of Richard and Margaret Hatton, and the niece of Secretary Thomas Hatton of Maryland.

COLONEL THOMAS BROOKE of "Brookfield," Prince George's County, Md., their eldest son, married first, Anne ——; second *Barbara* (1676-1754), the youngest daughter of THOMAS DENT of St. Mary's County, and his wife Rebecca, the daughter of the Rev. William Wilkinson; their daughter *Jane,* married ALEXANDER CONTEE, whose daughter *Jane,* married JOHN HANSON.

THOMAS (*Continued*)

The son of Dr. Philip Thomas and Jane (Contee) Hanson, *John Hanson Thomas,* was born in Fredericktown, May 16, 1779, and died there May 2, 1815. He married, October 5, 1809, *Mary Isham,* the daughter of Rawleigh and Elizabeth (Marshall) Colston, of "Honeywood," Va., who was born at "Honeywood," January 23, 1789, and died in Baltimore, Md., December 11, 1844. Their son was *John Hanson Thomas II.*

COLSTON

At the time of the Conquest, the Colstons, who descend from Robert de Colston, of Colston Hall, in the county of Lincoln, were a family of consequence. William Colston (1608), traced through sixteen generations.

His son, Edward Colston, the notable philanthropist of Bristol, Eng., born November 2, 1638, is buried in All Saints' Church, Bristol. On his tomb a long epitaph recites that he lived "84 years, 11 months, and nine days, and then departed this life 11 October, 1721, at Mortlake in Surrey, and lieth buried in a vault by his

CONTEE BOWL
Made in London. Tower Mark 1737

ancestors, in the first cross alley under the reading desk of this Church."

WILLIAM COLSTON, born in England 1660, and died in Virginia 1701, is the first from whom there is an authentic genealogical record. He came from Bristol, Eng., settled in Rappahannock County, Va., and was a gentleman of means as shown by his will, probated December 3, 1701. Therein he devises many tracts of land, negroes, etc., and "money in England." He

COLSTON

was Clerk of Rappahannock County 1683, and after the partition of that county was Clerk of Richmond County, from 1692 to 1701.[31] He was also Justice of the Provincial Court, High Sheriff of Richmond County and Burgess 1692. He had a certificate granted at a court held for Rappahannock County April 4, 1688, according to an act of the Assembly, "for eighteen hundred acres of land due for the importation of thirty-six persons, and himself, twice imported." From this it is inferred that William Colston came to Virginia and finding the country agreeable, returned to England for the purpose of bringing over a retinue of servants, for household and agricultural purposes. He married first, before 1687, Mrs. Ann Hull; had one son William; married second, *Ann,* the daughter of William Gooch of York County, Va., and the widow of Thomas Beall.

CAPTAIN CHARLES COLSTON of " Exeter Lodge," Va., their son, born April 17, 1691, and died 1724, was Cap-

---

[31] *Richmond County Records.*

tain of the Virginia Militia and Justice of Richmond County 1724. He married *Rebecca,* the youngest daughter of Samuel and Frances (Allerton) Travers, and the widow of John Taverner; she was born at "Exeter Lodge," Va., October 10, 1692, and died December 29, 1726.

TRAVERS COLSTON of "Exeter Lodge," Va., their son, born at "Exeter Lodge," Va., January 4, 1714, and died in November, 1751, was High Sheriff of Northumberland County 1745. He married second, *Susanna,* the daughter of John and Ann (Metcalf) Opie, and the widow of Rodman Kenner of "Kennerly"; she was born in Virginia February 5, 1719, and died at "Exeter Lodge," Va., 1750. Issue:

William, a Captain, married Lucy, the daughter of Colonel Langdon Carter, of "Sabine Hall," Richmond County, Va.

Rawleigh, born at "Exeter Lodge," Va., May 11, 1747, and died at "Honeywood," Va., 1823, married *Elizabeth,* the daughter of Thomas and Mary Randolph (Keith) Marshall, and the sister of Chief Justice Marshall; *Mary Isham,* their daughter, married *John Hanson Thomas,* whose son was *John Hanson Thomas II.*

GOOCH

MAJOR WILLIAM GOOCH, of English descent, settled near the present site of Yorktown. He represented York County in the House of Burgesses, November, 1654, and was one of the Councillors appointed by the General Assembly March 31, 1655.[32] The inscription

---

[32] *William and Mary Quar.,* Vol. V, p. 110.

Burke's Peerage and Baronetage, edition 1896, gives a William Gooch, uncle of the Governor of Virginia of that name, as having died in 1655. He may have been this William Gooch, who became a Major after his appointment as Councillor.

A CONTEE SILVER TEA SET
Made in London. Tower Mark 1737

on the very old tombstone on which his arms are carved at " Temple Farm," where Lord Cornwallis surrendered in 1781,[33] reads as follows:

Major William Gooch of This
Parish
Dyed, Oct. 29, 1655.
Within this tomb there doth enterred
Lie
No shape but substance true nobility
Itself though young in years Just twenty
nine
Yet graced with vertues morall and divine
The Church from him did good participate
In Counsell rare fitt to adorn a State.

GOOCH

His daughter, *Ann Gooch,* married, first, Captain Thomas Beall, and second, W I L L I A M COLSTON. Their son, *Charles Colston,* married *Rebecca Travers,* and their son was TRAVERS COLSTON.

TRAVERS

Two brothers, WILLIAM and Rawleigh Travers, English colonists, are recorded in Lancaster and Rappahannock and Richmond Counties early in the seventeenth century. In 1653, a patent for three hundred acres of land on the south side of the Rappahannock River was granted to Rawleigh Travers, and William Travers was witness to a will May 17, 1656. In 1661, a tract of five hundred acres on

TRAVERS

Morattica Creek was conveyed to him by Thomas Chetwood. He was also named as legatee under the will of Giles Hussey, 1668.

[33] *Ibid.,* Vol. IV, p. 197.

COLONEL WILLIAM TRAVERS, born in England 1630, and died in Virginia 1679, was given his title officially by the House of Burgesses of Virginia. As Captain, with Colonel John Washington, Captain John Lee, Mr. William Mosely, and Mr. Robert Beverly, he was appointed to settle the bounds of Northumberland and Westmoreland Counties; as Colonel of Rappanhannock County, in 1675, the Royal Council of Virginia appointed him one of a commission to employ Indians in defence of the colony.[34]   He was Burgess for Lancaster County 1677, and Speaker of the House.   He married Rebecca ——, who was administratrix of his will, the appraisement being made at " Exeter Lodge." (She married, second, John Rice.)   Issue:

SAMUEL.

Rawleigh, a Justice of Richmond County, 1701, married Sarah Taverner, to whom he devised " Exeter Lodge," which he had inherited from his father, during her widowhood, with reversion to his niece, Rebecca Travers.

William.

CAPTAIN SAMUEL TRAVERS, the eldest son of William and Rebecca, was Captain of the Virginia Militia 1685 to 1693; Justice of the Provincial Court of Rappahannock County, and Sheriff 1693.[35]   He married *Frances,* the daughter of Isaac and Elizabeth (Willoughby) Allerton.   Issue:

Elizabeth, married John Tarphy, a Justice and High Sheriff of Richmond County 1721.

Winifred, married Daniel Hornby of " Hornby Manor," on the Rappahannock River, which by his will, dated October 13, 1749, he bequeathed to Travers

[34] *Henning II,* pp. 299, 309, 330, 420, 428.
[35] *Records of Rappahannock County,* September 3, 1685; *Richmond County,* December 6, 1693.

Colston, Jr., who died between the date of said will and that of Travers Colston, his father, March 4, 1759. " Hornby Manor " thus descended to William Colston, the brother of Travers, Jr.

Rebecca, married, first, John Taverner; second, CHARLES COLSTON, whose son TRAVERS, married *Susanna Opie,* and their son was *Rawleigh Colston.*

ALLERTON

DEPUTY-GOVERNOR ISAAC ALLERTON, of the Allerton family of Suffolk, Eng., was born in 1585-86, " as we learn from a deposition made September 26, 1639, in which he is described as ' Isaacke Allerton, of New Plimmouth in New England, Merchant, aged about 53 years.' " He is named in the Leyden records as " of London," being admitted to citizenship there, February 7, 1614. He was one of the four signers of the letter from Leyden Church to Carver and Cushman, June 1, 1620. Save himself, his brother-in-law Priest, and the subsequent Governor of the Colony, William Bradford, none of the colony appear to have attained the honor of being freemen of Leyden. A *Mayflower* passenger 1620, and Signer of the Compact, Allerton was accompanied on the voyage to America by his first wife, Mary Norris, whom he had married at the Stadhius, Leyden, November 4, 1611. They brought with them three children, Bartholomew (who subsequently returned to England), Remember and Mary.

He started New England commerce, by building a vessel called the *Hope,* used in trading with the Dutch in New Amsterdam, and with the Virginia colonists. Tobacco was the staple export of Virginia, but he brought away in addition, a store of beaver which the planters had purchased of the Indians. In exchange

for these commodities, they left with the Virginians
supplies brought from England, from Barbadoes and
New England. When Bradford was chosen Governor,
after Carver's death in the spring of 1621, Allerton was
made Assistant, or Deputy-Governor, an office which
he held alone until 1624, when the number of Assistants
was increased to five, and in 1633 to seven, of whom he
was one. One of the "Undertakers" in 1627, and said
to have made five voyages to England as an agent for
the Colony, he was actively engaged in business in the
Massachusetts colonies from 1631 until 1637 or 1638.
He had a trading post at Machias, 1632-33, which was
pillaged by the French, and his fishing station at
Marblehead was burned 1635.

He appears to have had some trouble with his breth-
ren at Plymouth and removed to Marblehead, which
place he and his son-in-law, Moses Maverick, founded.
Soon he committed the unpardonable sin of sympathiz-
ing with the Quakers, opposing the measures used
against them, and he found it convenient to leave without notice.

The New Amsterdam records place him there February, 1639, and he probably became a resident in the
fall of 1638, thus being one of the earliest English
settlers. From that time for twenty years he played
a prominent and honorable part in the political and
business life of the Dutch colony. During the earlier
years of his life there, he was associated in business with
Govert Loockermans, one of the leading and most interesting figures in the history of those times, and it is
quite possible that he lived at Loockerman's house on
the Hoogh Street (the present Stone Street), when at
Amsterdam. January 20, 1642, he sold his yacht
"Hope" to Governor Loockermans of New Amster-

dam. The following year he and Loockermans had a grant there of two lots on the Great Highway. Evidently he resided some time at New Amsterdam, for when an uprising of the Indians in the neighborhood was feared, at the request of Director Kieft, the " Commonalty " elected, September 13, 1643, eight selectmen for counsel and advice on public affairs, Allerton being one of the number. He was the only one of the Pilgrim Fathers who became a resident of New York.

" In April, 1647, Isaac Allerton purchased from one Phillip de Truy the land lying between the Highway, now Pearl Street, and the shore line of the East River, which was then west of the present location of Water Street. This strip, which was probably not more than a few feet in width, extended from the present location of Peck Slip southerly, nearly if not quite, to where Fulton Street now is. At the upper end of this property, where it appears to have been the widest, and where a small bay or cove ran into the land just north of it, he increased the width by filling in and building a wharf, and on this he erected a large building for a warehouse, with a smaller one adjoining on the west for a residence, and from that time until long after his death, 'Allerton's Buildings' were a prominent landmark in the Dutch city. All the available evidence tends to prove that Allerton's buildings and wharf covered nearly the site now occupied by Nos. 6, 8, 10 and 12 Peck Slip."

The "Duke's Plan " of New York 1661, represents Allerton's buildings on the East River outside of the city limits, just south of the " Passage Place " to Long Island, and the same occurs on the " Nicholl's Map " in 1664-68.

" Although Isaac Allerton became a resident of New

Haven at about the time he purchased the land of de
Truy, seats in the Meeting House there being assigned
to him and his wife, on March 10, 1646, and where he
built himself 'a grand House on the Creek with four
Porches,' (the site of which on the corner of State and
Fair Streets has been marked with a tablet and inscription by the New Haven Colony Historical Society),
the New Amsterdam records show that he maintained
his business and residence there until his death, the court
records showing him to have been present in court July,
1658 . . . Isaac Allerton continued to have intimate
and friendly relations with the Massachusetts colonies,
after leaving Plymouth, a large share of the trade between them and the Dutch passing through his hands,
and he was always active in assisting natives of New
England, even giving his personal guarantee, for the
purpose of avoiding quarrels between his countrymen
and the people of New Amsterdam.

   " Great interest attaches to Isaac Allerton's connection with Virginia. For years he had been trading
there carrying them grain, flour, and other products
of the northern colonies, bringing back the tobacco
which formed almost their only crop, and in 1650 establishing a plantation for himself in what is now Westmoreland County, upon the Machoatick River, now
called the Machodoc, a small tributary to the Potomac.
He was the last survivor of those who are generally
counted the leaders of the Pilgrims . . ."

   A tablet was erected to the memory of Isaac Allerton, June 1, 1904, at No. 8 Peck Slip, New York City,
by the Society of the Mayflower descendants in the
State of New York. He died in New Haven 1659.
The records there show that his inventory was brought
into Court April 5, 1659, the son Isaac being away at

the time, probably in Virginia. The latter produced his father's will, July 5 following, and was appointed to settle the estate, but the next day relinquished the trust to certain others, although the Court endeavored to persuade him to the contrary as being the deceased's "eldest and onely sonne." In fact, Isaac is the only child referred to in his will, which mentions debts due him in Barbadoes, Delaware Bay and Virginia. No stone marks the grave of Isaac Allerton but on the corner of Union and Fair Streets, set in a brick wall is a marble slab, with this inscription:

"On this ground lived Isaac Allerton, a pilgrim of the *Mayflower*, The Father of New England Commerce."

The "House with four Porches," already mentioned, which stood on this ground, and had fourteen fireplaces, was said by a writer of that day to have been the finest between Boston and New Amsterdam. No remains of it are left.

His first wife having died February 25, 1621, Isaac Allerton married second, about 1626, *Fear,* the daughter of William Brewster, the first Elder of Plymouth Colony, or as he has sometimes been called "The Father of New England." Fear Brewster, a passenger on the *Ann,* 1623, died, December 12, 1634. How soon after this Allerton again married, is not apparent, but in 1644 a third wife, Johanna, is mentioned.[36]

COLONEL ISAAC ALLERTON, the only son of Isaac and Fear (Brewster) Allerton, born at Plymouth Colony 1630, and died between October 25, and December 30, 1702, lived some years with his grandfather, Elder Wil-

[36] Authorities: Biography of Deputy-Governor Isaac Allerton, from Brewster *Genealogy*.

N. E. Hist. and Geneal. Mag., July, 1890, p. 291.

Baylies' Hist. of N. E., Vol. I, pp. 72, 125.

liam Brewster. Graduating from Harvard College 1650, he is supposed to have settled in Virginia about 1655, on the plantation belonging to his father, on the west side of Machoatick River. The records of Northumberland County, (including Westmoreland) show that an order dated February 6, 1650, was made by the Governor and Council, concerning the complaint made by the Machoatick Indians about Mr. Allerton's plantation. The Court directed that "if the Indians were not content with Allerton being there, to remove them, but an inquisition being made, the said Indians and the Werowance Peckaton, declared they were well content with Mr. Allerton staying there so long as the land wherever he hath already cleared be useful, provided that no more housing be there built than is now upon it." This plantation is laid down on Herrman's map of Virginia and Maryland, engraved by Faithorne 1670, his nearest neighbors being John Lee, Henry Corbin and Dr. Thomas Gerrard. He was appointed by Sir William Berkeley, Governor and Captain-General of Virginia, with Colonel John Washington, Captain John Lee and five others, Justices of Westmoreland County, in 1663.

Neill, in his " Virginia Carolorum." states that in an expedition against the Indians (the Marylanders being under Major Thomas Truman, and the Virginians under Colonel John Washington), Colonel George Mason and Major Isaac Allerton united their forces about September 27, 1675. Finding no enemy, they laid seige for six weeks to a neighboring fort of friendly Susquehannás, who, finally stealing away by night, soon bitterly retaliated upon the whites. Colonel Isaac Allerton was appointed 1679, with Colonel Leger Codd and Colonel George Mason to superintend the build-

ing of a fort and magazine on the Potomac River. He
was one of the committee of the Association of Northumberland, Westmoreland, and Stafford Counties, November 1, 1667; second on the Commission of Peace for
Westmoreland and of the Quorum, November 5, of
that year; a Burgess 1676 and 1677; appointed by
James II 1680, Collector of Customs for York River;
Lieutenant-Colonel of Westmoreland County 1680 to
1682; of the Royal Council 1680 to 1683; Escheator-
General for Westmoreland County 1683, and at the
Council held at James City, October 18, 1688, with
others, including the Governor, Lord Howard of Effingham.

The will of Colonel Allerton, dated October 25, 1702,
and proved December 30 following, after a pious pre-
lude disposes of his estate. To his daughter Travers
(the wife of Samuel Travers), who "has had a sufficient part or portion of my estate given her in consideration of marriage, I do therefore for memorial sake
give unto her three daughters, Elizabeth, Rebecca and
Winifred Travers, the sum of one thousand pounds of
tobacco apiece," when seventeen years of age or upon
marriage. He made his son Willoughby Allerton, re-
siduary legatee and executor.[37]

As early as 1652 Colonel Isaac Allerton had a wife
Elizabeth;[38] he married second, *Elizabeth,* the daugh-
ter of THOMAS WILLOUGHBY, of Lower Norfolk, Va.
Issue:

Sarah, married (second wife), Hancock Lee of
"Ditchley," Va. They were the progenitors of Gen-

[37] Authorities: *Ibid.*
　　Henning I.
　　Lee of Va., p. 69.
　　N. E. *Reg.,* July, 1890.
[38] *N. E. Reg.*

Va. Mag. Vol. I, pp. 199, 245, 250.
William and Mary, Vol. IV, p. 87.
Richmond County Recs.

eral Robert E. Lee, Zachary Taylor, President of the United States, and Sarah Knox Taylor, the wife of Jefferson Davis, President of the Confederate States of America.

Daughter, married —— Newton.

Frances, married SAMUEL TRAVERS.

Willoughby, married Hannah, the daughter of William Keene and the widow of John Bushrod of Nominy Plantation. His will proved March 25, 1724/25, directs that he " be interred in silence, without any show of funebrious rites and solemnities, and that my grave be impalled with a brick wall, together with all the rest of my friends and relations, a years time after my death."

BREWSTER

ELDER WILLIAM BREWSTER, born 1566-67, was the son of William Brewster appointed by Archbishop Sandys in January, 1575-76, as receiver of Scrooby, and bailiff of the manor house in that place, belonging to the Archbishop, being given a life tenure of both offices. As the parish registers do not begin until 1695, no record of the son's birth, baptism or marriage has been found after careful research.[39] An affidavit

BREWSTER

made at Leyden, June 25, 1609, states that Elder William Brewster, his wife and son Jonathan declare their

[39] *Ibid.,* Vol. XVIII, 18-20.

ages to be respectively forty-two, forty and sixteen years. William Bradford's statement that Brewster was "nere fourskore years of age (if not all out) when he dyed," agrees with the affidavit. Therefore he was born in 1566 or 1567, and he " dyed at Plymouth in New England the 10th of April, 1644." [40]

" He matriculated at Peterhouse, Cambridge, December 3, 1580, but it does not appear that he remained there long enough to take his degree.[41] He is next found as a ' discreete and faithfull' assistant of William Davison, Secretary of State to Queen Elizabeth, accompanying that gentleman on his embassy to the Netherlands in August, 1585, and serving him at Court after his return, until his downfall in 1587. After the retirement of Davison, Brewster returned to Scrooby, where he lived ' in good esteeme amongst his freunds, and ye gentlemen of those parts, espetially the godly and religious, doing much good in promoting and furthering Religion.' In 1590 he was appointed administrator of the estate of his father who died in the summer of that year, leaving a widow, Prudence. His father was ' Post ' at Scrooby, at the time of his death, and it is said that the Elder's grandfather held the same office.[42] Sir John Stanhope, who became Postmaster General in June 1590, appointed one Samuel Bevercotes to succeed the deceased Brewster. Through the influence of Davison, however, the old postmaster's son William, was appointed to the office, which he held until September 30, 1607, (O. S.). His residence at Scrooby was the old manor house.[43] In this house the

40 Brewster Book.   41 Brown's Pilgrim Fathers of New England.
42 Arber's Story of the Pilgrim Fathers, p 50.
Brown's Pilgrim Fathers of N. E., p. 54.
43 Hunter's Founders of New Plymouth, 1854, pp. 17-18.
Raine's History of the Parish of Blyth, pp. 129-130.

members of the Pilgrim Church were accustomed to
meet on the Lord's day, where Brewster 'with great
loue entertained them when they came making prouis-
sion for them to his great charge.' The Pilgrims, attempting to remove to Holland in the latter part of
1607, were imprisoned at Boston, through the treach-
ery of the master of the ship that was engaged to trans-
port them.   Bradford says that Brewster 'was ye
cheefe of those that were taken at Boston, and suffered
ye greatest loss; and of ye seuen that were kept longst
in prison, and after bound ouer yo ye assises.' Through
Bradford also, we learn that Brewster after he reached
Holland, suffered many hardships and spent most of
his means in providing for his 'many children.' He
was not so well fitted as the other Pilgrims for the hard
labor which became their common lot, yet he bore his
condition cheerfully.   During the latter part of the
twelve years spent in Holland, he increased his income
very much by teaching and by the profits from a print-
ing press which he, by the help of some friends, set up
in Leyden. At the end of that time, 'for sundrie weigh-
tie and solid reasons' which are duly set forth in Bradford's *History*, among which was a true missionary
spirit, the Church at Leyden resolved to emigrate to
Virginia.

"Brewster, the Elder of the Church, who had been
chosen to that office during the Pilgrims stay at Leyden,
was desired by those chosen to go first, 'to goe with
them,' while John Robinson, the pastor, stayed with the
majority who should follow later.   Thus it happens
that we find Elder Brewster, his wife Mary, and two
young sons among the passengers of that famous vessel,
the *Mayflower*, which dropped anchor in Plymouth

harbor, December 16, 1620 (O. S.).   At Plymouth, Brewster bore an important part in establishing the Pilgrim Republic, not shrinking from even the severest manual labor, and ' when the church had no other minister, he taught twise eury saboth and ye both powerfully and profitably, to ye great contentment of ye hearers ' " . . .

He signed the Mayflower Compact; was member and Chaplain of the first military company organized at Plymouth ,Colony, under Captain Myles Standish, and served against the Indians; Deputy, 1636.

" His wife Mary, whose maiden namc has not been discovered, ' dyed at Plymouth in new England the 17th of Aprill, 1627.' [44]   Bradford says that though she died long before her husband, ' yet she dyed aged,' but by her affidavit of 1609, she was less than sixty years of age, and it is probable that the ' great & continuall labours, with other crosses and sorrows, hastened it (i. e. old age) before ye time.'   Elder Brewster survived his wife many years. . . .   August 20, 1645, a final division of the Elder's estate was made by Bradford, Winslow, Prince and Standish, between ' Jonathan and Loue his onely children remayneing.' " [45]

As has been said, on the voyage to America, Elder Brewster was accompanied by his wife and two younger sons, whose names were Love and Wrestling.   Jonathan, his eldest son, came in the *Fortune* 1621, and his daughters, Patience and *Fear* in the *Ann,* 1623. Patience married Thomas Prince, Governor of Plymouth Colony 1634, and *Fear* married (second wife) ISAAC ALLERTON, Deputy-Governor of Plymouth Colony.   Their son ISAAC, married second, *Elizabeth Willoughby.*

[44] Brewster Book.   [45] *Brewster Genealogy* (1908).

WILLOUGHBY

CAPTAIN THOMAS WILLOUGHBY, born in England 1601, and died in Virginia 1658, was according to a tradition in the family a nephew of Sir Percival Willoughby of Wallaton.[46] Coming to Virginia 1610, after reaching manhood he became one of the leading merchants of the colony. There is a certificate, dated 1627, by Thomas Willoughby of Rochester, aged twenty-seven years, in regard to a ship in which he was about to go to Virginia.[47] There can be hardly a doubt that he was the patentee returning from a visit home. He was a Justice of Elizabeth City 1629 to 1632, and of the Council 1644, 1646, and 1650. In 1654, he patented large tracts of land in lower Norfolk County, which his descendants owned for many generations, and part of which, (Willoughby's Point, near Norfolk, the Manor Plantation) is still owned by descendants of other names.[48] His wife's name is not known unless, as is probable, it appears under a patent to him in 1654 when *Alice,* Thomas and Elizabeth Willoughby were among the head rights. In the records of Lower Norfolk County is the following: "Att a Court held 16 Aug. 1658, upon the peticon of Mr. Thomas Willoughby, a Commission of Administration is granted unto him upon his father's estate. Captain Willoughby, who deceased in England, hee putting in Security according to law." Issue, two children, viz:

Thomas, born in Virginia, December 25, 1632, was educated at Merchants Tailor's School, London, where his name appears as the "only son of Thomas Wil-

[46] Va. *Hist. Mag.,* Vol. I, p. 447; Hotten.
[47] Sainsbury's *Calendar of State Papers,* Vol. I.
[48] *Ibid; Henning I; William and Mary Quar.,* Vol. III, p. 67; Vol. IV, p. 173.

loughby of Virginia, gentleman." He was Justice, Burgess and one of the Council.[49]

Elizabeth, married ISAAC ALLERTON. Their daughter, *Frances Allerton,* married SAMUEL TRAVERS, whose daughter, *Rebecca,* married CHARLES COLSTON.

OPIE

The first of the name in Virginia, Thomas Opie, of English descent, married Helen, the only child of Rev. David Lindsay. Their son: CAPTAIN THOMAS OPIE, of the Virginia Militia, died November 16, 1702. The name of his wife is not known. He is buried beneath the same tombstone as his grandfather, as the following inscription records:

OPIE

" Here also lyeth the body of Captain Thomas Opie, Jr., of Bristol, grandson of Mr. David Lindsay, who departed this life 16 November, 1702." [50]

His son, *John Opie,* of Richmond County, Va., who died 1722, married Ann, the daughter of Richard and Ann Metcalf, and the granddaughter of Gilbert Metcalf; she died 1725. Their daughter, *Susanna,* married first, Rodham Kenner, and second, TRAVERS COLSTON.

LINDSAY

The Lindsays are of ancient origin. The line of descent is from William de Lindsay of Ercildoun, who flourished about 1133, through sixteen generations to Rev.

[49] *William and Mary Quar.,* Vol. II, p. 155; Vol. III, p. 67; Vol. IV, p. 173.
[50] *William and Mary Quar.,* Vol. VI, p. 129.

David Lindsay, known to the world as the minister of
Leith, the celebrated Bishop of Ross,[51] who was Chaplain for King James I. of England and VI. of Scotland. He is said to have been a man of great ability
and deep learning, and held
several offices under the
crown. The Bishop had the
honor of being the only
minister of note who had
prayers for the beautiful
and unhappy Mary, Queen
of Scots, at the time of her
execution. He accompa-
nied King James on his
matrimonial voyage to Den-
mark, and performed the

LINDSAY

marriage ceremony. Their children, King Charles I.,
and his brother, Prince Henry, were baptized by Mr.
Lindsay. He died in 1613, leaving two children, viz:

Rachel, married Rt. Rev. John Spottswoode, Archbishop of St. Andrews, who died December 2, 1639,
and was the ancestor of the families of Spottswood,
Dandridge, Randolph, Lee, Carter of Shirley, and
others of Virginia.

Sir Hierome, of Annatland, and the Mount " Lord
Lion King at Arms " who died 1642, married first Margaret Colville, the daughter of a Scottish Knight.

Their son, Rev. David Lindsay (1603-1667), settled
in Northumberland County, Va., prior to 1655, as he
was granted a judgment that year in that County
Court, and was the Rector of Old Wicomico Church.
Not much is known of his life work, as the old parish

51 *Lindsay Geneal.*, by Margaret Isabella Lindsay.

records have been destroyed. His tombstone bears the following inscription:

" Here lyeth interred ye body of that Holy and Reverant Divine, Mr. David Lindsay, late Minister of Yeocomico, born in ye Kingdom of Scotland, ye first and lawful sonne of ye Rt. Honerable Sir Hierome Lindsay, Knt., of Ye Mount, Lord Lyon-King-at-arms, who departed this life in ye 64th year of his age ye 3rd April Anno Dom. 1667."

His will, is dated April 2, 1667; in it he bequeaths " all my goods, lands, chattels, debts, servants, moveables, or what else is mine unto my living daughter Helen, whom I constitute, appoint and ordain my lawfull execut[x] to this my last will and Testam[t] to be fulfilled, and I do hereby give and bequeath my whole estate to my loving daughter Helen Lindsay to her, her heirs, etc." His daughter, married Thomas Opie.[52]

METCALF

A merchant of London, Gilbert Metcalf, the son of Richard of North Allerton, York County, Eng., came before 1708, to Richmond County, Va., with his wife Jane, who died 1725. A deed is recorded in that county [53] from " Jane Metcalf wife, and executrix of Gilbert Metcalf, late of London, deceased." (Gilbert Metcalf was an uncle to Sir Gilbert, Knight, Lord Mayor of York, 1695). Issue:

METCALF

Richard, married Ann —— (she married second, Ed-

[52] Accord'ng to the records of Northumberland County Court House, 1667, " a probate of will was granted on petition of Mistress Helen Lindsay, daughter to Mr. David Lindsay, in April, 1667."

[53] *Deed Book,* No. 5, p. 12.

ward Barrow), and their daughter Ann married *John Opie,* whose daughter, *Susanna,* married second, TRAVERS COLSTON.

MARSHALL

CAPTAIN JOHN MARSHALL, born in Ireland 1610, served in cavalry under King Charles at the battle of Edge Hill. With his family, he emigrated to Virginia about 1650, and settled at Jamestown, afterwards removing to Westmoreland County, and was Captain of the Virginia troops in the Indian Wars.[54]

His son, *Thomas Marshall,* a planter, was born in Washington Parish, Westmoreland County, Va.; will probated May 31, 1704. He married Martha ———.

CAPTAIN JOHN MARSHALL of "The Forest," their son, born in Virginia, 1700, and died April, 1752, he was Captain of the Virginia troops in the Indian Wars. He married, 1722, Elizabeth (1704-1775), the daughter of John Markham, (born in England, and died in Virginia).

COLONEL THOMAS MARSHALL, their son, born in Virginia, April 2, 1730, and died in Kentucky, June 22, 1802. He is said to have attended with George Washington, the school of Rev. Archibald Campbell, Rector of Washington Parish, Westmoreland County. Here began the intimate friendship which lasted through life, between Washington and Marshall. He accepted the agency of Lord Fairfax to superintend his landed estates, to make leases, collect rents, etc., and often accompanied Washington in his surveying excursions for Lord Fairfax and others. He was a Burgess of Virginia, Lieutenant during the French War, and with Braddock in his ill fated expedition, though not present at the fight in which he was slain. One of that band of

[54] *Paxton's Marshall Family.*

early patriots which resolved to resist the encroachments of the British Crown at the hazard of all that is dear to men, when the Revolutionary War broke out. Their heroic spirit manifested itself in raising a patriotic company known as Culpeper Guards, and when formed into a regiment he was made Major. He distinguished himself at the battle of Great Bridge, the first engagement on Virginia soil, and was at Valley Forge with his sons, John (afterwards Chief Justice of the U. S.) and Thomas. At the battle of Germantown, when General Mercer was killed, he succeeeded to the command. It has been said that at Brandywine where a horse was killed under him, that Colonel Marshall saved the patriot army from destruction. For such distinguished services, the House of Burgesses of Virginia, through their Speaker, Edmund Randolph, presented him with a sword. In 1779, Colonel Marshall was sent with the third regiment to reinforce General Lincoln, in South Carolina. He joined Lincoln just in time to be shut up with him in Charleston, and to share in the surrender of that city to the British. But having been paroled, Colonel Marshall with other officers, visited Kentucky in 1780, travelling on horse-back through the wilderness. On that trip he selected his beautiful farm of " Buckpond," near Versailles, to which he subsequently removed his family from Virginia.[55] He married *Mary Randolph,* the daughter of Rev. James and Mary Isham (Randolph) Keith. She was born in Virginia, April 28, 1737, and died in Kentucky, September 19, 1809. Issue, fifteen children who attained maturity, among them: *Elizabeth,* who married *Rawleigh Colston;* Chief-Justice John; James Markham, and Dr. Louis.

[55] *Ibid.,* pp. 20, 21.

RANDOLPH

The Randolphs descend from Robert Randolph, of Sussex, Eng., who married Rose, the daughter of Thomas Roberts, of Hawkhurst, Kent.

Their son, William, was born 1572, and died 1660.

RANDOLPH

His son, William II., married second, Dorothy Lane, the sister of Sir Richard Lane.

Their son, Richard, born February 21, 1621, and died in Ireland 1671, married Elizabeth, the daughter of Richard Ryland.

COLONEL WILLIAM RANDOLPH, their son, of "Turkey Island," on the James River, Henrico County, Va., was born in Yorkshire, Eng., about 1651, and died April 11, 1711. He removed to Warwickshire, Eng., and emigrated from that place about 1674, being the first of the family in Virginia. The following inscription is on his tombstone at Turkey Island:

> Col. Wm. Randolph of Warwickshire, but late of Virginia, Gent, died April 11, 1711.
> Mrs. Mary Randolph, his only wife, she was the daug er of Mr. Henry Isham by Catharine his wife. He was of Northamptonshire, but late of Virginia, Gent.

He was Captain of the Militia of Henrico County 1680, Lieutenant-Colonel 1699; one of the Royal Council of Virginia; a Burgess 1700 to 1705; by appointment of Their Majesties, William and Mary, February 6, 1690, the founder and trustee of William and Mary College; and by appointment of His Majesty William III, Escheator-General for the south side of the James River.[56] He married, Mary, the daughter of Henry and Katharine (Royall) Isham of Bermuda Hundred; she was born 1660, and died 1735. Issue, seven sons and two daughters. Among others, Chancellor William; Isham, ancestor of Thomas Jefferson; and Richard, ancestor of John Randolph of "Roanoke."

COLONEL THOMAS RANDOLPH, of "Tuckahoe," their second son, born June, 1689, and died 1730, was a Burgess 1720 to 1722, and Justice of Henrico County, Va. He married Judith,[57] a daughter of Charles and Susanna (Tarlton) Fleming, whose daughter, *Mary Isham,* married Rev. James Keith (born in Scotland 1696, and died in Virginia 1758), and their daughter, *Mary Randolph Keith,* married THOMAS MARSHALL. Colonel Charles Fleming was the son of John Fleming who died 1686.

ISHAM

The Ishams descend from Sir Euseby Isham, Knight, of Pytchley and Braunston, who was born February 26, 1552-53, knighted May 11, 1603, and died June 11, 1626. He married Ann, the daughter of John Borlase, of Marlow County, Bucks, Eng. Their son, William,

[56] *Col. papers of Va.,* No. 63, 1680; *Va. Mag.,* Vol. I, pp. 225, 238.
Campbell's *Hist.,* p. 630; *Hist. of William and Mary College.*
[57] *Year Book Col. Wars,* 1899-1902.
William and Mary Quar., Vol. VII, p. 123.
Recent investigations prove that the name of Thomas Randolph's wife was not Churchh'll, but Judith Fleming, as was claimed by John Randolph, of "Roanoke."

baptized March 20, 1587-88, at Braunston, married, August 15, 1625, Mary, the daughter of William Brett and the sister of Sir Edward Brett.

Their son, Henry Isham, born in England 1627, came to Virginia and became a merchant at Bermuda Hundred, on the James River, Va., dying in 1675. He was Justice of Charles City County, Va., 1657, Captain and High Sheriff of Henrico County

ISHAM

1669 to 1670.[58] He married Katharine Royall who was born in England, and died in Virginia 1680. Their daughter Mary married WILLIAM RANDOLPH.

THOMAS (*Continued*)

The son of John Hanson and Mary Isham (Colston) Thomas, *Dr. John Hanson Thomas II.*, born in Fredericktown, Md., September 23, 1813, resided in Baltimore, and died at White Sulphur Springs, July 15, 1881. One of the City Council of Baltimore, and in the Legislature of Maryland, 1861 to 1862, he and other members were arrested by the Federal authorities and confined in several United States forts, until a new Legislature could be elected under military supervision. He married in Falmouth, Va., November 15, 1837, *Annie Campbell,* the daughter of Basil and Annie Campbell (Knox) Gordon, who was born in Falmouth, October 29, 1819, and died in Baltimore, March 17, 1886. Their son was *Douglas Hamilton Thomas.*

[58] *Year Book Colonial Wars,* 1899-1902, p. 679.

GORDON

The Gordons are of Scotch origin, the first with an ancestral record being Samuel Gordon, born 1656, the first of the name on " Stock-erton " farm, in the Parish of Kirkcubbright, Scotland, who died there April 15, 1732, aged seventy-six. In some way he was related to the families of Lord Kenmuir and the Gordons of G r e e n l a u. He married Margaret McKinnell, and their son John (1682-1738), married Grace New-all.

GORDON

Their son, Samuel Gordon, was the last person baptized by Rev. James Renwick, who was beheaded at the Cross of Edinburgh; he died February 22, 1799, and was the first of " Lochdougan." He married Nichola, the daughter of John Brown of Craigen Callie, and his wife, Margaret McClamrock, of Craigen Bay. Nichola Brown was from the Carsluth family her grandfather and uncle being ministers in the Parish of Kirkinabrook; she died November 18, 1795, aged seventy-one, and had issue, a large family, many of whom were born at " Stockerton," before their removal to " Lochdougan." Among them were two daughters who married; an eldest son John, who inherited the two " Lochdougans," at his father's death; and three younger sons, Samuel, Alexander, and Basil. These last emigrated to Virginia, where they engaged in mercantile business. Alexander returned to Scotland, and died there 1819, and Samuel married Susanna Knox.

The third one of the emigrants, Basil Gordon, born in Scotland 1770, and died in Virginia 1846, married at "Windsor Lodge," Culpepper County, Va., 1814, *Annie Campbell*, the daughter of William and Susanna (Fitzhugh) Knox; she was born September 14, 1784, and died in Baltimore, October 8, 1867. Their daughter, *Annie Campbell,* married *John Hanson Thomas II.*

KNOX

Of ancient Scotch lineage, the Virginia branch of the Knoxes descend from John Knox of Renfrew, Renfrewshire, w h o s e wife's name is unknown. John Knox II., of the same place, wife's name also unknown, had issue, John III., who married Janet, the daughter of John Somerville, "Baillie" of Renfrew; had issue, John, Robert, William, Anna, who married Mr. Campbell, and Agnes, who married Mr. Dunlop.   The three sons came to Virginia, where the Knoxes owned large landed estates, consisting of "Windsor Lodge," Culpepper County; "Berry Hill," Stafford County; "Orchard Fields," and "Belmont," also in Stafford County (where most of the old members of the family are buried) ; "Smith's Mount," and "Vaucluse," in Westmoreland County.

The eldest of the three sons, John Knox, lived a bachelor at "Orchard Fields," where he was murdered by his slaves, some one hundred and fifty in number, whom

HENRY FITZHUGH
Of Bedford, England

CHIEF JUSTICE JOHN MARSHALL

WILLIAM KNOX
Of "Windsor Lodge," Va.

SUSANNA FITZHUGH
Wife of William Knox

he had promised to set free by his will, which not being
made at the time of his death, the slaves were inherited
by his brother, William of " Windsor Lodge."

The second son, Robert Knox, settled in Charles
County, Md., and married Rose Townsend Dade, whose
son, Robert Dade Knox, married a Hanson.

The youngest son, William Knox, settled in Culpepper County, Va., and established himself, 1805, at
"Windsor Lodge." In 1767 he married *Susanna*
(1751-1823), the daughter of Thomas and Sarah (Stuart) Fitzhugh, of " Boscobel," whose daughter, *Annie
Campbell,* married Basil Gordon, and their daughter,
Annie Campbell, married *John Hanson Thomas II.*

FITZHUGH

Some of the Fitzhughs were high in office and favor
in England during the
fifteenth and sixteenth
centuries. The name is
a combination of Fitz
and Hugh, sometimes
one, sometimes the other
would precede, until at
length they were united
in Fitzhugh.

COLONEL WILLIAM
FITZHUGH, the son of
Henry Fitzhugh (born
1614), was born in Bed-
ford, Eng., January 9,
1651, and died at his
home "Bedford," Staf-

FITZHUGH

ford County, Va., October, 1701. The progenitor
of the well-known Virginia branch of this family, a lawyer of prominence, large planter, merchant and ship-

per, he was a Burgess 1678 to 1687; Lieutenant-Colonel of Westmoreland County 1683, and Colonel of Stafford County forces 1690.[59]   Bishop Meade of Virginia, in his " Families of Virginia " thus writes of him:

" There are some things in the life and character of the father of this large family of Fitzhughs worthy to be mentioned for the benefit and satisfaction of his posterity.   I draw them from his pious and carefully written will, and from a large manuscript volume of his letters, a copy of which was some years since gotten from the library of Cambridge, Mass., by one of his descendants, and which is now in the rooms of the Historical Society of Virginia.   It appears that he was, during the period that he exercised his profession, an eminent and most successful lawyer, and published in England a work on the laws of Virginia.   He was much engaged in the management of land causes for the great landowners, whether residing in England or America.   He was counsellor for the celebrated Robert Beverly, the first of the name, who was persecuted and imprisoned for too much independence.   He transacted business for, and purchased lands from Lord Culpepper, when he held a grant from King Charles for all Virginia.   In all these transactions he appears to have acted with uprightness and without covetousness, for in his private letters to his friends he speaks of being ' neither in want nor abundance,' but content and happy, ' though before he died he acquired broad acres which he divided among his children.' "

He married, May 1, 1674, Sarah (born August, 1663), the daughter of John Tucker, of Westmoreland

[59] *Letter Book* of Colonel Fitzhugh.
Va. Hist. Soc.
Va. Mag., Vol. II, p. 259.
Year Book Col. Wars, 1899-1902.

County, who was born in England, and died in Virginia 1671, and Rose his wife, who died 1712. Issue, five sons and one daughter. The eldest son, William of "Eagle Nest," died 1713; he married Ann Corbin, and they were the ancestors of Mary Anne Randolph Custis, the wife of General Robert Edward Lee. Another son was HENRY. Of the daughter, Bishop Meade writes as follows:

" But I must not lay down my pen, though the heart bleeds at its further use, without the tribute of affection, of gratitude and reverence to one who was to me as a sister, mother and faithful monitor, Mrs. Mary Custis, of Arlington, the wife of Washington Custis, grandson of Mrs. General Washington, who was the daughter of Mr. William Fitzhugh of ' Chatham.' Scarcely is there a Christian lady in our land more honored than she was, and none more loved and esteemed, for good sense, prudence, sincerity, benevolence, unaffected piety, disinterested zeal in every good work, deep humility and retiring modesty, for all the virtues which adorn the wife, the mother and the friend—I never knew her superior."

CAPTAIN HENRY FITZHUGH, of "Bedford," Va., the son of William, born January 15, 1686-7, and died September 12, 1758, was Captain of the Virginia forces.[60] He married, February 24, 1718, *Susanna*, the daughter of MORDECAI COOKE; she was born December 7, 1693, and died November 21, 1749.

THOMAS FITZHUGH, of "Boscobel," the son of Henry, born July 16, 1725, and died December 1, 1788, he was Justice of Stafford County 1765, and October 5, of that year, he signed the protest against the Stamp Act with Peter Daniel, W. Brent, J. Mercer, Thomas Ludwell Lee, Samuel Selden, Robert Washington and

[60] *Stafford County Recs.*
Fitzhugh Recs.

several other Justices, and sent it to Governor Fauquier. Hayden, in *Virginia Genealogies,* commenting on this protest says: "This document is one of the most remarkable of the many protests against the iniquitous Stamp Act which found expression in those days. The Justices not only protest against the measure, but ask the Governor to issue a new commission for their county, in which they *may be left out.*" Thomas Fitzhugh was also a signer of the Declaration of Freemen of Stafford County, July, 1774.[61] He married, June 19, 1750, Sarah Stuart, born February 21, 1731, and died November, 1783, the daughter of Rev. David Stuart, who was born in Scotland, and died in Virginia, January 31, 1749; his wife was Jane, the daughter of Sir John Gibbons, Bart., a Member of Parliament for Essex, Eng.; she was born in England, and died in Virginia, January 14, 1750.

A daughter of Thomas Fitzhugh, *Susanna Fitzhugh,* married William Knox, of "Windsor Lodge," whose daughter, *Annie Campbell,* married Basil Gordon; their daughter, *Annie Campbell Gordon,* married *John Hanson Thomas II.*

COOKE

MORDECAI COOKE, of Gloucester County, was born in England, and died at "Mordecai Mount," Va. The approximate date of his coming to America cannot be clearly established, nor has the name of his wife been disclosed, by careful investigations, but it is known that he had issue, Mordecai, Thomas, Giles, John, Mary. Francis, and *Susanna.* A grant was issued to him for one thousand one hundred and seventy-four acres on

[61] *Hayden*, p. 296.
 Amer. Archs.

"Mob Jack Bay," and it is a disputed question whether he was established at "Warham" or "Mordecai Mount," but the former seems more probable. He was High Sheriff of Gloucester County 1698, Justice 1702 to 1714, and Burgess for Gloucester County,[62] a staunch loyalist, devoted to his King, and the House of Stuart. He was an intimate friend of Sir William Berkeley, Governor of Virginia, and it was in his comfortable

COOKE

home at Warham that Governor Berkeley took refuge during the Bacon rebellion, when he crossed the York River into Gloucester. Mordecai Cooke received Governor Berkeley not only as a friend, but also as the representative of the King's person, and insisted that while he tarried in Gloucester, Warham should be his headquarters. His daughter, *Susanna Cooke,* married HENRY FITZHUGH, of "Bedford," Va.

THOMAS (*Continued*)

The son of John Hanson and Annie Campbell (Gordon) Thomas, *Douglas Hamilton Thomas,* born January 1, 1847, married, January 25, 1870, ALICE LEE, the daughter of Dr. John and Catherine (Cocks) Whitridge, of Baltimore. Issue:

Douglas H. Thomas, married Bessie Lyman Chadwick, of Boston.

John Hanson Thomas.

ALICE LEE WHITRIDGE THOMAS.

62 *Va. Mag.,* Vol. I, pp. 234, 366; Vol. II, p. 5.

WHITRIDGE

Tiverton, R. I. was the residence of Dr. William Whitridge, born February 13, 1748, and died April 5, 1831. He married Mary, the daughter of John and Deborah (Barker) Cushing, who was born 1759, and died 1846.

Their son, *Dr. John Whitridge,* born in Tiverton, R. I., March 23, 1793, and died July 23, 1878, moved to Baltimore, Md. and married Catherine Cocks, who was born in New York, September 23, 1801, and died in Baltimore, Md., March 21, 1895. Their daughter, ALICE LEE, married, January 25, 1870, *Douglas Hamilton Thomas,* of Baltimore, whose daughter is ALICE LEE WHITRIDGE THOMAS.

CUSHING

The English ancestry of the American Cushings begins with T h o m a s Cushing, of Norfolk County, Eng., who had large estates in Hardingham, Hingham, and other parts of the county. The earliest deed extant which bears his name, is dated 1466, and contains also the name of his eldest son and heir William, who lived at Hingham; will dated September 20, 1492. John Cushing, William's son, lived at Hardingham; will dated February 21, 1522; and his second son, Thomas, died at Hard-

CUSHING

ingham, April, 1558. His sixth son, Peter, buried at Hingham, March 2, 1615,[63] married, June 2, 1585, Sarah Hawes, who died 1641.

Their third child, Matthew Cushing, born in England 1588, and died in Hingham, Mass., September 30, 1660, embarked with his wife and children in the ship *Diligent* of Ipswich, which sailed from Gravesend, with one hundred and thirty-three passengers, April 26, and arrived at Boston, August 10, 1638. The same year, this company began the settlement of Hingham, which they named after the former home of the Cushing family in England. At a town meeting, held 1638, a house lot of five acres was given to Matthew Cushing, which was in the possession of a lineal descendant as late as 1877. He is the ancestor of all the Cushings of New England, rendered famous in the annals of American history as the " Family of the Judges." He married, August 5, 1613, Nazareth, the daughter of Henry Pitcher, who was born in England, 1585, and died in Hingham, Mass., January 1, 1681.

JOHN CUSHING, their youngest son, born 1627, and died March 31, 1708, moved to Scituate, Mass., 1662, where he purchased the farm on " Belle House Neck." He was Deputy to the Colony Court for many years, first in 1674; Assistant of the old colony government 1689, 1690, 1691; Selectman, and Representative of the General Court at Boston, the first year after the two colonies of Plymouth and Massachusetts were united, and for several succeeding years.[64] He married, January 20, 1658, Sarah, the daughter of Matthew Hawke,

Cushing Family, by Lemuel Cushing, M. A., B. C. L., Montreal, 1877.
[64] Cushing Family, p. 16.
Year Book Col. Wars, 1896, p. 307.

Town Clerk of Hingham; she was born 1641, and died 1678.

JOHN CUSHING II, their son, born in Hingham, Mass., April 28, 1660, and died January 19, 1737, was Deputy to the General Court 1692; Chief Justice of the Inferior Court of Plymouth from 1702 to 1710; Representative Member for Massachusetts, of the Governor's Council from 1710 to 1728, and Judge of His Majesty's Superior Court of Judicature of Massachusetts, from 1728 until his death. In 1732, he was Lieutenant-Colonel of the Plymouth regiment, which at that time embraced all the the local militia of the county.[65] He married, May 20, 1687, *Deborah,* the daughter of Thomas and Hannah (Jacob) Loring. She died June 9, 1713.

HON. JOHN CUSHING III, their son, born July 17, 1695, and died March 19, 1778, at Scituate, Mass., resided at "Belle House," Scituate, until 1743. Was Town Clerk from 1719 to 1744; Representative from Scituate 1721, and for several succeeding years; Judge of the Superior Court from 1747 to 1771, when he resigned; Councillor of the Province from 1746 to 1763, and one of the Presiding Judges at the trial of the British soldiers for the massacre at Boston, March 5, 1770.[66] He married first, April 1, 1717, *Elizabeth,* the daughter of Nathaniel and Sarah (Thaxter) Holmes, who died March 13, 1726.

Their son, *John Cushing IV.,* born August 16, 1722, resided at "Belle House." He married Deborah Barker of Scituate.

[65] *Ibid.,* p. 21.
   Ibid.
   Am. Archs., Series 4, Vol. IV, p. 1464.
[66] *Ibid.,* p. 31.

Their daughter, *Mary Cushing*, married Dr. William Whitridge of Tiverton, R. I.

JACOB-THAXTER

NICHOLAS JACOB, was born in England, and died in Hingham, Mass., June 15, 1657. He was Deputy to the General Court of Massachusetts 1648 to 1649.[67] His wife Mary, died in Hingham, Mass., June 15, 1681. Among their children were two daughters: *Elizabeth*, who married JOHN THAXTER, and *Hannah*, who married Thomas Loring (the son of Thomas and his wife Jane Newton). Their daughter, *Deborah*, married JOHN CUSHING II.

LIEUTENANT JOHN THAXTER, probably born in England 1626, died in Hingham, Mass., March 14, 1686. He was Lieutenant 1664, and afterwards Captain. Was in command of a troop of cavalry 1680 and Representative to the General Court 1666, and many following years. He married *Elizabeth Jacob*, and their daughter, *Sarah*, married NATHANIEL HOLMES, the son of Joseph and Elizabeth (Clapp) Holmes.

CLAPP-HOLMES

CAPTAIN ROGER CLAPP, the colonist, was born in Salcombe, Eng., April 6, 1609, and died in Dorchester, Mass., February 2, 1690. He was Lieutenant of the Dorchester Train Band 1644; afterwards its Captain, joined the Ancient and Honorable Artillery Company 1646; Second Sergeant 1647, Lieutenant 1655; Commander of Castle William 1665 till 1686; a Representative from Dorchester sixteen terms from 1647 to 1671.[68]

---

[67] *Hist. Hingham*, Vol. II, p. 371.
 Old. Col. Mass., Vol. II, pp. 166, 238; Vol. III, pp. 121, 147.
[68] *Anc. and Honl. Artil.*, Vol. I, p. 298.
 Hist. Hingham, Vol. III, p. 230.

He married Joan ——, and their daughter *Elizabeth,* married Joseph Holmes.

LIEUTENANT NATHANIEL HOLMES, the son of Joseph, was born at Roxbury, Mass., July 10, 1664, and died in Boston, 1710. He joined the Ancient and Honorable Artillery Company, and was First Sergeant of the company 1695.[69] He married in Boston, October 1, 1691, *Sarah,* the daughter of John and Elizabeth (Jacob) Thaxter, and their daughter, *Elizabeth,* married JOHN CUSHING III. The line descends as follows:

John Cushing IV. married Deborah Barker.

Mary Cushing married William Whitridge.

John Whitridge, married Catherine Cocks, whose daughter, ALICE LEE, married *Douglas H. Thomas.*

ALICE LEE WHITRIDGE THOMAS,

and her daughter,

ALICE LEE WHITRIDGE THOMAS,

Members of Chapter I., The Colonial Dames of America.

[69] *Ibid.*

XLIV

MALLETT

Arm: *Azure, three scollop shells or.*
Crest: *Leopard's head erased proper.*
Motto: *" Perseverando."*

One of the Huguenots of La Rochelle, France, David Mallett, went to England with his family, after the Revocation of the Edict of Nantes.

Their son, John Mallett, who died in Fairfield, Conn., 1745, married Johanna Lyon.

Their son, Peter Mallett, born March 31, 1712, and died in Fairfield, Conn., June 18, 1760, married Naomi ———.

PETER MALLETT, their son, born November 14, 1744, and died February 2, 1805, in Fayetteville, N. C., was one of the Wilmington Committee of Safety 1775; Commissary 5th Regiment, North Carolina Militia, April 23, 1776; Commissary 6th Regiment Continental Line, October, 1776; and in the North Carolina Legislature 1778. He married *Sarah,* the daughter of Robinson and Sarah (Coit) Mumford.

MALLET

Their son, *Edward Jones Mallett,* born in Fayetteville, May 1, 1797, and died August 20, 1883, married, September 11, 1820, Sarah, the daughter of James and Sarah (Jenckes) Fenner, born May 13, 1797, and died May 17, 1841.

Their daughter, *Sarah Fenner Mallett,* born August 14, 1821, and died December 25, 1904, married, April 30, 1840, Stephen States Lee.

MUMFORD

The pedigree of the Mumfords is as follows:

James Mumford, married *Sarah,* the daughter of Richard and Elizabeth (Saltonstall) Christophers. *Richard Christophers* was descended from William Brewster.

Robinson Mumford, married Sarah Coit.

Sarah Mumford (1765-1836), married, 1780, PETER MALLETT. (See pp. 187-193, Mallett to Lee.)

BREWSTER

ARMS: *Sable, a chevron ermine, between the stars, argent.*
CREST: *A bear's head, erased azure.*
MOTTO: *" Verite soyet ma gard."*

WILLIAM BREWSTER (1560-1644), the ruling Elder of the Plymouth Colony Church, acted as minister and teacher until 1629. He left four sons and a daughter. His sword and many relics of personal property are still preserved in the museum at Plymouth.[1] His wife's name was Mary. Some of his descendants are as follows:

Jonathan Brewster (his son), born August 12, 1593, in England, and died May 7, 1659, in Connecticut, married, April 15, 1624, Lucretia Oldham.

Elizabeth Brewster, born May 1, 1637, and died 1708, married, September 7, 1653, Peter Bradley, who died April 3, 1682.

Lucretia Bradley, born August 16, 1661, and died 1691, married, June 26, 1681, Richard Christophers I.

Richard Christophers II, born August 18, 1685, and died 1736, married, August 16, 1710,.Elizabeth Saltonstall.

Sarah Christophers, married James Mumford.

[1] *Life and Times of William Brewster, Chief of the Pilgrims.*

SALTONSTALL

ARMS: *Or, a bend between two eagles, displayed sable.*
CREST: *Out of a ducal coronet or, a pelican's head, azure, vulning itself gules.*

The colonist, Sir Richard Saltonstall, born in England 1586, and died 1658, was Justice of the Peace in West Riding of Yorkshire and Lord of the Manor of Ledsham, near Leeds. One of the grantees of the Massachusetts Company under the charter obtained from Charles I., on August 26, 1629, Richard Saltonstall, with Thomas Dudley, Isaac Johnson, John Winthrop and eight other gentlemen, signed an agreement to pass the seas and inhabit and continue in New England, provided that the patent and whole government of the plantation should be transferred to them and other actual colonials. The proposition was accepted by the General Courts of the Company, which elected Sir Richard Assistant to the new Governor. He arrived with Governor Winthrop on the *Arbella,* June 22, 1630, and began with George Philips, the settlement of Watertown. Owing to the illness of his two young daughters, however, who with his five sons, had accompanied him, he returned with them and two of the sons to England in 1630, from where he continued to display the greatest interest in the Colony, and to exert himself for its advancement. He was one of the patentees of Connecticut and sent out a shallop to take possession of that territory. The vessel, on her return trip, was wrecked off Sable Island 1635.[2] In 1644, he was sent to Holland as Ambassador, and was one of the Judges of the High Court that sentenced the Duke of Hamilton, Lord Capel and others, to death for high treason 1649. In 1651, he wrote a letter of remonstrance to

[2] Appleton's *Cycl. of Am. Biog.*

John Cotton and John Wilson against the persecutions of the Quakers. His wife was Grace Kay.

Their son, Richard Saltonstall, born 1610, and died April 29, 1694, emigrated with his father to Massachusetts in 1630, and was among the first settlers of Ipswich. He published a polemic against the council appointed for life, 1642, and in July, 1643, signed a letter urging the colonial authorities to take warlike measures against the French in Acadia. He befriended the regicides, who escaped to New England in 1660, and protested against the importation of negro slaves. Returned to England 1672. He married, 1633, Muriel Gurdon.

Their son, Nathaniel Saltonstall, born 1639, and died May 21, 1707, was chosen one of the Governor's Assistants 1679, and one of the Council under the charter of William and Mary. He was also appointed 1692 one of the Judges on a special commission of Oyer Terminer, to try persons accused of practising witchcraft in Salem. Reprobating the spirit of persecution that prevailed, and foreseeing the outcome of such trials, he refused to act. His wife, Elizabeth Ward, he married December 28, 1663.

Their son, Governor Gurdon Saltonstall, born March 27, 1666, and died September 20, 1724, was Governor of Connecticut 1708 until his death. His first official act was to propose a synod for the adoption of a system of ecclesiastical discipline. The Saybrook platform, the outcome of his suggestions, through his influence conformed in some essentials to the Presbyterian policy. For the purpose of conveying to Queen Elizabeth, an address urging the conquest of Canada, he was appointed agent for the colony 1709, and raised a large contingent in Connecticut for the disastrous expedition under Sir Hovenden Walker. The first printing-press in the colony was set up in his house 1709. His activity in establishing Yale College, influenced the decision to build at New Haven instead of Hartford. He made the plans and estimates and during the early years of the College took the chief part in the direction of its affairs. He married Jerusha Richards. They had a son Gurdon, and a daughter Elizabeth, who married *Richard Christophers II*, whose daughter, *Sarah,* was the wife of James Mumford.

FENNER

The Fenners came to this country in 1630, and married into many of the old New England families. Thus their descendants can claim as ancestors, makers of history whose names are now extinct.

ARTHUR FENNER I., the son of Thomas, born in England 1622, and died October 16, 1703, became Freeman, acted as Commissioner and Deputy, and was Chief Commander of King's Garrison

FENNER

of Providence, 1653 to 1688.[3] He married *Mehitable,* the daughter of RICHARD WATERMAN; she died 1684.

THOMAS FENNER, their son, born September, 1652, and died February 27, 1718, held the offices of Deputy to the General Assembly of Rhode Island; Assistant Justice of the Peace, 1683 to 1718, and Major from the Main. He married, July 26, 1682, *Dinah,* the daughter of Thomas and Mary (Harris) Borden.

Their son, *Arthur Fenner II.,* born October 17, 1699,

[3] *Geneal. Dict. of R. I.,* pp. 78-408.

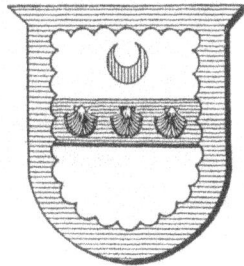

and died February 2, 1788; married, June 2, 1723,
Mary, the daughter of James and Hallelujah (Brown)
Olney; she was born September 30, 1704, and died
March 18, 1756.

GOVERNOR ARTHUR FENNER III, their son, born December 10, 1745, and died October 15, 1805, was elected
in May, 1790, the first Governor of Rhode Island, after
that State had ratified the Constitution of the United
States, and died in office. The town of Providence appointed him on the Committee of Inspection recommended by the Continental Congress, which held its
first meeting in the chamber of the Town Council, December 24, 1774. He married *Amy,* the daughter of
Gideon Comstock.[4]

Their son, *James Fenner,* born January 22, 1771, and
died April 17, 1840, married in November, 1792, Sarah,
the daughter of Silvanus and Freelove (Fenner)
Jenckes, who was born July 12, 1773, and died May 24,
1844. Their daughter *Sarah,* married *Edward Jones
Mallett,* whose daughter *Sarah Fenner,* married Stephen States Lee.

JENCKES

JOSEPH JENCKES, born 1622, and died January 4,
1717, was Deputy to the General Assembly of Rhode
Island 1680, holding office from 1679 to 1691. He
married Esther Ballard, who died 1717.

GOVERNOR JOSEPH JENCKES, their son, who died
June 15, 1740, was Deputy, Speaker of the House of
Deputies, Major of the Fourth Main, Assistant
Deputy-Governor, and Governor 1727 to 1732.[5] He

---

[4] *Col. Recs.* Congressional Library, Washington.

[5] *Gen. Dict. of R. I.,* pp. 112, 258.

Fragmentary Hist. of the Baptists, by Morgan Edwards, published
about 1790.

SILVER PITCHER
Brought to America by John Mallett

GOVERNOR JAMES FENNER OF RHODE ISLAND

married Martha, the daughter of John and Mary (Holmes) Brown.

Their son, *Obadiah Jenckes,* who died 1763, married, May 21, 1713, Alice, the daughter of Zachariah and Mercy (Baker) Eddy, who was born January 5, 1694, and died 1770.

Their son, *Ebenezer Jenckes,* married Alice ————.

Their son, *Silvanus Jenckes,* born May 22, 1746, and died May 25, 1781, married, July 7, 1772, *Freelove,* the daughter of James and Freelove (Whipple) Fenner, and their daughter *Sarah,* married *James Fenner,* the son of GOVERNOR ARTHUR FENNER.

WATERMAN-BORDEN-HARRIS

RICHARD WATERMAN (1590-1673), was Freeman, Commissioner, and founder of Providence, R. I., 1656 to 1658.[6] He married Bertha ————, who died December 3, 1680, and their daughter *Mehitable,* who died 1684, married ARTHUR FENNER I.

RICHARD BORDEN (1601-1671), was Assistant-Commissioner 1653 to 1659. His wife was Joan ————, and their son *Thomas,* married *Mary,* the daughter of WILLIAM HARRIS; their daughter *Dinah,* married, July 26, 1682, THOMAS FENNER.

WILLIAM HARRIS (1610-1681), one of the founders of Providence, was Deputy and Assistant Town Councillor, 1665 to 1677. His wife Susanna, died 1682.

BROWN

CHAD BROWN, who died in 1650, was one of the founders of Providence, R. I., signing the following agreement:

"We whose names are hereunder, desirous to inhabit

6 *Geneal. Dict. of R. I.,* pp. 408-410.

772 ANCESTRAL RECORDS AND PORTRAITS

in the town of Providence, do promise to subject ourselves in active or passive obedience to all such orders,
or agreements as shall be made for public good of the
body in an orderly way by the Mayor, assent of the present inhabitants, masters of families incorporated together into a townfellowship and such others as they
shall admit unto them, only in civil things."[7]

He served on a Committee to compile a list of the first
lots situated on the town street. His service in this direction is mentioned years after in a letter from Roger
Williams to John Whipple, Jr., July 8, 1689. Served
also on a Committee, with three others, to settle all matters of difference between Providence and Pawtuxet,
regarding the division of lines, and was the first settled[8] pastor of the First Baptist Church. His wife was
Elizabeth ———.

Their son, *David Brown,* who died 1710, married,
1669, Alice Hearnden, and their daughter *Hallelujah,*
married *James,* the son of Epenetus and Mary (Whipple) Olney, whose daughter *Mary,* married *Arthur
Fenner II.*

WHIPPLE-ANGELL

JOHN WHIPPLE (1617-1684), married Sarah ———.

JOSEPH WHIPPLE (1662-1746), Deputy, Town
Councillor, Assistant and Colonel in the regular Militia
on the main land, held office from 1698 to 1720. He
married *Alice,* the daughter of Edward Smith and his
wife *Amphilis Angell.*

Their son, *John Whipple,* born May 18, 1685, and
died May 18, 1765, married Abigail, the daughter of
Joseph and Sarah (Pray) Brown; their daughter, *Free-*

[7] *Gen. Dict. of R. I.,* p. 314.
[8] *Ibid.*

love, was born December 24, 1728, and died August 21, 1751; married *James,* the son of Arthur and Mary (Olney) Fenner, whose daughter *Freelove,* married *Silvanus Jenckes.*

THOMAS ANGELL (1618-1694), was Commissioner, Juryman, Town Clerk, Freeman, and Constable 1652 to 1658; signed with twelve others a compact incorporated together in town fellowship August 20, 1638; also signed with thirty-eight others, July 27, 1640, an agreement for a form of government.[9] His wife was Alice ———, and their daughter *Amphilis,* married Edward Smith, whose daughter *Alice,* married JOSEPH WHIPPLE.

COMSTOCK-ARNOLD

SAMUEL COMSTOCK, born May 27, 1637, was the son of Samuel who died 1660, and his wife Anne, who died 1661. He held the office of Deputy from 1699 to 1711. He married, November 23, 1678, Elizabeth, the daughter of Thomas and Phoebe (Parkhurst) Arnold. THOMAS ARNOLD (1599-1674), was Deputy and Town Councillor 1666, 1672.

Their son, *Hazadiah Comstock,* born April 16, 1682, and died February 21, 1764, married Catherine, the daughter of John and Sarah (Brown) Pray.

Their son, *Gideon Comstock,* born November 4, 1709, and died in 1801, married Amy ———, and their daughter *Amy,* who died September 2, 1825, married ARTHUR FENNER III.

LEE

ARMS: *Argent, a fess sable, three pellets in chief, martlet in second, sable.*
CREST: *Talbot's head, collared.*

The Lees descend from Francis Lee of Barbadoes, whose wife was Mary ———.

9 *Ibid.,* p. 4.

Their son, Thomas Lee, born February 6, 1710, and died August 8, 1769, married in Charleston, S. C., Mary Giles.

Their son, Stephen Lee, born January 21, 1750, during the Revolutionary war[10] was held as hostage by the British on the schooner *Pack Horse* in Charleston Harbor. He married Dorothea, the daughter of Paul Smizer, and the widow of the Rev. Hugh Allison.

LEE

Their son, Paul S. H. Lee, born September 22, 1784, and died April 20, 1852, married, January 10, 1809, Jane Elizabeth, the daughter of Jacob and Rebecca (Murray) Martin, of Charleston.

Their son, Stephen States Lee, born November 8, 1812, and died August 22, 1892, married, April 30, 1840, in Baltimore, *Sarah Fenner,* the daughter of Edward Jones and Sarah (Fenner) Mallett. Issue:

Edward Jones, was born August 18, 1841, and died May 17, 1842.

James Fenner.

Julian Henry, born November 2, 1845, married Elizabeth Dawson Tyson.

Hillyard Cameron.

Amabel, born June 14, 1858, and died March 1, 1895, married, December 18, 1879, John Cowman George.

The second son, *James Fenner Lee,* born July 9, 1843, and died January 24, 1898, married, June 28, 1866, MARY CORNELIA, the daughter of William George

10 *Hist. of S. C.*
Patriots in the Civil Line, p. 163.

THE MARTIN ARMS

and Sophia (Howard) Read, and the widow of Albert Henry Carroll. (See pp. 490-502.) Issue:

Mary Cornelia, died young.

Arthur Fenner, was born June 28, 1868, and died February 3, 1892.

SARAH FENNER, born December 17, 1870, married, October 2, 1901, John Mosely Walker, of North Carolina.

James Fenner, born June 9, 1872, married, February 19, 1906, Lillian Margaret Wathen.

Emily Harper, died in infancy.

Sophia Howard, born January 21, 1876, married, November 22, 1897, James Briscoe, Jr.

READ[11]

The emigrant, Sir William Read, died in 1736; his wife was Jane Spalding. Some of their descendants are as follows:

James Read, married Ellen, the daughter of JAMES BOND, of Georgia.

JACOB READ, born in 1752, and died July 17, 1816, married in September, 1786, Catherine, the daughter of David and Anna (French) van Horn.

William George Read, married *Sophia,* the daughter of JOHN EAGER HOWARD, of Belvidere, Baltimore, Md.

MARY CORNELIA READ, married first, Albert Henry Carroll, and second, *James Fenner Lee.*

SARAH FENNER LEE, married John Mosely Walker.

VAN HORN—PROVOOST

ABRAHAM VAN HORN, the son of Cornelius and Anna Maria (Jansz) van Horn, married, September 6, 1700,

---

[11] Read—Reade of Lincolnshire, Eng., and Newcastle, Del.

Maria, the daughter of David and Zyntje (Laurens) Provoost, from Amsterdam.

Their son, David van Horn, baptized July 20, 1715, married, September 25, 1744, *Anna,* the daughter of Philip and Anetjie (Philipse) French, and their daughter *Catherine,* married, September 13, 1785, JACOB READ, of South Carolina.

DAVID PROVOOST I, was born in Holland, and died January 16, 1656.

DAVID PROVOOST II, married Zyntje Laurens from Amsterdam.

FRENCH-PHILIPSE

JOHN FRENCH, died August 6, 1692.

PHILIP FRENCH, his son, married *Anetjie,* the daughter of FREDERIC PHILIPSE and his first wife Margaret (Hardenbroek) de Vries; (his second wife was Catherine van Cortlandt).

Their daughter *Anna,* married DAVID VAN HORN, whose daughter *Catherine,* married JACOB READ, of South Carolina.

HOWARD-EAGER

The Howards descend from Joshua Howard of Manchester, Eng., who married Johanna O'Carroll, and came to this country 1665.

His son, Cornelius Howard, married Ruth, the daughter of John and Jemima (Murray) Eager.

COLONEL JOHN EAGER HOWARD (1752-1827), their son, married, May 18, 1787, *Margaretta,* the daughter of BENJAMIN CHEW; their daughter *Sophia,* married *William George Read.*

CHEW

JOHN CHEW, the emigrant, married Sarah ———.

COLONEL SAMUEL CHEW, of Maryland, married Anne, the daughter of William Ayres.

Their son, *Benjamin Chew*, born February 13, 1671, and died March 3, 1699-1700, married, October 8, 1692, Elizabeth Benson.

SAMUEL CHEW II, born August 30, 1693, and died June 16, 1743, married first, October 22, 1715, Mary, the daughter of Samuel and Ann Galloway. (See pp. 499-501).

CHIEF JUSTICE BENJAMIN CHEW, their son, born November 29, 1722, and died January 20, 1810, married first, Mary, the daughter of John and Mary (Thomas) Galloway; second, Elizabeth, the daughter of James and Mary (Turner) Oswald. The line descends as follows:

Margaretta Chew, married JOHN EAGER HOWARD.

Sophia Catherine Howard, married *William George Read*, whose daughter, MARY CORNELIA READ, married second, *James Fenner Lee*, whose daughter is:

SARAH FENNER LEE WALKER,

Member of Chapter I., The Colonial Dames of America.

XLV

BONSALL

The colonist, Richard Bonsall, a member of the " Society of Friends," who died 1699, came to Philadelphia in 1688, having received a grant of three hundred acres of land from William Penn at Darby, now a part of Philadelphia. He brought his family from Derbyshire, England, where is the small town of " Bonsall," said to date back to the Norman Conquest, which contains a very interesting old stone church known as the " Bonsall Church." Richard, who married Mary Wood, is not to be confounded with his kinsman, Richard Bonsall, a younger brother of Sir Thomas Bonsall, who also settled near Philadelphia, but not until 1769.[1]

BONSALL

Their son, Obadiah Bonsall, born before 1683 and died 1732, married *Sarah,* the daughter of John and Frances Bethel, and their son was *Vincent Bonsall.*

BETHEL

JOHN BETHEL, who died in 1708, represented Chester County in the Provincial Assembly of Pennsylvania, 1707.[2] He married Frances ——, and their daughter *Sarah* married Obadiah Bonsall.

---

[1] *Family Papers.*

[2] Penn. *Arch.,* second series, Vol. IX, p. 683.

BONSALL (*Continued*)

The son of Obadiah and Sarah (Bethel) Bonsall, *Vincent Bonsall,* a large owner of real estate, died in Delaware 1796, where he moved from Pennsylvania. He married *Grace,* the daughter of Philip and Mary (Hoopes) Yarnall, his son, *Philip,* married in 1772, *Catherine,* the daughter of Caleb and Eleanor (Fairlamb) Harrison, and lived and died in Delaware. Their son was *Caleb Bonsall.*

YARNALL

In 1694, Philip Yarnall I., (who died 1734), married Dorothy, the daughter of John Baker.

Their son, Philip Yarnall II, born November 29, 1696, and died 1758, married, April 24, 1720, *Mary,* the daughter of Daniel and Jane (Worrilow) Hoopes, who was born November 22, 1700, and died 1765. Their daughter, *Grace,* married *Vincent Bonsall.*

HOOPES

JOSHUA HOOPES, who died 1723, represented Bucks County in the Provincial Assembly of Pennsylvania, 1686 to 1711.[3] He married Isabel ——.

DANIEL HOOPES, their son, born 1670, represented Chester County in the Assembly of Pennsylvania, 1708 to 1709.[4] He married, December 10, 1696, Jane, the daughter of Thomas and Grace Worrilow, and their daughter, *Mary,* married Philip Yarnall.

FAIRLAMB

NICHOLAS FAIRLAMB, who died in 1722, was a member of the Pennsylvania Assembly from Chester County,

[3] *Penn. Arch.,* second series, Vol. IX, p. 752.
[4] *Ibid.,* p. 683, etc.

1704 to 1718.[5] He married, 1703, Catherine, the daughter of Richard and Eleanor Crosby, and their daughter, *Eleanor,* married 1748, *Caleb,* the son of Caleb and Hannah (Vernon) Harrison, whose daughter, *Catherine,* married *Philip Bonsall.*

VERNON

RANDALL VERNON, born 1640, and died 1725, was a member of the Pennsylvania Assembly from Chester County, 1687.[6] He married, November 14, 1670, Sarah Bradshaw. Issue, among others, Hannah, who married, 1713, Caleb Harrison, whose son, *Caleb, Jr.,* married *Eleanor Fairlamb.*

BONSALL (*Continued*)

A young man, Caleb Bonsall, the son of Philip, was fond of going to the theatre, and on that account his membership in the Quaker Meeting came to an abrupt ending. He had strong literary tastes, and was considered an excellent Shakespearian scholar. While still quite young (born 1775), he moved from Delaware to Norfolk, Va. He married, 1813, *Sarah,* the daughter of Dennis and Elizabeth (Haynes) Dawley, of "Pembroke," Princess Anne County, Va. The wedding took place in the fine old brick house on "Pembroke Farm," ten miles from Norfolk. This house is in a good state of preservation, the inscription on the corner-stone showing that it was built in 1764. Having married into a large slave-holding family, he did not see much of his relatives in the North; nevertheless he inherited real estate in Delaware, part of which has been retained in the family during a period of one hundred and thirty

5 *Penn. Arch.,* second series, Vol. IX, p. 683, etc.
6 *Ibid.*

CALEB BONSALL

JOHN PURVIANCE LEIGH

OLD BONSALL SILVER

years. There is also a beautiful old English silver tea set, that has been in service for several generations. Their son was *Stephen Bonsal.*[7]

DAWLEY

The Dawleys have been in Virginia from the earliest times, and members for generations of the Vestry of Lynnhaven Parish. Dennis Dawley, who died in 1728, married Amey ——.

DENNIS DAWLEY II, their son, who died in ——, was one of the Committee of Safety, December 6, 1774.[8] He married a daughter of John Bonney.

CAPTAIN DENNIS DAWLEY III, their son, who died in 1805, was Lieutenant and Captain in the Virginia Militia, September 11, 1777.[9] He married Elizabeth Haynes, and their daughter, *Sarah,* married *Caleb Bonsall.*

LEIGH

FRANCIS LEIGH and his wife moved from Warwick to Norfolk County, Va., late in life. His will, probated in 1783, gives much information as to his family, but unfortunately most of the records of Warwick and the adjoining counties, were destroyed during the Civil War. Therefore the exact relationship of the Leighs in Virginia before this time is not certain, but records exist of the Leighs in Virginia prior to 1640. Francis Leigh was one of the Committee of Safety from Warwick County, Va., 1774 to 1775.[10] He married *Elizabeth,* the daughter of William, Jr., and Lucy (Bassett) Roscoe.

[7] A full account of the Bonsall family in this country has been compiled by Spencer Bonsall of Philadelphia. See *Penn. Hist. So.*

[8] *William and Mary Quar.,* Vol. V, p. 248.

[9] Princess Anne County *Recs.*

[10] *William and Mary Quar.,* Vol. V, p. 250.

Their son, *Dr. William Leigh,* married Sarah Hunter, the daughter of Andrew Purviance, of Philadelphia and Salem, N. J., and the granddaughter of Samuel Purviance (who died in 1781), whose wife was Mary, the daughter of the Rev. Andrew Hunter. Samuel Purviance was an uncle of Samuel Purviance, Jr., a chairman throughout the Revolution of the Committee of Safety of Baltimore Town.

Their son, *John Purviance Leigh,* married Frances Haynes Land, and their daughter, *Fanny Land,* married *Stephen Bonsal.*

ROSCOE

The Roscoes descend from William Roscoe, born in 1644, and died November 2, 1700, whose tomb, with its fine armorial bearings, may be seen at Blunt Point, on the James River. He married, 1695, *Mary,* the daughter of COLONEL WILLIAM WILSON, who was High Sheriff for Elizabeth City County, Va., 1693.[11]

WILLIAM ROSCOE, JR., their son, who died 1753, was a Burgess of Warwick County, Va., 1736, and one of the "Gentlemen Justices" 1752. He married, *Lucy,* the daughter of COLONEL WILLIAM and Joana (Burwell) Bassett, and their daughter, *Elizabeth,* married FRANCIS LEIGH.

BASSETT

The colonist, Captain William Bassett, who died in 1670, was appointed 1665 to superintend the erection of the fort at Jamestown, Va.[12] He married *Bridget,* the daughter of Colonel Miles and Anne (Taylor) Cary.

11 *Spottswood Letters,* Vol. II.
12 *Va. Mag. of Hist. and Biog.,* Vol. II, p. 231; Vol. III, p. 423.

"BASSETT HALL"
Williamsburg, Va.

"PEMBROKE HALL."

COLONEL WILLIAM BASSETT, of Eltham, their son
(1670-1723), a Burgess from New Kent County 1692
to 1696 and 1702, was of the Council 1707 to 1711;
Lieutenant Commander-in-Chief and County Lieutenant of New Kent County and King William 1715. His
tomb, bearing arms and epitaph, has been removed from
" Eltham " to Holywood Cemetery. Although " Eltham " was their home, the Bassetts also had a house
at Williamsburg, still preserved, where Burwell Bassett, Colonel William's son, frequently entertained General Washington and which was subsequently owned by
John Tyler, President of the United States. William
Bassett married *Joana* (1670-1723), the daughter of
Major Lewis and Abigail (Smith) Burwell.

Their daughter, *Lucy Bassett,* married WILLIAM
ROSCOE, JR., whose daughter, *Elizabeth,* married FRAN-
CIS LEIGH.

BURWELL

MAJOR LEWIS BURWELL, of Carter's Creek (1621-
1653), son of Edward of Bedfordshire, Eng., and Dorothy, the daughter of William Bedell, of Catsworth,
Eng., came to Virginia in 1643, was Burgess of Gloucester County, Va., and Major of the Militia. He married, 1645, *Lucy,* the daughter of CAPTAIN ROBERT
HIGGINSON, the colonist, who was Commander of forts
in the Middle Plantation, Williamsburg, Va., 1644-
1646.

MAJOR LEWIS BURWELL II, their son, who died 1710,
was Burgess, one of the King's Council, and Colonel
of Militia for Gloucester County, Va., 1702 to 1710.
He married Abigail Smith, and their daughter, *Joana,*
married COLONEL WILLIAM BASSETT, of " Eltham,"
whose daughter, *Lucy,* married WILLIAM ROSCOE, JR.

CARY

COLONEL MILES CARY, of Warwick County, Va., born in Bristol, Eng., and died June 10, 1667,[13] was Colonel-Commander of Warwick County; Lieutenant 1652; Burgess 1659 to 1663; His Majesty's Escheater-General for the County, 1663 to 1666; and one of the King's Council, 1663 to 1667. He married, *Anne,* the daughter of CAPTAIN THOMAS TAYLOR, of Magpie, Warwick County, Va., who died 1656; was Burgess for Warwick County 1646, and of the County Court 1652, etc.[14] Their daughter, *Bridget Cary,* married CAPTAIN WILLIAM BASSETT.

BONSALL (*Continued*)

The son of Caleb and Sarah (Dawley) Bonsall, *Stephen Bonsal,* married *Fanny Land,* the daughter of John Purviance and Frances Haynes (Land) Leigh. Their daughter, VIRGINIA PURVIANCE BONSAL, married Miles White, Jr.

VIRGINIA PURVIANCE BONSAL WHITE, Member of Chapter I., The Colonial Dames of America.

13 See tombstone at Windmill, Warwick Co., Va.
   Mr. Wilson Miles Cary, Genealogist.
14 Henning *Stats.*

XLVI
BLOW

The name of Blow occurs frequently in the earliest records in Lower Virginia, in fact the fourth recorded land grant was given to John Blow and his wife Frances in 1624, Northampton County. The first entry in the Land Book of Surrey County 1663 is to George Blow. This George had two sons, Richard and George, and his widow Marjory married Richard Smith, November 3, 1675. Richard died in 1687 childless. The Blows had, from the earliest days, many transactions in lands with the Nottoway Indians, and several of the deeds with the marks and signatures of the natives are still in possession of the family. For several generations, members of the Blow family were appointed trustees by the House of Burgesses of Virginia, in dealing with these Indians.

BLOW

SAMUEL BLOW, the first of the family of whom we have certain knowledge, born 1701, and died July 31, 1766, was buried at the "Old Place," Southampton County; his will proved in that county September 14, 1766. He was one of four brothers of Welsh descent, and Justice and High Sheriff of Southampton County. A land-owner, recorded deeds show he bought land from the Indians. He married Martha, the daughter of John Drew, and the wedding ring bearing the date of the marriage, is now in the possession of one of their descendants. She was a very energetic, capable woman, and managed the family estate after the death of her husband, who gave her in his will the life use of his plantation, "whereon I now live," and after her death it was to go to his son Richard. She received the labor of five negroes for life, and the use of the remainder of the estate after the debts and legacies were paid, this remainder to be divided among all the children after her death. To his son Richard he gave "Eight hundred & forty-seven acres of Land lying in the County of Southampton, known by the name of the Quarter; I also give unto my son, the following negroes, to wit; Will, Jenney, Sarah, Cabe & Old Pat, One horse called Dart, with a saddle and bridle, One feather bed & furniture, my silver-hilted sword, One gold ring & £50 current money, together with all profits that shall or doth arise from the partnership with Charles Briggs, also all stock of what nature or kind soever belonging to the said plantation." To each of his four daughters he gave negroes, a gold ring, and £50 in current money. Three of them received each a horse, saddle, and one feather bed with furniture. Samuel Blow had ten children, five of whom survived, viz.: Elizabeth, married Charles Briggs; RICHARD; Martha, married Mr. Hines, and one of her descendants married a son of John Tyler, President of the United States; Lucy, married Mr. Birdsong; Mary, married Mr. Mason.[1]

LIEUTENANT RICHARD BLOW, their sixth child, born October 17, 1746, and died February 3, 1833, was First-Lieutenant Fourth Regiment, in the Continental Army

[1] Copy from a record taken from the Blow *Family Bible*, by Mrs. Emma Blacknall.

the date of commission being March 11, 1776, and a bearer of dispatches at the battle of Great Bridge, near Norfolk. Finding, however, that he could be of more service to his country by owning and fitting out priva- teers, he left the army and gave his time to shipping interests, bringing supplies to the colonies, making sev- eral voyages to England in his own vessels, and after the war receiving a note of thanks from the United States Congress for services rendered during the war. He suffered severe losses at the time of the embargo in 1812, about which date he became President of the Farmers Bank in Norfolk, Va.   He was a very public- spirited citizen, having had much to do with laying out the city of Portsmouth, and in building the Dismal Swamp Canal.[2] He bought an estate from Harrison (of Berkley on the James River), who had a large grant of land from the British Crown.   It is said that he gave in exchange for it a fine race horse which he imported from England.   This is the Tower Hill tract of land, still in possession of the family.   On this farm were native African slaves who could tell the story of their capture and voyage from Africa.   One, who was named August, claimed to be the son of a native king, and said he was betrayed and sold into captivity by his uncle, who wished to wear the crown.   They had learned to speak imperfectly in English, and used to sit under the trees and " pick wool " when they were too old to work in the fields.[3] He married, April 5, 1786, *Frances,* the daughter of Stephen and Anne (Phripp) Wright, born September 25, 1767, died in Portsmouth, Va., November 19, 1838, and was buried in the family lot in Cedar Grove Cemetery, Portsmouth.   Richard

[2] Forces *Archs.,* Series 5, Vol. I, p. 21.
[3] From manuscript left by his granddaughter, Mrs. Emma Blacknall.

Blow was over forty years of age when he married Miss Wright, and his house in Portsmouth was large and well provided with furniture, silver and china, most of which was imported from England. In addition to his town house he kept a farm on Paradise Creek near Portsmouth, which supplied his table with fruit and vegetables. Here he passed the remainder of his life, dying full of years and honors in the eighty-seventh year of his age. Their son was *George*.

WRIGHT

The Wrights of Norfolk, Va., have long occupied a useful and honorable position. The first of the name in Virginia was Thomas Wright, who had land patented to him in 1635, "One hundred and fifty acres on the West Branch Elizabeth River." His will, dated January 10, 1654, is on record at the Norfolk County Court-house, Portsmouth, Va.

The will of his son, Thomas Wright II., is recorded October 15, 1678, and mentions six children.

WILLIAM WRIGHT, the son of Thomas Wright II., born 1668, was Justice of Nansemond County 1702, and Burgess 1714.

WRIGHT

His son, *Stephen Wright,* married twice; second, August 4, 1728-29, *Mary,* the daughter of Sampson and Anne (Church) Trevethan, and the widow of ——— Thoroughgood.

STEPHEN WRIGHT II, their son, was born 1730, and died 1779. A large landowner, he lived in Norfolk

County, Va.   He was a member of the Committee of
Safety for Norfolk County, July 20, 1775.   His will,
proved in the June court of 1779, bequeathed to his wife
the stock of all kinds, household furniture, plate, every
article of plantation utensils, the full use of the plantation where they lived, for her life, his "riding chair,"
harness and £2000 current money of Virginia, together
with all the land her father left her, "or all my right
and title to same."   Also seven female and eight male
slaves.   After bequeathing plantations and other real
estate to his three surviving sons, he gave to his four
daughters the residue of the current money due his estate, after legacies and debts were paid, and gave an
equal proportion of all his negroes not previously mentioned to his sons and daughters.   He married *Anne,*
the daughter of John and Frances (Mason) Phripp,
born 1740.   They had ten children, of whom the fourth,
Frances, married RICHARD BLOW.

TREVETHAN-CHURCH

The Trevethans were an old family in Cornwall,
Eng., descended from Sir John Trevethan 1450,
brother-in-law to "ye great Arundel of Lanhorne."

SAMPSON TREVETHAN is mentioned in a will of 1716.
He was Surveyor of Lynnhaven Bay 1714; Naval Offi-
cer of the Lower James 1716, and lived in Norfolk
County, Va., where he was a large land owner.   He
married *Anne,* the daughter of RICHARD CHURCH, of
Lower Norfolk County, a Burgess 1675 and 1702.
Their daughter *Mary Trevethan,* married (second wife)
STEPHEN WRIGHT.

PHRIPP-MASON-SEAWELL

In 1741, John Phripp (1684-1776), was an Alderman of the Borough of Norfolk, Mayor 1745 and 1757, and Warden of St. Paul's Church 1749. He married *Frances,* the daughter of George Mason. Their daughter *Anne,* married STEPHEN WRIGHT.

FRANCIS MASON (1584-1648), came to Virginia 163—, and was Justice from the formation of Norfolk County in 1637, until his death; Lieutenant of Militia 1640; Church Warden the same year, and High Sheriff of the county 1646. He was twice married, second to Alice ————.

LEMUEL MASON, their son, born after 1625, and died 1702, will proved September 15, of that year, was Justice 1649 until the year of his death; High Sheriff 1664-1668; a Burgess 1654, 1657-1660, 1663, 1675, and 1685; Presiding Justice and Colonel of Militia, Lower Norfolk County 1680. He married *Anne* (1635-1705), the daughter of HENRY SEAWELL, who was Burgess for Elizabeth City 1632, Burgess Norfolk County 1639, and gave the name to Seawell's Point, Elizabeth City. He had a son Henry.

GEORGE MASON, son of Lemuel, died 1710. He was Justice of Norfolk 1702, and Captain of Militia 1707. He married Phillis ——, and their daughter *Frances,* married John Phripp.

BLOW (*Continued*)

The son of Richard and Frances (Wright) Blow, *George Blow,* born in Portsmouth, Va., February 3, 1787, and died at Tower Hill, October 21, 1870, was buried in the family lot in Cedar Grove Cemetery. Mrs. Blacknall's manuscript gives the following account:

"When a small boy he was bitten by a mad dog, whilst at school in Belfield. The wound was cauterized, and he was immediately sent home. His parents at great expense and trouble, sent to North Carolina, procured a mad stone and applied to his hand, and then sent him to the Light House at Cape Henry for bathing, and there he spent the summer and the wound was cured and never troubled him after. . . . He was educated at Belfield Academy, Greensville County, Va. and at William and Mary College, Williamsburg, where he was a law student. It was here that he met his future wife, *Eliza,* the daughter of *Robert Hall Waller* and his wife *Nancy Camm.* They were engaged three years, and married when she was seventeen and he not twenty-one, as soon as he had finished his course at college. They went to Portsmouth to live with his father and chalk out their future life. They were married, December 12, 1807, about which time his father being well advanced in years began to settle up his mercantile affairs with a view of retiring from business. He therefore sent the young couple to his large plantation Tower Hill, Sussex County, Va., where they ever after lived and reared a large family. I wish I could describe that dear old place, as I remember it from 1812 to the present date. It contained over three thousand acres of ' forest and stream ' interspersed with ample clearings of corn and cotton fields, and lay for several miles on the Nottaway River. It had over a hundred servants to till the lands, and I have seen five generations on the place. They were carefully trained to be good mechanics, carpenters, blacksmiths, coopers, millwrights, etc., whilst the women were taken in the house and taught sewing, spinning, weaving, cooking, and to be such well trained domestics as we shall never see again. They lived in neat log-cabins, with pretty little gardens around them where they raised vegetables and even flowers adorned them sometimes. They had fruit trees and chickens and lived well and comfortably."

Besides the Tower Hill plantation, he owned the "Old Place" in Southampton County, and "Wheatlands," "The Flats" and "Waller's Neck" in James City County, Va., in all about six thousand acres; also valuable wharf property and other real estate in Portsmouth and Norfolk. He served in the war of 1812, and was Captain of the Fourth Virginia Regiment. He was an ardent Southerner, a firm believer in "States' Rights," and a member of a society that had for its object the returning of the slaves to Africa.

Thirteen children were born to George and Eliza (Waller) Blow, as follows:

Robert Waller died at the age of twenty.

Richard, married first Laura Townes of Petersburg, and second Laura Dunbar of Norfolk. He was a physician, and volunteered his services during the epidemic of yellow fever in Norfolk, but took the disease himself and died September 21, 1855.

Emma, married Dr. George Blacknall, U. S. N. and C. S. N.

George, married Elizabeth T. Allmand, and died at the age of eighty-one in 1894.

Fanny, died young.

Mary Frances, married Lieutenant Bushrod W. Hunter, U. S. N., Alexandria, Va., later Major, C. S. A.

Norborne, died in the seventies.

William Nivison, married Lavinia Cargill.

Nancy Camm and Eliza Waller died young, as did also a second Eliza Waller.

Atala, married *Dr. Joseph Beale,* U. S. A.

Robert Waller, was a clergyman of the Episcopal Church.[4]

WALLER

The Wallers of Virginia, belong to the same family as did the poet Edmund Waller, who died October 1, 1689.

COLONEL JOHN WALLER of Spottsylvania County, Va., was the first of his name to be definitely known. There exists a probability that he was the son of Dr. John and Mary Waller of Newport Pagnall, Buckinghamshire, Eng., who received patents of land in Virginia 1667, and whose son was John. By a division of King William County, Colonel John Waller (who had first settled in King and Queen County), was thrown into Spottsylvania County, where his plantations were called "Enfield" and "Newport." In his official career he was Sheriff of King and Queen County 1699 to 1702; Justice of King William County, 1703; a Burgess, 1713, 1720 and 1722; first Clerk of Spottsylvania County, and Vestryman of St. George's Parish. His will was proved October 1, 1754. His library included books on "Home Physicking both for Men and Animals," religious books of the Church of England, the standard poets of the day, a "Book of the Sufferings of King Charles," Prayer Book and Book of Practice, Shakespeare's Poems, three volumes of "Spectators Dissolved," etc. He married Dorothy King, and had several sons and one daughter: Mary, who married Zachary Lewis; John, William, Thomas, and BENJAMIN.

BENJAMIN WALLER, born October 1, 1716, and died May 1, 1786, was buried in Williamsburg, Va. The

[4] Taken from Family Bible, by Mrs. Emma Blacknall.

Misses Blacknall own the original commissions held
by him under the Crown. In 1737, he was Register of
the Court of Vice-Admiralty in Virginia, commission
signed by William Gooch, with the Royal Seal; Deputy
Clerk of James City County, 1737, commission signed
by John Carter, Secretary of the Colony, with the Carter seal; King's Attorney in Gloucester, 1738, commission signed by William Gooch, with Royal Seal;
Clerk of James City County, 1739, commission signed
by John Carter, Secretary of the Colony; King's Attorney in James City County, commission signed by
William Gooch, 1739; Clerk of the Court of Oyer and
Terminer 1739, commission signed by William Gooch;
Clerk's Assistant to the House of Burgesses, 1740,
commission signed by William Gooch, with Royal
Seal; with this is a certificate that the proper oaths
have been administered to Benjamin Waller, Gent.,
signed by Philip Lightfoot and Thomas Lee; Clerk of
James City County 1742, commission signed by John
Robinson, Secretary of the Colony, with the Robinson
Seal; a certificate that the proper oaths had been ad-
ministered to Benjamin Waller, Clerk of the Com-
mittees of Propositions and Grievances and Privileges,
and Elections, was signed by Cole Deggs and John
Tayloe; Clerk of James City County 1743, commission
signed by Thomas Nelson, Jr., with Nelson Seal. All
these Commissions were in the reign of King George
II, and William Gooch, Esq., was "His Majesty's
Lieutenant-Governor and Commander-in-Chief of the
Colony Dominion of Virginia." Benjamin Waller was
also Clerk of the Council, Burgess of James City
County, 1744 to 1759; on the list of the Committee of
Safety for the city of Williamsburg, December, 1774;
one of the Convention 1775, 1776; Judge of the Gen-

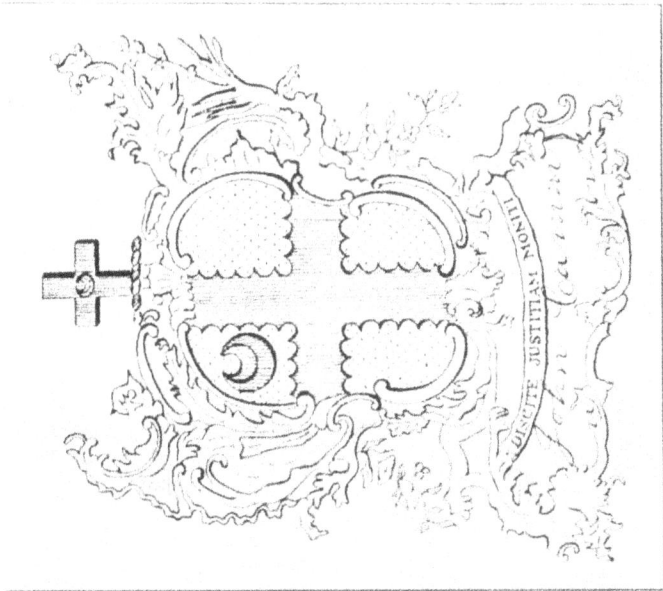

HERALDIC BOOK PLATE OF JUDGE BENJAMIN WALLER

HERALDIC BOOK PLATE OF JOHN CAMM

eral Court, 1779 to 1786; Judge of the Admiralty Court 1781; and Vestryman of Bruton Parish.[5]

" He was one of the Judges of the Supreme Court of Virginia 1778, and after the reorganization of this government, he was induced to accept a seat at the Council, having resigned all his offices under the Crown at the beginning of the Revolution and retired into private life. From thence he was made Chief Judge of the Court of Admiralty, and, for his convenience, as he was then quite an old man, the sessions of this Court continued to be held at Williamsburg after the seat of government had been removed to Richmond."[6]

His grandson, Governor Littleton Waller Tazewell, writes interestingly in his autobiography of his grandfather:

" . . . . When my Grandfather was about ten years of age, John Carter, Esq., the then Secretary of the Colony. . . . was occasionally detained at the house of old Mr. Waller by some difficulty he experienced in crossing the Mattapony River while making a journey from Williamsburg to his seat at Corotoman in the Northern Neck. In the course of the evening my Grandfather came in from school, and the Secretary, either to amuse himself or to please his host, calling the little boy to him, began to question and examine him, upon the subject of his school studies. Struck with the quickness and the correctness of the boy's replies, and supposing that he had found a boy of uncommon parts, which would not probably develop in his situation for the want of a proper education, the Secretary observed to old Mr. Waller that he must give him that boy and he would make a man of him.

5 Force's *Archives.*
6 *William and Mary Quar.,* July, 1898.

To this the old man assented very readily supposing, however, that the Secretary was not in earnest. Mr. Carter therefore stated that he would return that way on a certain day and expressed a wish that the boy might be got ready in the meantime to accompany him on his return to Williamsburg. On the very day appointed the Secretary again came to old Mr. Waller's, who, not believing the Secretary to be serious in what he said, and not supposing, therefore, that he would ever be called upon to comply with his promise, had done nothing towards getting his son ready to leave home, and so stated. Mr. Carter was vexed at this and insisted upon taking my grandfather with him as he was, and this being at last consented to by his parents, he was placed in the Secretary's chariot and carried by him to Williamsburg where he was immediately placed by the Secretary in William and Mary College and remained a student for several years, completing his college education when he was between sixteen and seventeen years of age. He was then placed in the Secretary's office."

(At the age of twenty the Secretary induced him to study law, and obtained permission of Lady Randolph, the widow of Sir John, former Attorney-General, to allow the young man the use of her deceased husband's excellent law library. He prosecuted the study of law at every leisure moment and obtained a license to practice about the year 1738, beginning his professional career in the county courts of the city of Williamsburg).

"For several years we lived together, seldom separated for a single day, and always to our regret even then; when the occasion passed which had taken me from him for even an hour, I flew to his bosom as to that of my best friend, and he pressed me there with a warmth that told me I was his precious treasure. I heard him breathe his last sigh, and although but a child, I felt I had lost what my heart valued most dearly, and would most willingly have gone down with him into the same grave."[7]

BENJAMIN WALLER married, January 2, 1746, Martha, the daughter of Robert Hall, of North Carolina, who was Burgess in 1714; she was born May 2, 1728. In the Waller Family Bible is this entry:

"My blessed wife and best of woman entered into immortality on Friday, August 4, 1780, a few minutes after six in the morning."

They had thirteen children, of whom the following survived:

Martha, married William Taylor.

Mary, married John Taylor Corbin.

John, married Judith Page.

Dorothy Elizabeth, married Henry Tazewell, whose son was Governor Littleton Waller Tazewell.

Anne, married John Boush.

Benjamin Carter, married Catherine Page.

Clara, married Edward Travis.

William, married Elizabeth Macon.

Robert Hall married *Nancy Camm.*

The eleventh child of Benjamin and Martha (Hall) Waller, *Robert Hall Waller,* was born in Williamsburg, Va., January 7, 1764, and died February 25, 1808, "about five in the morning" (buried in the Waller burying-ground) in Williamsburg, where he had lived and held offices ·connected with the courts of James City and York Counties. He married, March

---

[7] The Autobiography *of Governor Littleton Waller Tazewell.*

5, 1789, *Nancy,* the daughter of John and Elizabeth (Hansford) Camm; she was born in York County, Va., August 1, 1770, and died July 28, 1800; married second, Martha Cary Crafford, widow of John Crafford, of Warwick County, Va. His daughter *Eliza* (first wife), married *George Blow.*

CAMM

REV. JOHN CAMM, the son of Thomas of Hornsea, York County, Eng. (1718-1779), was educated in the school at Beverly, near Hornsea, admitted to Trinity College, Cambridge, June 16, 1738, elected to a scholarship April 10, 1741, and took the degree of B. A. 1741-42. In the faculty records of William and Mary College he is termed Master of Arts. He was minister of Newport Parish in Isle of Wight County 1745. September 18, 1749, he took the usual oath as Professor of Divinity in William and Mary College, and subscribed in York County Court the Abjuration test. Previously, on August 4, 1745, he subscribed before the Faculty, his assent to the Thirty-nine Articles of the Church of England, and took the oath *defideli*; was selected as agent by the clergy to represent their side in England in the celebrated "Parsons' Cause." He became President of the College in 1771, and continued as such until removed in 1779 by the Board of Visitors.[8] He was on the Colonial Council of Virginia, 1774.

In the traditions of William and Mary College, where he was Professor and President for twenty-eight years, Camm is preeminently known as "Old Parson." He remained unmarried up to the age of fifty-one, when he met his fate in a remarkable manner.

[8] *William and Mary Quar.,* Vol. I, p. 71; Vol. III, p. 64.
   Trinty College *Recs.*
   York County *Recs.*

" . . . . A fair Virginian, of name and kinship with the rebel Hansford of Bacon's day was one of Camm's parishoners, and it is said, induced by a love-smitten swain, he called upon her to urge the suit of the discarded one. Among other authorities, he invoked the Bible, which he said, enjoined matrimony as one of the duties of life. Persuasion was wasted, however, for the young lady declared that if the parson would consult Chapter XII, verse 7, of Second Samuel, he would note an injunction of the text which might suggest the reason for her refusal. Mr. Camm went home, and examined the Scriptures, when the words stood plainly revealed—'And Nathan said to David, Thou art the man.' Mr. Camm took the hint," and in 1769, he was married to Elizabeth or Betsey, the daughter of Charles Hansford III.[9]

" A memorable consequence of this marriage should be noticed. According to the monastic views entertained by colleges at this time, the President alone was authorized to enjoy the luxury of marriage. Camm was then a professor only, and accordingly the 'visitors' fulminated an order that 'All professors and masters hereafter to be appointed be constant residents of the College, and upon the marriage of such professor or master, that his professorship be immediately vacated."

The children of John Camm and Elizabeth Hansford were:

Anne or *Nancy,* married *Robert Hall Waller.*

Thomas, a clergyman, married Eliza Pescud.

Robert, drowned when eighteen or nineteen years of age.

John, died December 30, 1775. He studied law and

[9] Virginia *Gazette.*

removed to Amherst County where he was Clerk of the Court. There is an amusing tradition about him. He was bald at a very early age, and the crier who seems to have been facetiously inclined, was wont to call the Clerk to his duties at the courthouse door with "John Camm, John Camm! Little bald-headed man! Little bald-headed man!"[10] He married Elizabeth Powell.

Elizabeth, married Anthony Whitaker.

HANSFORD

As early as 1647, one John Hansford appears as an inhabitant of Hampton Parish, York County, Va., and

HANSFORD

in 1651, Richard Hansford was granted lands at West's creek in the same county. Among his head rights were Elizabeth and John Hansford.

COLONEL JOHN HANSFORD, for many years active in the affairs of York County, occupied a seat on the Justice's Bench in 1655. His will was proved November 24, 1661, and judging from the number of servants and the amount of silver mentioned in his inventory, recorded June 25, 1668, he was a man of birth, wealth, and position. He left four sons and three daughters. His widow married second, October 10, 1661, Mr. Edward Lockey, a merchant of Virginia, largely interested in the tobacco trade.

CHARLES HANSFORD, the youngest son, born 1647,

[10] From Dr. Thomas Ellis of Powellton County, Va.

and died 1702, was a Justice of York County and a Captain. He married Elizabeth, the daughter of Edward Folliott, and the widow of Josias Moody. They had issue, three sons, *Charles II.,* William and John, and four daughters. Rev. Edward Folliott, the father of Elizabeth, was the son of Sir John Folliott and his wife Lucy, the daughter of John Aylum, Bishop of London. Edward matriculated at Oxford, Hart Hall, April 13, 1632, aged twenty-two years; B. C. L., November 24,

FOLLIOTT

1632; Rector of Alderton, Northam, in 1634, until sequestered by the Parliamentary Committee. The family descends from Francis of Pirton.[11]

The elder son, *Charles Hansford II,* will proved June 15, 1761, married Susanna ——, and their children were *Charles III,* and Lucy.

The third *Charles Hansford* in direct descent, the son of *Charles II,* lived until 1778, his will being proved in December of that year. He had five children: Richard, Benjamin, *Elizabeth,* who married REV. JOHN CAMM, Mary and Martha.

Descendants of the Hansfords are among the Pattersons, Camms, Hydes, Hills, Custises, and many other well-known families in Virginia, to-day.[12]

BLOW *(Continued)*

The eleventh child of George and Eliza (Waller) Blow, *Atala Blow,* born August 15, 1826, was christ-

11 Nash's *Hist. of Worcestshire.*
12 *William and Mary Quar.*

Va. Hist. Papers, and especially Mrs. Tyler's paper on *Thomas Hansford.*

ened by the Rev. Mr. Wingfield, and died May 28, 1894. She married *Dr. Joseph Beale, U. S. N.*, later Surgeon-General of the Navy. Issue:

Margaret, died young.

ELIZA WALLER, married William Thomas Wilson.

Mary Burgoine.

Joseph, married Margaret Fales.

George Blow, married Elizabeth DeV. Lürman.

Florence, married John Graham.

BEALE

The son of Thomas and Catherine Beale, William Beale, was born near Calne, Wiltshire, Eng., August 4, 1709. About 1728 he came to Pennsylvania and settled in Whiteland near Downingtown, Chester County. He married first, Mary, the daughter of David Jenkin (who died in Uchlan, Chester County in 1743); she was born April 9, 1715, and died August 25, 1771; second, March 3, 1774, Rachel, the widow of Phineas Lewis. Issue: first wife, eight children, viz: Thomas, William, John, Susanna, David, Mary, Joshua and Edith.

Their son John Beale, born December 12, 1740, and served in the Continental army under Lafayette, died January 25, 1777, of fever at the Head of the Elk, during that terrible winter of privation and discouragement that almost wrecked the cause of liberty. He was a farmer and a Quaker, therefore, a non-combatant, but it is said having gone, as was his custom, to Philadelphia to sell his produce, he became so fired by enthusiasm over the Revolutionary cause, that he then and there sent back his wagons and horses by his servants, and enlisted in the army under Captain James McDowell. He married, Tamar, the daughter of

Joseph and Hannah (Price) Bourgoin, of Bradford, Chester County. She married second, William Huddleson and emigrated to Kentucky taking with her several children. Joseph Bourgoin, a French Huguenot, died 1764. He married, November 30, 1737, Hannah Price, who died in 1789. His French Bible from which these dates are taken, is still in the possession of his great-great-grandson, John Mills, of New York City. They had a large family, some of whom went west to Pittsburg, where the name was gradually changed to Burgwin.

The fifth child of John and Tamar (Bourgoin) Beale, Joseph Beale, after the death of his father, was brought up by his grandfather William Beale, went to Philadelphia and became an active and much respected business man. He married *Margaret,* the daughter of James and Elizabeth (Loughhead) McDowell. Issue: James, John, *Joseph,* married *Atala Blow;* Elizabeth, Harriet, Horace.

McDOWELL

CAPTAIN JAMES MCDOWELL, an Irishman of Scotch descent, born in 1740, and died September 12, 1815, was the only one of his family who came to this country. His Scotch ancestor went to Ireland with Cromwell, had lands given him and settled there. James McDowell was a man of strong personality, and a warm patriot. He was Captain of Militia in the Fourth Battalion of Chester County, 1776, and a Captain of Light Horse in the Militia after the Revolution. He married Elizabeth Loughhead, and their daughter *Margaret,* married Joseph Beale I.

Their son, *Joseph Beale II.,* married *Atala Blow,* whose daughter ELIZA WALLER, married William

Thomas Wilson. Issue: William Thomas, who died in infancy, and BESSIE BEALE, who married William S. Hilles.

ELIZA WALLER BEALE WILSON,

BESSIE BEALE WILSON HILLES,

Members of Chapter I., The Colonial Dames of America.

XLVII
MASON

COLONEL GEORGE MASON, said to have been an officer in the army of King Charles I, born in Staffordshire, Eng., emigrated to Virginia about 1651, settling at Doeg's Neck, in the County of Stafford, became a famous Indian fighter, and died in 1686. He was Justice of the County Court of Stafford and Captain of Militia 1655 to 1658; High Sheriff 1670; Colonel and County Lieutenant 1675. He married before 1658, Mary French (?)[1]

COLONEL GEORGE MASON II, their son, born at Doeg's Neck, was a Burgess 1676 and later. He held the offices of Justice of the County Court of Stafford, 1689 to 1715; High Sheriff 1698 to 1699, and 1705 to 1706; Burgess 1702 and later; Colonel and County Lieutenant from 1699. He married *Mary,* the daughter of Gerard and Anne (Thorowgood) Fowke, of Westmoreland County, Va., and Charles County, Md. Their son was GEORGE MASON III.

FOWKE

COLONEL GERARD FOWKE, of Westmoreland County, Va., and Charles County, Md., was the son of Roger and Mary (Bailey) Fowke, of " Gunston Hall," Stafford County, Eng., where the family were long seated. He emigrated to Virginia in 1651 with George Mason I, was commissioned Justice of the County Court of Westmoreland March 22, 1654, and was also of the

---

[1] See *Deed,* December 25, 1658, recorded *Westmoreland County Recs.,* made by Captain George Mason and wife Mary of Stafford County, and acknowledged in Court by their Attorney, Gerard Fowke.

Quorum. At the sessions of the court he is styled
"Captain" 1658, and "Colonel" August, 1662, and
third in the commission. Colonel and County Lieutenant 1660, he was also Burgess for Westmoreland
1663. In 1664 he removed to Maryland, became a Burgess 1665 for Charles County, and died at his seat near
Port Tobacco 1669, administration being granted to
his widow on October 30 of that year. He married
1661, *Anne,* the daughter of Adam and Sarah (Offley)
Thorowgood (Thoroughgood), and the widow of Colonel Job Chandler, of Charles County (Receiver-General of Maryland, and Member of Lord Baltimore's
Council; he died in 1659, leaving two sons, Colonel
William, who died 1685, and Richard, who died 1697);
she was living 1673. Issue of Gerard and Anne
Fowke, four children, viz:

Adam, died in infancy.

Gerard, of Charles County, was the father of Captain Chandler Fowke.

Mary, married COLONEL GEORGE MASON II.

Elizabeth, married Major William Dent, of Charles
County.[2]

THOROWGOOD, OR THOROUGHGOOD

CAPTAIN ADAM THOROWGOOD, of Princess Anne
County, Va., born at Grimston, Norfolk County, Eng.,
1602, was the son of William Thorowgood of Grimston, Commissary of the Bishop of Norwich, whose line
runs directly back through John of Felsted, Essex
County, John, Thomas, and John, all of Chelston-Tem-
ple, Hereford County. Adam Thorowgood came to

[2] Hayden, pp. 155-743-5.
Westmoreland *Recs.*
Va. Hist. Mag., Vol. III, p. 321.

Virginia in the ship *Charles,* and settled in 1621 at
Hampton, on the James, Elizabeth City County. He
married Sarah, the daughter of Robert and Anne (Os-
borne) Offley, of London (see pp. 347-349). Issue:
Adam; *Anne,* married GERARD FOWKE; Sarah, married Simon Overzee, and Elizabeth,[3] married John
Michael.

MASON (*Continued*)

COLONEL GEORGE MASON III, son of George II,
born at Doeg's Neck, was drowned in March, 1735,
while crossing the Potomac River to a plantation he
owned in Maryland, but his body was recovered and
buried at Doeg's Neck. He held the offices of Justice
of the County Court of Stafford from 1713; High
Sheriff, 1713 to 1714; Burgess 1718 to 1726; Colonel
and County Lieutenant from 1719. He married, 1721,
Anne, the only surviving child of Stevens Thomson,
Attorney-General of Virginia. One of their sons,
Colonel George Mason (1725-1792), of "Gunston's
Hall," Stafford, which he built about 1750, was the
author of the Virginia Bill of Rights 1776, and drafted
Virginia's Constitution. Another son was THOMSON
MASON.

THOMSON

STEVENS THOMSON, was born at "Hollin Hall,"
Stafford County, Eng., the son of Sir William Thom-
son(knighted October 31, 1689), Sergeant-at-law; Alderman of London and Member of the Parliament
1681; and grandson of Henry Thompson, who purchased "Hollin Hall," near Ripon, in 1658. Stevens
Thomson emigrated to Virginia on being appointed

[3] *Va. Hist. Mag.,* Vol. II, pp. 414-418; Vol. III, p. 321.
William and Mary Quar., pp. 169-171.

Attorney-General for the Colony 1704, holding the office until his death. He brought with him his wife, Dorothea, and five children, viz: Mary, Elizabeth, William, *Anne,* who married GEORGE MASON III, and Stevens; they all died young except *Anne,* his sole heir. His wife died in Williamsburg, July 12, 1713, and he also died there in 1713.[4]

MASON (*Continued*)

THOMSON MASON, the second son of George and Anne (Thomson) Mason was born at Doeg's Neck in 1730/ 33, and died February 26, 1785, it is said at his seat "Chippawamoie" in Stafford; but he was buried at "Raspberry Plain," his estate near Leesburg, Loudoun County, Va. He was educated at William and Mary College, Va.; studied law at the Middle Temple, London; was a Burgess, 1766 to 1775, from Stafford and Loudon Counties; in 1778 appointed a Member of the first Supreme Court of Virginia, which office he held for a short time, and was afterwards one of the five Judges of the General Court; in 1779 to 1783 a Member of the House of Delegates. He married in 1759, *Mary,* only daughter of Colonel Abraham and Mary (King) Barnes, and their daughter, *Anne Thomson Mason,* married *Richard McCarthy Chichester.* They had also two sons who gained distinction.

The elder, General Stevens Thomson Mason, (1760-1803), was United States Senator from 1795 until the year of his death. The second son, John Thomson Mason, (1764-1824), attained high rank at the bar

4 *William and Mary Quar.,* Vol. X, pp. 140, 166.
   Hayden, p. 110.
   Va. Hist. Col., Vol. X, p. 216.

but twice declined the office of Attorney-General of the United States when offered by Presidents Jefferson and Madison, and failed of election as Senator from Maryland by one vote.[5]

BARNES

COLONEL ABRAHAM BARNES, of "Tudor Hall," Leonardtown, St. Mary's County, Md., according to his deed filed in Westmoreland, Va., August 28, 1744, was "the eldest son and heir of Thomas Barnes of that county." He died at "Tudor Hall" in 1778, his will being proved January 13, of that year. He was a Justice of the County Court of St. Mary's as early as 1742; Burgess from 1744 to 1754 inclusive, when chosen a Delegate to represent the Assembly at the Albany Congress. He was a Delegate to the Maryland Convention 1774, and Chairman of St. Mary's Committee of Correspondence, 1775. He was a member of the first Vestry of St. Andrew's Parish from 1753 to 1771. Up to the year 1749, he had the rank of "Captain," then that of "Major," and finally that of "Colonel" in 1761. He married first, *Mary,* the only daughter of Colonel Robert King, and she died about 1740; married second, before August, 1744, Elizabeth, the daughter of Colonel John Rousby. His only

5 Hayden, pp. 109-110.

Appleton's *Cycl. of Amer. Biog.,* Vol. VI, p. 241, etc.

Va. Hist. Mag., Vol. I, pp. 251, —; Vol. II, pp. 13, 371; Vol. IV, pp. 380-386; Vol. VIII, pp. 246-247.

Councils of Va. Jours. 1689-1705, etc.   *Will of Colonel George Mason II,* in *Va. Hist. Soc. Archs.*

Va. Hist. Col., Vol. X, pp. 215, 224.

Va. Hist. Reg., Vol. IV, pp. 18, 66, 73.

Hennings *Stats.,* Vol. II, p. 330.

daughter, *Mary King*, (first wife), married THOMSON MASON.[6]

KING

MAJOR ROBERT KING I, of " Kingsland," Monohen, Somerset County, Md., died intestate 1697, administration being granted October 21, to " Madame Mary King," his widow. He held office as Justice of the County Court of Somerset 1689 to 1690, etc.; in 1689 held the rank of Captain and in 1690 that of Major in the County Militia, and the same year was Burgess; April 16, 1691, commissioned Justice of the High Provincial Court of Maryland, and Naval Officer for the Pocomoke District; Commissioner for laying out Courts 1683. He married Mary ——. Issue, three children, viz.: Mary, Eleanor, and ROBERT.

COLONEL ROBERT KING, of " Monohen, Somerset, but latterly residing also in Accomack," was born in 1689, only son and heir of Major Robert King. His will was proved June 26, 1775, and strictly entailed on his oldest son Nehemiah " any dwelling plantation at Monohen in Somerset, whereon my deceased father Major Robert King, in his life-time did dwell, containing about three hundred acres and I believe called ' Kingsland' with remainder to his male issue, failing which to male issue of deceased son Robert, then to female issue of Nehemiah, and to Nehemiah ' certain negroes' of which I was in possession before my last marriage."   He left to his granddaughter Mary Barnes, £100 in gold at sixteen, and to her father a ring. Robert King was Justice of the County Court

6 *Md. Archs.*

Records of St. Mary's County.

Md. Delegates to Albany Congress in *Dixie Mag.*, by Kate Mason Rowland.

of Somerset, and Colonel of the County Militia. The
name of his first wife is unknown, and by his second
wife Anne Makemie, he had no issue. His only daughter, *Mary,* married COLONEL ABRAHAM BARNES and
their daughter, *Mary King,* married THOMAS MASON,
whose daughter, *Anne Thomson,* married *Richard Mc-
Carthy Chichester.*[7]

CHICHESTER

The Chichesters trace back to Engeler, who was
seized at date of the Domesday Survey in 1080, of
lands in the Manor of " Cicestr " or Chichester, in the
County of Sussex, and also of divers lands in Somerset. His descendant, Sir Robert Chichester, knighted
by Edward III at the siege of Calais in 1347, and at
Poitiers with the Black Prince in 1356, died in 1370,
and was succeeded by his son John Chichester, Lord
of certain Manors in Somerset, which in 1384 he settled
on the issue of his marriage with Thomasine, the daughter and heiress of Sir John de Raleigh, who died in
1375, and was the head of that very ancient Devonshire house from which sprang the celebrated Sir Walter. The heiress brought to her husband the Manor
of Raleigh, near Barnstable, together with many others,
and by this marriage the Chichesters became one of the
most important families in North Devon. John Chichester thereupon assumed the Raleigh arms (*chequy
or and gules a chief vair*) and this coat has been borne
by his descendants ever since in lieu of their ancient
bearing (which was *ermine a canton sable*). Thomasine Chichester, outliving her husband, died in 1402,
and her monumental effigy still graces the chancel of
Arlington Church. John Chichester, the son of these

[7] *Md. Archs.* and Somerset *Recs.*

worthies, was born in 1386, and by his marriage 1424, with Alicia, the daughter and heiress of John Wotton, brought into the family, besides other Manors, that of Widworthy, in Somerset. Their great-great-grandson John Chichester, upon his marriage in 1538 received this Manor from his father and his line for six successive generations flourished at Widworthy.

RICHARD CHICHESTER, of Lancaster County, Va., the first immigrant of the family, came to the colony in 1702, bringing with him his son John. He was born at Silverton, in Devonshire, March 5, 1657, the second son of John Chichester, of Widworthy, Somerset County, and his wife Margaret Ware. The Lancaster records show that his first purchase of land was dated October 12, 1702, and the consideration paid was twelve thousand pounds of tobacco and forty shillings; the acreage is not stated, the land referred to being already in his possession. In 1710, he paid Robert Hall £300 for five hundred and twenty-eight acres on the Rappahannock River. He was Collector of Rappahannock River 1713, and High Sheriff of Lancaster 1722 to 1723. From 1714, if not earlier, he was a Justice of the County Court.[8] He married Anna ——.

His only son, *John Chichester, Gent.,* was baptized at Widworthy, May 10, 1681, and died intestate in Lancaster County, Va., October, 1728, his father giving bond October 9, as administrator. He married Elizabeth, the daughter of Thomas Symes, and wife Mary Richards, of Dorset County, Eng. Elizabeth was born in 1683, and died in England, January 1, 1728.

RICHARD CHICHESTER II, " GENT," their only son,

8 Hayden, pp. 93-94.
Va. Hist. Mag., Vol. II, p. 8.

"Fairweathers," Lancaster County, came from England as a child with his mother to his father, then in Virginia, and lived some years with his father and grandfather, and then returned to England with his mother. After the death of both parents, in 1728 he returned to his grandfather and lived with him some years before he died in 1734. In 1741 he returned to England and died at Exeter, December 30, 1743 and was buried at Powerstock, Dorset. He held the office of Justice of the County Court at Lancaster 1739 and probably earlier; was Vestryman of Christ Church Parish and Church Warden 1739 to 1741. He married, July 3, 1734, shortly after his grandfather's death, *Ellen,* the third daughter of Colonel William and Hannah (Beale) Ball. They had two sons and four daughters, viz:

John, married Jean Smith, died s. p. and made his brother Richard heir.

Richard.

Elizabeth, married William Glasscock, Jr.

Ellen, married Andrew Robertson.

Mary, married Rawleigh Downman.

Hannah.[9]

Their second son, *Richard Chichester III,* of Newington, Fairfax County, was born in Lancaster County 1736, and died 8th month and 22d day 1796 (buried in Fairfax County). In 1765, he moved to Fairfax, where he was Justice of the Peace and Lieutenant. He married first, Anne Gordon (1743-1765); second, *Sarah,* the daughter of Daniel and Sinah (Ball) McCarthy.

Their son, *Richard McCarty Chichester* (1769-1793), of Fairfax County, married *Anne,* the daughter

9 Hayden, pp. 91, 92, 93, 94, 95.

of Thomson and Mary King (Barnes) Mason; she was
born 1769, and died 1817 in Loudoun County, and
their daughter, *Anne Mason,* married Charles Pendleton, the son of Benjamin and Elizabeth (Pendleton)
Tutt.

BALL

COLONEL WILLIAM BALL (1615-1680), of Millen-
beck, Lancaster County, Va., married in London, July
2, 1638, Hannah, the daughter of Thomas Atherold,
of Burgh County, Suffolk. (See pp. 134-137.)

CAPTAIN WILLIAM BALL II., their eldest son, of Parish of White Chapel, Lancaster, was born June 2, 1641
in England, and died in Lancaster, September 30,
1694, (will proved 11th month 10th day). He was
Justice of the Lancaster County Court 1676 to 1680:
a Burgess and held the rank of Captain 1682 to 1692.
He married Margaret (?), only daughter and heiress
of —— Harris of "Bay View," Northumberland
County, Va.

COLONEL WILLIAM BALL III., of Lancaster County,
Va., their eldest son, was born there 1676, and died
1745 (will proved 3d month 8th day). He was Justice
of the County Court of Lancaster in the years 1699,
1702, 1714, 1720, 1722, and probably until his death;
Burgess and styled "Captain" from 1704 to 1711;
styled "Major" from 1712 to 1722, etc.; Colonel and
County Lieutenant from about 1720. He possessed
land in Lancaster, Richmond, King George and Westmoreland Counties, was Surveyor of Northumberland
County 1729, and Vestryman. He married Hannah
Beale, who died before 1744 and was living in 1719.[10]

[10] Hayden, pp. 50, 52, 53, 54, 55, 61, 62.
    Va. Hist. Mag., Vol. I, pp. 230, 368; Vol. VIII, pp. 245, 246.
    Henings *Stats.,* Vol. II, p. 239.
    William and Mary Quar., Vol. V, p. 260.

Their daughter *Ellen,* married RICHARD CHICHES-
TER II.

MAJOR JAMES BALL, of "Bewdley," Lancaster
County, Va., third son of William Ball II, was born
in Lancaster County 1678, and died there October 13,
1754 (will proved November 15). He was Justice of
the County Court of Lancaster from 1714 if not earlier;
Burgess 1715, 1722, 1734, 1740; Captain 'and Major
of the County Militia; Vestryman of Christ Church and
Church Warden 1743. He married first, June 15, 1699,
Eliza Howson, who died January 22, 1705, leaving
three daughters; married second, April 6, 1707, *Mary,*
the daughter of Edwin and Mary (Walker) Conway. They had ten children, of whom the youngest,
Sinah, married COLONEL DANIEL McCARTY. He also
had a third wife.[11]

CONWAY-WALKER

The colonist, Edwin Conway I., came to Virginia in
1640, from the County of Worcester, Eng. He first
appears as "Mr. Edwyn Conway, Clark of this Commonwealth in the County of Northampton." In his
first grant of land 1644, he is recorded as "Edwyn
Connaway of Northampton, Clarke" and was probably
born in Worcester, Eng., 1610, and died in Lancaster
County, 1675. His next grant was for twelve hundred and fifty acres, December 6, 1652, and in 1657 an
inclusive patent for twenty-five hundred acres to "Edwin Conoway Gentleman" was issued, September 26,

[11] Hayden, pp. 63, 64, 65.
William and Mary Quar., Vol. V, p. 261.
Va. Hist. Mag., Vol. VIII, p. 246.

1678, sixteen hundred and fifty acres was granted to "Edwin Conway, son and heir of Mr. Edwin Conway dec^d" who had patented it in 1659. He married in England, Martha, the daughter of "Richard Eltonhead, of Lancashire, Eng., Esquire." He probably married second, a sister or sister-in-law of Colonel John Carter I, of Corotoman.

EDWIN CONWAY II., his only son, was born in Virginia 1654, as in a deposition of 1679, in Richmond County Court, he stated his age as twenty-five. He died in Richmond County, will proved 9th month 7th day 1698. He was Justice of Lancaster County Court 1691, holding the office until his death. He married first, *Sarah*, the daughter of Lieutenant John Walker, of Rappahannock County, and second, Elizabeth Thomson. He had two children, (first wife), Edwin, and *Mary*, who married JAMES BALL.[12]

LIEUT.-COLONEL JOHN WALKER, of Rappahannock County, Warwick and Gloucester, born in England, was deceased by 1684. He was Justice of the County Courts of Warwick and Gloucester; Burgess for Warwick 1644, 1646, and 1649; removed to Gloucester and became Colonel of that County and Member of the Colonial Council 1656 and later. His first wife, name unknown, was the mother of his six daughters, who are mentioned in the will of their step-mother, Mrs. Sarah Walker (widow of Colonel Henry Fleet, who died in Rappahannock County in 1660, leaving one son, Colonel Henry Fleet). Mrs. Walker's will was proved in Richmond County, 12th month 30th day, 1679, and gave bequests to her six Walker step-daughters by name, all then unmarried. She was survived by her hus-

---

[12] Lancaster County *Recs.*
Notes of Wilson Miles Cary.

band, whose daughter *Sarah*, married EDWIN CONWAY II.[13]

McCARTY

CAPTAIN DANIEL McCARTY, of Cople Parish, Westmoreland County, the son of Dennis and Eliza (Billington) McCarty of Northumberland County, was born in 1679, and died May 4, 1724. His will proved the fifth month and twenty-seventh day of that year, disposed of a large estate.[14]   He was a Justice of Westmoreland County Court from 1706, if not earlier; Burgess 1706, and Speaker of the House 1715 to 1720; High Sheriff 1710 to 1711, Burgess 1720 to 1722. He married first, Mrs. Sarah Payne, widow of James Payne, and second (mentioned in his will) Anna Lee, the daughter of Richard and Lettice Corbin Lee, and the widow of Colonel William Fitzhugh. Her will was proved in 1732.

The wills of Luke Billington and his wife Barbara, of Rappahannock County, Va., were proved respectively in 1672 and 1674, and mention their children: Luke, who died s.p.; Elitia (Alicia), Elizabeth, who married Daniel McCarty; Jane, Barbara, who married William Joseph Tayloe, and Mary, who married ———— Daniel.

MAJOR DENNIS McCARTY, of Cople Parish, Westmoreland, subsequently of Prince William County, was the eldest son of Daniel McCarty. His will was proved the 1st month and 20th day, 1743, in Prince William County where he was a Justice of the County Court from 1731, Major of the County Militia, and

13 Henings *Stats.*, Vol. I, p. 422.
   William and Mary Quar., Vol. III, p. 67.
   Cary *Notes* from Richmond County Recs.
14 See tombstone, near Montross, Westmoreland.

Vestryman of Truro Parish 1732. He married, September 22, 1724, *Sarah,* the eldest daughter of COLONEL WILLIAM BALL III; she married second, Abraham Barnes.

COLONEL DANIEL MCCARTY, ".Gent.," of Cople Parish, Westmoreland, their eldest son, was born at Pope's Creek, Westmoreland, and died in 1791, at Cedar Grove, Fairfax County; will proved there 1792.[15] He was Justice of Fairfax County Court from 1770; Colonel and County Lieutenant, and Vestryman of Pohick Church, Truro Parish, 1774.[16] He married *Sinah,* the daughter of James and Mary (Conway) Ball; she was born February 14, 1727-28, and died 1798. Their daughter *Sarah,* married (second wife), *Richard Chichester III.*

TUTT

The pedigree of the Tutts is as follows:

Benjamin Tutt, of Spottsylvania County, Va.

Richard Tutt, of Spottsylvania County, married, 1731, Elizabeth, the daughter of Richard Johnson.

Richard Tutt, of Culpeper County, Va.

Captain James Tutt, of Culpeper County, will proved 1790, married Anne, the daughter of William Brown.

Benjamin Tutt, of Culpeper County, who died 1817, lived at "The Retreat"; married Elizabeth, the daughter of Nathaniel and Sarah (Clayton) Pendleton.

Charles Pendleton Tutt (1780-1832), married *Anne*

[15] Deed Book, Fairfax Co., Vol. III, p. 371 (1792).
[16] Hayden, pp. 86, 87, 89; Henning's *Stats.,* Vol. IV, p. 58.
    Va. Hist. Mag., Vol. VIII, pp. 246-247.

Mason, the daughter of *Richard McCarty Chichester* and his wife *Anne Thomson Mason;* she was born October 16, 1789, and died July 12, 1882 at Berkley Springs.

Eliza Pendleton Tutt, married Josiah Colston, U. S. N.

PENDLETON

The Pendleton pedigree is as follows:

George Pendleton, Esq., of Pendleton, Lancaster.

George Pendleton, moved to Norwich; married Elizabeth, the daughter of John Pettingill, Gent.

Henry Pendleton, married Susan Carmver.

Henry Pendleton, third son, married Elizabeth ——.

Philip Pendleton, came to Virginia 1674; married Isabella Hurt, and their daughter Elizabeth, married Samuel, the son of John Clayton.

Henry Pendleton (1683-1721), of Caroline County, married Mary (1688-1770), the daughter of Colonel James Taylor, of Carlisle, Eng., and Caroline County, Va., and Mary Gregory, his wife.

Nathaniel Pendleton, of St. Marx Parish, Culpeper (1715-1794), married Sarah, the daughter of Philip and Anne (Coleman) Clayton. Philip Clayton was the son of Samuel and Elizabeth (Pendleton) Clayton.

Elizabeth Pendleton, married Benjamin, the son of Captain James Tutt.

Charles Pendleton Tutt, married *Anne Mason Chichester.*

Eliza Pendleton Tutt, married Josiah Colston.

COLSTON

The Colston pedigree is as follows:

James Colston, tradition says "of Bristol," came

from England 1664, and settled on "Clay's Hope," in Talbot County, Md.

James Colston II., of St. Michael's Parish, Talbot County, Md., will proved April 9, 1729, inherited "Clay's Hope" two hundred acres, in Ferry Neck, on Third Haven Creek in Talbot County, on the north side of the Choptank River, purchased 1664, by his father, James Colston the emigrant, from Henry Clay and wife, the original patentees of 1662, and from these dates it is traced in deeds and wills to the present time. It was chiefly owned in the Colston name till 1850 and since, and now a portion is still owned in the female (Hardcastle) line. An old Colston house, probably one hundred and fifty years old, is still standing on the place. James Colston married, second, 9th month 14th day, 1714, Elizabeth, the daughter of Henry and Elizabeth (Clements) Bailey.

James Colston III., (1720-1773), of "Clay's Hope," married Alice (1725-1814), the daughter of Morris and Alice Orem.

Jeremiah Colston, of Dorchester County, Md. (1757-1800), married Elizabeth ———.

Josiah Colston, U. S. N. (1795-1870), married *Eliza Pendleton Tutt* (1809-1879).

Frederick Morgan Colston, born January 10, 1835, married, October 28, 1868, *Clara,* the daughter of John Archibald and Anne Esther (Goldthwaite) Campbell.

BESSIE MASON COLSTON, born September 19, 1879, married in 1901, Dr. Hugh H. Young, of Baltimore, Md. (M. A., University of Virginia).

BAILEY-OREM-MORRIS

The Bailey pedigree is as follows:

Richard Bailey "Gent.," came to Maryland 1658.

Henry Bailey, of Talbot County, minor in 1684, married Elizabeth, the widow of Lambert Clements.

Elizabeth Bailey, married, September 14, 1714, James Colston II.

James Colston III, married Alice Orem.

The Orem pedigree is as follows:

Andrew Orem, Quaker, of Talbot County, married Eleanor, the daughter of John Morris, Quaker, of Talbot County; she married second, Arthur Rigby.

Morris Orem, of Talbot County (1688-1765), married Alice ———.

Alice Orem, married James Colston III, whose descendant, Josiah Colston, married *Eliza Pendleton Tutt*.

GOLDTHWAITE

The colonist, Thomas Goldthwaite, born in England, and emigrated to Boston with Governor Winthrop in 1630, was supposed to have come from Lincolnshire, but was probably born in Yorkshire. In 1636 he was in Salem, and died March 16, 1683. His wife's name was Elizabeth.

Their son, Samuel Goldthwaite, was born 8th month, 20th day, 1637, at Salem; his will proved 12th month, 31st day, 1718. He married, 9th month, 6th day, 1666, at Charlestown, Mass., Elizabeth, the daughter of Eziekel Cheever, the famous master of the Boston Latin school, who was the son of William and Margaret Cheever.

Their son, Captain John Goldthwaite, of Boston, Mass., born at Salem, 1677, settled early in Boston, dying 6th month, 25th day, 1766. He was a Member of the Ancient and Honorable Artillery Company, from 1711, being Ensign 1730, Lieutenant 1732, and

Captain 1741 to 1766. He married second, Jane, the daughter of Thomas and Mary Tawley, of Boston, and the widow of John Halsey; she was born 1682.

COLONEL THOMAS GOLDTHWAITE, of Boston and Chelsea, and Fort Pownal, Me., born the 1st month, 15th day, 1717-18, and died 8th month, 31st day, 1799, was a merchant and removed to Chelsea 1750; Representative to the General Court 1757 to 1763; removed to Fort Pownal, Me.; Commander there 1764 to 1775; Justice of His Majesty's Court of Common Pleas, and in 1769, was commissioned Colonel of the 2nd Regiment of Lincoln County. Being a loyalist he went to England in 1779, and lived for twenty years at Walthamstow, Essex County. He married second, February 19, 1746, Katherine (1715-1796), the daughter of John and Elizabeth (Perrie) Barnes. Her father was a merchant of Boston, who died in 1739, at St. Clement's Bay, St. Mary's County, Md., and her mother died in Boston, 1742.

Their son, *Thomas Goldthwaite,* born in Chelsea, Mass., June 4, 1750, and died in England 1810, removed to Fort Pownal, Me., with his father in 1763. Being a loyalist, he went to England 1779; returned 1792, and afterward lived at Dalton, N. H., and Boston, Mass. He married second, 1791, Anne, the daughter of the Rev. Mr. Wilson of Woodbridge, Suffolk, Eng. She was born 1774, and died in Baltimore 1863; she removed from Boston to Montgomery, Ala., with her younger children in 1828.

Their daughter, *Anne Esther Goldthwaite,* was born in Dalton, N. H., 1806, and died February 13, 1883, in Baltimore. She married, 1831, Hon. John Archibald Campbell, of Montgomery, Ala., who was born June 24, 1811, near Washington, Wilkes County, Ga.;

died and was buried in Baltimore, 1889. He was Justice of the U. S. Supreme Court, 1853 to 1861, and Assistant Secretary of War, C. S. A., 1861 to 1865.

Their daughter, *Clara Campbell,* was born January 13, 1847, and married, October 28, 1868, *Frederick Morgan Colston,* and their daughter is:

BESSIE MASON COLSTON YOUNG,

Member of Chapter I., The Colonial Dames of America.

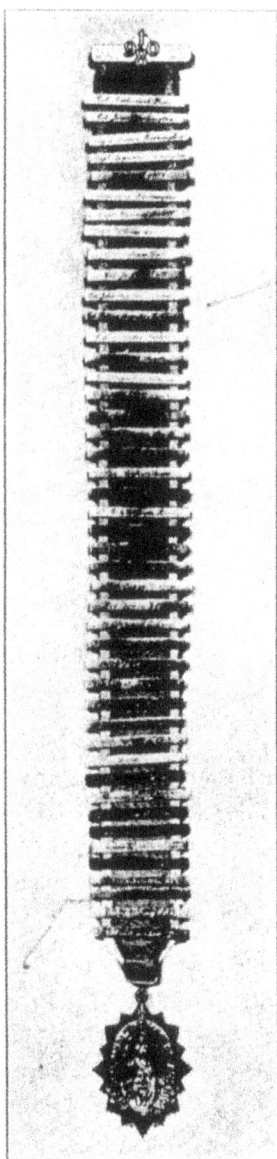

BADGE OF ONE OF THE MEMBERS OF CHAPTER I.,
THE COLONIAL DAMES OF AMERICA

INDEX

INDEX

Addison, 357 to 358, 671, 687

Alexander, 127

Allen, 298 to 299

Allerton, 733 to 740

Almy, 111

Alston, 368

Angell, 772

Arnold, 15 to 16, 112 to 113, 299, 773 to 774

Ashton, 446 to 448

Aston, 328 to 329

Aylett, 443 to 446

Bailey, 820 to 821

Baker, 314

Baker (Eng.), 560, 686-687

Baker (Va.), 54 to 55

Baldwin (Anne Arundel Co., Md.), 80, 81, 84, 92

Baldwin, (South River, Md.), 84

Ball, 134 to 137, 314, 814 to 815

Barker, 65 to 68

Barnes, 809 to 810

Barnett, 128

Barnwell, 378 to 381

Barroll, 475 to 476

Bassett, 782 to 783

Battee, 605

Baxter, 125 to 126

Baylor, 140

Beale, 802 to 803

Beall, 465 to 468

Beard, 247

Beekman, 507

Benson, 691

Bethel, 778

Bird, 650, 651, 654, 655, 657, 660

Bladen, 285 to 286

Bland, 279 to 281

Bland (Collateral), 281

Blount, 581 to 582

Blow, 785 to 788, 790 to 793, 801 to 802

Bolling, 325 to 326

Bond, 690 to 691

Bonsall, 778, 779, 780, 784

Borden, 18, 74, 190, 771

Bordley, 668

Boteler, 593 to 596

Bourne, 693

Bowdoin, 477 to 481, 486

Bowes, 36 to 37

Boykin, 44 to 49

Bradford, 705 to 707

Bradley, 256

Brandt, 194 to 198, 199 to 200

Brayton, 141

Brent, 521 to 525, 527, 528, 530, 532, 534 to 535, 536 to 538, 565 to 566

Brent (Collateral), 528 to 530

Brewer, 602 to 604

Brewster, 188, 740 to 743, 766

Brooke, 141, 357 to 358, 469, 553 to 558, 686, 727 to 728